The Economics of Development

The Irwin Series in Economics
Consulting Editor Lloyd G. Reynolds *Yale University*

The Economics of Development

EVERETT E. HAGEN, Ph.D.
Professor of Economics, Emeritus
Massachusetts Institute of Technology

1980   Third Edition

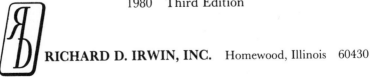

RICHARD D. IRWIN, INC.   Homewood, Illinois   60430

© RICHARD D. IRWIN, INC., 1968, 1975, and 1980

All rights reserved. No part of this publication may be
reproduced, stored in a retrieval system, or transmitted,
in any form or by any means, electronic, mechanical,
photocopying, recording, or otherwise, without the prior
written permission of the publisher.

ISBN 0-256-02318-2
Library of Congress Catalog Card No. 79-89466

Printed in the United States of America

2   3   4   5   6   7   8   9   0   7   6   5   4   3   2

Preface

The analysis of economic development, like any young discipline, is continually maturing. The changes during the past five years seem greater than those during any previous quinquennium. Perhaps this is not merely because they are closer to the retrospective eye. Perhaps even in a view not affected by the closeness of perspective they would seem greater.

In a sense all are matters of emphasis only. About a century ago Alfred Marshall quoted the dictum, "Natura no facit saltum"—nature does not make jumps; there are no discontinuities in nature; there is nothing new under the sun. But sufficiently great differences in degree are differences in quality, and some aspects of the study of economic development.have taken new shapes.

In part the change is one of available information. Over three decades overall data have been accumulated and increasingly refined by statistical offices of the United Nations. During the 1970s they have been augmented and subjected to econometric analysis by the development policy research staff of the World Bank. Meanwhile, increasingly, a host of academic researchers have contributed information, analysis, and viewpoints on specific topics to a group of journals devoted wholly to the study of economic development as well as to the general economics journals.

In part, also, new emphases have developed because of a change in reality as well as in information about reality. The less developed countries show a new hostility toward the more developed. The change may be only a superficial one. The sense of having been wronged that is overt now almost certainly existed previously in as great degree, suppressed. In any event, many of the LDCs now demand in concert what they used to ask individually and, their voices freed by a decade or two or three of independence and their hopes spurred by the success of OPEC, think of using their economic muscle to obtain concessions not obtained by request or negotiation. Evaluations of their prospects for success differ.

The new data make it necessary for even the most resistant to discard the view that the economic world consists of two groups of nations, each more or less homogeneous in income level, separated by a great chasm. The data show a continuum of countries ranging from the lowest- to the highest-income with hardly a break, though the population weight of China and India causes that half of the world's people to live in countries with very low per capita incomes.

The range of income even among the "less developed" countries is great. We used to use the terms "less developed" and "low income" countries interchangeably. Now we know that it is necessary to distinguish, within the "less developed" group, among the low-income, the middle-income, and if we wish to be precise the highest-income LDCs, a few of which have higher per capita incomes than do some members of the "more developed" group. Yet all but a few of the LDCs, ignoring the differences among themselves, unite in pressing the "more developed" or "industrial" countries for concessions which they (occasionally mistakenly but often correctly) believe will be of benefit to them all. Only a few of the most rapidly growing on occasion withdraw from the group on one issue or another.

With the new data and with increased understanding, a new concern about the distribution of income within the lower income countries is manifested by academics and by international practitioners of development. More specifically, they are concerned not merely about the LDCs as a whole but specifically about the welfare of the 800 million or so most impoverished individuals within the group. Unfortunately, in many of the LDCs that concern is not shared by the elites in power. In many instances their demand is for a new international but not a new internal economic order. Among observers in the more developed countries the response to this attitude varies from the view, "Let them turn to us when they have put their own houses in order" or at another extreme the view that there will be little change in income inequality within less developed countries except by social and political revolution, to the more temperate (not necessarily correct) view that rise in national income and amelioration of the inequality of its distribution will or at least can occur together.

A textbook must keep pace with this change in its field, and should make sense and order out of the increasingly rich and most recently available data. To do both, and for greater clarity of organization, in the revision of this text almost all of the text of the second edition has been revised and some chapters have been added. The following changes are illustrative:

The discussion of the noneconomic factors affecting economic development has been condensed. Discussion of the problem of unemployment in the LDCs has been expanded. Sections on the concept of a New International Economic Order and on international moves to attack directly the plight of the 800 million most impoverished have been added. A fairly brief chapter section on China has been added—the longest discussion of any individual country except Japan. Individual chapters on the role of each factor of production in growth, in part new, in part merely separated out for greater clarity, have been added. The discussion of customs unions has been moved to the chapter on Scale, and the discussion of commodity pricing to a new chapter on trade problems. On the judgment that the requests of some students and teachers reflects a more general demand, a short chapter has been added on the classical, neoclassical, and Marxist theories of growth, and another on the neo-Marxist, the "dependencia" school, and a more eclectic somewhat related tenor of thought that is found here and there in American, British, and European academic institutions.

The basic analytical approach remains unchanged.

I am indebted to Francisco Rivera-Batiz and Luis Tovaria for efficient research in the late stages of preparation of the manuscript.

December 1979   Everett E. Hagen

Contents

List of Figures

List of Tables

I

Introduction

1

Some Facts about
Economic Growth

When the serious study of the economic development of the lower income countries of the world began three decades ago, it was common to think of "the low-income countries" and "the high-income countries," separated by a wide gulf. The latter were the countries of Western Europe and three major countries of European colonization—the United States, Canada, and Australia. The former were all of the other countries and colonies of the world—seen as not only impoverished but stagnant.

The lower income countries were not stagnant even in 1950. They were growing. The remainder of the characterization, though overly simple, was not grossly distorted. But one of the remarkable results of economic development since 1950 is that this conception is no longer even grossly correct.

The first paragraph of the World Bank's *World Development Report, 1978* reads:

> The past quarter century has seen great progress in developing countries. In virtually all of them, income has risen faster than population, with a consequent rise in income per person. Three countries containing 1 percent of the population of the non-Communist world are exceptions. Economic growth has been accompanied by a rapid expansion of education systems, growing literacy, improvements in nutrition and health conditions, increasing technological sophistication, and structural changes, including a growing industrial base and greater urbanization. Progress on such a wide front and the steadily growing capacity of developing countries to manage their economies effectively are impressive achievements.

Even more remarkable, per capita income has risen so much more rapidly in some of the lower income countries—some whose income was already relatively high within the group—than in some of the higher income countries that with respect to their per capita incomes the countries of the

3

world today form a continuum. The simple conception of low- and high-income countries is obsolete.

And the more rapidly growing countries, which have moved into a "middle income" group, are rather angrily demanding "more." They are demanding that there shall be a "New International Economic Order."

Yet many millions of the people in the lower income countries still have an abysmally low level of living. To call attention to the lowest incomes Mr. Robert S. McNamara, president of the World Bank, has presented the conception of "absolute poverty," which he describes as "a condition of life so degraded by disease, illiteracy, malnutrition, and squalor as to deny its victims basic human necessities," "a condition of life so limited as to prevent realization of the potential of the genes with which one is born"[1] He adopted as the line dividing "absolute" from merely relative poverty a per capita income level in 1969 of $50 per year or less. In 1980 prices, that would be a level of about $100 as incomes have been conventionally measured. The World Bank staff, estimating the distribution of income within countries on the basis of highly uncertain but not implausible data, calculated that nearly 800 million people, 40 percent of the 1970 population of the "developing world," had incomes this low.[2] The income line drawn is an arbitrary one, and the entire conception of absolute poverty is very fuzzy. Moreover, the estimates may somewhat overstate the number of persons with the indicated incomes. However, the concept makes vivid the existence of extremely low incomes, quite possibly incomes that would have been deemed very low even in 1500, when the modern era was still in the future.

Most of the world's "absolutely poor" persons are in the lowest income countries, but some of them are in middle-income countries whose elites have contempt for their low-income classes.

In a sense this book is wholly devoted to exploring and explaining these four facts: that the lower income countries have developed greatly, that there is no longer a dichotomy of country income levels, that the middle income countries are aggressively demanding more, and that abysmal poverty still exists.

THE RANGE OF INCOMES

In 1977, 125 countries had populations of 1 million or more. For 121 of them the World Bank has made estimates of per capita gross national prod-

---

[1] *Address to the Board of Governors, September 24, 1973* (Washington, D.C.: World Bank, 1973).

[2] Hollis Chenery, M. Ahluwalia, C. L. G. Bell, J. Duloy, and R. Jolly, eds., *Redistribution with Growth* (London: Oxford University Press for the World Bank, 1974). To employ the term *developing* for the term *less developed* is a particularly perverse language usage, apparently adopted by many international organization officials out of a sense that the term *less developed* will be offensive. Some of the countries referred to are not developing, while the excluded high-income countries *are* developing.

uct in 1977 and the growth rate from 1960 to 1977.[3] Since the list is a long one, the data are not presented here but in Table 1–2 at the end of this chapter. Figure 1–1 is based on the data of that table.

At the bottom, three countries—Bhutan, Cambodia, and Bangladesh—are shown with per capita GNP per year below $100 and 23 countries are shown with per capita GNP below $200. In size, India dominates this group. Its per capita income, $150, is about the average for the group. At the top, even excluding little oil-rich Kuwait, the average per capita GNPs of the four highest income countries (Switzerland, Sweden, Norway and the United States) is $8,580—58 times that of India.

But an important fact concerning the table and figure is that these data exaggerate the true differences. The data were arrived at by the conventional method of estimating each country's per capita GNP in its own currency, then converting to a common currency, in this case dollars, by the use of the exchange rate between the two. This was the only method of comparison available until recently. That it much overstates the differences will be explained, and approximate corrections suggested, in Chapter 2. But even with correction of this distortion, in 1977 India had a per capita income only, say, one twelfth of the Western European average and one fourteenth that of the United States, and there were 15 countries with per capita incomes lower than that of India.

More than one half of the people of the world live in countries with very low average incomes. China and India alone contain more than 35 percent of the world's people (perhaps 37 percent: the population of China is uncertain), and another 16 to 18 percent (depending on one's estimate of China's per capita income) live in other countries with average incomes equal to or lower than that of China. But even these low-income countries have a range of incomes, and above them an unbroken continuum of countries rises steadily to the highest.[4]

---

[3] These are presented in the *World Development Report, 1979*. Estimates of per capita GNPs and growth rates are also prepared by the United Nations (see its *Yearbook of National Income Accounts*) and by the U.S. Agency for International Development.

[4] The per capita income estimate for China presented in Table 1–2, $390 in 1977, is that of the *World Development Report, 1979*. It is much higher than previous estimates—more than 2½ times that for India by the exchange rate method of comparison. Adjusted as in Chapter 2, it is a little less than twice that of India, perhaps one sixth that of Western Europe, and one ninth that of the United States.

The estimate is almost certainly too high. It was presumably arrived at by estimating China's aggregate GNP, then dividing by China's estimated population. But while population experts differ concerning China's probable population, the lowest of their estimates is 100 million higher than the 823 million estimate presented by the World Bank. An official Chinese estimate of the country's 1978 population released in August, 1979, the first official estimate since World War II, implies a 1977 popuation of some 930 million. The World Bank also probably considerably overstates the rate of increase in China's aggregate GNP. (See the scholarly summary of information in Nick Eberstaat, "Has China Failed?" *New York Review of Books*, April 5, 1979, pp. 33–39.) Correction on these accounts would reduce China's estimated per capita income in 1977 to no more than $330, a more plausible estimate, though still a surprisingly high one. Substituting this estimate, one would say that China's per capita income is considerably less than twice that of India, perhaps one seventh

6

FIGURE 1–1   Income levels, 1977, and growth rates, 1960–1977

Only a mind with preconceptions could see dichotomy rather than continuum in these data. Even apart from the oil countries, the fastest-growing countries were not the highest income ones.

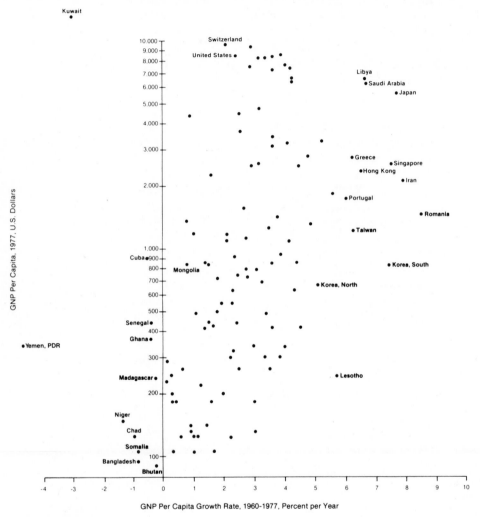

GNP Per Capita Growth Rate, 1960-1977, Percent per Year

Source: Table 1–2.

A CLASSIFICATION OF COUNTRIES

Even though national per capita incomes form a continuum, countries must be classified for convenience of discussion. How shall a classification be made?

that of Western Europe, and one eighth that of the United States. China would still rank high among the lowest income countries.

FIGURE 1–2   Income levels, 1975, and growth rates, 1970–1975

By comparing Figures 1–1 and 1–2, note the effect of the 1974–75 recession in industrial countries on growth rates in the lowest income countries.

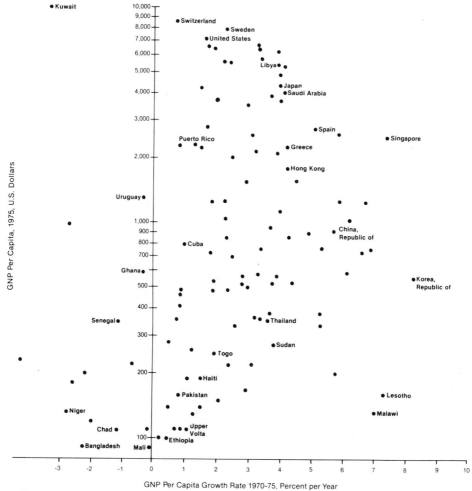

Source: Table 1–2.

It would be interesting to classify countries according to the state of their techniques. The ranking of some countries in this respect would differ greatly from their rank in income. The oil-producing countries provide the conspicuous example. They rank much higher in income than in technical capability. On the other hand, Japan and Israel, working with sparse natural resources, should be ranked higher among other nations in technical capability than in income. But for lack of a good measuring stick we cannot rank countries even approximately with respect to technical capability. With regard to per capita incomes, we can.

The World Bank's *World Development Report, 1979* classifies countries as "low income" (per capita GNP of $300 or less in 1977), "middle income," and "industrialized." The "industrialized" countries are the Western countries plus Japan. The *Report* classifies separately "Capital Surplus Oil Exporters" and "Centrally Planned Economies."

Though by now the reader will have had a surfeit of classifications, one other should be noted. In 1971 the United Nations formally established a class of "least developed countries." The criteria for inclusion were a low gross domestic product ($100 or less per capita in 1968), a low share of manufacturing in GDP, and a low literacy rate. Initially, 25 countries were included: 16 in sub-Sahara Africa, 6 in Asia, and the Maldives, Western Samoa, and Haiti. However, there were advantages in being included; special attention in technical assistance and United Nations economic aid was to be given to these countries. As a result, so many other countries pressed to be included that the list has grown to 42 and has lost its original significance.[5]

However, the concept of "least developed countries" should not be discarded. In some 12 to 15 very low income countries, per capita income is not rising or is rising more slowly than that of other countries. This is why these countries are at the bottom of the income list. The rest of the world is gradually drawing away from them. They are commonly regarded as likely to develop, if at all, only with an exceptional amount of economic and technical aid. Most are in Africa. Some have very limited natural resources. In some a spirit of entrepreneurship seems to be almost wholly lacking. These countries are reasonably classed as "least developed"—though again it must be noted that the qualities which distinguish them are a matter of degree and that there are differences of opinion concerning which countries should be included. (Observe on Figure 1-1 the impossibility of making a sharp distinction.)

Some writers refer to the Third World and the Fourth World, and thus implicitly to the First and Second worlds. In this terminology, the First World is the high-income non-Communist countries; the Second, the "centrally directed" or Communist countries; the Third, the lower income countries; and the Fourth, the "least developed" countries. Table 1-1 shows that part of the Second World is in fact in the Third World. The table, which classes the OPEC countries (members of the Organization of Petroleum Exporting Countries) in a separate column, also shows that not all oil countries are affluent. In Indonesia, Nigeria, and Ecuador, which are OPEC members, oil production forms too small a share of total economic activity to have raised per capita income greatly.

---

[5] UNCTAD (the United Nations Conference on Trade and Development) lists 31 countries as the "least developed." UNCTAD is an organization, not merely a conference.

TABLE 1–1   Selected groups of countries, classified by 1977 income levels*

	Number of Countries			
Per Capita Income (1977 U.S. dollars)	Population above 1 Million			Population below 1 Million (1975)
	OPEC Members	Centrally Directed	Other	
> 9,600	1		1	2
4,800 < 9,600	3		13	10
2,400 < 4,800	1	6	9	7
1,200 < 2,400	2	1	9	13
600 < 1,200	2	4	19	9
300 < 600	1	1	19	12
150 < 300			18	5
< 150			14	1

* Cambodia not included, for lack of an income estimate.
Source: Countries with population below 1 million (1975 data in 1975 dollars), *World Bank Atlas, 1977*; other data, Table 1–2.

Table 1–1 also shows the rather remarkable range of incomes in countries with populations below 1 million. Almost all of these tiny countries are islands. The two with per capita GNP above $9,600 and one in the $4,-800–$9,600 group are oil countries. Most of the other higher income contries with populations below 1 million are Caribbean islands.

GROWTH AND DEVELOPMENT

The terms *economic growth* and *economic development* will be used frequently. They do not have identical meanings.

"Economic growth" refers to increase in the production (gross domestic product) per capita or the income (gross national product) per capita in a country. The two are not necessarily identical—some of the income flowing from production may flow to foreigners.

The term *economic development* has two meanings. It is used to refer to economic growth plus improvement in the distribution of material welfare within the low-income countries. In this usage it implies improvement in the nutrition, health, and education of the lowest income families; reduction in infant mortality among these families; and increase in the dignity of their lives. These changes do not necessarily accompany economic growth; indeed, economic growth may make the poorest families even poorer.

The term *economic development* is also used, more technically, to refer to all the complex effects of growth, planned or unplanned, beneficial, detrimental, or neutral: to changes in the kinds of goods produced, the methods of producing them, and employment patterns; in the rate of population growth, foreign trade, urbanization, and so on; and in the distribution of material welfare. The term will be used in this book in both senses.

IS ECONOMIC DEVELOPMENT WORTHWHILE?

Before plunging further into the study of economic development, the reader may consider a philosophic question: Is that development worthwhile? The desired end product is increase in happiness. That economic development makes people happier is not self-evident.

An American student, considering how miserable he would be if his level of living were reduced to that of, say, the cultivators of India or northeast Brazil, may take it as axiomatic that those cultivators are miserable. But he is looking at their lives from the standpoint of what he is accustomed to. It will not do to judge the cultivators' happiness or the causes of their unhappiness from the outside. These must be judged from the cultivators' point of view.

"Seven years ago," wrote an American author in 1979,

> I traveled by train from Cairo to Aswan in Upper Egypt. . . . All along the way the train passed people standing in the fields, squatting by roadside fires, sitting in village stations, the women invariably wrapped in black from the eyes to the toes, the men in white or black tunics and turbans. . . . to my Western eyes they seemed, almost, a people made in a time before time, as though molded from the earth on which they stood. I remember shuddering with gratitude that the accident of birth had made me as I was rather than as they were. A month later I spent a few days in one of those villages the train had passed. Those days were a revelation: so alive with humor, intelligence, and intensity did the fellaheen prove to be, so complex was the life and culture of the village.[6]

Affluence certainly does not ensure happiness. The American society presents an example in point. Americans have been much the most affluent people in the world for a century. Comparison on a happiness scale with non-Western peoples is difficult, but among Western peoples Americans are probably the most anxious, that is, the least happy. The simple evidence is that in addition to the tranquilizers, sleeping pills, pep pills, pills to relieve headaches, and potions to relieve stomach distress that Americans can buy across the drugstore counter without a prescription and in addition to the illicit drugs to which a number of Americans resort, almost one half of American adults must relieve the anxiety of their lives or mitigate their state of depression by taking tranquilizers, soporifics, or antidepressant medications so dangerous that they can be obtained legally only through prescription by a physician. Historical accounts of American colonial life do not leave one sure that Americans of the 20th century are happier than were their colonial forebears at a time when per capita income was perhaps $250 or $300 per year. The contrary seems more likely.

---

[6] Vivian Gornick, in the *New York Times Book Review*, January 21, 1979.

In a distinguished early (1954) text on economic development W. Arthur Lewis presented arguments pro and con. The clincher for arguing that a rise in income increases human happiness was that it opens up more alternatives to human beings. We know now that this is hardly relevant, that it is dubious whether a correlation exists between happiness and the number of alternatives available.

The psychophilosophers who ponder such things know that a person's contentment with his life depends on his sure sense that he is a valuable being, that his life has some worth. Psychoanalysts know that the presence or absence of such a sense within an individual depends on whether or not he was given a sure sense of being valued during the earliest years of his life, and that its persistence within him thereafter has little to do with his absolute level of affluence. It depends rather on whether he feels that he is a part of a community of human beings by whom he is valued and on whom he can depend for recognition, respect, and, as he needs it, support.

In one of her novels, Willa Cather has one of her characters argue that (European) man has never been as happy since the Renaissance as he was before it. She does not spell out the argument; let me sketch it briefly here. On a well-run manor, the smithy, the miller, the carpenter, the peasant farmer each knew that his contribution to the life of the manor was needed and respected. A contemporary daily account of life on a certain medieval manor records that the lady of the manor visited the miller's wife because the latter's baby was sick. The incident symbolizes the best features of the manorial relationship. Alexis de Tocqueville, commenting on American life after a 1831 visit to the United States, remarked that in an aristocracy a chain of social responsibility ran from king to peasant, whereas democracy seemed to cause each person to withdraw into the solitude of his own heart. One need not agree that democracy was the cause of this phenomenon, or assume that a sense of social responsibility was strong on every manor or in every aristocracy, to appreciate the point.

By the same argument, before Western invaders disrupted the premodern social order of non-Western societies, in many of those societies a sense of social responsibility may have run from king or chieftain down to peasant and even the lowest members of those societies may have felt that their position was valued and secure. Such bits of historical evidence as are available concerning day-to-day life in these societies before the Western incursion do not suggest a lack of contentment. If one was respected, as was the miller on that manor, then one's income was enough. Today the elites of many non-Western societies feel contempt toward the peasants, and abuse them. This, it has been suggested, is a reaction to the contempt for their non-Western culture and society that was manifested by Western conquerors. The peasants have thus become the scapegoats for the humiliation that was experienced by the elites. The peasants' demand today for material improvement is evidence not that they have always felt impoverished but only that they feel unrespected today. Although this argument somewhat idealizes the past, it may contain a large element of truth.

E. J. Mishan, among others, has argued that affluence brings unhappiness because of its objective effects, such as pollution and urban dishevelment, and because of its destruction of old virtues.[7] Although most economists, including this writer, feel that Mishan strains pretty hard in making some of his points, there is a different sort of point that is hardly escapable. The location and arrangement of production are perpetually changing in a technically progressing society because of technical change and because of the changing patterns of life that rising income brings. Because each man's job is therefore also forever changing, and because almost every man's job is different from that of his father, a man has no roots. He feels no sense of community or security because he does not live long enough in one place, with the same set of neighbors. His neighbors are strangers, not members of a web of community. He tends to become a nameless atom. The increasing affluence that brings this result is hardly a bearer of happiness.

When one has no other basis for a feeling that one is valued and has value, the argument runs, one must seek that feeling in material goods. This is the basis of the sense of American families, the most affluent in the world, that they do not have quite enough but must keep gaining more—for example, by the wife working while young children are cared for in a day-care center. This—it is argued—is also the cause of the demand for more by the low-income classes of low-income countries. They are not respected, and so long as they are not respected, they will remain unhappy, as Americans remain unhappy.

If, then, it is dubious that the ascent of a society to affluence decreases unhappiness, is economic development worthwhile? The answer is yes, for four reasons.

First, history will not turn back. Neither any human power nor the wheel of fortune can restore the non-Western social structures that were destroyed by Western imperialism. Neither the elites nor the masses of non-Western societies any longer have a sense of secure place and secure valuation within a good society. This being so, both grasp for reassurance. The rod for which they grasp is economic development. They want it, badly. Their desires should be respected.

Second, a distinction must be made between the level of income and change in that level. People who are grasping at material goods to assuage their anxiety feel relief if they live better than they did previously. Rising income can give members of each generation a sense of affluence, and so a certain minimum but precious degree of assurance.

It is true that especially in the early generations of development the de-

---

[7] E. J. Mishan, *The Costs of Economic Growth* (New York: Praeger, 1967). See also his, *The Economic Growth Debate: An Assessment* (London: George Allen & Unwin, 1977).

velopment process may not raise the income of the mass of the people. It may leave their absolute level of income as low as before, or even reduce it. But economic growth carries with it the possibility of rising income for the lowly. If that possibility is realized, their sense that they are looked upon with contempt will be at least somewhat assuaged.

Third, economic growth carries with it the possibility, if by no means the certainty, of lessening the inequality of income distribution. This, if achieved, almost certainly increases human happiness. The argument is parallel to that of the preceding paragraph. It is relative status that is important.

Last, economic growth can alleviate the condition described by Mr. McNamara as absolute poverty. It is not possible to state with scientific assurance that the millions of people of the earth with the very lowest incomes will be happier if they receive minimum adequate food, health care, and education. Their present horizons may be so limited that they feel no sense of deprivation; no one has proved the contrary. But they will be fuller human beings if they are provided with the nutritional intake and health protection necessary for more adequate development of their bodies and their brains. Only a boldly cynical person would argue that this would not be good.

The reader will have noticed the stress in the above argument on improvement in the absolute and relative status of the low-income classes of the lower income societies. However, if the elites of those societies, deprived of the emotional security that their ancestors may have felt, grasp for more to relieve their anxieties, their grasping will cause them to resist accepting a lessened share of the benefits of growth in order to give the lowly an increased share. If traditional elites are in control, low-income countries are not likely to have egalitarian social policies. The groups in control may

Table 1–2   Population, income levels, and growth rates

	Population, Mid-1977 (millions)	GNP Per Capita		
		Level, 1977 (U.S. dollars)	Average Annual Growth (percent)	
			1960–77	1970–75
Low income countries				
Bhutan	1.2	80	−0.2	—
Cambodia	8.4	—	—	—
Bangladesh	81.2	90	−0.4	−2.3
Lao PDR	3.2	90	—	−15.9
Ethiopia	30.2	110	1.7	0.4
Mali	6.1	110	1.0	−0.1
Nepal	13.3	110	0.2	0.7
Somalia	3.7	110	−0.4	−0.2
Burundi	4.2	130	2.2	−1.1
Chad	4.2	130	−1.0	−2.0
Rwanda	4.4	130	1.0	0.2

14

Table 1–2 *(continued)*

	Population, Mid-1977 (millions)	GNP Per Capita		
		Level, 1977 (U.S. dollars)	Average Annual Growth (percent)	
			1960–77	1970–75
Upper Volta	5.5	130	0.6	1.1
Zaire	25.7	130	1.1	1.5
Burma	31.5	140	0.9	0.9
Malawi	5.6	140	3.0	7.0
India	631.7	150	1.3	0.5
Mozambique	9.7	150	0.9	−2.6
Niger	4.9	160	−1.4	−2.8
Viet Nam	50.6	160	—	—
Afghanistan	14.3	190	0.2	2.1
Pakistan	74.9	190	3.0	0.8
Sierra Leone	3.2	190	1.3	−0.5
Tanzania	16.4	190	2.6	2.9
Benin	3.2	200	0.2	−1.1
Sri Lanka	14.1	200	2.0	1.1
Guinea	5.0	220	1.3	1.3
Haiti	4.7	230	0.1	1.5
Lesotho	1.3	240	5.8	7.3
Madagascar	8.1	240	−0.2	−2.2
Central African Empire.............	1.9	250	0.2	−0.7
Kenya	14.6	270	2.5	2.4
Mauritania	1.5	270	3.6	2.6
Uganda	12.0	270	0.7	−4.5
Sudan	16.9	290	0.1	3.8
Angola	6.6	300	2.3	3.2
Indonesia	133.5	300	3.3	3.5
Togo	2.4	300	3.8	2.0
Middle income countries				
Egypt	37.8	320	2.1	1.3
China, People's Republic (CP)	930	330	4.0	4.2
Cameroon	7.9	340	2.9	0.5
Yemen, PDR	1.7	340	−4.8	−5.8
Ghana	10.6	380	−0.3	−0.3
Honduras	3.3	410	1.5	0.8
Liberia	1.7	420	1.8	0.9
Nigeria	79.0	420	3.6	5.3
Thailand	43.8	420	4.5	3.6
Senegal	5.2	430	−0.3	−1.1
Yemen Arab Republic	5.0	430	—	5.8
Philippines	44.5	450	2.5	3.7
Zambia	5.1	450	1.5	0.9
Congo, People's Republic	1.4	490	1.1	4.3
Papua New Guinea ..	2.9	490	3.4	3.3
Rhodesia	6.7	500	1.8	2.8
El Salvador	4.2	550	1.8	1.9

Table 1–2 (continued)

	Population, Mid-1977 (millions)	GNP Per Capita		
		Level, 1977 (U.S. dollars)	Average Annual Growth (percent)	
			1960–77	1970–75
Morocco	18.3	550	2.2	3.0
Albania (CP)	2.5	630	4.3	3.8
Bolivia	5.2	630	2.3	3.4
Korea, North	16.7	670	5.1	0.9
Ivory Coast	7.5	690	3.3	1.9
Jordan	2.9	710	1.8	1.9
Colombia	24.6	720	2.7	3.9
Paraguay	2.8	730	2.4	3.3
Ecuador	7.3	790	3.1	6.1
Guatemala	6.4	790	2.8	2.8
Korea, South	36.0	820	7.4	8.2
Mongolia (CP)	1.5	830	0.8	2.3
Nicaragua	2.4	830	2.5	2.5
Dominican Republic	5.0	840	3.6	6.6
Peru	16.4	840	2.3	3.4
Tunisia	5.9	860	4.3	6.9
Cuba (CP)	9.6	910	−0.4	1.0
Syrian Arab Republic	7.8	910	2.3	1.8
Malaysia	13.0	930	3.9	5.3
Algeria	17.0	1,110	2.1	4.3
Turkey	41.9	1,110	4.1	4.9
Mexico	63.3	1,120	2.8	2.3
Jamaica	2.1	1,150	2.1	4.0
Lebanon	2.9	—	—	—
Chile	10.6	1,160	1.0	−2.7
Taiwan	16.8	1,170	6.2	5.7
Panama	1.8	1,220	3.5	2.2
Costa Rica	2.1	1,240	3.2	3.7
South Africa	27.0	1,340	2.1	1.7
Brazil	116.1	1,360	4.9	6.2
Uruguay	2.9	1,430	0.8	−0.3
Iraq (OE)	11.8	1,550	3.8	6.7
Romania (CP)	21.6	1,580	8.5	10.2
Argentina	26.0	1,730	2.7	2.9
Portugal	9.6	1,890	6.0	4.5
Yugoslavia	21.7	1,960	5.6	5.9
Iran (OE)	34.8	2,160	7.9	13.3
Trinidad and Tobago	1.1	2,380	1.6	2.5
Bulgaria (CP)	8.8	2,580	4.4	3.9
Hungary (CP)	10.6	2,580	2.9	3.2
Hong Kong	4.5	2,590	6.5	4.2
Venezuela (OE)	13.5	2,660	2.7	1.5
Greece	9.2	2,810	6.2	4.2
Israel	3.6	2,850	4.8	4.0
Ireland	3.2	2,880	3.1	1.3
Singapore	2.3	2,880	7.5	7.3
USSR	258.9	3,020	3.7	3.1

Table 1-2 *(continued)*

	Population, Mid-1977 (millions)	GNP Per Capita		
		Level, 1977 (U.S. dollars)	Average Annual Growth (percent)	
			1960–77	1970–75
Poland	34.7	3,150	4.1	5.8
Spain	36.3	3,190	5.2	5.1
High income countries				
Italy	56.5	3,440	3.7	1.7
Czechoslovakia (CP) .	15.0	3,890	2.6	3.0
New Zealand	3.1	4,380	1.9	1.5
United Kingdom	55.9	4,420	2.5	2.0
German Democratic Republic (CP)	16.9	4,680	3.2	3.7
Japan	113.2	5,670	7.7	4.0
Saudi Arabia (OE) ...	7.6	6,040	6.7	4.1
Austria	7.5	6,130	4.2	4.0
Finland	4.7	6,160	4.2	4.1
Libya (OE)	2.6	6,680	6.6	3.9
Netherlands	13.9	7,150	3.7	2.2
France	53.1	7,290	4.2	3.4
Australia	14.1	7,340	2.9	2.4
Belgium	9.8	7,590	4.0	3.9
Denmark	5.1	8,040	3.1	1.7
Germany, Federal Republic	61.4	8,160	3.3	1.9
Canada	23.3	8,460	3.6	3.3
United States	220.0	8,520	2.4	1.6
Norway	4.0	8,550	3.9	3.3
Sweden	8.3	9,250	2.9	2.3
Switzerland	6.3	9,970	2.1	0.7
Kuwait (OE)	1.1	12,270	−3.1	−3.3

Methods: GNP per capita converted to U.S. dollars by the conventional method (see text). Growth rates, 1970–75, compound rate from initial to terminal year. Growth rates, 1960–77, least squares trend line fitted to real GNP data for all years of the period.

Symbols used:
— Not available.
CP Centrally planned economy.
OE Major oil exporter, i.e., country whose petroleum production contributes a large share of its GNP. Note that the oil countries Bahrain, Gabon, Qatar, and United Oil Emirates, with 1977 per capita GNPs ranging from $3,790 to $14,420 are not included because the 1977 population of each is below 1 million.

Sources: Population, GNP level, and growth rates, 1960–77, except People's Republic of China, *World Development Report, 1979,* Table 1. Growth rates, 1970–75, except China, *World Bank Atlas, 1977.* All data for China estimated by present writer.

demand more from the higher income countries as their moral right, but they are not likely to feel a moral obligation to share that "more" with their own lowly. Only when the forces of the market cause a decrease in the inequality of income distribution—or when social revolution occurs—will inequality decrease, unless in some way pressures from outside the lower income societies can bring about the result. This is one of the dilemmas of economic growth.

FOR FURTHER READING

Concerning national product data, see the suggestions for further reading following Chapter 2.

Ezra Mishan, *The Costs of Economic Growth* (New York: Praeger, 1967). Mishan's *The Economic Growth Debate: An Assessment* (London: George Allen & Unwin, 1977) is not an assessment but a restatement of his criticisms.

Dudley Seers, "What Are We Trying to Measure?" *Journal of Development Studies*, Vol. 8, No. 3 (April 1972).

E. F. Schumacher, *Good Work* (New York: Harper & Row, 1979). A collection of Schumacher's lectures and essays, some presenting examples of "intermediate technology," some expounding an almost religious belief in the virtues of the simple life.

❖ ❖ ❖ ❖ ❖

In "For Further Reading" in subsequent chapters, three recent collections of essays and a fourth book which excerpts a large number of essays will be listed repeatedly. They will be referred to hereafter by author and title only, that is, without full bibliographic reference. These are:

Jagdish N. Bhagwati, ed., *The New International Order* (Cambridge, Mass.: MIT Press, 1977).

Edgar O. Edwards, ed., *Employment in Developing Nations* (New York: Columbia University Press, 1974).

Gerald K. Helleiner, ed. *A World Divided: The Less Developed Countries in the International Economy* (Cambridge: Cambridge University Press, 1976).

Gerald M. Meier, ed., *Leading Issues in Development Economics*, 3d ed. (New York: Oxford University Press, 1976). Meier excerpts a wide range of essays concerning development. He has cut most of them—skillfully, but rather drastically. He presents introductory notes to each section.

The following journals are devoted to the economics of development and of the LDCs: *World Development, Journal of Developing Areas, Journal of Developing Economics,* and *Journal of Development Studies. Economic Development and Cultural Change* presents articles concerning both economic and cultural aspects. Articles on development are of course also found in all of the general economics journals.

2

A Closer Look at
Income Levels and
Growth Rates

INCOME LEVELS

One's first reaction, when one considers the data presented in Table 1–2, is that they are incredible. If one considers carefully what share of the goods and services consumed by the average American family that family could do without, assuming that the family lived in a warm climate and obtained its food in simple, not processed, form from nearby, one will conclude that the family could live healthfully on one fifteenth or conceivably one twentieth of its actual income, but certainly not on one fiftieth. Surely at this level of income 70% or 80% of the people of the lowest income countries would be dead within a year. Yet they do not merely exist; they exist with a margin that permits them to increase in number. Their number is increasing at a much faster rate than that of the populations of the high-income countries.

The data, then, not only seem incredible. They are incredible. The second thing to observe about them is that they are not true.

One of the difficulties is that national income measurements are imprecise; another is that national income concepts as used in these measurements were devised in the high-income countries and are better adapted to those countries than to lower income countries. In the latter, many goods and services are produced in the home, and not included in the measurement, that in high-income countries are purchased in the market and included.

The major source of error, however, is that the comparison among countries is made by estimating the national product of each country in its own currency, then converting the figure to another currency—in this case U.S. dollars—by use of the exchange rate between the two currencies. Whatever

18

the exchange rate measures, it does not measure the relative purchasing power at home of the two currencies.

An alternative procedure is to estimate directly the value that the goods and services produced in one country would have in another. To record the goods and services produced in, say, India, determine the prices they would have in the United States, and so calculate India's per capita income in dollars and compare it with that of the United States. Or, conversely, to value the national product of the United States in rupees and so compare it with that of India. Or, since the two procedures will yield quite different comparisons, to take an average (the geometric mean is usually used) of the two.

The process of such direct comparisons among countries began with comparison of European countries with the United States, more than 20 years ago. Steadily, estimates of varying degrees of reliability have been made for additional countries. On the basis of these purchasing power comparisons for some countries, statistical adjustments have been made to exchange rate comparisons to yield approximations to purchasing power comparisons for other countries. In 1978 Irving Kravis and two coauthors published one for more than 100 countries.[1] It shows, for India, per capita income in the early 1970s not one fiftieth but perhaps one sixteenth that of the United States. This is the geometric mean variant; the variant by which Indian production is priced in dollars would show the per capita income of Indians to be a larger fraction of the per capita income of Americans.

By and large, the greater the difference in income levels between two countries, the greater is the correction. If the correction could be applied to all the countries shown in Figure 1–1 and Table 1–2 it would considerably compress the range of incomes shown. However, it would not alter the ranking of countries greatly. The data based on conversions between currencies by means of exchange rates are used in this book because they are available for more countries, are familiar to economists, and do show with approximate accuracy the income rankings of countries. The reader should remember that these data exaggerate the income differences.

However, the differences are impressive even in corrected figures. A per capita income ratio of 14 to 1, or of 20 to 1 between the high-income countries and the very lowest income countries, is still enormous.

The Geographic Distribution of Income

Technical progress, it would seem, is a process that has diffused from a center of contagion in Western Europe. Table 2–1 shows average per capita incomes by geographic areas, with, however, the oil countries of the Middle East and the highest income countries other than the oil-rich ones set out as separate groups. (The data are for per capita GNPs calculated by use of ex-

---

[1] Irving B. Kravis, Alan W. Heston, and Robert Summers, "Real GDP Per Capita for More than One Hundred Countries," *Economic Journal*, 88 (June 1978), 215–42

TABLE 2-1   The world's geographic regions showed a wide range of income levels in 1975 (countries with populations of more than one million)*

	Population Mid-year (millions)	Per Capita GNP (U.S. dollars)
Northern America†	237	7,080
Australia–New Zealand	17	5,290
Japan	112	4,450
Europe, excluding Communist countries	419	3,950
USSR and Communist Europe	384	2,500
Affluent oil countries‡	83	2,070
Latin America, excluding Venezuela	408	960
Africa, excluding South Africa	383	332
Asia, excluding Japan and Israel	1,952	277

   * Three affluent oil countries with smaller populations are included in the oil country group.
   † United States and Canada.
   ‡ Algeria, Iran, Iraq, Kuwait, Saudi Arabia, and Libya, plus three tiny countries: Gabon, Qatar, and the United Arab Emirates.
   Source: World Bank Atlas, 1977. The tabulation omits Israel, with per capita income of $3,790, and the Republic of South Africa, with per capita income of $1,207.

change rates. In purchasing power, the range between Asia and Northern America is about one half of that shown in the table.) One observes a steady rise in income, with increasingly wide intervals, from the areas with which the West has had the least contact to those with which it has had the most. Japan is the exception (and now Hong Kong, Taiwan, and Singapore). Explanatory factors other than diffusion from the West exist and will be presented, but that diffusion seems a plausible important cause.

RATES OF GROWTH

The Countries of the West

Historians trace the economic rise of the West in the modern era back to the Western scientific and technical heritage from the ancient Middle East, from India via the Middle East, and from ancient Greece. A geographer asserts the causal influence of a superior climate. Some non-Westerners see the seed in the exploitation of lands conquered and ruled as colonies.[2] But the primacy of this factor is belied by the fact that the net economic exploitation, however one defines that phrase, was *quantitatively* small. In

---

   [2] A social-psychological argument may also be adduced. In the countries that Westerners conquered or ruled, they trod on ancient religious practices and taboos and in these and other ways indicated by their actions that they thought the traditional culture, and thereby the traditional people, worthless. They in turn seemed uncouth, barbaric, to the

some instances it was negative—the imperialists poured more money into some colonies than they took out. These quantitative observations should not be read as a defense of colonialism. On moral grounds colonialism is indefensible, but our moral indignation should not cause us to exaggerate its significance for the West's economic growth.

The proximate cause of the present high level of income of Western countries is simply that they have been growing economically for a long time. Even in 1700 their per capita incomes were significantly higher than those of the non-Western countries, possibly three times as high on the average. There are few data concerning the Western rate of growth during the two centuries before 1700. It cannot have been more than 1 percent per year per capita, and indeed it cannot have been much more than that during the 18th century, for projection of a higher rate of growth backward from the beginning of the 19th century yields an impossibly low level of income in, say, 1500. But during the 19th and 20th centuries it has been faster. For the last four decades of the 19th century and for the 20th century, there are estimates. Table 2–2 presents them for seven Western countries, Russia–USSR, and Japan.

TABLE 2–2   Western countries have been growing for a long time

Country	Annual Rate of Growth in Per Capita Income (percent)	
	1860 or 1870 to 1900	1900 to 1975
Japan	3.0	4.1
United States	2.5	2.0
Sweden	2.4	2.7
Canada	2.2	2.1
Germany*	2.0	2.1
France	1.5	1.5
Great Britain	1.4	1.3
Russia–USSR	1.0	2.6
Italy	0.8	2.3

* Since World War II, West Germany.
Sources: Estimates from Kuznets, in *Economic Development and Cultural Change*, October 1956, for the period up to 1950 have been combined with estimates by the International Bank for Reconstruction and Development for subperiods of 1950–75.

Though Japan's rate of growth during the period covered by the data is the fastest in the world (apart from almost vertical rises in oil countries), Japan is not the world's highest income country, because it entered the race at a low income level. The performance of Sweden and Switzerland (the

indigenous people. For an indigenous individual, to imitate their ways of living would be to admit that they were right, that he was worthless. Yet they had power. The mental and emotional confusion thus created in the colonial peoples must have given use to a strong unconscious barrier to adopting Western technical practices.

latter not shown in Table 2–2) during this period has received less attention than it deserves. By their steady rates of growth since 1870 as well as, undoubtedly, many decades before 1870, these two countries have become by conventional measures the highest income countries in the world apart from Kuwait, the United Arab Emirates, and Qatar. (However, purchasing power comparisons show that the United States still has the world's highest level of per capita income except for these oil countries.)

The growth of the Western countries as a group illustrates the "miracle of compound interest." Plotted on a semilogarithmic graph, a constant exponential rate of growth is a straight line, but plotted on a graph with an arithmetic scale, it rises slowly at first but in due time seems to be rising almost vertically.

Recent Growth: The Less Developed Countries

If the per capita income of China is one tenth, of India one fourteenth, or perhaps only one eighteenth, and of the lowest income countries one twentieth that of the United States, this is not because part of the labor, land, or capital of the low-income countries is unemployed. Or, where this is true, it is only a minor part of the explanation. The explanation of such large income differences is that the productivity of the low-income countries' land, labor, and capital is low even when these are fully employed. And the proximate cause of the low productivity of the low-income countries is that their productivity has been increasing for only a short time. With the possible exception of India this is not because of exploitation by the West but because until recently technical progress has not been a part of their culture or their behavior.

India may have been entering upon a period of "merchant capitalism"—artisans becoming traders of their products and then manufacturers—when the English invaded the subcontinent. If so, had India had contact with Western methods without colonialism, it might have undergone an industrial revolution not long after the West. The imperial powers were hostile to industrialization in their colonies, or at best were not interested in fostering it. The British found a flourishing cotton textile industry in India, and they tried to discourage it by taxing it (but did not succeed). When the Indians adopted modern methods, because of their lower wages and transportation costs they competed successfully with the British in making cheaper cotton cloths in India and in selling yarn to other Asian countries.

One economist has suggested an alternative or additional cause for the lack of technical progress in non-Western lands: that progress was deterred by the flooding of workers from India and China to other countries. Their willingness to work for low wages, Arthur Lewis argues, kept wage incomes so low that no market for industrial products existed. Hence industrialization did not proceed, and therefore incomes did not rise.[3] However, one must reject this argument as a general explanation, for there are too many countries that were not flooded by Indian or Chinese workers in which income nevertheless remained low. To the present writer, it seems likely that a much more important explanation lies in two other factors in combination: the inherent difficulty of technical progress even when the helpful example of advanced methods exists elsewhere, and differences in the degree of innovational talent and zeal that exists among countries at any given era in their histories. The first of these two points is argued in Chapter 6, the second in Chapter 13.

It may be reasonably assumed that in many of the present lower income countries growth began quietly decades and in some instances generations before World War II. Industrialization was proceeding fairly rapidly in Russia between 1860 and 1900, and at that time it was also beginning to be seen in eastern and southern Europe. Industry had begun to emerge in India and Japan before 1900. There was economic vigor and some manufacturing industry in Argentina in 1900, and the beginnings of manufacturing industry appeared in Brazil and Colombia soon after. Detailed historical study would probably show similar stirrings in a number of other countries at this time. However, in non-Western countries economic growth was certainly slow. It accelerated after World War II.

Only for the period since 1960 are there data for a large number of countries. Those data show that the present lower income countries are raising their per capita incomes much faster now than did Western countries in the early generations of their growth. From the viewpoint of the less developed countries or of sympathetic Westerners the present economic progress of the lower income countries is painfully slow, but from the viewpoint of history it is fast.

Yet in recent years only the middle-income countries as a group have been raising their per capita incomes more rapidly than the industrialized countries. Table 2-3 presents data for the period 1960-77. The table reflects the melancholy fact, considered further in Chapter 4, that growth begins slowly and accelerates slowly. Only after a period of some and perhaps many generations, during which a country's income rises to the level that is now considered "middle income," does it begin to catch up with the high-income countries, in the sense of growing at a faster rate than they do. This, it will be suggested in Chapter 6, is a rule that is likely to hold true in the future as it has in the past, even if the allocation of economic aid is biased in favor of the low-income countries.

But behind these group figures lie the large differences in growth rates among countries at any given income level that are shown in Figure 1-1

---

[3] W. Arthur Lewis, *The Evolution of the International Economic Order* (Princeton: Princeton University Press, 1978).

TABLE 2-3   Median and average growth rates, 1960-1977, in countries with populations of 1 million or more, classed by structure and income levels

Economic growth accelerates, then slows down, if these comparisons among non-oil non-Communist countries indicate its course in any given country over time.

Country Groups	Annual Growth Rates in Per Capita GNP, 1960-1976, in %	
	Median	Average, Weighted by Population*
Countries not separately classed below, by income levels, mid-1977 (U.S. dollars)		
80-300 (34 countries)	1.1	1.5
310-1,200 (42 countries)	2.5	3.0
1,210-3,200 (15 countries)	4.2	4.5
>3,200 (17 countries)	3.4	3.8
Centrally planned (12 countries, including Romania; low to high income levels)	3.9	4.0
Saudi Arabia, Libya, Kuwait, and Iran	6.7	7.4

* Weighting by population gives equal weights to the same percentage increase per person, regardless of absolute income level.

Source: Table 1-2.

and Table 1-2. There is among countries, as among individuals, a "circulation of the elites." Many countries at any income range are growing faster than some of the countries at higher income levels. There is no reason to suppose that the two or three highest income countries of today will be the two or three highest income countries 50 years from now. Nor even to suppose that two decades from now the high-income group, the middle-income group, the lower-income group, or even the least developed group will have the membership of those groups as they are identified today.

One may doubt that there will ever be even approximate equality of income among nations. One may speculate that some of the present middle-income countries will continue to grow faster in per capita income than the present high-income countries until they pass those countries, and that in turn, by the same process, they will eventually be passed by countries that are now below them. However, so many imponderables will affect the world's long-run economic growth that this must be a highly uncertain speculation.

THE DEMAND FOR A NEW INTERNATIONAL ECONOMIC ORDER

In any event, "a stern chase is a long chase." Differences in rates of growth will only very slowly decrease a wide income gap. Suppose that per capita income in a country with an average income level of $3,200 grows at a rate of 2.5 percent per year while per capita income in a country with an average income of $400, one eighth as high, grows at 3.5 percent per year.

The income gap between the two countries, calculated as the ratio between their per capita incomes, will begin to diminish at once, but the absolute difference in income level will continue to increase for some 182 years, and 214 and a fraction years will pass before the lower income country reaches equality with the higher—at an income in each of about $634,000 per capita. In a more or less finite world, this is hardly a realistic scenario.

In his 1977 address to the World Bank's Board of Governors, Mr. McNamara presented a related calculation. Suppose that the industrial countries of the world, as a group, continue their historical rate of growth in per capita income (not the unprecedentedly fast rate of the 1960s). If, then, each of the LDCs continues its growth rate of the 25-year period 1950–75, in 100 years only seven would reach equality with the average level of income in the industrial countries, and—so great is the difference in growth rates between these few and other LDCs—in 1,000 years, only another nine.

The lower income nations, perhaps especially the higher income nations among them, are impatient. They want an increase in income not merely through increasing productivity but through the transfer of wealth and income from the high-income nations to them. They feel that they have been abused and exploited. They believe (contrary to fact) that the terms on which they exchange their goods for the industrial products of the high-income countries have been worsening during the past century and more. Some statements of their leaders imply that if they had not been abused and exploited they would now have incomes that would equal, or at least approach, those of the West. They want not merely a transfer of wealth and income but a greater voice in world affairs. They propose, so far as they can, to reach these goals by means of their control over raw materials that the industrial nations use.

In a United Nations Special Assembly convened in September 1975 and in the United Nations General Assembly meeting in the autumn of 1976, the LDCs, which constitute a majority of the United Nations, adopted resolutions calling for a "New International Economic Order." The fourth meeting of UNCTAD, in March and May 1976, had issued a similar call, as had a World Economic Conference held in April 1976. The General Assembly resolutions asserted the need for change from the present world economic system to one "founded in equity and justice," and sketched the steps that the participants thought necessary to bring it about.

Specifically, these various resolutions called for: provision for "more participation" (meaning a larger share of control) in the international monetary system by the LDCs and the issuance by the International Monetary Fund of "Special Drawing Rights" (the equivalent of money; see Chapter 18) to the LDCs; cancellation of some of the foreign debts that the LDCs have accumulated through borrowing, and refinancing of the remainder at easier terms; "equitable participation" by the LDCs in world shipping (meaning transfer of ownership of ships and shipping facilities to them);

greater access of LDCs to the markets of the high-income countries; sovereignty (meaning ownership) by each nation over the natural resources within its boundaries that foreign firms may now be developing; an end to (mythical) declining terms of trade and an increase in the prices of LDC exports; an international code that would shorten the term and narrow the scope of patent rights; an increase in the transfer of technology; and effective regulation of the operations of international corporations.

The reader from a high-income country who may be incredulous and a little aghast that the LDCs feel that they should be *given* all of these things must remember the sense of injustice and frustration that lies behind the demands. Each of these demands is discussed at an appropriate place, later in this volume.

The call for a New International Economic Order contains no reference to redistribution of income within LDCs, and LDCs whose elite groups have no interest in such redistribution as well as individuals not in power who favor it join in the call.

Early in the 1970s the Club of Rome, a private group that has concerned itself with world economic growth, commissioned a study of the changes that would be needed to diminish rapidly the "income gap" between low- and high-income countries. The study, directed by Jan Tinbergen, was published in 1976, under the title *RIO—Reshaping the International Order.*[4] At about the same time, in anticipation of the concerns of the General Assembly, the United Nations had commissioned a more massively econometric study of the problem, this one to be directed by Wassily Leontief. It was published in 1977, and it employs the "input-output" technique which is identified with Leontief's name.[5] (This is described briefly in Chapter 22.) The Leontief study, inhibited by the sensitivities of United Nations members, makes no reference to restricting either population growth or the various arms races in the LDC world. The Tinbergen study is not thus inhibited.

Both studies envision a massive rapid transfer of technical knowledge and capital from high-income countries to low-income countries, and both assume that the low-income countries would be able to absorb the techniques of the high-income countries and develop industrial complexes with extreme rapidity. The changes would of course require the present industrialized countries to accept rapidly increasing flows of manufactured products from the erstwhile low-income countries. In the Leontief study the world's nations are divided between high- and low-income countries at such an income level that the income ratio between the two (with relative incomes calculated by use of exchange rates) in 1970 was 12 to 1. In one vari-

---

[4] Jan Tinbergen, coordinator; Antony J. Dolman, editor; and Jan van Ettinger, director, *RIO—Reshaping the International Order: A Report to the Club of Rome* (New York: E. P. Dutton, 1976).

[5] *The Future of the World Economy: A United Nations Study* (New York: Oxford University Press, 1977).

ant of the calculations, this gap is reduced to 7 to 1 by the year 2000. In another, it is eliminated by 2050. Heroic assumptions about the possible speed of change are required in both. The Tinbergen study envisions income parity between the two groups of nations a century from now. Tinbergen sketches a program by which the low-income countries, through their control of raw materials and the use of other economic weapons, might force the higher income countries to make the necessary changes.

FOR FURTHER READING

World Bank Report, 1979 presents a very useful textual summary and a set of 23 tables concerning various aspects of economic development in 120-odd countries. It is the second of an intended annual series of such reports.

The United Nations annual *World Economic Survey* presents a much longer summary concerning the non-Communist economically more developed countries, the Communist countries, and the less developed countries. Each volume also deals with a selected special topic. See also the reports of the United Nations regional commissions.

Statistical publications of the United Nations and its specialized agencies are comprehensive sources of data. Of most general coverage are three annual publications of the United Nations itself: the *Demographic Yearbook*, the *Statistical Yearbook*, and the *Yearbook of National Income Accounts*. The United Nations quarterly *Statistical Bulletin* presents current data. The standard source for statistical series relating to financial and some economic matters, for members of the International Monetary Fund and for the world as a whole, is the fund's monthly *International Financial Statistics*.

W. W. Rostow, *The World Economy: History & Prospect* (Austin, Texas: University of Texas Press, 1978) presents and discusses a large volume of varied data.

The United Nations General Assembly resolutions concerning the New International Economic Order are found in United Nations, General Assembly, "Resolutions Adopted . . . during Its Sixth Special Session," Official Records: Sixth Special Session, supplement no. 1 (A/9559), 1974; and "Resolutions Adopted . . . during Its Seventh Special Session," Official Records: Seventh Special Session, supplement no. 1 (A/10301), 1975.

See also the article by Kravis and others and the volumes by Tinbergen and Leontief listed in notes 1, 4, and 5, respectively, of this chapter.

3

A Description of
Low-Income Economies
and Their Growth

We turn now to a closer survey of the lower income economies and some aspects of their growth.

THE LDCs AS A GROUP

The Political-Social-Cultural Framework

1. Only about seven of the LDCs have reasonably full political democracy. I write "about seven" because the boundary line is not a clear and sharp one. For example, I include Mexico and Egypt. Are they democracies? Some persons would say no.

Since the democracies include not only Mexico and Egypt but also India, they include about one half of the total population of the non-communist LDCs and about one third of the population of all LDCs, including the Communist. Political control in the nondemocracies is by an individual who is hailed as the country's natural and right leader; a small traditional (usually landed) elite, with which a smaller new business elite may be associated; a military clique, representing that elite, which seized control when social revolution threatened to oust the old leader or leading group; or, where social revolution has succeeded, by a new authoritarian leader or group, Communist or non-communist. In some countries the authoritarian leader is an individual to whom there is tribal loyalty. In other countries he is merely an individual who seized the public's emotions during or after the struggle for independence from colonial rule. So long as the leader seems to have concern for the people, they hail him; if he seems to become highly oppressive, they may try to overthrow him. If they succeed they hail an authoritarian successor.

The Soviet Union provides the only clear example thus far of a continuation of authoritarian rule by popular choice as income rises to a high level. However, it should not be concluded that economic development necessarily breeds democracy. It may merely be that the same qualities that caused the countries of Western Europe to be the first to advance technically in the modern era are the qualities that also caused them to move steadily to democracy.

2. Of all the world's non-Western areas, only Japan, which has recently risen rapidly to a high-income level, did not experience Western domination during its modern history. China was never a Western colony, but Western domination was great there. All the areas of Africa and the rest of Asia other than a bit of Southeast Asia and part of the Middle East were made colonies. In the Middle East, Western domination was indirect rather than direct. The countries of South America, except for a few small ones on the northern edge of the continent, have been independent for a far longer time than other ex-colonies, but it was the Spanish and Portuguese invader-conquerors, not the indigenous population, who led the independence movements. They were the landed elite, and they remained in control. As it is sometimes put, colonialism became domestic. Rhodesia and South Africa are more extreme similar cases.

Demography

3. Until the post–World War II period the LDCs had barely entered upon the "demographic revolution." Death rates had been reduced during the preceding generation, but not much except in Ceylon (now Sri Lanka), Taiwan, and Singapore, where they had fallen during the 1930s. Elsewhere birth rates were high, death rates not much lower, and the population growth rate still low. Death rates were brought down sharply during the first decade following World War II, not by economic growth but by public health and preventive medicine programs introduced throughout the low-income world by the U.S. Public Health Service and the World Health Organization. Very rapid population growth ensued.

The Economic Base

4. One of the fictions commonly believed about the LDCs is that in all of them people jostle each other for space. Actually, population density varies greatly among them. It is high in countries in which settled agriculture has long been practiced. It is evidence of their success but lack of technical progress in agriculture. The two huge low-income countries, China and India, are densely populated; hence the bulk of the world's low-income population lives in densely populated countries. Population density is also high in island plantation economies—the West Indies, Fiji, Mauritius, Sri Lanka—to which immigrant labor was brought and in which some endemic

diseases were controlled.[1] Except for these plantation islands, wherever social organization was tribal and the economic base was hunting, herding, or fishing until modern times, population density is low. It is low in many countries in Southeast Asia, South America, and Africa. It is nevertheless true that no low-income country today has the unused rich land that was available in the United States, Canada, Australia, and New Zealand when European settlers came to them, and that few low-income countries today have as low person-land ratios as did the countries of Western Europe in 1700.

5. Because producers seeking minerals have first explored their homelands, geologically the less developed countries are still little explored. Geologists state that these countries surely have important undiscovered mineral resources.

6. An important band of LDCs lies just north of the Tropic of Cancer—African countries north of the Sahara, Afghanistan, Iraq, Iran, Pakistan, Bangladesh, and China. Chile lies below the Tropic of Capricorn. Apart from these, every LDC lies in the tropics, and every country in the tropics except Singapore, with its recent rapid rise in income, is a low-income country. The significance and causes of this association of location in the tropics with lack of development have been much disputed among economists. The question is discussed in Chapter 8.

There is little land in the South Temperate Zone. All but a few of the more developed countries of the world lie in the North Temperate Zone. For this reason the problem of economic development is sometimes referred to as the North-South problem. (South of the tropics, Uruguay and Argentina, with per capita GNPs of $1,430 and $1,730 in 1977, have become middle-income countries.)

7. In most lower income countries, agriculture is predominantly peasant agriculture: cultivation by peasant proprietors, who are renters in some countries and owners in other countries, on very small holdings. Even where land is plentiful, the typical holding will be no more than six to eight hectares (15 to 20 acres), since for most crops this is the greatest area that can be cultivated with one yoke of oxen or water buffalo or other beasts of burden, using primitive plows and drag harrows. Where population density is high, the size of a typical holding may be as little as one to three hectares. In these countries plots much larger than eight hectares are mainly tracts on which "dry cultivation" is practiced.

In other countries, large estates or ranches are common. They are of two types: large unproductive estates or ranches of individuals to whom operation of the establishment is more a way of life than an economic activity, and estates or plantations on which rubber, tea, cacao, or some other prod-

---

[1] Hla Myint makes these points in his *Economics of the Developing Countries* (London: Hutchinson, 1964), p. 32.

uct adapted to large-scale production with wage labor is produced for the world market. The first type of large estate is most common in South America, the second in Asia, though in Argentina a commercial orientation is important on the large cattle ranches and wheat farms. Estate cultivation of both types was begun by invaders from the West.

8. The ratio of exports to GDP varies greatly among low-income countries, as among higher income countries. The main causes of variation are two: the size of the country, and whether the country has a valuable mineral resource that is being exploited on a large scale, or a climate that causes it to specialize in production of a tropical agricultural or forest product for the world market. Not only are small countries in which a valuable natural resource is being exploited large exporters; more generally, a small country cannot satisfy the varied demands of its people as well as a larger one can, and it specializes for export in order to import. The ratio of exports to GDP or GNP also varies with the state of economic development.

9. Economies at all levels of income within the less developed group are inevitably and inextricably meshed with the world economy. During the last half of the 19th century, the industrial countries began to exert a large demand for the mineral and other products of the lower income countries, and the spread of railroads and the increased use of the steamship revolutionized transportation. Since that time there has been a world economic system that encompasses every country. Only the extreme case, Cambodia before the Vietnamese invasion of 1979, seemed almost closed to the world, but even it had to trade.[2] Some intellectuals of the LDCs, resentful of the influence of the countries, companies, and cultures of "the center" upon them at the "periphery," would have their countries withdraw from the international system, but this is impossible, or it is possible only at a drastic reduction in living levels that would constitute a price too high to pay. In their desire for improved techniques of production, their need for goods that they do not themselves produce or can produce only inefficiently, their producers' inevitable need for markets larger than one economy can provide, their knowledge, whether or not they would like to forget it, of consumption levels and patterns in other countries, and in the intellectual, social, and political relationships that affect these economic relationships, the LDCs are part of a world economy. We must study them as such rather than in isolation.

THE LOWEST INCOME COUNTRIES

This section does not discuss the "least developed countries," but those countries with settled agriculture and per capita GNPs of, say, $150 to $300 in 1977.

---

[2] The Arabian Peninsula provided another extreme instance of isolation before the discovery of oil on the peninsula.

1. Every one of these countries is a dual economy. Set in the midst of traditional agriculture, trade, and services is a modern enclave consisting of plantation agriculture and the processing of its products, minerals extraction and perhaps some processing of the ores, or the collecting and perhaps the processing of other natural resource products for export. These enterprises are run by foreigners, and they are owned by foreigners except as they have recently been expropriated.

2. The methods of production elsewhere are traditional. Those in agriculture are sometimes termed "biblical." The wooden plow, planting seeds by hand, threshing by walking oxen around and around over the heads of grain—these are symbolic of the methods in use. Nonagricultural production is largely "cottage industry": family-sized enterprises using little mechanical power. The contrast is spoken of as modern versus traditional, capitalist versus precapitalist. The methods used in the modern enclave are so far removed from those that traditional producers could manage that there is little if any transfer of technology from the enclave outward, though there may be some training in skills.

3. Except as foreign entrepreneurs are extracting a valuable mineral resource, some 60% or more of the aggregate output of the very lowest income economies is in agriculture, forestry, and fishing. Most of the remaining 40% of output is in trade, transport, and other services, and less than half of it is in mining, manufacturing, utilities, and construction—say 25% in the tertiary sector (services) and 15% in the secondary.

4. Value productivity is even lower in agriculture than in other sectors of the economy, and an even higher percentage of the labor force than of the value of production is in the primary sector—say 70% or 80%—with perhaps 10% in the secondary sector and 15% in the tertiary. A generation or two ago the share in the primary sector may have been 90%—the estimated share in the United States in 1776.

The reason for the concentration of production and employment in primary production is the economy's low productivity. As in any economy, the first priorities of demand are for food, clothing, and shelter. Since because of low productivity each agricultural family produces little more than enough for its own needs, a large agricultural labor force produces a surplus only large enough to supply a small nonagricultural population. Conversely, a small fraction of the labor force in nonagricultural employment produces enough other products to meet the small demand for them. The agricultural sector is larger than it would otherwise be because some of the demand for nonagricultural products is met by importing them and paying for them with agricultural exports.

Low productivity also dictates that the agricultural products shall be largely cereals and raw materials. The grains fed to cattle produce meat of much lower total nutritive value than that of the grains consumed; the nutrition gained from meat is expensive. At low levels of income the demand for meat is therefore small, even apart from noneconomic forces such as religious taboos that may bar meat consumption.

5. Little equipment per worker, and that equipment primitive, is associated with little output per worker. However, the amount of capital per unit of output is pretty much the same as in higher income LDCs or even in high-income countries. With more capital per worker, and that capital embodying progressively improving techniques, there is more output per worker, but in spite of large changes in given countries at some times, overall there is no dramatic change in the volume of output per unit of capital. Technical progress in capital equipment is, roughly, offset by diminishing returns to capital as its volume increases relative to the volume of labor. There is rather wide variation among countries in the capital-output ratio (discussed in chapter 10), but in low-income countries as in high-income countries the value of a country's capital is likely to be between, say, three and six times its gross product per year.

6. As one would expect, the share of the national income that is saved is very low in the lowest income countries in which the rate of economic growth is low. Correspondingly, the ratio of capital formation to the national product is low.

7. The family unit is the extended family—a group of several generations—in contract to the nuclear family of the West. This arrangement is commonly regarded as deterring economic progress. If one family member does save a little, other members have the right to demand that the savings be shared with them. However, there is sometimes an obverse advantageous effect. Where an entrepreneurial spirit is present, the entire extended family may support the individual. He is then able to entrust his finances and accounts to an extended family member as he could not to anyone else.

8. The society is still a village society, though towns and one or more cities of moderate or large size exist. The large cities are centers of government and administration or entrepôts for foreign trade, not the complex foci of economic life that they are in industrial countries. The flooding of people from the countryside into the largest cities, increasing their size at a rate not known before in urban history and making some of them very large indeed, has been a feature of the 1960s and 1970s. This migration has surely changed the nature of village family life.

9. There is only a small and weak middle class. The emergence of a middle class of small businesspersons, managers, and professionals is a function of economic development.

10. Written communication does not serve the function that it does in more complex societies, and literacy is low. So also is the level of education, newspaper circulation, attendance at cinemas, and radio ownership.

11. The distribution of income is highly unequal. Though the degree of

TABLE 3–1   Normal variation in economic structure with level of development

	Predicted Values at Different Income Levels (stated in 1964 prices)										
	Mean under $100*	$100	$200	$300	$400	$500	$800	$1,000	Mean over $1,000†	Total Change	Y at Midpoint
Accumulation Processes											
1. Investment											
a. Saving	.103	.135	.171	.190	.202	.210	.226	.233	.233	.130	200
b. Investment	.136	.158	.188	.203	.213	.220	.234	.240	.234	.098	200
c. Capital inflow	.032	.023	.016	.012	.010	.009	.006	.006	.001	−.031	200
2. Government revenue											
a. Government revenue	.125	.153	.181	.202	.219	.234	.268	.287	.307	.182	380
b. Tax revenue	.106	.129	.153	.173	.189	.203	.236	.254	.282	.176	440
3. Education											
a. Education expenditure	.026	.033	.033	.034	.035	.037	.041	.043	.039	.013	300
b. School enrollment ratio	.244	.375	.549	.637	.694	.735	.810	.842	.863	.619	200
Resource Allocation Processes											
4. Structure of domestic demand											
a. Private consumption	.779	.720	.686	.667	.654	.645	.625	.617	.624	−.155	
b. Government consumption	.119	.137	.134	.135	.136	.138	.144	.148	.141	.022	
c. Food consumption	.414	.392	.315	.275	.248	.229	.191	.175	.167	−.247	250
5. Structure of production											
a. Primary share	.522	.452	.327	.266	.228	.202	.156	.138	.127	−.395	200
b. Industry share	.125	.149	.215	.251	.276	.294	.331	.347	.379	.254	300
c. Utilites share	.053	.061	.072	.079	.085	.089	.098	.102	.109	.056	300
d. Services share	.300	.338	.385	.403	.411	.415	.416	.413	.386	.086	300

6. Structure of trade

a. Exports	.172	.195	.218	.230	.238	.244	.255	.260	.249	.077	150
b. Primary exports	.130	.137	.136	.131	.125	.120	.105	.096	.058	-.072	1,000
c. Manufactured exports ...	.011	.019	.034	.046	.056	.065	.086	.097	.131	.120	600
d. Services exports	.028	.031	.042	.048	.051	.053	.056	.057	.059	.031	250
e. Imports	.205	.218	.234	.243	.249	.254	.263	.267	.250	.045	250

Demographic and Distributional Processes

7. Labor allocation											
a. Primary share	.712	.658	.557	.489	.438	.395	.300	.252	.159	.553	400
b. Industry share	.078	.091	.164	.206	.235	.258	.303	.325	.368	.290	325
c. Services share	.210	.251	.279	.304	.327	.347	.396	.423	.473	.263	450
8. Urbanization	.128	.220	.362	.439	.490	.527	.601	.634	.658	.530	250
9. Demographic transition											
a. Birth rate	.459	.446	.377	.338	.311	.291	.249	.229	.191	-.268	350
b. Death rate	.209	.186	.135	.114	.103	.097	.091	.090	.097	-.112	150
10. Income distribution											
a. Highest 20%	.502	.541	.557	.554	.547	.538	.511	.494	.458	-.044	
b. Lowest 40%	.158	.140	.129	.127	.128	.130	.138	.143	.153	-.005	

* Approximately $70. Mean values of countries with per capita GNP under $100 vary slightly according to composition of the sample.
† Approximately $1,500. Mean values of countries with per capita GNP over $1,000 vary slightly according to composition of the sample.
Source: Hollis B. Chenery and Moises Syrquin, Patterns of Development, 1950–1970 (New York: Oxford University Press for the World Bank, 1975), pp. 20–21.

inequality varies considerably among these countries, in general it is much greater than that in income after taxes in the industrial countries.

CHANGES WITH GROWTH

All of these conditions change as growth proceeds and income rises. The savings rate and the ratio of investment to GNP rise; the share of income spent for nonagricultural products increases; the shares of the three sectors in the national product change; government takes and spends an increasing share of the national income, the largest single increase being for education; cities grow; literacy increases; a middle class gradually emerges; the birth and death rates fall, but not equally; imports and exports both increase, not only absolutely but also more rapidly than does the national product; and so on and so on.

Hollis Chenery and Moises Syrquin, using some 20,000 observations concerning 130 variables, from 101 countries for the period 1950–70, have estimated the most likely relationship of these and various related variables to the level of income and the size of the country's population. Table 3–1 presents their results. The income levels shown are per capita GNP in U.S. dollars at 1964 prices. For 1980 prices, each figure should be doubled. Since the two researchers used quadratic equations to calculate the most likely values of each variable, the extreme values are not good estimates; hence for per capita income levels below $100 and above $1,000, they used the mean values of their data rather than the values arrived at by means of their equations.

The data are impressive. Saving rises from 10% of GNP at incomes below $100 to 23% at incomes above $1,000, and investment rises from 14% to 23%. The proportion of school-age youngsters in school rises from 24% to 86%. Private consumption falls from 78% of the gross national product to 62%, and food consumption falls from 41% to 17%. The primary sector share of production falls from 52% to 13%; the industry share rises from 12% to 38%. Primary sector employment falls from 72% to 16% of the labor force. Primary sector exports fall; exports of services and industrial products rise. The distribution of income becomes more and then less unequal. And so on. Discussion of these changes occupies a fairly large share of the rest of this book.

It may merely be noted here that no implication of causal associations should be drawn from Table 3–1. By showing the statistical association between progressively higher levels of income and progressively different shares of variables in GNP or in other relevant totals, the table may seem to imply that the rise in per capita income causes the various changes. It does cause some of them, but for others the causation lies in complex aspects of the growth process, of which a rise in per capita income, along with other changes, is the result. The student should withhold until later chapters any judgments about causation.

FOR FURTHER READING

Hollis B. Chenery and Moises Syrquin, *Patterns of Development, 1950–1970* (New York: Oxford University Press for the World Bank, 1975).

B. F. Johnston, "Agriculture and Structural Change in Developing Countries: A Survey of Research," *Journal of Economic Literature*, 8 (June 1970), 369–404.

4

Economic Growth,
Unemployment,
and Income Distribution

We may speak of the *process* of economic growth. We speak of the *problem* of the material welfare of those 800 million persons, or by now perhaps 900 million persons, whose lives Mr. McNamara has described as lives of "absolute poverty." This implies human intervention, rather than merely the dispassionate analysis of an economic process. The appropriate intervention has been little studied.

"The development strategies advocated during the past twenty years," writes one development economist, "have consistently sought an increase in the level of incomes, but certainly no levelling of incomes."[1] He exaggerates somewhat, but not much.

The first effect of technical progress, it is shown later in this chapter, is to increase the inequality of the distribution of income.

Income distribution is discussed at various points throughout this book, since most of the topics discussed affect it. This chapter provides an extensive introduction to it. To begin the discussion, it will be useful to define a conceptual tool that is used later in the chapter, the Lorenz curve. A closely related tool, the Gini ratio, is also defined.

THE LORENZ CURVE AND THE GINI RATIO

Inequality of income distribution is often portrayed on a "Lorenz curve," as in Figure 4–1. If the distribution of income were entirely equal, it would be represented by the 45° line. Along that line, each 1% of the population

---

[1] L. S. Jarvis, in *Employment in Developing Nations,* ed. Edgar O. Edwards (New York: Columbia University Press, 1974), p. 168.

38

FIGURE 4-1   Two Lorenz curves yielding the same Gini ratio

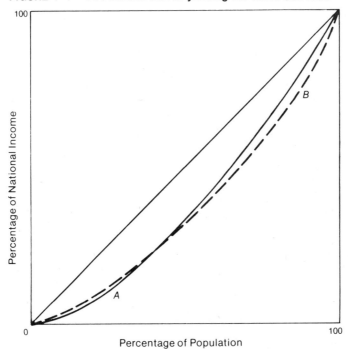

receives 1% of national income. In fact, however, the curvé of income distribution in any country (say curve A) sags below the 45° line. The lowest income 10% of the population receive less than 10% of the income, and the next 10% almost certainly also receive less than 10%, and so on up to some point at which, graphically, the curve A has a slope of just 45°, after which point higher income deciles each receive more than 10%.

The Italian mathematician Gini proposed an algebraic measure of the degree of inequality: the ratio of the area between the line of equality and the income distribution curve to the entire area below the line of equality. In the case of perfect equality, the Gini ratio is zero. If one person, represented at the extreme right of the box, received all of the income, the Lorenz curve would follow the perimeter of the box, and the ratio would be unity. If one Lorenz curve lies entirely below another, the Gini ratio will necessarily be higher for the lower curve. However, two Lorenz curves may cross. The Gini ratio may be identical for the two, even though these show markedly different distributions of income. Because of such ambiguities, the quantitative discussion in this chapter will usually make comparisons between countries in terms of the income shares of given segments of the array of income receivers (for example, the shares of the bottom 40% or of the top 20%) rather than by means of Gini ratios.

THE DETERMINANTS OF INCOME DISTRIBUTION

The distribution of income in any country depends on whether aggregate demand for the goods and services that the country is capable of producing is sufficient to provide full employment for labor and other productive resources, on the distribution of the ownership of land and capital, on whether through effective innovation the country's entrepreneurs are earning large incomes, on the supply of and demand for unskilled labor and labor of various types and degrees of skill and training, and on the secondary distribution (that is, redistribution) of income through the progressivity or regressivity of the tax system and of public services and transfer payments.

Whether aggregate demand for goods and services is high or low will depend on the vigor of entrepreneurship, the government's fiscal and monetary policies, and foreign demand. Before growth begins, the distribution of landownership is an important determinant of the distribution of income. As growth proceeds, the distribution of capital ownership becomes increasingly important. In private enterprise economies, the distribution of capital ownership is always highly unequal. Effective innovation always increases the income share of innovating entrepreneurs, and so for a considerable period of time increases the inequality of income distribution.

The income share of labor is presumably lower, and the national distribution of income is more unequal, the faster the labor force is growing. Where all agriculture is primitive, with possible qualification concerning landless laborers, the income of cultivators is low but equal. When some segments of agriculture become more capital-intensive, the income of cultivator-owners of the capital rises above that of other cultivators. The more capital-intensive manufacturing production is, the less is the total share of labor in the national product. Manufacturing becomes more capital-intensive with the increase in the degree to which government policies subsidize capital, raise manufacturing wages, and protect capital-intensive production from foreign competition. The more labor-intensive production is, the greater is labor's share and the greater is the demand for skilled and probably also for technically trained labor. Income then becomes more unequally distributed among laborers. Among the bottom 70 percent or so of income receivers, income then becomes more unequally distributed, because of the relatively high incomes of the top decile or two of this group, but among the top 50 percent or so of income receivers, the distribution of income becomes less unequal. A narrowly based educational system and one which extends advanced education only to a selected group increases the inequality of income distribution. An educational system which extends widespread elementary and vocational education decreases inequality.

Lastly, a regressive tax system increases the inequality of the distribution of disposable income, whereas inequality is lessened by a program of governmental expenditures which stresses transfer payments and free public services for the masses (education, water supply, sanitation, health, recreation).

INCOME DISTRIBUTION IN LOW-INCOME COUNTRIES

We turn from these generalizations to more specific empirical observations.

In economies (mostly in the past) in which the soil was cultivated by small-farm proprietor families, each owning its land, the distribution of income among cultivator families was a flat plain, and the distribution of income in the economy as a whole was relatively equal. No one should suppose that the Lorenz curve for the entire economy approached congruence with the 45° line. There was a capital city, if not a trading city or an industrial city with at least small factories, and there were towns serving regional needs. There were high-income governmental and professional leaders. If there was a group of "big traders," they too had high incomes, perhaps the highest in the country. Urban incomes surely averaged not less than two and almost certainly three or more times rural incomes. And even among farmer-owned family-sized farms there were differences in size, soil quality, operational efficiency, and income. Yet, relatively, income inequality was moderate.

There are few such societies today. In a study of income distribution and economic growth in 43 LDCs, Irma Adelman and Cynthia Morris classed the countries into groups whose members had common characteristics. One of the groups contains the six countries of Burma, Chad, Dahomey, Ecuador, Niger, and Surinam.[2] Using as a yardstick of income inequality the share in income of the lowest income 60% of the population, the researchers present this group as having the least unequal incomes. The average share

_____

[2] Irma Adelman and Cynthia T. Morris, *Economic Growth and Social Equity in Developing Countries* (Stanford: Stanford University Press, 1973). The method of analysis is "hierarchical." Units (in this case countries) that differ with respect to some quality being investigated (in this case inequality of income distribution) are divided into two groups on the basis of some relevant important characteristic with respect to which the two groups differ but the members of each group are fairly homogeneous. If the two groups are also found to differ with respect to the quality being explored, it is concluded that causation may be present. Each of the two groups may then be subdivided into two, on the basis of some other relevant characteristic, and the difference with respect to the dependent quality noted. The process may be continued for one or more groups as far as seems fruitful.

The six countries have another common characteristic: concentration of exports. Four commodities comprise more than 75% of the value of each country's exports. Apart from Surinam, which exports bauxite, these exports are tropical agricultural products. One should not conclude that concentration of exports causes low inequality of income distribution. Within another subgroup of 24 countries, the more diversified exports are, the higher is the income share of the lowest income 60%. These facts illustrate the truism that causation must be deduced from the logic of a relationship; statistical correlation does not prove it.

in total national income of the lowest income 60% in the entire statistical universe of 43 countries, the researchers calculated, was 26 percent; the share in this group of six was 34%. (Among the 43 countries the highest percentage share of the lowest income 60% was 38%, in Israel.)

In a comparable study of income distribution, the World Bank staff estimates that in only three of these six countries—Chad, Nigeria, and Surinam—do the lowest 40% of income receivers receive a relatively high share of income, that in Burma and Dahomey they receive a moderate share, and that in Ecuador they receive a low share. Burma and Dahomey are placed just outside the "low-inequality" group, but, based on the income share of the lowest 40%, the World Bank study would rank five additional countries—Sri Lanka, Pakistan, Uganda, Thailand, and India—as having as low inequality as Burma and Dahomey.

Contrasting with these countries is the larger number of countries in which before modern growth began a class of individuals held large tracts of land that they operated as estates or rented to peasant tenants. In many of the countries in which this was true, the large landowners were descendants of alien conquerors, as in Latin America. In India, which was not an integrated nation until the last half of the 19th century, the large landlords are in many cases the descendants of conquerors from other regions of the subcontinent. (Their presence in India makes the classification of India as a country with low inequality seem anomalous.) There also were and are large landowners in some countries of the Middle East whose population seems to have once been relatively homogeneous ethnically and religiously. Tribal land may have gradually become the personal possession of descendants of tribal chieftains.

In countries in which there is such a landed group, this relatively small number of persons, receiving at least one third of the aggregate net income from agriculture, had very high incomes, and the top 2, 3, or 4% of income receivers, including these landed persons plus the governing group and the professional persons associated with it, received a considerably larger share of the national income than was the case elsewhere.

If the cultivators were proprietor-renters, incomes within agriculture were fairly equal, though lower relative to the average level of income than where the cultivators were also owners. Only where a group of cultivators had become detached from the land and had become agricultural wage earners (as on estates or other large farms) did gross inequality among agriculturists develop.

Not only were and are urban incomes considerably higher than rural ones; wages in large industrial establishments were and are exceptionally high—because these establishments want to attract the best workers, because the belief that all "modern" establishments earn large profits and can afford high wages creates expectations that cause workers to resist wage levels that are regarded as normal in other employment, and because in one way or another governmental regulations in many countries enforce the high wages. Full-time workers in these establishments and in utilities, transportation, and the like, are probably all within the top 20% or 30% of income receivers.

Between them and the cultivators stands a band of income earners who have sometimes been overlooked. In countries in which there has been any stir of growth at all—that is, in all but a dozen or so of the lowest income countries—many urban earners are self-employed or are employed in small shops, and many of these shops are manufacturing, not service, establishments. Persons with colonial experience have long known this. Students of economic growth have rediscovered this economic sector and have named it the urban "informal sector."

> The popular view of informal-sector activities is that they are primarily those of petty traders, street hawkers, shoeshine boys and other groups "underemployed" on the streets of the big towns. The evidence suggests that the bulk of employment in the informal sector, far from being only marginally productive, is economically efficient and profit-making, though small in scale and limited by simple technologies, little capital, and lack of links with the other ("formal") sector. Within the . . . informal sector are [workers] offering virtually the full range of basic skills needed to provide goods and services for a large though often poor section of the population."[3]

Incomes in the informal sector—commodity- or service-producing—average much below those in larger scale industry but much above those in peasant agriculture. The impact of the informal sector on income distribution probably does not vary greatly from country to country at a given stage of growth. Differences among countries in the inequality of income distribution as growth begins, then, are determined mainly by whether aggregate demand for goods and services is high or low, the distribution of landownership, whether manufacturing is capital-intensive or labor-intensive, the educational system, and the growth rate of the labor force.

In both the Adelman-Morris study and the World Bank study, in a multiple correlation analysis the average level of education (or degree of literacy) in a country was inversely associated with the degree of inequality of the income distribution.

LABOR FORCE GROWTH, URBANIZATION, AND INCOME DISTRIBUTION

The more rapidly the labor force increases, the greater, it may reasonably be supposed, will be the number of persons who are unemployed or employed at unusually low income jobs.

---

[3] International Labor Office, *Employment, Incomes, and Equality: A Strategy for Increasing Productive Employment in Kenya* (Geneva: ILO, 1972). Although the statement refers to Kenya, it is equally applicable elsewhere.

The decline in infant and child mortality after World War II brought an unprecedentedly rapid increase in the labor force in many LDCs, beginning in the mid-1960s. In the mid-1960s it was possible to forecast fairly accurately the increase in the labor forces of LDC areas, for almost all of the entrants to the labor force up until that date were already alive. Table 4-1

TABLE 4-1   The labor forces of LDCs are growing at unprecedented rates

	Average Percentage Rates of Growth per Year	
	1950–1965	1970–1980
Developed countries	1.1	1.0
Less developed countries	1.7	2.3
LDCs by regions		
Central Africa	1.0	1.2
Temperate South America	1.5	1.5
East Africa	1.3	1.8
Middle South Asia*	1.4	2.0
Caribbean	1.8	2.3
West Africa	2.0	2.3
Southeast Africa†	1.9	2.5
North Africa	1.1	2.6
Southwest Asia‡	1.9	2.8
Tropical South America	2.7	3.0
Other East Asia	1.8	3.1
Central America	2.8	3.4

Note: The tabulation excludes Sino-Soviet countries.
* Includes Sri Lanka, India, Iran, and Pakistan.
† Includes Burma, Cambodia, Indonesia, Malaysia, the Philippines, and Thailand.
‡ Middle East countries.
Source: D. Turnham and I. Jaeger, *The Employment Problem in Less Developed Countries: A Review of the Evidence* (Paris: OECD, 1971). The labor force projections presented were made in 1966.

presents the data. Birth rates have been declining in some of these countries since the mid-1960s (see Chapter 9), but even in 1977 the percentage of the population under 15 years of age averaged about 43% in Asia, Africa, and Latin America, whereas in Europe it was 26% and in the United States 23.[4] Because of the declines in birth rates, the average rate of labor force growth in LDCs as a group during the 1970s was the fastest they will ever know. The rate of growth in the labor force in all but a few LDCs will be very high until the end of this century. In the present high-income countries the labor force doubled in about a century. It will have doubled in the present low-income countries in 30 years.

That with this rapid increase in the labor force the marginal product of labor in rural areas is very low is perhaps indicated by the flooding of better-educated rural youths (those with a few years of schooling) to the cities.

---

[4] *Development Cooperation—1978 Review*, p. 11.

The surging growth of LDC cities has been one of the more spectacular phenomena of the 1960s and 1970s. A few examples:[5]

	Population in about 1950	Population in about 1970
Abidjan	69,000	Well over 500,000
Lagos	Less than 250,000	1,500,000
Bangkok	Less than 1,000,000	3,000,000
Bogota	650,000	2,500,000
Mexico City	3,100,000	13,000,000

It is projected that by the year 2,000 Mexico City will have a population of at least 30 million and be the world's largest city.

Cities grow as centers of governmental administration, as ports of entry and exit for goods and people, as centers for the processing of some of the goods imported and perhaps of those exported, and by an "agglomeration" effect. Many types of industrial production are done most economically where other types of industrial production are going on. On the average, wages and nonwage incomes are higher in cities than in the countryside. Higher wages must be paid initially to attract the labor needed for the expanding production. An expanding sector provides other opportunities for increased incomes. Other reasons for urban growth are mentioned in Chapter 9. But the postwar flocking of people to the cities has the appearance of flight from the countryside.

There is a large amount of unemployment in the larger cities of many LDCs—about as much unemployment among young males as among young black males in the larger American cities. Yet, as noted, many of the better-educated young men of lower income countries are flooding to the larger cities. There may be noneconomic reasons. The same desertion of farms for the cities, though much less extreme in degree, occurred in the United States after World War I. That desertion was memorialized by the song "How ya gonna keep 'em down on the farm, after they've seen Paree?" But John H. Harris and Michael Todaro, after research in Africa, suggested a purely economic reason in the LDCs.[6] Even if a young man is unemployed in an LDC city for a large part of the year, his annual income may be as great as it would be as a member of a cultivator family. Moreover, he has the prospect of obtaining a relatively high income full-time permanent job.

The flight to the cities creates great new problems in city administration, and a great need for infrastructure for the many in-migrants, a need that the

---

[5] The data for the first four cities are from a World Bank Sector Working Paper, *Urbanization* (Washington, D.C.: World Bank, 1972); those for Mexico City, by Alan Riding, appear in the *New York Times,* February 11, 1979.

[6] "Migration, Unemployment, and Development: A Two-Sector Analysis," *American Economic Review,* 60 (March 1970), 126–42.

elites who may determine urban and national policies are reluctant to meet. Hence slums and shantytowns ring the cities.

Much research has treated rural and urban life in lower income countries as "bipolar." The individual remains in the village; or he moves to the city and adopts a new life; or he moves to the city, finds that the move was not satisfying, and moves back. This view of a bifurcation of life is apparently wrong. It results because the research worker goes to either an LDC city or an LDC village and makes a static study there. Ready travel now exists between village and city. The young family member who seeks a job in the city lives with a relative already there while he searches, or is supported by his family back on the farm. If he is successful he may send income home. Family decisions may still be made by the family acting corporatively. The move to the city, Uzzell writes, does not cause a break in family life but a change in its emphasis.

Most of the comments above apply to the rural-urban migration of young men. Most research workers have assumed that women migrate only as family members. However, recently reported surveys in cities in seven Latin American countries show that the number of women migrants, including wives, is greater than the number of men. The single women migrants therefore outnumber the men.

In their relation to the urban labor force they live in a separate world. Most become domestic servants. A survey in Lima, Peru showed that the typical woman migrant lives for a short time with relatives who migrated previously, then seeks a household job, moves repeatedly to successively better-paid jobs in better neighborhoods, and in her mid-twenties, after seven years of work is six households, leaves the gainfully employed labor force to start her own family.

This large market for domestic servants no doubt stimulates migration, and the large supply of domestic servants perhaps enables middle-class women to enter the labor force in other types of jobs.[7]

ZERO MARGINAL PRODUCT OF LABOR?

Sample surveys in a number of LDCs in the late 1960s and early 1970s showed open unemployment of more than 10% of the labor force in four of the countries surveyed—Ceylon, Colombia, Puerto Rico, and Trinidad and Tobago—but ranging down to as low as about 3% in Egypt and averaging some 7% or 8%. Open unemployment, then, averaged about as great as it

---

[7] Concerning the question of bipolarity, see Douglas Uzzell, "Ethnography of Migration: Breaking Out of the Bipolar Myth," mimeographed, Rice University Program of Development Studies Paper No. 70, Houston, Texas, 1976. Concerning women migrants, see Elizabeth Jelin, "Migration and Labor Force Participation of Latin American Women: The Domestic Servants in the Cities," in *Women and National Development: The Complexities of Change*, edited by the Wellesley Editorial Committee (Chicago: University of Chicago Press, 1977), excerpted in *Development Digest*, 17 (January, 1979), 67–74.

did in Western Europe, the United States, and Canada during the recession of the mid-1970s. But the open unemployment surely understates the problem in the LDCs. Workers who cannot find urban employment may not only take petty service jobs; they may also take shelter with their farm families. Unemployment is disguised.

Disguised unemployment appears in industrial societies, in two forms. A family member who would like to work outside the home but cannot find employment may give up the search and thus not be counted as unemployed. And a person who cannot find employment that will fully use his or her training and ability may take a less productive job. The resulting low productivity, then, is not due, at least directly, to lack of technical ability or capital. In industrial economies the problem is usually thought of as mainly cyclical, and the proximate cause is thought to be simply slack in aggregate demand. It is asserted that in many LDCs disguised unemployment of both forms is a persistent situation, and that disguised unemployment of the second form is so great that in agriculture and some other occupations the marginal productivity of labor is zero. The concept is that if a small amount of labor were withdrawn from production in the sector in question, the same volume of aggregate production could be obtained with no improvement in the quality of management and with no increase in the aggregate amount of capital used, though it is agreed that in a realistic definition there might have to be some change in the form of the capital equipment. The implication of the concept is that in peasant agriculture no important change in tools and equipment would be necessary.

On the basis of considerable familiarity with LDCs, W. Arthur Lewis asserted as long ago as 1954 that in many of the LDCs there were large reservoirs of labor whose marginal productivity was "negligible, zero, or even negative."[8] This labor was found, he stated, in agriculture, in petty trades and services, in the domestic service of wealthy men who kept retainers because their position required them to do so, and in other areas. That such labor existed, he wrote, was "obviously the relevant assumption for the economies of Egypt, of India, or of Jamaica," though not for the economies of some parts of Africa or Latin America.

Lewis's assertion has aroused both theoretical and empirical controversy. The question is of some importance, since a feasible remedy for disguised unemployment is simply an increase in the aggregate demand for goods and services, whereas the problem of general low productivity is far less tractable.
lr012

Zero Marginal Productivity?: The Theoretical Argument

Employers who behave as "economic men" would not hire workers unless the marginal productivity of those workers equaled the wages paid

---

[8] Arthur Lewis, "Economic Development with Unlimited Supplies of Labor," *Manchester School*, 22 (May 1954), 139–91.

them. But a peasant family may continue to support an added family member who cannot do better elsewhere, even though his or her presence merely spreads among five persons work that could be done by four. A wealthy patron may feel an obligation to support unneeded retainers.

However, the presence of unneeded retainers does not necessarily imply zero marginal labor productivity. The retainer may be incapable of performing any task of a complexity beyond bowing or opening a door. If so, his support is a transfer payment; there is no underemployment or hidden unemployment. Moreover, the member of the elite who supports the retainers may gain significant positive product from the "conspicuous consumption," from knowing that his neighbors see that he recognizes that "noblesse oblige." Hawkers on the street may also be incapable of more demanding work than the work they do.

If unneeded labor is present on farms, this is more important evidence. The procreation of an "extra" farm family member may be deliberate. It may lessen the risk that there will be no male heir to perpetuate the family. Yet such an heir could assume the family headship when the time came even though he worked elsewhere meanwhile. Unless the psychic cost of the separation to the family is as great as the value of the added material income, then his presence on the farm does imply zero or very low marginal productivity.

Empirical Controversy

But does zero marginal productivity of labor exist? To a tourist or even a research worker visiting a low-income country, its presence may seem obvious. One can see that "all those workers are not doing anything useful." Yet, as just suggested, the visual impression that they could do something more useful may be quite incorrect. Several empirical studies bring the existence of labor with zero marginal productivity into question. Two of them relate to the two countries which Lewis thought provided egregious examples of the phenomenon. A statistical study of prices and wages in Egyptian agriculture after World War II found seasonal relationships between price and wage movements, and variation in the two among different geographic areas, that were consistent with the absence of surplus labor at peak seasons and very difficult or impossible to reconcile with the presence of surplus labor.[9] In a study of Indian farm management, it was found that in each of five regions analyzed separately output per acre declined as the size of the holding increased.[10] This suggests that additional labor per acre on the

---

[9] Bent Hansen, "Marginal Productivity Wage Theory and Subsistence Wage Theory in Egyptian Agriculture," *Journal of Development Studies*, 2 (July 1966), 367–99.

[10] M. Paglin, "Surplus Agricultural Labor and Development: Facts and Theories," *American Economic Review*, 55 (September 1965), 815–33. From an analysis of the rela-

smaller plots increased yields, hence that there was no zero marginal labor productivity on plots of any size. In the province of Bangladesh, then East Pakistan, of which Comilla is a central city, a program of labor-intensive public works, inaugurated in order to provide employment, was carried out during the four years 1962–65 and on a reduced scale for several years more. Even though the program was executed mainly during the off-season, it was strenuously opposed by landlords because it forced them to pay higher wages to obtain agricultural labor. That fact, though not conclusive, raises the question of whether labor with a zero marginal product had been present.[11]

Certain historical events are pertinent. When European conquest, improvement of transportation facilities, and the arrival of traders offered new markets for agricultural staples in Africa, there was a spectacular flooding of cultivators onto previously unused lands to clear them, put them under the plow, and take advantage of the new opportunities. When similar developments, including the opening of the Suez Canal, opened new markets for Burmese rice, there was a similar mass movement of labor from Upper Burma to the jungles of Lower Burma. During the 25 years following the opening of the Suez Canal in 1869, Burma's rice exports rose to seven times the 1869 level, and Burma became the "rice basket of Asia." Between 1913 and 1953, Nigeria's oil and oilseed exports increased to 7 times the initial level, even though its cocoa exports were also expanding rapidly, and during the same 40 years Ghana's cocoa exports increased to 13 times the initial level. Between 1918 and 1950, the area under cotton in Uganda increased about 11-fold, and the area under subsistence crops about 7-fold. (The introduction of estate agriculture by European immigrants was important in Uganda.)[12]

At first glance these facts seem to show that there had been zero marginal productivity of labor. (In a previous edition of this book the present

---

tionship of the assumed loss of farm labor force members in India during the severe influenza epidemic of 1918–19 to the loss of production that resulted, T. W. Schultz concluded that there had been no redundancy of labor. However, since A. K. Sen argues plausibly that the loss of output is explainable in a way consistent with previous labor redundancy, this evidence is less sturdy than that of the other two studies. See T. W. Schultz, *Transforming Traditional Agriculture* (New Haven: Yale University Press, 1964), and a criticism by Sen, a reply by Schultz, and a rejoinder by Sen in *Economic Journal*, 77 (March 1967), 154–65.

[11] The Comilla program is described in Richard V. Gilbert, "The Works Program in East Pakistan," *International Labor Review*, 89 (March 1964), 213–26, and more fully in John W. Thomas, "Rural Public Works and East Pakistan's Development," mimeographed (Cambridge, Mass.: Harvard University Development Advisory Service [now the Harvard Institute for Economic Development], 1968).

[12] The data for Burma are from J. S. Furnivall, *Political Economy of Burma* (Rangoon: Burma Book Club, 1931). Hla Myint, *Economics of the Developing Countries* (London: Hutchinson, 1964, pp. 38–39 and 43, cites the other data. He draws the conclusion that the marginal productivity of labor must have been zero.

writer drew this conclusion.) But on reflection they seem evidence only of a movement from lower to higher average productivity.[13]

The surging growth of LDC cities is not evidence of zero marginal labor productivity in rural pursuits. It is evidence that there is some level of income on the farm at which added farm family members leave for the cities, but it does not indicate what that level is.

No research studies give evidence of zero marginal labor product.[14] In 1969 the International Labor Organization, an agency of the United Nations, announced the launching of a World Employment Program. Its basis was the judgment that the creation of added productive and adequately remunerated jobs in LDCs would reduce world poverty in an especially effective way. That is, the program was based on belief in the existence of a great deal of disguised unemployment. The ILO sent teams of researchers to four countries: Colombia, Ceylon, Kenya, and Iran to determine the facts and recommend activities. Rather to the surprise of the research teams, one suspects, they found relatively little open unemployment and could not adduce evidence of the existence of disguised unemployment.[15] They found the most open unemployment in Colombia and Ceylon. In Ceylon (Sri Lanka), 90% of the men between the ages of 15 and 19 with secondary school education, and two thirds of such men between 20 and 24, were unemployed. Yet workers to weed fields or tap palm trees had to be imported from southern India. This is evidence, not of zero marginal productivity of labor, but of voluntary unemployment arising out of a cultural view that manual labor is demeaning and out of dreams of the positions that education would open up.

The question is still a controversial one, but as the evidence has grown, this writer has been moved to the conclusion that disguised unemployment

[13] Research that determined whether there was considerable abandonment of land in the several cases would provide pertinent evidence.

[14] The literature up to about 1962 is reviewed in C. H. Kao, K. R. Anschel, and C. K. Eicher, "Disguised Unemployment in Agriculture: A Survey," in Agriculture in Economic Development, ed. C. K. Eicher and L. Witt (New York: McGraw-Hill, 1964). The economics journals contain no later accounts of research leading to that conclusion, unless one regards Sen's criticism of Schultz, mentioned in note 10, as such evidence. In an analysis of the data of the 1970–1971 Indian National Sample Survey, Deepak Lal concluded that there is very probably no surplus labor among Indian agricultural wage workers. From other data sources, he concluded that there is very little among farm family workers. See his "Supply Price and Surplus Labor," World Development, 4 (Oct.–Nov. 1976), 889–905.

[15] See the following, all published by the ILO in Geneva: Towards Full Employment: A Program for Colombia (1970); Matching Employment Opportunities and Expectations: A Program of Action for Ceylon (1971); Employment, Incomes, and Equality: A Strategy for Increasing Productive Employment in Kenya (1972); and Employment and Income Policies for Iran (1973). Or see a summary volume: J. Mouly and E. Costa, Employment Policies in Developing Countries: A Comparative Analysis, ed. P. Lamartine Yates (London: George Allen & Unwin, 1975). These reports recommend many pertinent and useful measures for increasing the productivity and income of the poor. A later ILO study, in the Philippines, is reported on in International Labor Review, 110 (July 1974), 18–24. The ILO plans studies in still other countries.

is not an important part of the problem of low income or of the highly un-equal distribution of income in low-income countries. The problem of low income is rather one of low average productivity, a much more complex problem to attack.

UNEMPLOYMENT AND INCOME DISTRIBUTION DURING GROWTH

Technological Disemployment

Technical progress in the early stages of economic growth is virtually certain to increase unemployment and the inequality of income distribution.

One of the ways in which it will increase inequality is simple and obvious. Innovation will not occur everywhere at once. Where it occurs, income will rise relative to that in the rest of the economy. Early innovation is likely to occur in cities, which are already high-income areas. Thus innovation is likely to raise relatively high incomes even higher. As the cities grow, capital gains in the value of city land will increase the effect.

That unemployment will almost necessarily increase is less obvious. Consider the sequence of events.

An improvement in methods of production will yield either production of the same outputs with fewer inputs or improvement in the product with no more inputs than existed previously. The improvement will typically use more capital and less labor, with the increase in capital cost less than the decrease in labor cost. The innovator will therefore be able to sell the good at a price that will widen his profit margin. Suppose that in the case of a reduction in cost per unit he charges the same price as before. He will then receive the same gross revenue. He is employing fewer workers and paying out fewer wages; the extra profit margin flows into his pocket. In the case of an improvement in the quality of the product, he is enabled to sell the same number of units as before even though he charges a higher price. There will be no less or only a little less employment in his factory than previously, but consumers who are now spending more money for his product than before will have less to spend elsewhere, so that some workers will be "laid off"—"disemployed," to use the convenient English term—elsewhere. In either case, then, the innovation will not directly cause any change in aggregate GNP. The direct effects will be (1) an increase in unemployment, and (2) an increase in the innovator's income, and on both counts, an increase in the inequality of income distribution. The innovator may of course charge a lower price, or in the case of an increase in quality either a lower or a higher price, than in the examples above. Tracing the quantitative results is then more complex, but by working through the logic the reader can see that in every case the direct result is "technological unemployment" and the concentration of income in fewer hands.

In addition to this "technological unemployment," there will be a downward multiplier effect if the innovator does not spend his increased income, for the workers who have been laid off will necessarily reduce their spending. Only if the innovator increases his spending by as large an amount as the disemployed workers reduce theirs will the downward multiplier be avoided. His spending will not cause reemployment of the disemployed workers; it will only keep unemployment from spreading. If he spends as much of his added income as the disemployed workers had been spending of theirs, the level of aggregate GNP will be maintained. If he spends less, aggregate GNP will fall.

There is a temporary offset. The innovation will commonly involve an increase in the amount of capital equipment used. Assume that this capital equipment is too costly to be purchased out of the innovator's current income so that its purchase requires the use of previously accumulated savings, his or someone else's, or the creation of bank credit. If so, its construction will cause an increase in employment. But once the equipment has been constructed, the temporary stimulus will end. Only the disemployment will remain.

This is the situation in the early stages of economic growth. Technical progress is bound to be slow, one bit at a time, for a rapid sequence of innovations will not suddenly spring forth in a static economy. Each bit of investment will end, and with it its temporary demand for labor, and only the disemployment will remain. Increased unemployment is the price of the initiation of technical progress, unless the government intervenes effectively to counter unemployment at a time when it does not yet understand the situation well enough to intervene and probably also lacks the will to intervene, or unless reemployment is provided by increasing foreign demand for a product whose output the country is able to increase.

When the pace of technical progress and investment becomes faster, a series of temporary stimuli may combine to become a continuing one. Suppose that a number of innovations occur close enough together in time to produce overlaps in the bulges in employment and income caused by the construction of capital equipment. Suppose, that is, that there is a continuing stream of innovation and of capital formation financed not out of the current receipts of innovators but out of accumulated past savings or credit creation. The resulting continuing creation of income, plus the multiplier effect which it in turn creates, may cause not merely an increase in aggregate income but a rise in employment more than equal to the technological disemployment.

Moreover, the demand for the construction of capital equipment plus the consumer spending of the increased income received may press upon the productive capacity of the relevant section of the economy, and may thus cause producers other than the innovators to engage in capital formation to increase the productive capacity—an accelerator effect. This secondary capital formation and the multiplier effect which flows from it will create reemployment and increase GDP. Through this total process of technological disemployment plus reemployment, a secular expansion of aggregate and per capita income—economic growth—occurs.

This is the classic process of economic growth. Even a fairly slow pace of growth may bring reemployment equal to disemployment. But full employment and the maximum benefit of growth will not be achieved unless growth or increase in the demand for exports is sufficient to employ in addition the full increase in the labor force.

Because of technological disemployment, early development may bring "immiseration," that is, decline in the absolute level of income of the lowest income groups. While some writers assert that this occurs, all of the available data indicate secular increases, not decreases, in industrial employment as industrial output rises. However, data do not exist for the very earliest stages of industrialization.

The Absorption of Labor in Manufacturing

The joint presence of disemployment and reemployment in LDCs is reflected in the fact that between 1964 and 1976 manufacturing production in those countries rose by about 7% per year and manufacturing employment by about 5% per year.[16] The increase in employment was not necessarily net; disemployment in petty shops because of their replacement by larger factories may not be caught in the data. However, in principle it is. To illustrate the limited power of increase in manufacturing to solve the unemployment-underemployment problem, let us assume that it is, and let us also make a further assumption. Associated with an increase in manufacturing is an increase in employment in transportation, communication, other utilities, and trade. Let us assume that because of this an increase in manufacturing output has associated with it an equal percentage increase in manufacturing and related employment. This is a crude but not unreasonable rule of thumb.

The rate of increase in manufacturing output was rising during the 12-year period. From 1969 to 1976 it was 7.5%, in spite of the depressing effect of the 1974–75 recession in the high-income countries. It is reasonable to assume that during the 1980s the rate of increase will be 8%. On our assumptions, the rate of increase in associated employment will also be 8%.

---

[16] United Nations *Yearbook of Industrial Statistics*, 1976, vol. 1 (in former years titled *The Growth of World Industry*). Data are available from 1955 on. The data on the relationship between the rate of increase in manufacturing output and the rate of increase in manufacturing employment vary so erratically from period to period and from region to region that only the data for the most recent 12-year period are used here and even these data must be regarded as having an appreciable margin of error. In Latin America, in the 1960s, manufacturing output grew more than twice as fast as did employment in manufacturing.

But even if these assumptions are realistic, consider the limited magnitude of the effect on total employment. In countries with per capita GNP of $200 or $300, employment in manufacturing plus associated employment may total, say, 10% of the labor force. If such employment increases at 8% per year, that increase will absorb only 0.8% of the labor force annually, while the labor force is increasing at 2% or perhaps 2.5% or 3%. Only if manufacturing output is 30% of total GDP and manufacturing plus associated employment totals some 30% of the labor force will an 8% rate of increase absorb annually a percentage of the labor force equal to the likely average annual rate of increase in the LDC labor force during the 1980s. Manufacturing output does not constitute 30% of total GDP until countries are at, say, the $800 to $1,000 level of per capita GDP. For countries below that level the absorption of the increase in the labor force, to say nothing of the absorption of technical disemployment other than that in manufacturing, must occur elsewhere if it is to occur at all. And the lower the level of per capita GDP, and therefore the less the creation of employment in manufacturing, the greater is the problem.

Disemployment, Reemployment, and Income Distribution

An increase or a decrease in unemployment affects the distribution of income indirectly as well as directly. Disemployment obviously widens the income disparity between, say, the top decile and the disemployed decile or so of the labor force. The disemployed worker may have come from a peasant family, and may return to it rather than become unemployed, but if he does he reduces the per capita income of the family. The existence of surplus workers also depresses industrial wages or keeps them from rising as much as they would otherwise.

Reemployment has opposite effects. Every withdrawal of a worker from agriculture to industry raises not only his income but also that of the remaining family members who share the family's food or the income from it. A worker in industry may eat more than he did when he was a low-productivity and low-income member of a rural family. More certainly, the remaining members of a farm family will eat better now that their income per capita has increased. The amount of produce marketed will not increase by the full amount that the migrant member of the family was eating while still within the family. This is well attested by empirical evidence. On both counts, the terms of trade will turn in favor of agriculture, even if the shift of a worker from agriculture to industry did not appreciably reduce agricultural production. Change in terms of trade in favor of agriculture tends to lessen income inequality. As reemployment continues and the marginal productivity of farm workers rises, each successive shift of labor out of agriculture will cause a greater reduction in agricultural production (or lessen its increase), and the change in the terms of trade will be greater. At the same time, increasing real wages will have to be paid in industry to obtain workers. These influences are not great in the lowest income countries, but they exist. If there are overt unemployed in the cities, a rise in food prices will injure them. This fact plus a bias by virtue of which many governments favor nonagriculture quite apart from unemployment may cause them to prevent food price increases if they can. Yet where the poor are predominantly in agriculture, reemployment and a rise in the pieces of agricultural products lessens the inequality of income distribution by almost any measure.

The effect, of course, may be more than offset by increase in the labor force.

The Rate of Growth and Income Distribution

On account of the considerations just stated, one would expect income distribution within any country to become less unequal if the rate of growth is rapid and more unequal if it is slow. There are not many countries for which data to test this exist. The World Bank publication, *Redistribution with Growth*, presents data for 18 countries.[17] Figure 1-1 in that book is presented here as Figure 4-2. A vertical line has been added at a rate of growth in GNP of 6%. Of the 7 countries growing at a lower rate, the income share of the lowest income 40% of the population decreased in 6; of the 11 countries growing at a faster rate, the income share of the lowest income 40% increased in 5.

The wide scatter of the data indicates that factors other than the rate of growth were exerting important effects on the distribution of income, but the data also indicate a relationship between the rate of growth in GNP and change in income distribution that can hardly be mere coincidence.

THE LEVEL OF INCOME AND THE DEGREE OF INEQUALITY

This relationship between the rate of economic growth and change in income distribution leads to an important thesis about the relationship between per capita income levels and income distribution. The data presented in Chapter 2 show that the rate of growth is slow in the lowest income countries as a group, and that at least up to an intermediate level of per capita income it is increasingly fast (or increasingly less slow) as income rises. This is not surprising: as has been noted, growth does not gain its full speed suddenly. It may be expected, then, that at low levels of per capita income, with slow growth, inequality of income distribution will increase, but that at some level of per capita income economic growth may reach a

---

[17] Hollis B. Chenery, M. Ahluwalia, C. L. G. Bell, J. Duloy, and R. Jolly, eds., *Redistribution with Growth* (London: Oxford University Press for the World Bank, 1974).

FIGURE 4-2   Growth rates affect the inequality of income distribution

Above the 45° line, the income share of the lowest income 40% is increasing; below that line, it is decreasing. The correlation with growth rates above and below 6% per year, respectively, is striking.

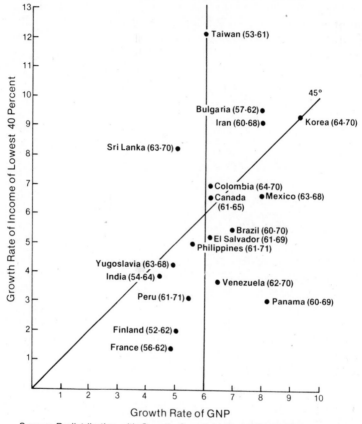

Source: *Redistribution with Growth.* Copyright World Bank, 1974.

rate sufficiently fast to more than counter the technological disemployment effect, so that income inequality will decrease.

Redistribution with Growth tests that thesis by showing the distribution of income in 66 countries at levels of per capita GNP ranging from the lowest to the highest. The shares of the national income received by the lowest income 40% and the highest income 20% are shown for each country. The estimates were derived by fitting a freehand Lorenz curve to whatever data concerning income distribution were available for each country. The underlying data were uncertain, varied conceptually among countries, and were for different segments of the income distribution in different countries. "The data are weak," writes Montek S. Ahluwalia, who was in charge of this work, "but they are also the only data we have." Moreover, deriving income distribution estimates from freehand Lorenz curves is a notoriously uncertain process because slight changes in the slope of a Lorenz curve may represent fairly large changes in income distribution. For these reasons, the estimates finally arrived at are necessarily somewhat subjective and the margin of possible error is obviously great. Nevertheless, the data merit careful study because of what they seem to show.

Table 4–2 summarizes them. The table shows the income share of the lowest income 40 percent of the population decreasing and that of the highest income 20 percent increasing until a per capita income of $300 in prices of the 1960s is reached. Above that level the trend reverses; inequality decreases. But in capitalist countries even at national per capita income levels above $1,000 the distribution of income is still slightly more unequal than in the very lowest income countries. The reader should note that these per capita income levels correspond to much higher ones—say twice as high—in prices of 1980.

The data of the table are for income before the payment of income taxes. The highest income 20% of income receivers in high-income capitalist countries pay heavy income taxes. (Italy may be an exception; tax evasion there is extreme.) To a much greater degree, in low-income countries they do not. Data for the distribution of aftertax income would show the income share of the highest income 20% in capitalist countries with per capita incomes above $1,000 to be much less, and the income share of the highest income 20% in the $501–$1,000 per capita income countries to be appreciably less, than in Table 4–2, and the shares of the lower income 80% to be correspondingly greater.

Yet even if the indicated adjustments were made, the data would show the inequality of income distribution in capitalist countries to be increasing until a per capita income level of some $300 is reached, and not becoming as favorable as in the lowest income countries until per capita incomes

TABLE 4–2   As income rises, income inequality increases, then decreases*

(1)	(2)	(3)	(4)
		Income Share (in %) of	
Income Level	Number of Countries	Highest Income 20%	Lowest Income 40%
$100 or less	8	46.1	16.4
$101–$200	5	57.9	13.4
$201–$300	13	67.9	11.1
$301–$500	8	57.6	11.6
$501–$1,000	12 (15)	54.0 (50.6)	13.5 (15.3)
Above $1,000	15 (17)	46.6 (44.9)	14.8 (16.1)

* Only the data in parentheses include the socialist countries.
Source: Table 4–3.

58

above \$500 and probably as high as \$1,000 (in prices of the 1960s) are reached.

The U-shaped effect of increase, then decrease, in inequality as one moves from low-income to higher-income countires was first mentioned by Simon Kuznets, and is known as the Kuznets effect. Both the data and their interpretation have been challenged. It has been suggested that the change occurs not because economic growth causes an increase, then decrease, in inequality, but because many middle-income countries are Latin American countries, where inequality is high because "colonialism was domesticated." Also, Gustav Papanek has argued that the effect disappears when certain strongly dualistic countries are omitted from the sample. However, even after allowance for these factors, the effects persists in Table 4–3 (which is based on a larger sample than was previously available).

Wilfred Beckerman has argued, perhaps more cogently, that a spurious statistical effect occurs. As development gets under way, he notes, young workers leave their parental families, and what was formerly one household is then recorded in surveys as two or three households with, of course, lower income per household. He cites as evidence an ILO study of Japan.[18] It seems doubtful that this effect fully accounts for the U-shape, and it is assumed in the discussion in this chapter that it does not—that the data do reflect an effect of economic growth.

Table 4–3 shows the individual country data that are averaged in Table 4–2. (To avoid cells with very small numbers of cases, the two income classes with incomes of \$200 or less are combined in Table 4–3.)

Both tables show the inequality of income distribution to be much less in higher income socialist countries than in capitalist countries. The data taken at face value much overstate the difference. The income distribution shown for capitalist countries is of pretax incomes. Aftertax incomes, which correspond to the data shown for socialist countries, are much less unequal. Moreover, the great perquisites given to the elites in socialist countries— such as cottages in the country, official cars, and the privilege of purchasing at special stores which have superior goods at very low prices—are not reflected.[19] Yet on a comparable basis[20] inequality in socialist countries would probably be shown to be considerably less than in capitalist countries, for two reasons. One is the absence in socialist countries of incomes from capital. The other is that socialist regimes tend to provide lower income families

---

[18] Kuznets presents the U-shape hypothesis in his "Quantitative Aspects of the Economic Growth of Nations," No. 8, *Economic Development and Cultural Change*, 11, No. 2, Part 2 (January, 1963). Beckerman's is presented in his "Some Reflections on 'Redistribution With Growth,' " *World Development*, 5 (August, 1977), 665–76.

A comprehensive analysis of the apparent determinants of income distribution during growth is presented in Montels S. Ahluvalia, "Inequality, Poverty, and Development," *Journal of Development Economics*, 3 (December, 1976), 307–41.

[19] See Hedrick Smith, *The Russians* (New York: Quadrangle/New York Times Book Co., 1976).

[20] Full comparability is impossible because of the differences in economic structure.

with a broader band of free public services—education, health and medical care, water supply and sanitation systems in the cities, and a variety of other amenities—than do nonsocialist countries at comparable levels of income. This is notable in Cuba and China, less so in the USSR and the Eastern European Communist countries. However, some non-Communist countries, notably South Korea, Taiwan, and Singapore, also provide these.

The individual country data show that the average inequality in the highest income capitalist countries, weighted by population, is probably less than the simple averages of Table 4–2, for smaller countries are numerous in the high- and moderate-inequality groups.

As Table 4–3 shows, there is much variation among countries at any income range, and group averages are affected by one or two unusual countries. But, taking group averages, the data show curious trends. In the high-inequality group the share of the lowest income 40% remains virtually constant above the $200 level, and in the moderate-inequality group it is almost the same at all per capita income levels except between $300 and $500. Only in the low-inequality group of countries, then, if these intercountry comparisons give an indication of trends over time, may the low-income 40% of the population expect to increase their share as national income rises. But in the high-inequality countries even the pretax share of the highest income 20% falls abruptly at the $200 level and then falls again at high incomes. In the moderate- and low-inequality groups, excluding the effect of the single case of Korea, the pretax share of the highest income 20% rises and then falls.

But what shall one make of the division of countries into three classes? In *Redistribution with Growth* this is done as a way of separating out a large number of country data into more easily analyzable sets. But can one assume that some countries are high-, moderate-, or low-inequality by nature, and will remain so at whatever level of income?

The answer may be a qualified yes. The writer, who is acquainted with the economic institutions and the social structure of some of the low-income countries listed, recognizes in a number of these countries in the high-inequality column a structure that will tend, in the absence of social revolution, to perpetuate high-income inequality as income rises (even though the inequality may lessen somewhat). He sees fewer such countries in the other two columns—though he would have placed Iran before the 1978 revolution, Chile, and Argentina in this group, and in the World Bank analysis all three are in the moderate-inequality class. On the other hand, by virtue of forces present in their early history the United States, Canada, and Australia were destined to have low inequality of income distribution, and by virtue of the nature of their economic development Japan, South Korea and Taiwan seem destined to have low inequality. Perhaps the history of other low-income countries similarly constrains them in one direction or the other.

Yet past histories or present circumstances are hardly a sure guide to the

TABLE 4–3 Differences among countries in the degree of inequality at various income levels

There are large differences among countries in the degree of inequality, at all income levels. The share of the highest income 20% decreases much more than the share of the lowest income 40% increases. Inequality is least in the socialist countries.*

	High Inequality Share of Lowest 40% Less than 12%			Moderate Inequality Share of Lowest 40% between 12% and 17%			Lowest Inequality Share of Lowest 40%, 17%*	
	Lowest 40%	Top 20%		Lowest 40%	Top 20%		Lowest 40%	Top 20%
0–$200								
Kenya	10.0	68	Burma	16.5	44.8	Chad	18.0	43.0
Sierra Leone	9.6	68	Dahomey	15.5	50.0	Sri Lanka	17.0	46.0
Iraq	6.8	68	Tanzania	13.0	61.0	Niger	18.0	42.0
			India	16.0	52.0	Pakistan	17.5	45.0
			Madagascar	13.5	61.0	Uganda	17.1	47.1
						Thailand	17.0	45.5
Average	8.8	68	Average	14.9	53.9	Average	17.4	44.8
$200–$300								
Philippines	11.6	53.8	Zambia	14.5	57.0	Korea	18.0	45.0
Ivory Coast	10.8	57.1				Taiwan	20.4	40.1
Senegal	10.0	64.0						
Rhodesia	8.2	69.0						
Tunisia	11.4	33.6						
Honduras	6.5	65.0						
Ecuador	6.5	73.5						
Turkey	9.3	60.8						
El Salvador	11.2	52.4						
Average	9.5	61.1	Average	14.5	57.0	Average	19.2	42.5
$300–$500								
Malaysia	11.6	56.0	Dominican Republic	12.2	57.5	Surinam	21.7	42.6
Colombia	9.0	61.0	Iran	12.5	54.5	Greece	21.0	49.5
Brazil	10.0	61.5						
Peru	6.5	60.0						
Gabon	8.8	67.5						
Average	9.2	61.2	Average	12.4	56.0	Average	21.3	46.0

$500–$1,000

Country		
Jamaica	8.2	61.6
Costa Rica	11.5	58.5
Mexico	10.5	64.0
South Africa	6.2	58.0
Panama	9.4	59.4
Average	9.2	60.3
Guyana	14.0	45.7
Lebanon	13.0	61.0
Uruguay	16.5	48.0
Chile	13.0	56.8
Average	14.1	52.9
Yugoslavia	18.5	41.5
Bulgaria	26.8	33.2
Spain	17.6	45.7
Poland	23.4	36.0
Japan	20.7	40.0
Average	19.1 (21.4)	39.3 (42.8)

$1,000 and up

Country		
Venezuela	7.9	65.0
Finland	11.1	49.3
France	9.5	53.7
Argentina	16.5	47.4
Puerto Rico	13.7	50.6
Netherlands	13.6	48.5
Norway	16.6	40.5
Germany, West	15.4	52.9
Denmark	13.6	47.6
New Zealand	15.5	42.0
Sweden	14.0	44.0
United Kingdom	18.8	39.0
Hungary	24.0	33.5
Czechoslovakia	27.6	31.0
Australia	20.0	38.8
Canada	20.0	40.2
United States	19.7	38.8
Average	9.5	56.0
Average	14.4	46.7
Average	19.6 (2.17)	39.2 (36.9)

* Only the data in parentheses include the socialist countries.
Source: *Redistribution with Growth.* Copyright World Bank, 1974.

future of income distribution because at least seven new forces will be at work. First, many of the lower income countries have just undergone severe strain associated with the attaining of independence. That transition in their histories surely interferes with the simple projection of the past into the future, even though one may not know in what direction the shift will be. Second, throughout the world today there are social expectations that were not present even 40 years ago; surely these will exert pressure upon the factors that determine income distribution. Third, expenditures for education are greater today than they were previously during the early stages of growth. Both presumptive logic and empirical evidence, which have been mentioned, indicate that increased education, if it is widespread rather than elitist, is associated with lessened income inequality. Programs of education differ somewhat among countries. Fourth, agricultural innovation may lessen inequality. Fifth, the future economic growth rates of the lower income countries may be faster than either their past growth rates or the historic growth rates of Western countries. Sixth, deliberate measures may be taken to lessen or to increase the inequality of income distribution. These may not merely duplicate measures of the past. Last, social pressures may in a number of instances lead to social and political revolution, with effects on income distribution that will depend on the nature of the revolution.

HUMAN INTERVENTION: GENERAL OBSERVATIONS

No more than the course of growth itself is the distribution of income inexorably determined by market forces. Policy measures of LDC governments affect income distribution greatly, and international institutions may also intervene with some effect. Major governmental measures that affect income distribution are discussed in later chapters. Some introductory comments are made here.

The distribution of income in LDCs is as unequal as it is because the governments of those countries adopt measures that increase income inequality or fail to take measures to alleviate it. They fail to do this not (or not only) because their countries are poor but because the lowest income groups are looked upon as unworthy of help or because (the obverse of the same coin) the groups in power have economic privileges that they have no intention of giving up. Alexis de Tocqueville, noting the insensitivity of highly cultured aristocrats of his and earlier times toward the suffering of the poor, commented that "the same man who is full of humanity toward his fellows when they are at the same time his equals becomes insensible to their afflictions as soon as the equality ceases."[21] The feeling of elites in many low-income countries that their inferiors "hardly belong to the same race" ex-

---

[21] Quoted by Arthur Schlesinger, Jr., in *Foreign Affairs*, 57, no. 3 (1979), 504.

plains their resistance to notions that the fruits of economic growth should go to the poor of their countries—and to the not uncommon pressure of proponents of a "new international economic order" to have added benefits go, not to the poor of their countries, but to themselves. Even groups that come into power as reformers often think of reform as reducing the income of the highest income receivers rather than as improving the material welfare of all the poor.

Governments may lessen the inequality of income distribution in three ways: by lopping off incomes at the top through taxation, by increasing the income of the groups at the bottom, and by reshaping the forces of the market so that the distribution of the income from production is less unequal in the first place.

Heavy taxation of the affluent does not benefit the poor unless the governmental revenues obtained are used to provide services for the poor. Heavy taxation of high incomes may cause the emigration of professional and technical personnel and perhaps also managerial personnel. Heavy taxation of interest and profits may cause capital flight. Moreover, enforcement of these taxes is difficult; the necessary institutions, records, and attitudes do not exist in low-income countries. Hence these policies, carried to an extreme, may be more attractive politically than beneficial economically.

The government may increase the real income of the poorest by altering the tax system to lessen its burden upon them, by providing money transfer payments to them, by increasing the governmental services provided without charge, or by directly providing employment for the unemployed or underemployed poor. Tax systems are discussed in Chapter 16. Programs to employ the unemployed or the underemployed in labor-intensive public works are discussed in Chapter 15.

Market forces may be reshaped to benefit the poor in four ways: by adopting a population policy which reduces birth rates and thus reduces the future rate of increase in the labor force; by providing education that will increase the productive capabilities of workers; by redistributing the ownership of property so that the income from it is spread more equally; and by freeing or restraining the forces of the market which determine the relative demand for, prices of, and incomes from capital and labor and different types of labor.

Population policy and educational policy are discussed in Chapter 9, land reform in Chapter 8, and freeing or restraining the market forces that determine relative demand and prices are discussed briefly in the second and third paragraphs below and in more detail in Chapter 21.

There is no easy effective way of redistributing the ownership of business property other than giving land to the poor. The socialization of business property does not benefit the poor unless after socialization it is run efficiently, so that profits continue, and the profits are used to relieve tax burdens on the poor or to provide services to them. Inheritance taxes, another means of redistributing wealth, are subject to the same fiscal difficulties and limitations as other taxation of the affluent in low-income countries. The adoption of socialism in a country is the result of social, political, and cultural conditions within which economic analysis is a rather minor element.

The cruder measures of interference with market forces—direct price and quantity controls—often have indirect effects that worsen the conditions they are intended to improve. Fixing the prices of selected commodities is likely to cause only limited quantities of those commodities to be available at those prices, and often to favored individuals; others needing the commodities may have to find them on the black market at prices higher than unrestrained market prices would have been. Restricting the quantities of products deemed unessential that may be produced or imported may reduce the use of productive resources or foreign exchange to supply them but may also increase further the already high incomes of dealers or smugglers. If the products are used only by the affluent, this transfer of income from one affluent group to another may be of little concern to the government. There are such products. However, import restrictions on more widely used consumer goods, so that foreign exchange may be used to import capital goods or components in domestic manufactures, may worsen the distribution of income considerably.

The more important measures to restrain or guide the play of market forces are intended to foster domestic manufacturing or the use of "modern" methods. It is argued by many development analysts that such measures are misguided. These arguments are discussed and the empirical evidence presented in Chapter 21.

The major redistributive measures mentioned above may be politically impossible. In many LDCs the groups who would yield up income under them are the groups who control the government. Some of the measures may also be opposed because of the appeal of "modernity" in industry, meaning capital-intensive production, or they may be impossible administratively because of the lack of the necessary administrative institutions, talent, and energy and of the data on which administration must be based. The political, attitudinal, and administrative difficulties have made many observers pessimistic about the likelihood of lessening inequality except through the possible effects of growth upon it. As growth proceeds, some of the attitudes change and some of the abilities improve. This and the direct economic effects of growth discussed in this chapter may be reasons why inequality tends to diminish after a certain point in growth.

INTERNATIONAL RECOMMENDATIONS: MEETING BASIC NEEDS

By 1976 it had become apparent to the ILO, according to its director general, that "an employment-oriented strategy, by itself, will not suffice. . . . employment issues are intimately connected to wider issues of poverty and inequality."[22] He therefore proposed to an international conference convened by ILO a strategy to satisfy the "basic needs" of the poor of the LDCs. He defined basic needs as including two elements: first, food, shelter, and clothing; and second, essential services provided by the community, such as safe drinking water, sanitation, public transport, and health and educational facilities. He estimated that in "developing countries" other than China and the oil-producing countries, minimum basic needs could be met by the year 2000 only by land reform in a number of countries, substantial fiscal redistribution of income, and a rate of economic growth appreciably faster than the rather rapid rates of the preceding years to create added income to finance the government services and the fiscal redistribution.

INTERNATIONAL ACTION: RAISING THE PRODUCTIVITY OF THE POOREST

The ILO has neither a carrot to offer lower income countries nor a stick with which to beat them, except the stick of moral suasion. The World Bank does have a carrot: money to lend. In the 1973 address to the Board of Governors of the World Bank in which Mr. McNamara presented the concept of absolute poverty, he said that the bank planned "to place far greater emphasis on . . . assistance designed to increase the productivity of that approximately 40 percent of the population of our developing member countries who have neither been able to contribute significantly to national economic growth nor to share equitably in economic progress." The member countries do not include the People's Republic of China. The figure of 40% included 550 million persons in "absolute" poverty plus 200 million in "relative" poverty. Mr. McNamara defined as relative poverty income below one third of the average income of the country.

Of these 750 million persons 600 million were rural: owners of very small plots of land, tenants, sharecroppers, and landless rural workers. The 150 million urban persons included very small scale shopkeepers and unemployed or underemployed workers. In his 1977 address to the Board of Governors, Mr. McNamara stated that "to the extent that the poor possess some tangible assets, however meager—a small farm, a cottage industry, or a small-scale commercial operation in the urban sector—it is possible to help them to become more productive through better access to credit, extension assistance, and production inputs." In effect, he was conceding that the bank's aid could reach principally those who possess some property, though he also stated that the bank had financed labor-intensive urban activities with low capital costs in Tanzania, India, and Indonesia, and that it ex-

---

[22] Report of the Director General, International Labor Office," chap. 2 of *Employment and Basic Needs* (Geneva: International Labor Office, 1976).

pected to increase its annual financial commitment to such projects to $300 million (at 1976 prices) by 1980. The bank planned to work through local financial institutions, creating them where necessary.

The shift in emphasis in World Bank loans had begun before either address. In the three years July 1968–June 1971, loans and credits by the bank for agricultural development equaled the total for the preceding 21 years of the bank's operations. Most of these loans and credits did not reach the smallest scale farmers, but as an example of the new emphasis, in Kenya a bank project related to tea production provided credit and extension services for smallholder tea producers scattered throughout the tea-growing areas of the country and also financed processing factories and access roads. In the fiscal year 1977, the bank made loan commitments of $2.3 billion, 33% of its total commitments during the year, to "agriculture and rural development," and just over three fifths of these commitments were for "rural development."[23] The bank defines rural development loans as those of which more than one half of the direct benefits, the bank estimates, will go to rural families who are among the absolute or relative poor. Of the 10 million farm families or 60 million individuals who, it is estimated, will benefit from the agriculture and rural development loans of 1974–77, an estimated 35 million will be among the rural poor.[24]

Yet Mr. McNamara's statements are themselves an implicit acknowledgment of the limits of the bank's efforts. The poor who "possess some tangible assets, however meager," are a small fraction of the 750 million persons in absolute and relative poverty, the most well off among them. Moreover, the bank acknowledges that "a country's commitment to project objectives is an essential precondition to success." In the main, despite the best efforts of international institutions, an increase in the material welfare of the poorest persons within LDCs must come from the policies of their governments or from sufficiently rapid economic growth.

FOR FURTHER READING

Among the articles and books listed in footnotes to this chapter, the following are especially recommended for further reading: Adelman and Morris (note 2), Harris and Todaro (note 6), W. Arthur Lewis (note 8), Chenery and others (note 17), and *Employment and Basic Needs* (note 22). Lewis's article is a classic in development theory. His sequel article in the *Manchester School*, 26 (May 1958), 1–24, makes penetrating comments on disemployment.

Edgar O. Edwards, ed., *Employment in Developing Nations*.

[23] The term *the bank* is used here to include the International Bank for Reconstruction and Development and the International Development Association, two of the three agencies within the World Bank group.

[24] Mr. McNamara referred to "almost 40 million" in his 1977 address to the Board of Governors, but the percentages for the three years given in the 1977 World Bank annual report indicate a total of about 35 million.

Henry J. Bruton, "Economic Development and Labor Use: A Review," pp. 49–81 of this work, is an elegantly stated comprehensive survey.

David Morawetz, "Employment Implications of Industrialization in Developing Countries: A Survey," *Economic Journal*, 84 (September 1974), 491–542.

David Turnham and I. Jaeger, *The Employment Problem in Less Developed Countries: A Review of the Evidence* (Paris: OECD, 1971).

Amartya Sen, *Employment, Technology, and Development* (London: Oxford University Press, 1975). An International Labor Office study.

A number of other publications of the International Labor Office, the Organization for Economic Cooperation and Development, and the World Bank deal with the problem of employment.

Frances K. Stewart, ed., *Employment, Income Distribution, and Development*. Constitutes vol. 11, no. 2 (January 1975), of the *Journal of Development Studies*. Also published as a book (London: Frank Cass, 1975).

Cheryl Lassen, *Reaching the Asset-less Poor: An Assessment of Projects and Strategies for Their Self-Reliant Development* (Ithaca: Rural Development Committee, Cornell University, 1978). Excerpted in *Development Digest*, 17, no. 1 (January 1979), 3–26.

G. M. Meier, ed., *Leading Issues in Development Economics*, 3d ed., chaps. 1 and 4.

John Friedmann, *Urbanization, Planning, and National Development* (Beverly Hills, Calif.: Sage Publications, 1973). John Friedmann and William Alonso, eds., *Regional Policy: Readings in Theory and Applications* (Cambridge, Mass.: MIT Press, 1975). These two volumes deal mainly with urban and regional development but also tangentially with the urbanization of the unemployed or underemployed.

II

Development Theories

5

The Grand Theories

There are three "grand" theories of economic development: the classical, the neoclassical, and the Marxist. They are grand not only in the sense that they are comprehensive, but also in an architectonic sense. They are rounded, elegant, intellectually beautiful. All three evolved to describe the behavior of technically advanced societies. Classical theory was displaced by neoclassical theory a century ago. Neoclassical and Marxist theory, which have survived to the present day, have been extended by their advocates to apply to the LDCs. They are therefore of more interest here, but classical theory, from which they sprang, is discussed briefly.

These three theories plus a fourth that is grand by intention are discussed in this chapter. That fourth is the theory of stages of development. In one variant it is merely descriptive, and in another it is almost empty of content. It is treated briefly.

THE MEANING OF TECHNICAL PROGRESS

Classical theory is a theory of economic growth without technical progress. To understand classical theory, we must understand clearly what technical progress is.

A method or procedure used in production is a technique. An entrepreneur presumably selects the techniques that will yield the highest return on his capital. We may think of a list or schedule of capital instruments embodying all of the techniques known at a given time, from those with the highest marginal productivity of capital down to those with the lowest. The techniques which yield a rate of return down to the present rate of interest are in use; it is not yet worthwhile to use the others. In time, if more income

71

is saved and seeks investment and no new techniques have been devised, the new savings will be offered at lower rates of interest than previously, and some of the capital instruments not previously worth using will be constructed. Their use will increase the productivity of labor and land, and therefore the productivity of all inputs combined, though not by as much as previous increments of capital did.

The introduction of the new capital instruments is not technical progress; there has been no change in known technology. Technical progress is (a) the inventing or devising of new, more productive technology plus (b) its introduction into production.

SMITHIAN ECONOMICS

Adam Smith, the founder of modern economics, whose *Inquiry into the Nature and Causes of the Wealth of Nations* was published in 1776, was a growth theorist. Specialization in production—the division of labor—follows from the "natural propensity" of human beings to "truck, barter, and exchange," Smith wrote. Not only does the division of labor lead to an increase in the dexterity of workers and elimination of the wastes of time involved when a person does more than one task; when people focus their attention on a narrow process they are likely to improve the methods of accomplishing it, through the invention of machinery and in other ways. That is, they will achieve technical progress. The division of labor, Smith noted, is limited by the extent of the market. But he also noted that increase in productivity increases income ànd enlarges the market, and that the process may thus go on indefinitely.

Though he perhaps would not have regarded himself as such, Smith was a sociologist as well as an economist. England was the world leader in economic advance, he argued, because its institutions were so conducive to it. Within very modest constraints, for example to ensure honesty, England permitted individuals and firms to produce what they wished by whatever methods they wished to use. In this "laissez-faire" atmosphere the "invisible hand" of their desire to maximize profits guided resources into the most efficient, that is, the most productive, uses.

CLASSICAL THEORY: GROWTH WITHOUT
TECHNICAL PROGRESS

The fact that stared men of Smith's time in the face was "accumulation," that is, capital formation. The classical economists who followed Smith, of whom the greatest were David Ricardo and Thomas Malthus, treated that accumulation as the engine of growth, overlooked the fact that it was so productive because a separate process, technical progress, was accompanying it, and considered the effect of the accumulation of capital and population growth in the absence of technical progress.

The first edition of Malthus's *Essay on the Principle of Population* appeared in 1798. His last statement of his thesis was contained in an article for the 1830 edition of the *Encyclopaedia Britannica*. The first edition of Ricardo's *Principles of Political Economy* appeared in 1817, with subsequent editions in 1819 and 1821. By these dates the fact of indefinitely continuing technical progress in Britain was inescapable. It is testimony to the tendency of evey brilliant minds to consider only one new intellectual concept at a time that in their theorizing neither man took that technical progress into account.

The classical economists distinguished among three "factors of production"—land, capital, and labor. Land, which by extension includes natural resources, was the noncreatable and nonreproducible input into production. Capital was instruments of production created by human beings from natural resources. Labor was simply the work force. The distinctions are overly simple ones, for much land is created by investment and much of the productive capability of labor is created by education and training, that is, investment in human capital. However, the three categories are still convenient in simple models of growth.

Successive inputs of capital and labor into production will be less and less productive if the quantity of a third input, land, is limited in quantity. This fact was the basis of Malthusian and Ricardian theory. The theory of the two men centered on the way in which the fixity of the total supply of land must cause economic growth to taper to an end. They were concerned with the change in income distribution that must occur as the end of growth (in their view) approached inexorably. Malthus popularized the horrifying effects of continuing population growth, but his analysis and that of Ricardo led to essentially the same conclusions.

Ricardo's analysis was more subtle. Malthus ignored variations in the quality of land. Ricardo took into consideration that producers would turn to poorer and poorer qualities of land as the pressure of population growth and production on land already in use increased. However, the Ricardian conception and a simple version of the Malthusian can be portrayed on the same geometric figure. Figure 5–1 introduces the reader to a geometric presentation of a production function, and Figure 5–2 presents a Ricardian and a Malthusian model.

In Figure 5–1, each isoquant $(X_1, X_2,$ etc.) represents a constant amount of output, produced at different points along the isoquant with different proportions of land to capital-plus-labor. $0ABC$ is a path which increasing production might take. The numbers 6, 8, 10, and 12 represent units of output.

Figure 5–1 is drawn on the assumption of land and capital-plus-labor increasing in equal proportions and of constant returns to scale. Because the two inputs increase in equal proportions, their relative price remains constant. Thus there is no reason to alter the proportions of the two used in production, and the "expansion path" or "growth path" $0ABC$ is a straight line. Because returns to scale are constant, if successive increments of inputs are

FIGURE 5–1 With two inputs increasing in amount in equal proportions, output may increase indefinitely

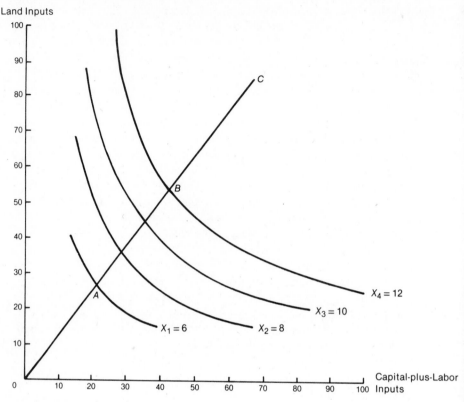

Land Inputs

Capital-plus-Labor Inputs

$X_1 = 6$ $X_2 = 8$ $X_3 = 10$ $X_4 = 12$

equal, successive increments of production are equal. (The isoquants, drawn to represent equal increments of output, are equal distances apart.)

Figure 5–1 presents only the central portion of a production function, corresponding to a small lower left portion of Figure 5–2. The portions of each isoquant sloping "northeast" (at both ends) represent inputs with negative marginal productivity. On the left, above the point at which the slope of an isoquant is vertical, an increase in the amount of land diminishes output; more capital-plus-labor is required to produce the same quantity of output. On the right, beyond the point of horizontal slope, added capital-plus-labor decreases output; more land is needed to produce the same quantity of output.

Figure 5–2 assumes, with Malthus and Ricardo, a fixed amount of land and increasing amounts of capital and labor. The aggregate quantity of land is $O\overline{N}$. For the Malthusian model, all land is assumed to be homogeneous in quality. Not all land is used initially; in this simple presentation of the Malthusian model, when the quantity of capital-plus-labor increases, the

FIGURE 5-2   If one of the inputs is fixed in amount, output must eventually reach a limit, perhaps asymptotically (if there is no technical progress)

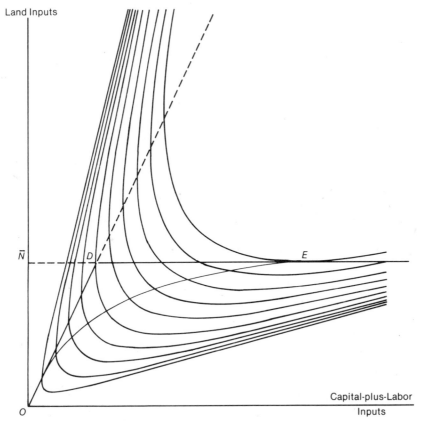

quantity of land used increases in the same proportion until the limit to the aggregate supply of land is reached. Up to this point, D, output is subject to constant returns to scale. Since it is assumed that only one method of production, using fixed proportions of the inputs, is known, at D aggregate output comes to an abrupt halt, regardless of increases in capital-plus-labor.

The Ricardian model is less primitive. $O\bar{N}$ is again the aggregate amount of land, but it is assumed to be of decreasing quality. Successive increments of capital-plus-labor, working with progressively poorer land, will produce successively smaller additions to output, until at point E the increase in output comes to an end.

In discussing their theories, both Malthus and Ricardo allowed for more intensive cultivation of land with additions to capital-plus-labor. Whether or not all land is assumed to be of equal quality, the expansion path would then take the shape OE.

Ricardo, like Malthus, assumed that any increase in wages above the subsistence level would cause an increase in population, hence an increase in the labor force and an increase in competition for jobs, that would return wages to that level. Initially, with a surplus of the best quality land, no one would need to pay rent for the use of land. Capital would obtain profit equal to the difference between the aggregate value of output and total wage payments (equal to the number of workers times the subsistence wage rate). When with increasing amounts of capital and labor the best quality of land was all in use and producers had to turn to poorer land, by bidding for the use of the better land they would cause rents to be paid equal to the difference between its productivity and that of the land at the margin. Profits per unit of output would fall. Gradually, as competing producers turned to poorer and poorer land, output would rise less and less per unit of added capital and labor and at the same time the competition for the better land would increase rents and hence reduce profits, until at point E there would be handsome rental income for landowners, no profits for capitalists, and no further investment. There would be no added demand for labor, so that wages would forever after remain at the subsistence level. There would be no further population increase, but also no further growth. The economy would have reached a miserable steady state.

NEOCLASSICAL GROWTH THEORY

It is amazing to some observers that "neoclassical" economists who followed the classical economists ignored, as had the classical economists, the technical progress that was going on around them. However, they were not unaware of it. Like the classical economists, they were concerned with the contribution of land, labor, and capital to production and with the distribution of the income from production among wages, profits, and rents. They could develop more precise reasoning in their analytical models if they held the "state of the arts" constant, and so they did.

Throughout the lifetimes of Malthus and Ricardo real wages did remain approximately constant (see the discussion in Chapter 4 of the early stage of growth), and the subsistence theory of wages did seem realistic. However, during the next generation wages rose progressively. The next generation of economists saw that rise, and saw that the productivity of labor was increased by investment in education and training, that population increase so great that it caused wages to return to the subsistence level did not occur, and that land could be literally created, and its productivity increased, by investment. Gradually the gloom spread by Malthus and Ricardo dissipated.

The new economists saw that land, labor, and physical capital were not homogeneous. Gradually the conception emerged of a very large number of producers competing for the use of these inputs, using a little more of one, a little less of another (moving along an isoquant in Figure 5-1 or Figure 5-2) as their relative prices and productivity indicated. In this model inputs in excess supply were offered at reduced prices, thus inducing an increase in their use. Competition for the use of inputs in short supply caused an increase in the payment offered for their use, until at a higher price there was no excess demand. Simultaneously producers made more of one product, less of another, as profitabilty indicated.

In the final formulation, an intellectually elegant model emerged of a system in which there was a very large number of competing producers (competition was said to be atomistic), every type of input was priced at just the price that would involve use of all of it, and every product was priced at the price at which all that was produced, and no more, was wanted and at which no producer could gain by producing more of one product and less of another, and each input was used in a way that caused it in combination with other inputs to yield the maximum value of output. The value of aggregate output in the entire system was maximum, and each unit of each input received an income just equal to the value of its contribution. Profit was not a residual, as in classical models; no special rule applied to entrepreneurship or management. They too were inputs whose earnings and use were determined by competition among them. It could be proved mathematically, and in due time it was, that in this system the value of aggregate output would just equal the aggregate payments to inputs. Incomes just exhausted the value of output.

The economy of the neoclassical system was the entire world. Each country would naturally produce the type of products for which it had relatively the greatest quantity of inputs adapted to that production—if land, land-intensive agricultural products, if labor, labor-intensive products, since the inputs available in large supply in a country were relatively cheaper there. Yet, conversely, by creating the greatest demand for its most plentiful type of input, the country obtained the highest possible income for its inputs. Thus, as each country followed its greatest comparative advantage, its economic self-interest was harmonized with the maximum welfare of the world. Harmony and almost infinitely great flexibility and adjustment—these were the keynotes of neoclassical economics.

There were no early masters of this neoclassical system; it was evolved gradually by many thinkers. In the 1870s, Austrian economists (the "Austrian school") elaborated the conception of marginal adjustments. In the almost innumerable editions of his *Principles of Economics,* during the last decade of the 19th century and the first of the 20th Alfred Marshall presented workmanlike versions of the evolving body of theory. Its precise statement must be mathematical. The statement of the general equilibrium summarized above was first made (mathematically) by the Swiss mathematician Léon Walras, in a three-volume work published in 1874–77. In his *Foundations of Economic Analysis,* published in 1947, Paul Samuelson provided the magisterial statement of the dynamics—the approach to equilibrium—as well as the statics of the model.[1]

It was necessary, it is true, to make certain adaptations in the model in recognition of certain aspects of reality. In the neoclassical system there was no government. However, in reality there was such a thing as monopoly. A monopolist would charge too high a price for his product, and to obtain that price he would produce less of it than would maximize the world's welfare. Government must then exist to step in and end monopoly. Or, where monopoly was the most efficient way of rendering services, as with many utilities, government must regulate. In some instances a sufficient scale of production for greatest efficiency could be attained only by a single producer—a monopoly. A product might have external economies, that is, might yield benefits that the producers could not corral and sell. Here, the government should subsidize or otherwise stimulate a greater volume of production of the product than the market would induce. Or, there might be external diseconomies, such as pollution. In this case, the government must prevent the undue noxious side effect, either by forbidding it or by levying a cost that induces the producer to end or curtail it. Where the external economies are great, as with education, the government may wish to provide the good itself, free of charge. Similarly, there are "public goods," goods whose benefit, within wide limits, anyone may obtain without lessening that received by someone else, and for whose benefit reimbursement from the individual user could be collected only at undue cost. The light from a lighthouse is a simple example. National defense and crime prevention are important examples. These too the government itself should provide without charge.

There was also another type of problem. In the neoclassical model there was always full employment of labor and all other productive resources. There must be, not only because competition among inputs for employment and competition among producers for their use would provide employment for all inputs, but also because, given full employment, there would always be enough demand for goods and services to sustain it, since—as the French economist Jean-Baptiste Say first stated formally and other economists repeated—the supplying of goods creates an equal demand. But in fact "crises" and depressions repeatedly shook the economic world. For a generation and more, economists offered *ad hoc* explanations of these. Malthus had maintained, without a clear or complete explanation of how it could be true, that there could be continuing "underconsumption" and lack of demand, but neoclassical theory passed Malthus by.

Then in the 1930s John Maynard Keynes offered his well-known full-fledged theory of continuing unemployment.[2] It was not exactly neoclassi-

---

[1] Paul Anthony Samuelson, *The Foundations of Economic Analysis* (Cambridge, Mass.: Harvard University Press, 1947).

[2] J. M. Keynes, *The General Theory of Employment, Interest, and Money* (New York: Harcourt, Brace, 1936).

cal, but neither was it antineoclassical. A little later Roy Harrod in England and then Evsey Domar in the United States offered a different explanation,[3] which, like the Keynesian one, need not be presented here.

These cases of monopoly, externalities, public goods, and unemployment were regarded by neoclassical economists as minor qualifications of the broad general usefulness of their model. For over a century—up until World War II—the neoclassical model was the central arch of economic thought in the Western world. It is significant that neither in the work of Keynes nor in that of Harrod and Domar is there technical progress.

Yet there is a neoclassical literature of economic growth. Continuing technical progress, bringing continuing economic growth, was introduced explicitly into neoclassical theory in the 1950s by the simple assumption that the same quest for maximum income that leads to an economic optimum in static theory also leads to technical progress. This is illustrated in James E. Meade's book *The Neo-Classical Theory of Economic Growth*, published in 1960.

Stated algebraically, the neoclassical production function in its most general form is:

$$Y=F(K,L,N),$$

that is, the quantity of output is a function of the quantities of capital, labor, and land. Meade's production function is:

$$Y=F(K,L,N,t),$$

in which t (for time) reflects continuing technical progress at a constant rate over time. Beginning with a simple estimate by Moses Abramovitz in 1956 and an analytically more intriguing one by Robert Solow in 1957, some economists have estimated that between 80% and 90% of the increase in private nonagricultural output in the United States has been due to something other than increase in inputs, and so is comprehended under Meade's t. These estimates are discussed in Chapter 12.[4] For the low-income countries, the most important aspect of the neoclassical theory of growth is its assumption—or conclusion—that technical progress and economic growth will proceed smoothly and optimally if the government adopts appropriate policies, among them abstention from an inflationary level of government

---

[3] See Roy F. Harrod, "An Essay in Dynamic Theory," *Economic Journal*, 49 (1939) 14–33, and his *Toward a Dynamic Economics* (London: Macmillan, 1948); and Evsey D. Domar, "Capital Expansion, Rate of Growth, and Employment," *Econometrica*, 14 (April 1946), 137–47, and "The Problem of Capital Accumulation," *American Economic Review*, 37 (March, 1947), 34–55. Or see Domar's articles in his *Essays in the Theory of Economic Growth* (New York: Oxford University Press, 1957).

[4] Much advanced growth theory centers on the conditions for an indefinitely continuing steady state of growth, and of the rules under which such a state will be approached from given initial conditions. This theory includes studies of the implications of models incorporating capital instruments of various "vintages" (ages) in which progressive advances in techniques are successively adopted as capital of each vintage replaces capital of an earlier vintage that has just worn out. The treatment is abstract and mathematical.

deficit spending, education of its citizens, openness of trade with the rest of the world, granting private enterprisers freedom to pursue the courses that they judge most profitable, and opening the country to foreign private enterprise—in general, permitting the forces of the market to exercise their beneficial effects, while the government limits itself to activities relating to monopolies, externalities, and public goods.

MARXIST THEORY

Karl Marx based his theory of history on the Hegelian doctrine that development proceeds by thesis, antithesis, and synthesis. For Marx the most recent thesis and antithesis were feudalism and capitalism, respectively. The synthesis would be socialism, but this would not form a new thesis in the Hegelian manner. Rather, it would be the culmination of history; with it, historical process would end. Here we need deal only with Marx's theory of the evolution of socialism from capitalism.

Marx was born in 1818. When he grew up, classical economics was still the current theory. His economics is based on Ricardo, and there is no technical progress in his analysis, but only capital accumulation.

The true value of any good, Marx wrote, is measured by the amount of labor embodied in it. Capitalists, because they are monopolists, are able to charge a price for goods above their true value. Because of this "surplus value," the income paid out in the process of production is not sufficient to take all goods off the market. Because of this inadequacy of demand there is always unemployment. Because a "reserve army of the unemployed" exists, capitalists can hold wages down to the subsistence level. Capitalists will always be searching for markets for their goods; this search is the source of imperialist colonialism.

The successive economic crises that must occur under the capitalist system will increase in magnitude, until in the ripeness of time the workers will arise, throw off their chains, seize control of the means of production, and establish socialism. At first a dictatorship of the proletariat will be needed, but as human evil gradually ceases to exist under the just socialist economic system, the need for coercion by the state will cease and the state will wither away.

It was not the logic of Marx's theory of historical evolution that caught the attention of the world, but his denunciation of inequality and injustice and his analysis of its causes. Marx was a bitter man, and he gained a followership among millions of other people who were bitter about life under capitalism. As was noted, the extension of his theory to the LDCs is discussed in the following chapter.

STAGES OF GROWTH SCHEMAS

Lastly, note should be taken of several schemas of stages of growth.

The Historical School

During the 19th century, the German "historical school" (really, two or three schools of writers, in successive generations) evolved schemas of the stages of economic development. Friedrich List wrote of the pastoral, peasant, agricultural-manufacturing, and agricultural-manufacturing-commercial stages. Bruno Hildebrand referred to the stages of exchange: natural (that is, barter), money, and credit. Gustav Schmoller thought that the evolution from village or manorial to town to territorial to national economies was significant. Karl Bücher and Werner Sombart introduced classifications with greater sociological content. Bücher contrasted closed household, town, and national socioeconomic systems, and Sombart described fairly richly concepts of precapitalist and early, high, and late capitalist systems.

Stages: Rostow's Schema

Walt W. Rostow's later stage schema is a distant relative rather than a lineal descendant of these.[5] In Rostow's schema, once the static stage of traditional life has been disturbed, the society passes through the later stages of establishment of the preconditions for growth, takeoff, drive to maturity, and high mass consumption. During the period of establishment of the preconditions, "the insights of modern science [begin] to be translated into new production functions"; the idea spreads that economic progress is possible, an effective centralized national state is built, education broadens, new types of entrepreneurs come forward, commerce widens, economic institutions change, and so on.

The period of takeoff is "the interval when the old blocks and resistances to steady growth are finally overcome." The changes sketched above proceed. During a period of "a decade or two" or "two or three decades" investment rises rapidly, the basic economic, political, and social structure of the society are transformed, and thereafter a steady rate of growth can be sustained.

During the drive to maturity, a period of about 60 years after the beginning of takeoff, the nation acquires mastery of the most advanced existing technology, and it can produce anything it chooses, at least in its chosen area of specialization. Thereafter, in the age of high mass consumption, the economy's leading sectors shift toward durable consumer goods, and a large share of the population acquires a high level of living.

---

[5] The first presentation of the schema is in Rostow, "The Take-off into Self-Sustained Growth," *Economic Journal*, 66 (March 1956), 25–48. Rostow's most comprehensive presentations are in *The Stages of Economic Growth* (Cambridge: Cambridge University Press, 1960) and in W. W. Rostow, ed., *The Economics of Take-off into Sustained Growth* (London: Macmillan, 1964).

Rostow has been sharply and correctly criticized for two aspects of his presentation:

1. The limited content or the tautological nature of most of his distinctions between his stages. As one reads his essays quickly, the stages seem to be given distinctive characteristics, but as one searches more carefully for distinguishing marks, most of them vanish. Thus "basic economic, social, and political transformation" turns out to be indistinguishable from earlier or later economic, social, and political transformation. The "drive to maturity" turns out to have the same characteristics as the earlier process of growth. High mass consumption turns out to exist at any time, relative to earlier times. The use of consumer durables, now that they have been invented, occurs earlier in real life than does the "drive to maturity" that is supposed to bring it about. And so on. Except for the one specifically stated criterion of the change in the rate of investment during the period of takeoff, no one scrutinizing a society with Rostow's book in hand would know what to look for to distinguish the stages.

2. The invalidity of his one quantifiable criterion. The supposed upward surge in the rate of investment (and presumably also the rate of growth) during a crucial period of takeoff turns out to exist in only a few countries. The facts elsewhere contradict the schema.

Rostow may have based his concept of such a period on the history of the country with whose growth he was most familiar, England. A surge of industrialization did occur there, beginning early in the 1970s. Similar surges occurred in the Soviet Union and in Japan, where political revolution burst the bonds that had previously been hampering growth. These are special cases. As data for other countries have been accumulated, it has become clear that in economic development there is usually no such phenomenon as a takeoff. Gross and net capital formation rose fairly steady in most Western European countries from about 1850—the date when data begin—until World War I. To divide the rise into periods would be entirely artificial.[6]

Hence there are no stages, one following another. But Rostow's essays present rich and perceptive suggestions of the changes that must occur if a country that was traditional is to become technically progressive.

FOR FURTHER READING

Standard texts on the history of economic thought discuss the classical and neoclassical schools.

Paul Anthony Samuelson, *The Foundations of Economic Analysis* (Cambridge, Mass.: Harvard University Press, 1947).

---

[6] Data are presented in S. S. Kuznets, "Quantitative Aspects of the Economic Growth of Nations," no. 7, *Economic Development and Cultural Change*, 10, no. 2, part 2 (January 1962), appendix tables.

James E. Meade, *A Neo-Classical Theory of Economic Growth*, 2d ed. (London: Unwin University Books, 1962).

V. I. Lenin, *Imperialism: The Highest Stage of Capitalism* (New York: International Publishers, 1933). First published in 1917.

W. W. Rostow, *The Stages of Economic Growth* (Cambridge: Cambridge University Press, 1960).

W. W. Rostow, ed., *The Economics of Take-Off into Sustained Growth* (London: Macmillan, 1964). Contains criticisms of the schema by other economists.

G. M. Meier, ed., *Leading Issues in Development Economics*, 3d ed., chap. 2.

For the student who has proceeded beyond elementary mathematics, A. K. Dixit, *The Theory of Equilibrium Growth* (London and New York: Oxford, 1976) provides an exhaustive and demanding account of the abstract propositions that have been built upon neoclassical growth theory.

6

The Structuralists, the Dominance-Dependence School, and Technoeconomic Facts

This chapter deals with the structuralists, and with a group—or several subgroups—of theories which I shall call collectively the dominance-dependence theories. They are held by the so-called radical theorists, the neo-Marxists, the *dependencia* school, and a number of recent writers, not wholly committed to any one of these views, who reflect one or another of them in part. On occasion I shall refer to these latter as "the partisans."[1] They would undoubtedly assert that it is the more conventional economists who are partisan.

Structuralism and the other theories have common elements. The analysts of all these schools write in terms of dichotomies: low-income countries versus high-income countries, developed countries versus underdeveloped countries. They sometimes write as though growth were not occurring in the lower income countries; they seek to explain its absence. All of them believe that the lower income countries have been wronged. I single out the structuralists because of an element in their theory that is not present in the others: the judgment that in addition to other causes certain aspects of the economic structure of the lower income countries prevent them from developing.

THE STRUCTURALISTS

The first structuralist theory was that certain economic conditions in low-income countries create vicious circles that prevent these countries

---

[1] In a review in the *Journal of Development Economics*, 3 (1976), 299, of G. K. Helleiner, ed., *A World Divided: The Less Developed Countries in the International Economy* (Cambridge: Cambridge University Press, 1976), C. P. Kindleberger applies the term *the partisans* to these recent writers.

84

from growing. The theory of vicious circles was advanced immediately after World War II. It was a forerunner of the later theses that were specifically termed structuralist. The theory has been outmoded by the course of events; development found impossible by the theory has occurred in dozens of countries. Yet it is worthwhile to examine the views of low-income countries on which the theory rests, for those views, still held more or less unconsciously, are the basis for theories and attitudes that still color much thinking and comment.

VICIOUS CIRCLES?

The theory is that two mutually reinforcing vicious circles perpetuate low income. Either alone would be sufficient to do so. One consists of the relationships among lack of capital, income, and saving. Because income is low, there is little capacity to save. The low income is a reflection of low productivity, which in its turn is due largely to the lack of capital. The lack of capital is a result of the small capacity to save, and so the circle is complete.

The other vicious circle relates market size, income, and investment. "The inducement to invest," Ragnar Nurkse wrote, "may be low because of the small buying power of the people, which is due to their small real income, which again is due to low productivity. The low level or productivity, however, is a result of the small amount of capital used in production, which in its turn may be caused at least partly by the small inducement to invest." The circle is complete; there is little inducement to invest because, income being low, the market is small; so long as there is little investment, income will remain low and the market small.

If there were inducement to invest, there would be no savings to finance investment, and if there were savings, there would be no inducement to invest them. There is no way in which the circles can be converted into upward spirals.[2]

When the thesis of two vicious circles is heard by persons who have a mental image of low-income countries as immobilized in a morass of poverty, it seems so self-evidently true that no investigation seems needed to confirm it.

Critique: Market Size?

Nurkse cited as examples of the smallness of the market the impossibility of profitable shoe production in a hypothetical economy with income so

[2] The best-known presentation is that by Ragnar Nurkse in his *Problems of Capital Formation in Underdeveloped Countries* (New York: Oxford University Press, 1953). Hans W. Singer had made a brief but fairly complete statement of the doctrine earlier, in "Economic Progress in Underdeveloped Countries," *Social Research*, 16 (March 1949), 1–11. See also his "Obstacles to Economic Development," *Social Research*, 20 (Spring 1953), 19–31.

low that few persons wear shoes, and a volume of use of steel too low to absorb an economic level of output of a modern steel mill. But this is irrelevant. A growth process does not require that a low-income country have a market sufficient to justify the production of every industrial product, but only a market large enough to justify improved methods in the production of a considerable range of goods, to get the process of economic growth and increase in income under way.

Demand for a range of goods large enough in amount to take the output of more productive plants off the market was present in virtually every low-income country except tiny island nations before the process of modern economic growth began, and it was present not merely in the low-income country as a whole but in separate regions or cities. Examples of such products are soap, matches, sandals, rice or wheat flour, sugar and various sugar products, textiles, clothing and other textile products, and bricks, cement, and some other construction materials.[3] The first manufacturing enterprises are small due to lack of the managerial talent and boldness that are needed to launch larger ones rather than to market limitation. Hla Myint has coined a relevant phrase. The economies that are relevant, he wrote, are not economies of scale but "economies of experience."[4]

At some stage in the growth process, limited market size will surely curtail growth, since many high technologies are associated with large-scale production. This quite separate question is discussed in Chapter 11.

Critique: Inability to Save?

The notion that small low-income countries have too low income to save and thus to invest is inconsistent with the facts of their history. There seems to be no society in history that was too poor to wage war, even a large-scale war relative to the size of the society, when emotions were aroused. Any considerable war requires a share of the nation's work force and other productive resources that would be sufficient for a significant rate of capital formation. And while the disruption of war has often caused hardship and death, historical records suggest that the diversion to war of a considerable fraction of the resources of the population at large, in even the lowest income societies, has often occurred without causing starvation or death.

The lowest income societies have often been able to build magnificent monuments. Alec Cairncross has written: "Anyone who looks at the pyra-

---

[3] In an earlier book, *On the Theory of Social Change* (Homewood, Ill.: Dorsey Press, 1962), the present writer noted examples of the successful introduction of modern methods in the production of such products in the first years of the 20th century in two valleys of Colombia that were then isolated (Antioquia and "The Valley"), the larger of which could not have had a gross product of much more than $100 million (in 1965 prices) at the time.

[4] "An Interpretation of Economic Backwardness," *Oxford Economic Papers*, n.s., 6 (June 1954), 132–63.

mids, cathedrals, and pagodas that civilizations have bequeathed, can hardly regard the construction of railways, dams, and power stations as imposing an unprecedented burden on a poor community."[5]

No one would expect the lowest income groups in low-income countries to contribute savings for investment. But they do not do so in any society. Apparently the families forming the two or three lowest income deciles of any population dissave. At least this is true in the highest income society of the world, the United States. Saving is roughly zero in the next decile or two and a low fraction of income in the decile or two next above. It is only because of the relatively high rate of saving by families and single individuals in the highest several deciles of the income distribution in any society (saving both out of their personal incomes and through the companies of which they are the major owners) that there is a considerable net flow of consumer saving in the economy as a whole. In 1950 the highest 10% of U.S. income receivers after taxes, who received 29% of aggregate income, saved 20% of their income. The bottom 90%, on the average, saved only 3%.[6] To understand the saving potential of any economy, it is necessary to consider the highest income groups, and the highest income groups obtain a larger share of the country's income in low-income countries than in high-income ones.

The income shares of the highest income 20% and the lowest income 40% of income receivers in LDCs were discussed in Chapter 4. For seven low-income and seven high-income countries, Kuznets has presented estimates of the share of national income received by the highest 10%. These are shown in Figure 6-1. The contrast is notable. If the estimates were of incomes after the payment of income taxes, the difference would be still more striking, for the affluent in high-income countries pay high income taxes, whereas the affluent in LDCs pay none. W. Arthur Lewis draws a moral: "Least of all can those nations plead poverty as an excuse for not saving in which 40% or so of the national income is squandered by the top 10% of income receivers, living luxuriously on rents."[7]

Historically, some of the landed rich have on occasion been innovative. The "agricultural revolution" that preceded the industrial revolution in England was carried out by them. The German Junker class modernized German agriculture. In Iran, large landowners have established food-processing plants to process products of their land—and have thereby raised the level of income in the country. Such instances are apparently rare, but it seems fairly clear from the available data that if there is little saving and productive investment in a low-income country, this is because people are not motivated to make it, not because they cannot.

---

[5] A. K. Cairncross, "Capital Formation in the Take-off," in W. W. Rostow, ed., *The Economics of Take-off into Sustained Growth* (London: Macmillan, 1964).

[6] S. S. Kuznets, "Quantitative Aspects of the Economic Growth of Nations," no. 5, *Economic Development and Cultural Change*, 8, no. 4, part 2 (July 1960), 22.

[7] *The Theory of Economic Growth* (London: George Allen & Unwin, 1955), p. 236.

FIGURE 6–1 Income shares before taxes of upper 10% of income units (families or tax returns, selected countries, late 1940s and early 1950s)

The very highest income groups receive a larger proportion of the national income in low-income countries than in high-income countries, even before taxes

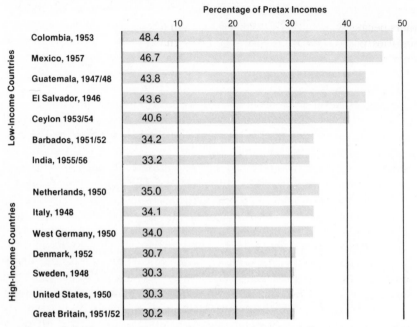

Source: S. S. Kuznets, in *Economic Development and Cultural Change*, 11, no. 2 (January 1963), table 3, p. 13.

Saving is likely to be, as it was early in the industrial revolution in England, by entrepreneurs who innovate, profit on a small scale, and invest the profits in their business, expand the profits, plow them back again, and expand further. "A country's saving rate is low," Lewis writes, "not because the country is poor but because its capitalist [i.e., entrepreneurial] class is small." As those of a country's businesspersons who have capitalist temperaments invest, profit, save, and invest, the country's saving rate and investment rate rise and growth proceeds.[8]

THE "BIG PUSH" THESIS

On the basis of the vicious circle thesis plus two added considerations that were given little emphasis by Singer or Nurkse, Paul Rodan has argued

---

[8] "Economic Development with Unlimited Supplies of Labor," *Manchester School*, 22 (May 1954), 131–91.

that a "big push" (better termed a big pull) is needed to initiate growth.[9] The first of the two added considerations is that low-income countries (Rodan argues) are often on dead center because no potential investor anticipates investment by other persons, and therefore no one anticipates a market large enough to justify an investment. No one anticipates action by others because the market information system (the price, cost, interest rate, securities price changes, etc.) that sends signals in advanced countries is nonexistent. In advanced countries the general expectation that there will be growth yields external pecuniary economies—in this instance, capital gains—that help to justify the investments.

Second, the lack of infrastructure makes other investment uneconomic. Transportation, power, and communications facilities and some other facilities must be built in large lumps. Because of low saving capability the lumps of capital needed cannot be amassed.

The remedy, Rodan argues, is a comprehensive investment program, by which many investment projects, undertaken simultaneously, will create the demand for each project that will make it profitable, and by which infrastructure facilities will be made available. Rodan acknowledges that capital would have to be provided from outside, but he argues that the labor needed could be found in the disguised unemployment that he asserts is present in the agriculture of low-income countries. He adds that the vision of such a bold and promising program might stir imaginations and evoke enough energies to make a "big push" a success even though a society had not been motivated to carry out a lesser program.

Critique: Market Signals

The conception of inefficient markets is plausible, and it was generally accepted when it was first pronounced, but it has been belied by empirical research. Surprisingly, markets in traditional economies seem to work very well. Studies cited in Chapter 8 show that peasant producers react rationally and quickly to changes in prices.

Critique: Are Lumps of Capital Needed?

The need for expensive investment projects if infrastructure is to be available, like the market signals argument, was stated as axiomatic. It seems axiomatic in an industrial country. But in fact almost any type of infrastructure facility can be built in various grades or sizes. Roads may be dirt, graveled, blacktopped, or paved, light-duty or heavy-duty, and they

---

[9] He has presented his argument in various places, but most comprehensively in his "Notes on the Theory of the Big Push," in *Economic Development for Latin America*, ed. H. S. Ellis and H. C. Wallich (New York: St. Martin's Press, 1961).

may be built in any width the traffic calls for. Electric generators vary in size from small diesel units to the largest hydro or nuclear plants. Local telephone systems and even microwave transmission towers are relatively inexpensive. A city can afford the urban utilities it "needs," since these are proportional to its size and functions. Railroads are perhaps the least divisible type of infrastructure, but until a heavy volume of bulk traffic calls for the service of a railroad, road or water transport is a fairly good and finely divisible substitute. And while unit cost varies with the facility, the view that there is a dichotomy in costs—that unit cost is "high" in small or lower grade facilities and "low" in large, higher "quality" ones—is overstated. The services of a large infrastructure facility built as early as the argument implies would be exorbitantly costly per unit, since for a long time only a small fraction of the capacity would be used. The role of infrastructure facilities in development is coordinate with that of many other pieces of capital equipment and with changes in management practices and in institutions. Increasingly large infrastructure facilities have their place in the course of development, but they deserve no special niche as absolute or near-absolute prerequisites to growth.

Critique: Lack of Realism

Perhaps the most damning criticism of the big push thesis, as of the theory of vicious circles, is that growth has begun in less developed countries without a big push and without massive intervention, quietly, gradually, "like a thief in the night." Obviously, there are no internal barriers to the gradual beginning of growth. The vicious circles and big push theses are models with little empirical relevance.

Counterpoint: Hirschman on the Strategy of Growth

In a 1958 book, *The Strategy of Economic Development*, Albert O. Hirschman attacks the big push proposal as unnecessary, impossible, and undesirable. "It combines a defeatist attitude toward the capabilities of underdeveloped economies," he states, "with completely unrealistic expectations about their creative abilities." A people that is "entirely uninterested in change and satisfied with its lot is . . . expected to marshall sufficient entrepreneurial and managerial ability to set up at the same time a whole flock of industries."

The scarcest factor in the LDCs, Hirschman asserts, is the ability to make decisions. The approved policy for an economy desiring to stimulate growth is to make the nonobvious initial decisions that create bottlenecks, or at least scarcities, and thus make the advantages of further investment steps obvious. For example, establishing "directly productive activities" that create a bottleneck in infrastructure will make the desirability of improving infrastructure obvious and thus induce a decision within government for its construction.

In general, Hirschman suggests, growth proceeds by advances that create bottlenecks. Responding to those bottlenecks creates others, at other points, and thus development proceeds, transmitted from one sector to others through linkages, in a continuing moving picture of unbalance.

Critique

Hirschman's prescription for initiating growth is as removed from reality as Rodan's. An economy that had somewhere within it the capacity to make the nonobvious decisions needed to initiate growth would hardly be an economy of ineffective decision makers in the first place. However, Hirschman's argument that growth proceeds by a series of moving imbalances is a more fundamental one. The question of balance or imbalance is discussed in Chapter 7.

STRUCTURALIST THEORY PROPER

Latin American economists striving to explain why economic growth in Latin America was not proceeding more rapidly in the 1960s conceived that certain aspects of their countries' economic structures were the cause. Raul Prebisch (writing in publications of the United Nations Economic Commission for Latin America), Celso Furtado, and Osvaldo Sunkel were among the most prominent of these economists.[10]

In contrast to the harmony and infinite flexibility that neoclassical theory portrays, the structural theory of (lack of) growth is one of rigidity and disconnectedness. Whereas the neoclassical theory sees economic actors as responsive to small changes in prices and opportunities, structuralist theory views the behavior of LDC producers as rigid, inflexible, unresponsive. This is true, in structuralist theory, not (or not merely) because entrepreneurs are inept but because (a) a market network that would give them information is lacking, (b) the actions of monopolistic subsidiaries of multinational corporations (MNCs) deter growth, and (c) the cultural and economic dependence of the LDCs on the economically advanced countries creates certain difficulties.

The supposed absence of a market network has been discussed. Even though there is an opportunity to sell more agricultural products, cultiva-

---

[10] Representative writings are Prebisch, "The Economic Development of Latin America and Its Principal Problems," *Economic Bulletin for Latin America*, 7 (February, 1962), 1–22; C. Furtado, *Development and Underdevelopment* (Berkeley: University of California Press, 1964) or *Economic Development of Latin America* (Cambridge: Cambridge University Press, 1970); and O. Sunkel, "National Development Policy and External Dependence in Latin America," *Journal of Development Studies*, 6 (October 1969), 23–48.

tors do not perceive it and do not gear up to produce more. Even though there is a large enough market for production of a manufactured product by modern methods, producers do not appreciate it and do not act. All of this presumably happens because of the absence of the sensitive signals that move entrepreneurs in advanced countries to action. It has been suggested above that this supposed lack of a market system is unfactual. Further evidence is given in Chapter 8.

The structuralist writers, or some of them, see multinational corporations as embodying the "monopoly capitalism" that Marx portrayed. In a nonindustrial country there may be a market for only a single firm in a single industry. This firm has a situation of at least monopolistic competition. If it is a foreign firm, through its dealings with its head office and with subsidiaries in other countries it may be able to conceal profits, evade government regulation of foreign exchange transactions, and so on. There is a factual basis for these claims. Nationals of the country may have reason to feel aggrieved. However, the claim that this behavior materially deters growth both overlooks the positive contribution of MNCs, and greatly exaggerates their adverse financial dealings. Calculation of such firms' sales, maximum possible profits, and maximum possible "excess" profits and "excess" foreign exchange withdrawals in relation to total national income or total foreign exchange transactions will indicate how improbable it is that these excesses reduce the national market for other goods by an appreciable percentage or are a significant source of the country's foreign exchange problem. The operations of MNCs are discussed in Chapters 11 and 18.

The structuralist writers note that the elites of the LDCs, having become addicted to Western culture, buy imported luxuries. Because they spend the country's foreign exchange for these luxuries, it is argued, there is too little foreign exchange for the importation of needed investment goods. Moreover, because the elites are addicted to these luxuries, they do not save. Also, producton of the goods that the elites buy is capital-intensive; if those goods are produced within the country, their production uses so much capital that too little is left for enterprises that would produce by advanced methods for a mass market. And in any event because of the inequality of income distribution and these tastes of the elites who receive too much of the income, the remaining domestic market is too small to induce efficient mass production.

The arguments are not persuasive. With respect to these elites, as with respect to the excesses of MNCs, the magnitudes involved are not great enough to cause the results asserted. The argument concerning the mass market is a peculiar one. It is presented as applying to all the LDCs. Since the LDCs vary greatly in size, the argument could apply to all of them or to any considerable number of them only if the size of the market needed to justify mass production differed in every country.

Empirical studies do not support the argument concerning capital intensivity. Studies in Mexico, Brazil, Venezuela, and Colombia show that the variation among income classes in consumption patterns is not as great as the structuralist writers had supposed.[11] Although studies in Pakistan, Turkey, and Colombia indicate that the goods and services consumed by the rich are produced by more capital-intensive methods than are used to produce the goods consumed by the poor, they also indicate that the difference is modest.[12] Econometric models based on data from Ecuador, Chile, and Korea suggest that redistribution of income from rich to poor may actually increase the capital intensivity of producton (largely because it would increase the demand for food and reduce that for personal services).[13] These various studies would suggest that differences between the poor and the affluent in the consumption of imported goods are less than is commonly assumed, though the goods differ.

That the traditional highest income classes in LDCs contribute little capital for productive investment in their countries is true. That they would contribute more if they had not been infected with "modern" tastes by contact with high-income countries is much less certain. Those tastes may determine the nature, not the magnitude, of their consumption expenditures.

The structuralists view rigidity in their economies as not only deterring growth but also as causing inflation. This aspect of their theory is discussed in Chapter 16.

THE DOMINANCE-DEPENDENCE THEORIES

Even more than the structuralists, the dominance-dependence theorists sweep aside the observation that economic growth is a difficult and cumulative process and the contentions that the present high-income countries have higher incomes primarily because they and the West were beneficiaries much sooner than others of the scientific and technical advances of the ancient and medieval worlds and have been building upon them for a long time. The important cause of underdevelopment, these writers believe, is none of these, but rather the neocolonialist policies of the imperialist powers. Those nations, having been forced to end their political

---

[11] W. R. Cline, "Distribution and Development: A Survey of the Literature," *Journal of Development Economics*, 1 (February 1975), 359–400.

[12] These are reported on in the Rice University Program of Development Studies Discussion Paper no. 46 (Pakistan by Ronald Soligo, Turkey by Tuncay M. Sunman), and for Colombia in John G. Ballentine and R. Soligo, "Consumption and Earning Patterns and Income Redistribution," *Economic Development and Cultural Change*, 26 (July 1978), 693–708.

[13] V. Tokman, "Income Distribution, Technology, and Employment in Developing Countries: An Application to Ecuador"; concerning Chile, A. Foxley, "Redistribution of Consumption: Effects on Production and Employment," *Journal of Development Studies*, 12 (April 1976), 171–90; and I. Adelman and S. Robinson, *Income Distribution Policy in Developing Countries: A Case Study of Korea* (Stanford: Stanford University Press, 1976).

colonialism, scheme to maintain domination over the countries of "the periphery." Virtually every aspect of the economic and political relationships of the corporations and governments of the developed nations—corporations and governments act in concert—perpetuates it.

The arguments of these theorists run through the various resolutions adopted by the United Nations Conference on Trade and Development (UNCTAD) since its formation in 1964, the statements of the Committee of 24 within the World Bank and the Committee of 77 within the United Nations General Assembly, and many resolutions adopted by the General Assembly. The partisans' arguments are expressed in the writings of many Latin American economists and are reflected in the writings of growth economists scattered here and there in American, Canadian, and English academia. They are presented in many articles in the periodical *World Development*.[14] They are presented in extreme form, fervently and rather elegantly, in an article by Osvaldo Sunkel, along with structuralist arguments.[15]

The underdeveloped countries, Sunkel writes, suffer not only from low income and slow growth, but also from regional disequilibrium, economic instability, inequality, unemployment, dependence on foreign countries, specialization in the production of raw materials, and economic, social, political, and cultural marginality.

Underdevelopment, he states, is an element in the process of development of the international system. Underdevelopment and development are two facets of a single process. Both internal and international structures are causes. International trade brings polarization because the low-income countries are assigned the production of primary products, which are processed in the home countries; because the economies of the low-income countries lack the work force, the entrepreneurship, and the physical and institutional infrastructure to seize export opportunities; because of worsening and unstable terms of trade; and because of generally monopolistic arrangements by which profits flow out from the underdeveloped countries to the developed. In Sunkel's view, even import substitution, the substitution in the underdeveloped countries of domestic manufacturing for exports behind the protection of import restrictions, is a way of integrating underdeveloped countries into a new type of polarized international capitalist system.

In this neocolonialism multinational corporations play a major role. In their home countries they plan new products and new methods, the machinery for both, and the manufacturing strategy. They specialize in the generation of new technical knowledge which is consumed in the underde-

---

[14] And reflected in half a dozen essays in Helleiner, ed., *A World Divided.*

[15] "Transnational Capitalism and National Disintegration in Latin America," *Social and Economic Studies,* special number, 22, no. 1 (March 1973); reprinted in G. M. Meier, *Leading Issues in Development Economics,* 3d ed. (New York: Oxford University Press, 1976), pp. 692–702.

veloped countries but not shared with them. Integrated scale of production, capital, planning, market power, techniques, finance, and other choices belong mainly to the home country. The MNCs intrude into the law, politics, foreign policy, and cultures of the underdeveloped countries—and escape regulation. Among the results are the persistence of the exporting of primary products (whose prices are held low by MNC bargaining) by the underdeveloped countries, exogenous dynamism, exogenous decisions, indebtedness, denationalization, subsidiarization, the danger that regional integration will favor the MNCs and lead to the liquidation of local enterprises, and a growing income gap between the developed countries and the underdeveloped countries.

The broadest criticism to be made of this group of theories is that, like most "devil theories" of history, they caricature or ignore facts. The condition of few LDCs is stagnant. Polarization is not occurring. If it has existed, it is decreasing, not increasing. The LDCs do not form a low-income group far removed from the MDCs. Their incomes, almost all of them rising, range up to those of the middle-income countries. Those countries used to be LDCs. Some other LDCs will soon join the group, and some will move on up through it, though only slowly. For good or ill, modernization is spreading in the LDCs as their incomes rise. It is possible to argue that it is deterred by adverse policies of high-income country governments and of MNCs, a question that is discussed in Chapters 18 and 19, but it is unfactual to assert that it is not occurring. However, it is true that the mass of the people in LDCs do not share in the fruits of early growth.

Some of the partisans do not present their attacks in the extreme form exemplified in Sunkel's article, and they do not make his extreme claims about the results of the policies of the MDCs. They say only that if higher income countries altered certain of their policies the progress of lower income countries would be faster. Waiving the question of the motivations underlying MDC policies, almost every growth economist would agree with the statement. Many growth economists would add that many of the policies that the partisans recommend that LDCs adopt would harm, not help, the LDCs. Those policies of MDCs and of LDCs are discussed here and there throughout this book.

Here the specific viewpoints of two subgroups may be noted.

Neo-Marxism

The only rounded application of Marxist logic to the problem of economic growth, an extremely urbane one, was presented by Paul Baran in a book published in 1957.[16] The main ingredients of Baran's presentation are two:

---

[16] P. A. Baran, *The Political Economy of Backwardness* (New York: Monthly Review Press, 1957).

1. A version of all of the hypotheses of peculiar barriers. The market is too small because of the profits retained by the ruling coalition of owning classes. These classes receive income ample for saving for investment, but they do not invest. In general, the situation is marked by monopolistic market arrangements and by production that yields no external economies, contributes nothing to public welfare, and stimulates no investment for growth.

2. An alliance between feudal landlords, industrial royalists, and the rising bourgeois capitalist middle class, imposing a government that can take no forward-looking step. The conception of constructing infrastructure "transcends by far the financial and mental horizon" of these groups.

No technical or entrepreneurial problems exist. If the ruling alliance had the will, economic development and social progress could proceed without difficulty.

A decade later, in a more vehement but less coherent statement, André Gunder Frank presented a neo-Marxist view of the causes (as he saw them) of slow or negative development in Latin American countries.[17]

Some of the neo-Marxist writers would have lower income countries end their dependence and end exploitation by the economically advanced nations in various vigorous ways: by forming cartels through which to extract more income from the higher income countries; by expropriating foreign-owned enterprises or forcing their sale to domestic investors; by withdrawing recognition of patent rights; by defaulting on their debts. A few, such as some writers of the *dependencia* school, recommend almost complete autarky. To this proposal it is replied that while this might or might not eliminate the sense of dependency, it would be suicidal economically.

Dependencia

Writers of one group cry out with especial anguish at one aspect of their condition as they feel it: their dependence—in Spanish, *dependencia*—on the countries of "the center." These writers are distinguished not so much by the content of their analysis as by the tone of their writings. They feel that a strong foreign presence hangs heavily over them. Multinational corporations, loans, aid, trade, a foreign cutural presence: they object to all of these. They feel that they are wards, not free persons.

The aspects of economic dependence that the writers of this group assert most commonly are: (*a*) a heavy penetration of foreign capital; (*b*) the use of advanced, foreign, capital-intensive technologies in a relatively small industrial sector; (*c*) specialization in exports of primary commodities or labor-intensive manufactures; (*d*) elite consumption patterns determined by those of the advanced countries; (*e*) "unequal exchange" in various senses. (*Un-*

---

[17] André Gunder Frank, *Capitalism and Underdevelopment in Latin America* (New York: Monthly Review Press, 1967).

equal Exchange is the title of a 1962 book by Arghiri Emmanuel.)[18] Among the results are (*f*) growing inequalities in income distribution, even immiseration, and rising unemployment ("marginalization"), especially in urban areas.[19]

The reader will recognize five of these aspects of "dependence" as common conditions of early growth: the penetration of foreign capital; the use of foreign advanced capital-intensive techniques in a small sector; the "modern" consumption patterns of the elites; growing income inequality, even perhaps an absolute decline in the level of living of the poorest; and the importance of primary commodities or labor-intensive manufactures among exports. Conventional growth economists deny completely only the reality of "unequal exchange." But these economists would also note that the other conditions result from the growth process itself, regardless of the relationship between the LDCs and the advanced countries.

If LDCs are to export at all before they have developed modern industry, their exports will have to be either primary commodities or labor-intensive manufactures. The complaint is that the advanced countries ostensibly force continuation of this pattern.

It is noted in Chapter 19 that the evidence for the supposed secular worsening of the terms of trade between the LDCs and the industrial countries is nonfactual, though, omitting oil, there has been decline since 1950.

This section of this chapter has criticized the excesses of this group of theorists. One must sympathize with their plaint, but that sympathy should not cause one to overlook the fact that the conditions of which they complain do not add up to a sufficient explanation of the difficulties of economic growth, even insofar as the complaints are justified.

THE TECHNOECONOMIC STAGES OF GROWTH

A close "enfant terrible" scrutiny of the process of economic growth indicates reasons why growth must be slow and gradual that are quite alternative to those of the vicious circles, structuralist, or "accuser" theories. These reasons lie in "the nature of the beast."

A technique that is highly efficient in an industrial country is likely to be extremely costly—costly in the fundamental economic sense that it will use many units of capital-plus-labor input per unit of output—in a nonindustrial or less industrial country. The process of economic growth is in part a process of overcoming this difficulty by a sequence of creative adaptations. The sequence in its general outlines cannot be short-circuited or leaped

---

[18] Arghiri Emmanuel, *Unequal Exchange: A Study of the Imperialism of Trade*, translated from the French by Brian Pierce (New York: Monthly Review Press, 1972).

[19] This summary is from Sanjaya Lall, "Is 'Dependence' a Useful Concept in Analyzing Underdevelopment?," *World Development*, 3, nos. 11–12 (November/December 1975), 799–810.

over. There is a more fundamental problem than lack of knowledge. The problem may be understood by considering the nature of industrial production in an industrially advanced economy.

Few products manufactured in an industrial country are wholly or even largely produced in a single factory. The producer of even a moderately complex final product obtains components or materials from perhaps several dozen firms, each of which produces on a large scale because it has a number of customers for a single component or several variants of it, and each of which, in producing that component, may in turn purchase items from a number of other firms, each of which has multiple customers. (Some of these firms may incorporate products of their customers or their customers' customers into their own products; branches of the chains form circles.) The production methods used in this complex network involve advanced technology: mechanical, metallurgical, chemical, electronic, biological. And they are capital-intensive.

Advanced technology is embodied in the elaborate or massive machines; without the machines it is lost. Seemingly, many chemical or metallurgical processes, often the shaping of metal, and much manufacture to fine tolerances is impossible without the machines. This may not be true in all cases. Perhaps in part, the heavy machinery exists only because the thrust of invention in the West for generations has been to save labor by substituting capital equipment. It is conceivable that in some instances technical genius could achieve the advanced techniques without elaborate capital. However, technical genius is scarce in any country, and this is an academic possibility not of great practical importance.

Methods using elaborate machinery are economic because of the large volume of production. This marriage of capital-intensive high-technology methods with large-scale production gains the high productivity per unit of capital-plus-labor that is the hallmark of industrial society and the source of its high level of living.

Because income in a low-income country is low, the volume of demand is low. The market will take only a small volume of products. Hence, if a typical process were lifted out of the industrial complex of a high-income country and placed in a low-income economy, the capital, interest, and maintenance cost of an elaborate machine would have to be allocated over a small number of units of output, and the cost per unit of output of using the machine would be prohibitive. The use of the nation's resources in production by this method would lower, not raise, the level of living.

Furthermore, the advanced plant will need feed-ins of materials and components that it itself does not produce and cannot produce except at extremely high unit cost. In an advanced industrial country they flow in smoothly from the rest of the industrial complex. In a country in which the advanced plant operated in isolation, they could be provided (from abroad, by expensive stockpiling, or by relatively small scale production) only by an extravagant expenditure of inputs per unit of output. Altogether, the venture would increase poverty, not affluence, in the country.

Typical advanced techniques, then, become burdensome, costly techniques if they are transferred individually to an economy with no or little industry. But neither can the entire industrial complex be created there full-blown. Industrialization, it would seem, is impossible.

There is, of course, a solution, since industrialization did proceed in the West and is proceeding in non-Western economies. The possibility of the solution lies in the fact that not all processes that would increase productivity per combined unit of inputs require an elaborate supporting industrial complex. Some such processes are relatively self-contained. With these, industrialization begins.

The Schema

Early successes in every country have been in processes of this kind, processes that require few inputs of materials or components from other plants, and these, inputs that can be imported and stocked without undue cost. Such more or less self-contained processes will usually be employed in the production of goods already familiar and widely used in rougher form in the traditional society, for example, sugar, soap, matches, rice or wheat flour, leather and leather products, textiles and textile products, bricks, cement, beer. Their production involves no radically new technical problems and only a modest amount of managerial experience and skill, and low cost can be achieved without an extremely large volume of production. Such plants appear before the casual observer thinks of the modernization of production as having begun, but they are crucial first steps in it.

For one or another component or material that has been imported or made in low quality in traditional ways, several of the fairly simple industrial enterprises in combination may then become a market large enough so that it pays a local entrepreneur to enter upon its production by nonprimitive methods. Examples are cardboard cartons, simple cast parts, wire, sulfuric acid, caustic soda, light reinforcing rods, simple tools and machines. "Linkages" emerge.[20] Especially important, small casting, forging, and machining shops develop capability to do increasingly elaborate and precise work, and to work in metals other than merely iron. Local repair and maintenance thus improve. If they did not, other aspects of industrial production could hardly progress. Methods also become more capital-intensive and farther removed from traditional techniques.

---

[20] The term is Hirschman's. A. O. Hirschman, *The Strategy of Economic Development* (New Haven: Yale University Press, 1958).

The early industrial history of a number of countries, and probably that of every country if the history were known, shows a generation or two of attempts and failures (too poor quality, too high direct costs, two few customers to cover overhead costs) before successes are achieved by entrepreneurs who are more capable and resourceful or perhaps merely have the good fortune to be born later.[21]

The expansion of light engineering may be expected to follow. (The production within the country of almost all component parts of bicycles is symbolic evidence that this stage has been reached.)

Then there occurs a long stage or stages of progressive improvements in metallurgy, in industrial chemistry, in the control of quality and of size tolerances in metalworking industries. These, like the simpler steps before them, are prerequisites to further industrial advance. They are associated with increase in scale, either through expansion of the domestic market or through success in exporting; the use in this larger volume of production of machines and machine tools permitting greater precision; and improved understanding and management of chemical processes. The somewhat larger plants, the use of precision-yielding machinery, and the mastery of complex chemical processes are possible not so much because the market has expanded as because management ability has been increased through experience and increased understanding. Increasingly complex interrelationships of supply develop. Strands of interrelationship begin to take on the character of a net. [22]

Then expansion and increase in the technical capability and the complexity of the metallurgical and chemical industries may steadily occur, and ultimately, if the market is large enough, heavy metalworking processes and perhaps an advanced electronics industry may develop. The transition from light engineering to heavy engineering and advanced industrial metallurgy, chemistry, and electronics has not been studied. To casual observation the technical jumps involved in this transition seem very large. How they are accomplished is puzzling. A guess may be ventured that the explanation is twofold. Progress into the most advanced techniques may be by a series of not very large steps that go unnoticed, only the fairly spectacular final result attracting attention. On the other hand, by this stage in industrialization entrepreneurs may be ready to make rather large jumps.

In a country of even moderate size that advances far into these final stages, there may develop a productive system which, perhaps with the im-

---

[21] A vivid and scholarly account of failures by one group of early industrial entrepreneurs and successes by a more resourceful group a generation later is given in Luis Ospina Vasquez, *Industria y Protección en Colombia, 1810–1930* (Bogota: Editorial Santafe, 1955).

[22] The source of these observations is research by the writer in fieldwork in Colombia, and discussions of the order of emergence of industrial enterprises in other South American countries—discussions with young officials and scholars gathered together in a training course in Fortaleza, Brazil, in 1963.

port of the components embodying the world's latest technical advances, will be able to produce any known product within some area of specialization. Japan's technical advances illustrate that a latecomer may become the world leader in technical progress in some fields. However, a country need not enter upon this ultimate stage to have an industrial complex that will yield a high level of per capita income. (And of course high income may be yielded by technical advance in fields other than manufacturing industry.)

Even the very largest countries will specialize. The United States has the most diversified advanced industry in the world. Shipments of components and products that are international in Western Europe are interregional in the United States. Yet the United States too specializes, partly because of differences in comparative advantage, partly because of superior techniques elsewhere.

This process of industrialization is truly one of stages. A country cannot develop a highly productive network of production in manufacturing, agriculture, transportation and communication, or other sectors except by a progressive evolution of an industrial structure that may appropriately, even though figuratively, be termed epigenetic.

National Positions on the Growth Ladder

For convenience, this long development may be treated as consisting of six stages, each prerequisite to the one that follows, except that the sixth is merely a continuation of the fifth.

1. The emergence of self-contained factory processes.
2. The development of initial interrelationships.
3. The expansion of light engineering.
4. The improving control of quality and tolerances.
5. The elaboration of the industrial complex.
6. The stage of industrial complexity.

By this classification—and recognizing a margin of error in the placement of any country—the six "Sahelian" countries, those just south of the Sahara desert, have hardly yet entered state 1, and the other of the countries labeled the world's 25 least developed in 1971 by the United Nations Committee for Development Planning are barely within this stage. This was also true of the countries of the Arabian Peninsula before the discovery of oil there. The countries of central Africa below the Sahelian six are still in stage 1 or entering stage 2, as are Paraguay and Bolivia. Indonesia is probably still in stage 2. Colombia is entering upon stage 3; Mexico, Argentina, Chile, and Venezuela are farther within that stage. Spain and Portugal are in stage 4. Much of India is in stage 1, but there is an industrial band stretching across the country from Bombay toward Madras that is in stage 4 or even early stage 5. Parts of Northern Brazil are in stage 1, but São Paulo is well into stage 5. Southern Italy is hardly in stage 3 but northern Italy is in stage 4 and moving into stage 5. South Korea, Taiwan, and industrial centers of China are well advanced in stage 4. Western Europe, which can be treated as a single economic entity, the Soviet Union, Japan, and the United States are in stage 6.

Growth Points

The significance of the development of a web of interfirm and interindustry relationships in industrialization is illustrated by the importance of "growth points."

Because of technological external economies arising from proximity to appropriate other firms, growth in industry and in some types of service tends to be concentrated geographically. It centers on "growth points" or "growth centers," or, to use the stronger French term, *pôles de croissance*. It is argued that the geographic spot at which growth begins in an economy will form a focus of growth, and that the attractiveness of this center for further growth will at least for a time increase regional disparities in income and innovational energy.

One of the external economies involved is the availability to each firm of semiskilled, skilled, white-collar, or technical workers who have been trained by other firms. Any firm training workers loses some of them. If other firms are clustered nearby, those losses are offset by the recruitment of workers whom other firms have trained.

Much more important is another technological external economy that results from clustering. This is the advantage that results from the mere closeness of sources of supply, maintenance and repair services, and technical consultancy. Any firm in a low-income country that has to stockpile machinery components or to send 1,000 miles to obtain technical advice understands keenly the advantages of clustering.

The importance to a firm of having these and other needed facilities nearby is illustrated by the difficulties encountered by the government of Italy in its attempts after World War II to attract firms to the region in and near the "heel" of Italy's "boot." When the construction of infrastructure plus the rather generous financial incentives offered by the Italian government during the 1950s had induced a much smaller movement of industry to the area than had been hoped, the European Economic Commission underwrote a research study to determine the conditions needed to encourage an industrial enterprise or a group of interlocking enterprises to move.

That study, as reported in the London *Economist* (November 7, 1964), concluded that

> . . . most firms, despite the incentives, could not afford to sacrifice the "external economies" (i.e., benefits that come from the industrial environment

rather than from the particular firm's own efforts) that they would enjoy if they invested in the north.

It was found

> ... that external economies depended on something much more specific than being surrounded by a lot of other industries. For many firms it was vital to have several highly specialized auxiliary firms close at hand, providing them with components, carrying out a single operation in the productive process, or looking after servicing or retooling. . . . It appeared that for many industries the vital consideration was closeness to their auxiliaries rather than closeness to markets or basic supplies. For their part, some auxiliaries might need to have several large firms to serve before they could operate on an economical scale. . . . It appears that the common classification of industries into supply-orientated, market-oriented, and footloose . . . is inadequate, unless supply-orientation is taken to cover the much more specific requirement of closeness to auxiliary industries.

The industrial development of the Italian south has progressed modestly in recent years, but even this moderate success would not have been achieved had it not been for the industrial projects established in the region by the large government-owned business enterprise, the Institute for Industrial Reconstruction, whose decisions were heavily influenced by nonmarket considerations.[23]

And so industrial enterprises as well as some types of service enterprises tend to cluster, up to the point at which congestion, the main external diseconomy of clustering, other than pollution, outweighs the advantages of closeness.

The tendency is not all-encompassing. For types of production in which economies of scale are small or end at a small size, location near rural markets or near sources of supply may be economic. Keith Griffin reports that textiles production, food processing, and the production of construction materials appear in all parts of Taiwan, and that in the northern and central areas over 60% of rural income is from nonfarm sources.[24] In China, also, there is much dispersion of some industry to rural areas.[25] In China this was done predominantly by decree, to lessen urban congestion, and in Taiwan there are apparently considerable direct and indirect subsidies to rural industry, so that it is not clear in either case whether the result is uneconomic or whether it is the social optimum when the diseconomies which urban

---

[23] The work of IRI is discussed in S. Holland, ed., *The State as Entrepreneur: New Dimensions for Public Enterprise: The IRI State Shareholding Formula* (London: Weidenfeld & Nicholson, 1972).

[24] Keith Griffin, "An Assessment of Development in Taiwan," *World Development*, 1 (June 1973), 31–42.

[25] C. Howe, *Employment and Economic Growth in Urban China* (New York: Cambridge University Press, 1971); and J. Sigurdson, "Technology and Employment in China," *World Development*, 2 (March 1974), 75–85.

producers impose on the community, but for which they are not required to pay in other economies, are taken into account. In Japan some small-scale rural industry still persists. Mainly, these small enterprises make components or materials for large-scale industry. Their continued existence is due largely to the lower incomes which none-too-mobile producers will accept, and as the income differential between rural and urban Japan shrinks, the number of rural industrial enterprises is also rapidly shrinking. The income differential is also important in Taiwan and presumably in China, so that in these countries also the existence of all the present types of rural industry is hardly an equilibrium situation.

Whatever may be optimum in some instances, the net advantage for much the larger share of manufacturing lies in clustering. As economic development proceeds, industrial concentration increases. At a late stage, some local decentralization occurs and, also, "megalopolises" emerge in which for, say, 300 miles there is no countryside but only industrial urbanism of varying intensity. "Spread" has occurred from growth points until they merge.

Perroux, the author of the term *pôles de croissance*, saw nothing ominous in this tendency. [26] On the contrary, he recommended locational concentration to take advantage of the natural forces (mainly technological external economies). Myrdal saw a danger in the tendency.[27] He complemented or extended the concept of growth points with his thesis of "spread" and "backwash" effects. Growth, he said, tends to spread from the growth point, but a contrary effect may more than counteract this one. The growing center is attractive to firms by reason of the external economies that it presents, but not only to firms. It is also attractive to individuals as consumers. As a result, it will attract the most talented and alert individuals and leave outer areas denuded of capital and talent. This "backwash" may not merely retard the development of other regions but actually lower their economic level below what it would have been if the growth center had never emerged. Myrdal advocated policy measures to prevent this adverse effect. The importance of the effect and the necessity for the policy measures are matters of controversy.

There is a phenomenon in agricultural growth that may be termed a variety of growth point effect. Tang[28] and Nicholls [29] portray the growth point and spread effects in rural development in the Southern Piedmont during

[26] F. Perroux, "Note sur la Notion de 'Pôle de Croissance,'" *Économie Appliquée*, 8: 307–20.

[27] G. Myrdal, *Rich Lands and Poor* (New York: Harper, 1957).

[28] A. M. Tang, *Economic Development in the Southern Piedmont, 1860–1950* (Chapel Hill: University of North Carolina Press, 1958).

[29] W. H. Nicholls, "Industrialization, Factor Markets, and Agricultural Development," *Journal of Political Economy*, 69 (August 1961), 319–40.

the past century. The greater efficiency of agriculture near industrial centers is striking. More recently Nicholls has documented the close correlation between industrial growth and agricultural modernization in the Brazilian state of São Paulo.[30]

Adaptation and Creation

Engineers, scientists, and on occasion growth economists refer to the "transfer of technology." The phrase, though it contains an element of truth, is simplistic and misleading. A central fact of the industrialization process which I have thus reduced to a schema is this: with few exceptions even the simplest first processes cannot be lifted bodily from an industrial country and established unchanged in a nonindustrial country, and this holds even truer for more advanced, more industrial processes. In almost every instance there will have to be adaptations in order to accomplish something in the nonindustrial country for which the facilities by which it is done in the industrial country do not exist. And there is no automatic advance from one stage to the next. At every point new problems must be solved whose solution cannot be observed anywhere else. The course of industrialization in any country must to some degree be created within that country.

Moreover, continuing advance in productivity is not simply a process of adaptation of successively more complex processes from an industrial country. It requires continuing and progressive improvement and replacement of methods in place. The building into behavior of such perpetual change is the cornerstone, the keystone of the arch, the fount, of continuing rise in real income. No more than the ability to adapt methods successfully can this essential ingredient in the process be taught or transferred. It must spring from the energies, motivations, values, and creativity of indigenous entrepreneurs.

The necessarily sequential nature of technical progress holds true in agriculture, transport and communications, and some other services, as well as in industry, but it is most conspicuous and most complex in industry, and the other fields will not be considered here.

One should think of these progressive steps in economic growth as occurring in generations, not years or decades. To repeat what was said or implied at the beginning of this section: there is no need for any theory of obstacles, oppression, deliberate deterrence, or structural difficulties to explain the slowness of economic growth. These may be present, but they need not be posited merely because growth is slow. It is slow because of the technical nature of the growth process.

---

[30] W. H. Nicholls, "Agriculture and the Economic Development of Brazil," in *Modern Brazil: New Patterns and Development,* ed. J. Saunders (Gainesville: University of Florida Press, 1971).

Comments on the Technoeconomic Schema: Historical Variation

An early factory need no longer depend on a waterwheel—or a generation later, a steam engine, or several generations after that, an internal-combustion engine—for power; it can have a diesel engine running an electric generator. It is difficult to know whether such changes telescope somewhat the early stages of advance. However, it would seem that entrepreneurs adapting advanced techniques that are in use elsewhere should be able to move forward more rapidly than could entrepreneurs in the past who had fewer advanced techniques from which to select. This should be true, at least, when a country has a considerable number of resourceful entrepreneurs who are seeking to profit by introducing effective advanced techniques. This fact may explain the rapid advance of countries in the middle range of the LDCs. As was noted in Chapter 2, productivity and per capita income in these countries is rising more rapidly than it did in the Western countries in any historical period of their economic development. However, no country can "leap from the 17th century to the 20th."

The Pace of Advance: Differences among Countries

The pace of advance may differ from country to country, depending much less on the natural resources available than on two other factors: the country's economic and social institutions and the degree of entrepreneurial resourcefulness of the people. The surge of industrialization in Japan beginning in the 1880s is the classic example of advance in "two-league boots" if not "seven-league boots," and to state that it occurred "because they are Japanese" is not merely a superficial quip. Since the sixth century the Japanese have shown a unique ability to adapt from abroad what was useful for their national life. The Meiji Restoration of 1868 had cleared away the deadwood of feudal controls and had set in motion a high degree of governmental cooperation with eager entrepreneurship. Social institutions and national character combined to bring about a remarkable pace of economic advance. Yet one should not overstate the abruptness of industrialization even in Japan. Japanese innovation did not begin in 1868. There had been progressive advance in agricultural techniques for three centuries before the Meiji Restoration, and in handicraft production and business methods for two centuries. A small cadre of individuals had been experimenting with some Western industrial techniques since soon after 1800. Before 1850 there were metallurgical laboratories in Japan, and in 1850 or a year or two later there were reverberatory steel furnaces.

South Korea and Taiwan are repeating, several generations later, Japan's speed of early advance. No forecast is implied that they will also rush into the later stages as rapidly as Japan has done.

Latecomers

Japan, South Korea, and Taiwan are latecomers. As their examples illustrate, latecomers may benefit handsomely by taking advantage of techniques already developed elsewhere. Latecomers are not always rapid comers, as is illustrated by the examples of Greece, Portugal, and Spain in southern Europe, and of tens of lower income countries elsewhere. The examples of the three Asian latecomers suggests that instances of rapid industrialization are cases in which entrepreneurial talent and energy were present but repressed and surged forward when constraining social and political institutions were burst. However, this is retrospective inference. We deduce that the energy and talent had been present because of the results that we observe. It is difficult to separate the influence of social institutions from that of national character, because national character goes far to determine the nature of the social institutions.

Attempts to Escape the Sequence

Many low- or moderate-income countries try to move directly from little industry to "modern" production by introducing the production of one or a few modern products. Automobile production is a current frequent example. The process may begin as a "screwdriver industry." Parts are imported and assembled ("screwed together") into a finished product. The money and resource costs of the product are high; assembly in volume at the point of manufacture is more economical. A high tariff or the complete prohibition of imports prevents competition from the foreign producers.

The next step is to require that the assembling company shall produce or purchase within the country certain of the components, then an increasing number. The money cost and the underlying resource cost are still higher. Even when the country is producing almost all of the components, it is doing so at a very high cost in labor and capital, in the absence of the more fully developed industrial complex that lends efficiency to the production of such an elaborate product. The country's level of living is reduced.

It is argued that this forced advance to an advanced product has external economies. Production methods are learned, mechanics are trained, and so on. True, but almost certainly no more so than in the industrial ventures more suited to the country's state of advance that might have emerged otherwise, and meanwhile the diversion of energies from those ventures has probably deprived the country of more balanced support for industrial advance. On balance, industrialization has probably been retarded.

Qualifications to the Schema: Enclave Activities

If the mineral resources of a country are sufficiently valuable, a modern extractive industry and perhaps also industry that partially processes mineral products may be established in a country by foreign firms even in the complete absence of a supporting industrial complex. The extraction of the mineral may be so advantageous that it pays to proceed with it by the only feasible methods, namely, capital-intensive modern ones, even if these are encumbered by all the inefficiencies that lack of an industrial surround entails. Among the many examples are tin, tungsten, and lead mines in Burma early in the 20th century; copper mines in Zambia and the Congo; a huge hydroelectric, mining, and aluminum refining complex in Ghana; and oil extraction in the Middle East.

Such activities are commonly termed "enclave activities," because they are usually almost wholly detached from the domestic economy. They are cysts—in the economy but not of it. They may teach some of its indigenous workers mechanic's skills, and they may train indigenous individuals to produce some needed supplies, but in general the highly capital-intensive methods are so far removed from the methods present elsewhere in the economy that very little transfer of techniques takes place.

Footloose Industries

A quite different sort of industry may be in an economy but not of it. This is a small shop in which dexterous indigenous workers perform labor-intensive work on lightweight components of a larger product. A Western company ships in the component, pays wages that are very low by industrial standards but high by the standards of the country, and ships the processed component back home to be incorporated into the final product. The archetypal component of this sort is a tiny wafer which is the heart of a semiconductor; workers using microscopes guide a delicate instrument that solders fine gold wires to the terminals. Another example is cloth cut in the United States and shipped abroad to be sewn into garments which are shipped back. In 1973 such imports to the United States from LDCs were valued at $1.5 billion, 3.7% of all dutiable imports. The ideal location for footloose industries before the 1970s was Singapore, Taiwan, Hong Kong, or South Korea, but as wages in those countries rose rapidly with the rapid development of the countries, many firms with footloose processes have moved them elsewhere. Some 80,000 Mexican workers (almost all of them women) are now employed in such plants located just south of the Mexican-American border.[31]

---

[31] *New York Times*, February 22, 1979.

TABLE 6-1   Average hourly earnings of workers in some foreign countries in the late 1960s were one-fourth to one-eighteenth of those of workers doing similar work in the United States

	Average Hourly Earnings Abroad (dollars)	Average Hourly U.S. Earnings (dollars)	Ratio of U.S. Earnings to Earnings Abroad
Consumer electronic products			
Hong Kong	0.27	3.12	11.8
Mexico	0.53	2.31	4.4
Taiwan	0.14	2.56	18.2
Office machine parts			
Hong Kong	0.30	2.92	9.7
Mexico	0.48	2.97	6.2
Korea	0.28	2.78	10.1
Singapore	0.29	3.36	11.6
Taiwan	0.38	3.67	9.8
Semiconductors			
Hong Kong	0.28	2.84	10.3
Jamaica	0.30	2.23	7.4
Mexico	0.61	2.56	4.2
Netherlands Antilles	0.72	3.33	4.6
Korea	0.33	3.32	10.2
Singapore	0.29	3.36	11.6
Wearing apparel			
British Honduras	0.28	2.11	7.5
Costa Rica	0.34	2.28	6.7
Honduras	0.45	2.27	5.0
Mexico	0.53	2.29	4.3
Trinidad	0.40	2.49	6.3

Source: U.S. Tariff Commission, *Economic Factors Affecting the Use of Items 807.00 and 806.30 of the Tariff Schedules of the United States* (Washington, D.C.: U.S. Tariff Commission, 1970), cited by G. K. Helleiner, *Economic Journal,* 83 (March 1973), 45.

Table 6-1 shows the saving in wages gained by shipping materials abroad for processing or assembling.

Footloose processes are a sort of enclave activity, and like other enclave activities they may contribute little to the process of industrialization in the country in which they are carried out.

THE SCOPE OF INDUSTRIALIZATION

Much of the preceding section has been written as though economic growth consisted of the development of manufacturing industry. The view is a myopic one, implicitly adopted in that section for purposes of exposition. Industrialization may mean either of two things: the emergence of manufacturing industry or the adoption of more and more productive methods, typically involving the use of more and more capital equipment, more and more "industrial" methods, throughout the economy. Only in the latter sense are industrialization and economic growth congruent. Sequential progress is a necessary part of a country's advance in productivity in any sector, though the sequence is more binding, some steps more rigorously necessary before others, in some sectors than in others. Thus, some types of increase in productivity in agriculture are possible separately from industrialization elsewhere, but others cannot be achieved until farm machinery repair and maintenance services in towns have developed sufficiently.

FOR FURTHER READING

Concerning "vicious circles," see the writings of Nurkse and Singer cited in note 2 of this chapter; concerning the "big push," see Rodan—note 9; for a clear statement of the structuralist-partisan viewpoint, see Sunkel—note 5; for a lucid general statement of the neo-Marxist view, see Baran—note 16.

Gunnar Myrdal, *Asian Drama* (New York: Pantheon Books, 1968), presents at length a view concerning India that is not unrelated to the structuralist theses.

Hla Myint, *Economics of the Developing Countries* (New York: Praeger, 1965), presents a clear, balanced economist's view of more prosaic difficulties.

Albert O. Hirschman, *The Strategy of Economic Development* (New Haven: Yale University Press, 1958).

Essays by Maizels, Streeten, Stewart, Vaitsos, and Green, in *A World Divided*, ed. G. K. Helleiner, reflect viewpoints that might be termed "eclectic partisan."

Gerald M. Meier, *Leading Issues in Development Economics*, 3d ed., chap. 10.

Celso Furtado, *Obstacles to Development in Latin America* (New York: Anchor Books, 1970).

Michael Sharpston, "International Sub-contracting," *Oxford Economic Papers*, 27 (March, 1975), 94–135, reprinted as World Bank Reprint Series, No. 19.

7

The Proximate Causes
of Growth

Abandoning the search for underlying causes, this chapter asks two questions: (1) how does growth begin, and (2) what keeps it going? Given the supposed barriers to growth—technoeconomic, structural, or whatever—or the ease of growth that neoclassical theory assumes, what are the proximate causes of the initiation of growth? What exogenous force initiates it? And what are the requirements for keeping it going? Specifically, does growth begin with the pull of an increase in demand, or with a push from creative entrepreneurs even in the absence of change in demand? And does its continuation require balance or the series of spurts here and there in the economy that constitute imbalance?

DEMAND AS THE ENGINE OF GROWTH

Many economic historians have noted the remarkable association between high world demand for the exports of a number of countries and rise in their per capita incomes. Ragnar Nurkse, advancing the thesis that exports were the "engine of growth" in the 19th century, mentioned seven countries in evidence: Argentina, Australia, Canada, New Zealand, South Africa, the United States, and Uruguay.[1] Kindleberger cites England as the classic example of "export-led growth."[2] Other writers agree. Gustav Papanek cites market expansion in Pakistan after its separation from India in 1947 as perhaps the most important cause of the rapid technical progress

---

[1] R. Nurkse, *Equilibrium and Growth in the World Economy* (Cambridge, Mass.: Harvard University Press, 1961).

[2] C. P. Kindleberger, "Foreign Trade and Economic Growth: Lessons from England and France, 1850 to 1912," *Economic History Review*, 14 (December 1961), 289–305.

that occurred in Pakistan subsequently.[3] More recently, when the U.S. military offered an almost open-ended demand for supplies from South Korea and Taiwan during the Vietnam War, productivity and income in those two countries soared. But important changes in economic policy were made in those countries at the same time. Was the increase in demand or these policy changes the engine of growth?

The Staple Theory of Growth

Out of the association between increasing exports and economic growth in Canada, the "staple theory" of growth was born. The Canadian economist Harold Innis expounded it in the 1930s.[4] In a critique of the theory Richard Caves summarizes it succinctly.[5] The theory, Caves writes,

> describes a sequence of events whereby the rapid expansion of some commodity exports, requiring a substantial input of natural resources but relatively little local processing, induces higher rates of growth of aggregate and per capita income through a higher rate of capital formation, inflows of capital and labor to the region, and expansions of output and productivity in other sectors via various linkages, externalities, induced innovations, and the like. The resource-based product is called a staple, and the term is used equivalently to name the model.

Each phrase in that summary states one link in the theory. In Canada the commodity in point was wheat. It will be noted that, though the term is not used, the theory assumes a "leading sector" and linkages from that sector to others.[6]

It may be granted that where there are "empty lands" or idle workers and plants, an increase in demand will increase output and income. This "Keynesian" effect is not economic growth, or if one chooses to call it growth, it is a limited and analytically unimportant type of growth. An important question is whether or in what circumstances an increase in demand stimulated technical progress.

---

[3] G. F. Papanek, *Pakistan's Development: Social Goals and Private Incentives* (Cambridge, Mass.: Harvard University Press, 1967).

[4] Harold Innis, *Problems of Staple Production in Canada* (Toronto, Ryerson Press, 1933). Melville Watkins gives a rounded statement of the theory in "A Staple Theory of Economic Growth," *Canadian Journal of Economics and Political Science*, 29 (May 1963), 141–58.

[5] R. E. Caves, " 'Vent for Surplus' Models of Trade and Growth," in *Trade, Growth, and the Balance of Payments: Essays in Honor of Gottfried Haberler*, ed. R. E. Baldwin and others (Chicago and Amsterdam: Rand McNally and North Holland Publishing Co., 1965), pp. 95–115. Caves pursued the subject further in *Trade, Balance of Payments, and Growth: Essays in Honor of Charles P. Kindleberger*, ed. J. N. Bhagwati and others (Amsterdam: North Holland Publishing Co., 1971).

[6] Though the concept of leading sector is usually associated with the name of W. W. Rostow, the term and analysis was presented earlier by Albert O. Hirschman in *The Strategy of Economic Development* (New Haven: Yale University Press, 1958).

Instances may be cited: Whitney's invention of the cotton gin; McCormick's invention of the reaper; England's spectacular innovation in textile-processing machinery in the 18th century, to cater to a world waiting for its textiles; the invention of the Bessemer process of making steel in 1856 and of the Siemens-Martin method a decade later; Colombia's entry upon coffee production in response to the opportunity offered by the increased demand for coffee in Europe and the United States in the last half of the 19th century; innovations in steel refining in Sweden and in dairy products in Denmark in the last quarter of the 19th century. Most of these inventions preceded the surge in exports, but undoubtedly they were made out of awareness of the opportunity.

However, there are contrary considerations and contrary examples. Why should not an increase in demand that is making a country prosperous without innovating make it content with the methods it has? Argentina's income increased at a good rate in the late 19th century and early 20th century while immigration was filling empty lands and its exports of wheat and meat were mounting. Improved methods would have accelerated its rise in income, but none followed. Bolivia remained inert while tin exports soared. (Admittedly, Bolivia may have obtained little increase in domestic income.) A 70-year rising tide in world demand for Burma's rice failed to set a growth process in motion. Kindleberger draws a judicious conclusion: "Exports can lead to growth, but they need not."[7]

Kravis's Analysis

These few examples may suggest that a country that is more developed technically will respond to an increase in demand, whereas a less developed country will not. But even this is not certain. There has been one fairly rigorous analysis of increase in demand as the stimulating factor. Irving Kravis has presented a critique of the thesis that exports to the industrial countries were the "engine of growth" in newly developing countries in the 19th century.[8] If exports were the engine, he argued, we should expect to find one or more of the following features in the economic history of the periphery countries:

A large and/or growing share of exports in domestic production.

An accelerated increase in GNP following the increase in exports.

A concentration of exports in sectors that are growing relatively rapidly, and/or rapid growth in industries linked to the export industries.

---

[7] C. P. Kindleberger, *Foreign Trade and the National Economy* (New Haven: Yale University Press, 1962), p. 204.

[8] I. B. Kravis, "Trade as a Handmaiden of Growth: Similarities between the Nineteenth and Twentieth Centuries," *Economic Journal*, 80 (December 1970), 850–72. N. F. R. Crafts has a criticism of Kravis's article, and Kravis a reply, in *Economic Journal* 83 (September 1973), 875–89.

The attraction of foreign capital to export industries or to industries supported by them.

Kravis surveyed data concerning the seven countries listed by Nurkse. The seven countries were characterized by none of the six features.

He then turned to a GATT study of the exports of 58 less developed countries during the period 1951–61 to 1964–65. The study showed that the difference between superior, middle, and inferior export performance by these countries depended very little on differences in world demand for their products. Some energetic and innovational countries gained an increased share of the world market. Others lost part of their share. Kravis drew a conclusion:

> The idea that there was a powerful expansionary impact from the center's demand for food and raw materials, which was the main factor generating growth, can be true, if at all, for but a few countries. . . . nor was export expansion by periphery countries the differentiating factor determining the extent and quality of their growth.

Exports, Kravis concluded, are the handmaiden, not the engine, of growth. One may put that conclusion in another way. If a vigorous innovating spirit is present among the people of a country at a time when world demand for one of the country's major products is rising or is in prospect, the opportunity presented is likely to channel innovational talent into improvement in the methods of making the product. If a vigorous innovating spirit is not present, the country is likely to rest on its oars without innovating and enjoy the prosperity that has come its way.

If innovational ferment is present, will it manifest itself whether or not there is increasing demand?

Examples of purely exogenous innovation, or at least innovation without the carrot of increasing demand, are numerous. Exports played virtually no role in the Russian economy either during the period of its early fairly vigorous growth, 1860–1914, or subsequently until after World War II. The rapid rise in Japan's exports after about 1890 was the planned result of a feverish search for industrial and handicraft products that could be produced cheaply enough to earn foreign exchange, rather than a response to world demand for primary products in which Japan's natural resources gave it a comparative advantage; with the exception of silk, such primary products were nonexistent. Although increasing demand is given as the stimulating cause for England's advances in textile technology in the 18th century, the cause given for its advances in steel refining late in the 19th century is that demand for its steel was falling—it was losing the steel market to continental competitors that had lower labor costs and better ores.

Two noted development economists have expressed the judgment that economic growth begins with innovative improvement in supply, not through the stimulus of demand, and a third has presented a model that may be interpreted in the same way. Adam Smith, who may appropriately be termed the first development economist, thought this. As mentioned in Chapter 5, he believed that division of labor, and thereby technical progress, was occurring more vigorously in England than elsewhere not because England's market was expanding but because England's institutions were favorable to technical progress.

In the 20th century, Joseph A. Schumpeter argued that innovation occurs when innovational persons exist. The (business) entrepreneur acts, Schumpeter said,

> ... to found a private kingdom, usually, though not necessarily, also a dynasty. The modern world really does not know any such positions, but what may be attained by industrial or commercial success is still the nearest approach to medieval lordship possible to modern man. *Its fascination is specially strong for people who have no other chance of achieving social distinction....*
>
> *Then there is the will to conquer: the impulse to fight, to prove oneself superior to others, to succeed for the sake, not of the fruits of success, but of success itself....* The financial result is a secondary consideration, or, at all events, valued as an index of success and as a symptom of victory, the displaying of which very often is more important as a motive of large expenditure, than the wish for the consumers' goods themselves....
>
> Finally, *there is the joy of creating, of getting things done, or simply of exercising one's energy and ingenuity.* This is akin to a ubiquitous motive, but nowhere does it stand out as an independent factor of behavior with anything like the clearness with which it obtrudes itself in our case. Our type seeks out difficulties, changes in order to change, delights in ventures.[9]

The italics are mine.

Chapter 15 discusses W. Arthur Lewis's conception that a country's savings rate rises, and growth proceeds, when persons of a capitalist spirit are present. Lewis's conception seems to make a point similar to Schumpeter's. For Lewis's "capitalist" it would be reasonable to substitute "entrepreneurial."

The evidence seems to favor the Smith-Schumpeter-Lewis view. Rising demand seems to channel the innovational or "capitalist" spirit, rather than to cause it.

EXPORTS AS THE COMPLEMENT TO TECHNICAL PROGRESS

However, exports are not thereby demoted in growth theory. Economic growth requires technical advance, but as noted in Chapter 4, technical advance alone merely concentrates income and may be immiserating, as Marx

---

[9] J. A. Schumpeter, *The Theory of Economic Development* (Cambridge, Mass.: Harvard University Press, 1934). Originally published in German in 1912.

charged all capitalism is. An increase in aggregate demand reemploys the disemployed factors. By doing so, it at least maintains the level of income in the noninnovating sectors of the economy, perhaps increases it, and in either case enables the income average in the economy to rise. An increase in exports has often been the form of that increase in demand. Exports, then, are neither the engine of growth nor merely its handmaiden. If exports are in harness with technical progress, the two together will draw aggregate and per capita income in the economy upward.

In at least six of the seven countries listed by Nurkse—all but Uruguay—the outpouring of exports was accomplished by the filling of "empty lands," not by technical advance. (Perhaps this was true of Uruguay also.) The producers occupying the empty lands probably improved on previous techniques, but this was a secondary cause. However, the filling of empty lands was followed by the (1) multiplier and (2) accelerator effects that the staple theory notes. (3) A further income-spreading effect may have also followed. The induced increase in demand for the products of the rest of the economy may have increased prices and thereby incomes in the sectors of the economy that were already fully employed. In all three of these ways, the staple-producing sector may have been a fount from which increasing income flowed to the rest of the economy.[10] These effects rather than the inducing of technical progress are probably the important consequences of increasing world demand during the growth process.

BALANCE OR LACK OF BALANCE DURING THE GROWTH PROCESS

The Theses

Some economists, and not merely those who have adhered to the vicious circles or big push hypotheses, have argued that there must be balance during the growth process if it is to continue. In its weakest form the principle asserted is merely that as growth occurs there will be expansion in all sectors of production except in the production of "inferior goods" and except as imports satisfy demand. In its strongest form the thesis states that as growth occurs the output of the several sectors of the economy must be increased in proportions rigidly determined by the changing composition of rising demand and by input coefficients in production.

In a closed economic system, if the price elasticity of consumer demand were zero, and if there were fixed input coefficients in production (that is, if only one production method, involving fixed proportions of the various

---

[10] The present writer presents a model of "the fount" at work in the petroleum-exporting countries in "Economic Growth with Unlimited Foreign Exchange and No Technical Progress," in *Development and Planning*, ed. J. Bhagwati and R. S. Eckaus (London: George Allen & Unwin, Ltd., 1972).

inputs, were known), then an absolutely inflexible balance would have to be maintained. The allocation of increasing consumer demand among final goods would be completely determined by the income elasticity of demand for various products, the output of each industry feeding other industries by the input coefficients of each industry, and the output of capital goods by production requirements. In such an economy, only by coincidence would the demand for each type of input equal the available supply; except by coincidence or by a knife-edge balance, only one type of input, the bottleneck input, would be fully employed. No balance theorist quite argues that this extreme theoretical case is realistic, but some growth theorists vigorously argue the hampering effects of imbalance.

The opposing theory is that in its essence the growth process is one of imbalance. An innovator makes an advance in one field and expands production in it in order to meet the resulting demand. This creates increased demand and shortages of components or materials and a rise in their price, thus inducing expansion in those fields. Perhaps infrastructure now becomes congested. The government or a private entrepreneur is induced to provide it. Moreover, input coefficients are not fixed. Adjustments can be made.

Schumpeter, who proclaimed that innovation occurs in bursts or waves, lesser persons following the great innovator who first makes an advance, would have found the conception of rigid balance in growth incredible. He described the growth process as follows:

> Progress—in the industrial as well as in any other sector of social or cultural life—not only proceeds by jerks and rushes but also by one-sided rushes. . . . Evolution is . . . more like a series of explosions than a gentle, though incessant, transformation.[11]

The balanced growth theory, Hirschman writes,

> . . . is essentially an exercise in retrospective comparative statics. If we look at an economy that has experienced growth at two different points in time, we will of course find that a great many parts of it have pushed ahead: industry and agriculture, capital goods and consumer goods industries, cars on the road and highway mileage—each at its own average annual rate of increase. But surely the individual components of the economy will not actually have grown at these rates throughout the period under review. Just as on the demand side the market can absorb "unbalanced" advances in output because of cost-reducing innovations, new products, and import substitution, so we can have isolated forward thrusts on the supply side as inputs are redistributed among users through price changes, and at the cost of some temporary shortages and disequilibria in the balance of payments or elsewhere.[12]

---

[11] J. A. Schumpeter, *Business Cycles* (New York: McGraw-Hill, 1939).

[12] *Strategy of Economic Development*, p. 62.

The balance theory is a theory of markets, the imbalance theory one of decisions.[13]

Criticism

For a considerable share of the goods and services used in a country, growth is best served if production rises in at least roughly the same proportion as demand. Yet the balance thesis in strong form is untenable, for three reasons. First, even in the fairly short run, and even more so over periods of a few years, some input coefficients are not rigidly fixed. Entrepreneurs can and do adapt to differential relative pricing and differential relative availability of inputs. Second, with some qualification, goods whose production it does not seem economical to expand can be imported and goods whose production is expanded at a rate faster than that at which domestic demand expands can be exported. Third, capital goods can be built in larger units than are needed immediately, at the cost of temporary high unit costs of production, but with a resulting productive plant capable of producing later at lower cost than would two or more smaller plants built seriatim.

Dualism

The need for balance most cogently argued is that between agriculture and industry. The desirability of balance in production is being recognized when it is observed that the agricultural sector must be producing an adequate surplus if industrialization is to proceed, and must augment the urban market for industrial goods if industry is to thrive; or that there must be an excess of exports over the value of consumer goods imports.

Putting the agriculture-industry relationship in the way in which it is stated above is singularly agricocentric; it could as well be stated that the industrial sector must produce a sufficient surplus and must provide a sufficient market for agricultural products; but the Physiocratic viewpoint is the one commonly taken. There is reason for it. The demand for food is highly price-inelastic. Significant increase in demand without increase in supply will produce sharp price rises, and these will have serious income effects. Food and other agricultural products may of course be imported, but if the country has been agriculturally self-sufficient and its prices for agricultural products have been below the world prices, its prices for those products must rise to the world prices plus transportation costs before market forces will induce imports. (If the country has been an exporter of agricultural

---

[13] Paul Streeten's terms, in "Balanced versus Unbalanced Growth," *Economic Weekly*, April 20, 1963, pp. 669–71, reprinted in G. M. Meier, ed., *Leading Issues in Economic Development*, 3d ed.

products, any increase in the domestic prices for those products relative to the world prices should cause supply to be diverted from export to the domestic market.)

Some writers see as a major problem in growth the transfer of resources from agriculture to finance the expansion of industry. Not only must agriculture provide the produce; it must save enough to lend industry the funds to finance the transfer of that produce to feed and clothe the increasing number of nonagricultural workers. A worker coming from a rural family to an urban job must "bring his own lunch."

The argument is fallacious. There is no such logical necessity. Savings out of the income of industry, rather than out of the income of agriculture, may purchase the food of the new urban worker until the time when his industrial produce is available to finance it. Because of the large size of agriculture and the small initial size of manufacturing industry, if early development is financed out of taxes, these are likely to be taxes levied on cultivators or landowners. However, the earliest finance may be and typically is from the plowed-back profits of early innovators.

The question of the agriculture-industry relationship is discussed further in Chapter 8, and the question of financing early growth in Chapter 15.

FOR FURTHER READING

See the writings by Nurkse, Kindleberger, Innis, Caves, Hirschman, Kravis, and Schumpeter cited in notes 1, 2, 4, 5, 6, 7, 8, 9, and 11. Add W. A. Lewis, "Economic Development with Unlimited Supplies of Labor," *Manchester School* 22 (May 1954), 139–91.

Clifford Geertz, *Peddlers and Princes* (Chicago: University of Chicago Press, 1963), gives an insightful account of the difficulties of the transition from bazaar to fixed-price retail store in an Indonesian village. It is presented in shorter form as chap. 16 of E. E. Hagen, *On The Theory of Social Change* (Homewood, Ill.: Dorsey Press, 1962).

III

The Factors of Growth

8

Land. Will There Be Enough Minerals?

The discussion turns now to the constraints placed on growth by the limited quantity of the "factors in growth." In the theory of production, all of the myriad inputs into production can be classed under the "factors of production"—land, labor, physical capital, and, if management is separated out from other labor, management. The theory of production is not concerned with innovation, but innovation is at the center of the theory of growth. Entrepreneurship, whose input is innovation, is thus a factor in the theory of growth but not in the theory of production. And each of the traditional factors in production must be looked at not merely in the traditional way as a factor in production, but as a factor in growth.

A production function that includes growth may be written: $Y = a + bR + cL + dK + eM + ft$, where Y = output, R = land, L = labor, K = capital, M = management, and t represents "the residual," all of the changes over time that bring increase in output per unit of input—conspicuously, technical progress and increase in scale, both of which are discussed here, and also many other changes.[1]

First, then, land or, more precisely, natural resources.

About one sixth of the earth's land area is desert. Desert may contribute inputs into production—minerals—but in discussing agriculture it may be ignored. According to an estimate derived from United Nations publications, one fourth or a little more of the world's land area is arid or semiarid land capable of supporting human life. Together with deserts, it comprises

---

[1] Since we are centrally interested in income per capita, if we intended to use this statement of a production function as more than a symbolic introduction, we should restate it with the independent variable as Y/N, in which case the function would become more complex.

43% of the world's land area. The definition of arid and semiarid land reflected in this figure must be rather comprehensive, since it is estimated that in 1975 some 630 million people, one seventh of the world's 1975 population, lived on such land.[2]

Only some 11% of the earth's land area is cultivated. According to an estimate by the (U.S.) President's Science Advisory Committee, another 13% is potentially cultivable if it is cleared, irrigated, drained, or otherwise prepared, without the use of technology beyond that now in use in U.S. agriculture.[3] This estimate may overlap with the United Nations–based estimate of the amount of arid and semiarid land.

The remaining one third of so of the world's land area is occupied by cities and roads or other structures or is barred from cultivation by its physical nature, topography, or climate. Higher productivity is gradually drawing more and more land into use for cities and roads.

Land contributes extension, fertility, and minerals to production. Its fertility is its most important contribution to the lowest income economies. Before the discovery of oil, fertile little Yemen, in the southwest corner of the Saudi Arabian peninsula, supported more people, and at a higher level of living, than did all of the rest of the peninsula. In 1950 the fertility and plentiful supply per person of the land of primitive Burma yielded a higher level of living to the people of Burma than that of technically much more advanced but more densely populated India. But technology may be dynamic; since then, India has steadily advanced relative to Burma.

Next in time come minerals, if a technically more advanced country wants them and will pay for them. Possessing fertile and mineral-laden land becomes of decreasing importance as income rises; in increasing degrees a people needs only space on which to build factories or trading or financial centers whose produce can be exchanged for the fruits and the minerals of the earth. Ultimately, the most productive quality of strategically placed land is merely its extension, its existence as a base on which people may build buildings in which to conduct financial and trading activities.

Japan and Israel provide the extreme examples of "making bricks without straw"—building a high-income economy with few physical resources. Switzerland with only hydroelectric power and the Netherlands with little soil per capita add further illustrations.

If a country must start with agriculture (except as the demand of other countries for its minerals hauls its income upward), one may ask how, with minimal resources, Japan and Israel could have risen so far so fast. The answer must be the qualities of the people, though in the case of Israel one must also recognize a pouring in of capital from the countries of the West to

---

[2] Erik Eckholm and Lester R. Brown, *Can Desert Encroachment Be Stopped?*, Ecological Bulletin no. 4 (Stockholm: Swedish Natural Science Research Council, 1976).

[3] *The World Food Problem: A Report of the President's Science Advisory Committee*, vol. 2 (Washington, D.C.: The White House, 1967).

which Jews have dispersed. But except as providing space, land played a relatively small part.

The productivity of land depends not only on its qualities but on the other inputs that are combined with it. The United States obtains a much lower yield of rice per hectare than does Japan and a much lower yield of wheat than do countries of Western Europe, yet it derives a higher income from agriculture than does either.

In classical economic theory, land is the nonproducible factor in production, capital the man-made one. In fact, the line between land and capital is blurred. Land as space, as agricultural resource, and as minerals is created. Many major cities have been built upon swamps, because near the rivers that made the locations economically strategic the land was swampy. The plaque that marks the site of the Boston Tea Party stands two blocks from the present seashore. Agricultural land is created physically by landfill, economically by irrigation, drainage, improvement in transportation, and technical change. In economic effect land was created progressively in Europe by the invention of the horse collar (which permits draft animals to pull heavily without choking), a crop rotation system that made it unnecessary to let one third or one fourth of the land lie idle each year, and the curved steel plowshare; in the United States when the Erie Canal was built, when railroads were extended to the Mississippi and then on to the Pacific, when McCormick built his reaper, and when the refrigerator car was invented; in Asia and Latin America by the "green revolution." The land area of the Chinese economy, if not of the Chinese polity, increased greatly in the mid-17th to the mid-19th centuries when the introduction of early-ripening rice, peanuts, and sweet potatoes permitted the Chinese to move north to areas where the summer is shorter.

Natural resources in LDCs have often been created, in an economic sense, through the discovery by explorers from industrial countries of resources not previously known locally or known only to local citizens to whom they had little value, or through the introduction of technical change. The most spectacular example, of course, is the discovery and extraction of petroleum that elevated Saudi Arabia, Iran, and Libya from poverty to affluence and made the poor sheikhdoms of Abu Dhabi and Qatar the highest income countries of the world.[4] There are many other examples.

The teak forests of Burma and Thailand were of only petty local value until they were discovered by foreigners. Southern Burma, which had been only malarial jungle, became the "rice bowl of Asia," supplying most of Europe's rice, when the opening of the Suez Canal made it worthwhile to clear the jungle.

---

[4] Now that these two sheikhdoms have combined with the emirates to their south to form the United Arab Emirates, the merged income data show high income but not the world's highest income.

The value of certain tropical lands soared as new techniques increased the number and improved the quality of finished products that could be made from natural rubber, and as the rubber tree productivity of those lands was discovered. Then the natural resources were destroyed in large part when synthetic rubber was discovered and improved. The discovery of a method of extracting aluminum from bauxite made deposits valuable that previously had little value. The invention of nuclear fusion did the same for uranium deposits.

Michael Roemer has described the results in Peru of a different sort of natural resource discovery.[5] Fishing with nets, including fishing for anchovies, had long been a source of Peruvian income. Then, in the mid-1950s, the development of sonar "fish-finders" revealed the tremendous schools of anchovies that were being missed, and at about the same time nylon nets replaced the weaker, heavier, and less durable cotton ones. The catch multiplied from 59,000 tons to 8.5 million tons between 1955 and 1966. Among the results were the creation of four new industries serving the fishing industry (making boats, fishnets, processing equipment, and jute sacks); the employment of not far from 3% of the nonagricultural labor force in fishing, the fish meal industry, and the four supplier industries; and earnings from the fishing and fish meal industries that constituted one fourth of the country's total foreign exchange earnings.

Land is destroyed as well as produced. Possibly as much as one sixteenth of the earth's land surface has been converted from productive use to desert by the actions of people—by overgrazing and the removal of shrub and tree cover.

LAND AS AGRICULTURAL RESOURCE

The meaning of landownership or land possession differs greatly among cultures and legal systems with rspect to the use to which the possessor may put the land; his control over its surface, its water, and the minerals beneath it; his right to dispose of these uses, and of possession of the land; the duration of those rights; and his access to income earned from the land. Here only use of the land surface is discussed, and it is assumed that, as is commonly true, ownership has the same significance with respect to such use in non-Western cultures as it has in Western cultures.

Climate, topography, and the physical and chemical characteristics of land determine its agricultural quality. In general, deserts are unproductive not because their soils contain no nutrients but because they receive no rain. Yemen, mentioned above, is fertile not because its soil is chemically superior to other Arabian soil but because the mountain range that runs

---

[5] Michael Roemer, *Fishing for Growth: Export-Led Development in Peru, 1950–1967* (Cambridge, Mass.: MIT Press, 1970).

along Yemen's northeast border causes the monsoon rains to drop their moisture on Yemen, while beyond the mountains lies desert.

CLIMATE

The tropics, as defined by geographers, lie from about 1,600 miles north to about 1,600 miles south of the equator, but geophysically they are wider. There are three principal types of tropical climate, all hot. In a band 1,000 miles wide, centering on the equator, it is "always" raining (every month). On either side of these "humid tropics" lies a 500-mile band that has its annual season of heavy rains lasting for several months, then no rain until the next year. Still farther north and south, in bands up to 1,000 miles wide, lie the dry tropics, desert or hot and arid.

There is controversy about why the tropics have not developed economically. All of the theses relate to climate. Something about the tropical climate is hostile to economic development. One explanation is the Toynbeean one of challenge and response. Life was too easy in the tropics, too hard near the poles. In the temperate zone the climate was sufficiently rigorous to stir people to creative effort, and not too rigorous to be overcome. The hypothesis, if it is to be accepted at all, should be modified. The "easy life," in which there was early material development that then stopped, was in the Fertile Crescent, which lies in the subtropics, not the tropics. Perhaps the challenge of the tropics, like that of the polar regions, was too great.

In several books the geographer Ellsworth Huntington argued a different climatic thesis.[6] Human creativity and energy are greater, he wrote, where the climate is not only moderate but also variable. Occasional thunderstorms, which increase the quantity of ozone in the air, are especially favorable. (Amused critics noted that his description of a climate ideal for human achievement coincided remarkably with that of New Haven, Connecticut, where he lived and worked.) Huntington argued that the advance of material civilization in China, the Middle East, and other areas occurred when the climate was more favorable than it is at present, and that the advance stopped when the climate changed. He bolstered his thesis of historical changes in climate with much ingenious evidence, but geographers no longer give much credence to the thesis.

In *The Tropics and Economic Development*[7] Andrew W. Kamarck emphasizes a different and plausible explanation. Because winter, "the great exterminator," never comes, the parasitic diseases and the insect pest ene-

---

[6] See especially his *Mainsprings of Civilization* (New York: John Wiley, 1945).

[7] Subtitled *A Provocative Inquiry into the Poverty of Nations* (Baltimore: Johns Hopkins University Press for the World Bank, 1976). My data concerning tropical climate areas are from this book.

mies of plants, animals, and people flourish. For animals, the result is try-panosomiasis, which prevented the development of either cattle or transport animals, and left Africa divided into isolated communities. For people, there are parasite-caused diseases—hookworm disease, bilharzia, malaria, river blindness, and many others—that debilitate (and kill). Kamarck adds that where jungle is removed from the soil in the humid tropics the rains leach nutrients from it. Only soils annually renewed by alluvial overflow remain fertile. Shifting or slash-and-burn cultivation, practiced over much of the humid tropics, is sometimes pointed to as demonstrating the primitive thinking and the ignorance of the local population. Actually, short of the use of modern artificial fertilizers this is the most efficient method in the circumstances. It permits jungle growth to restore fertility after it has been lost in a few years' use of the land.

Mechanical transport is now available in the tropics. The tropical diseases can be attacked. Tropical conditions do not prevent future economic development. However, they probably explain the lack of material progress in the past.

THE PROBLEM OF PRODUCTIVITY INCREASE

Introductory comments have already been made. This section discusses further the process and the problems of increase in agricultural productivity.

Most agricultural production in low-income countries is by peasants cultivating small plots, which they may own or rent. It is estimated that in India some 25% of cultivators are tenants and some 50–60% owner-operators, and that in Pakistan some 25% are tenants and some 70% owner-operators.[8] Presumably the remainder are owners whose land is operated for them by managers, though the residual figure of 15–25% for India seems impossibly high.

Much technical advance in the agriculture of low-income countries must be by the adaptation to a country or a region of methods developed elsewhere. The small size of cultivators' plots creates difficulties for this transfer of technology.

Peasants respond with alertness to economic inducements. The first evidence is large scale and historical: the surge of peasants in Southeast Asia and West Africa to new lands when the opening of export trade created new markets for the products. Various pieces of research done since World War II have given impressive evidence that within the limits of the prod-

---

[8] Carl H. Gotsch, "Economics, Institutions, and Employment Generation in Rural Areas," in *Employment in Developing Nations,* ed. Edgar O. Edwards (New York: Columbia University Press, 1974).

ucts and the production methods in which they are traditionally skilled, peasants are judicious in shifting among products, production methods, and capital-to-labor ratios in order to maximize their income. Perhaps the first such study, concerning the Punjab region of India-Pakistan, was by Raj Krishna. There have been several other studies of the responses of farmers to price and cost changes in India and Pakistan; several in Africa; one in Thailand concerning rice, cassava, corn, and kenaf; one in Brazil concerning the degree to which price expectations affected the intensiveness of coffee tree cultivation and the abandonment and replacement of coffee trees; and one concerning the responsiveness to price changes in Costa Rica. The verdict is unanimous; in this respect peasants and other cultivators are alert and resourceful "economic men."[9]

But shifting to new methods and new crops is much more difficult than shifting among known ones, and it may involve large risks. The peasant cannot afford large risks. A single year's failure because a new method turned out not to be adapted to his soil or climate may mean, if not starvation, loss of his animals, his equipment, and even his land, for he has no margin of income or savings to fall back on. Hence by himself he cannot experiment with improved methods. Moreover, because of the small size of his operations it would not pay him to expend his resources in order to seek technical advances. The cost of finding improved varieties and practices, even if there were no cost of adaptation, would almost invariably be much greater than his small benefit. The cost of adaptation compounds the impossibility. The technical advances must be brought to him. Then, even though some risk is still involved, he seems to seize them eagerly.

The Difficulties

Large-scale investment can play its part in increasing agricultural productivity. Irrigation projects may permit multiple cropping on land already under the plow, or may convert land from waste to cultivation; drainage may do the latter; and roads or railroads may open up new regions. Irrigation has been important in India, China, the Middle East, and many other areas, and drainage in a few areas—for example, Israel. The Soviet Union

[9] See T. W. Schultz, *Transforming Traditional Agriculture* (New Haven: Yale University Press, 1964), chap. 3; P. T. Bauer, *West African Trade* (Cambridge: Cambridge University Press, 1954); E. R. Dean, *The Supply Responses of African Farmers* (Amsterdam: North Holland Publishing Co., 1966); W. O. Jones, "Economic Man in Africa," *Food Research Institute Studies*, 1 (May 1960), 107–34; W. P. Falcon, "Farmer Response to Price in a Subsistence Economy: The Case of West Pakistan," *American Economic Review*, 54 (May 1964), 580–91; Jere Behrman, "The Price Elasticity of the Marketed Surplus of a Subsistence Crop," *Journal of Farm Economics*, 48 (November 1966), 875–93 (concerning Thailand); M. Arak, "The Supply of Brazilian Coffee," unpublished Ph.D. dissertation, Massachusetts Institute of Technology, 1967; and C. E. Staley, "Response to Agricultural Prices in Costa Rica," *Economic Journal*, 71 (1961), 432–36.

has opened up large areas, in many of which, however, the growing season proved too short for effective cultivation. The opportunities for and the effects of these measures, though important, are limited. Moreover, these projects will not achieve their full benefits unless the glamorous large projects are accompanied by effective local administrative arrangements. Premier Chou En-lai stated in 1959 that only one half of the area of Chinese land claimed to be under irrigation at that time could be adequately irrigated. Bardhan, who notes this, also calculates on the basis of official Indian data that "only about 48% of the additional major and medium irrigation potential created since 1950–51 was utilized by 1955–56; the figure has gone up to 77% by 1964–65." The reason was not merely that administrators interested in the glamorous projects were less interested in the detail of making them work effectively, but also that administrative action to assure favored large landowners plenty of water made the supply to small peasants so uncertain that it did not pay them to make use of the facilities.[10] Only in the 1970s were some of these difficulties overcome, and then not all of them.

Although an occasional new plant variety introduced from the outside may be immediately useful, many—probably a large majority—will not be effective without adaptation. The problem may be one of soil chemistry, temperature, rainfall, length of season, and even length of day. A strain of cereal that does well in one country may do poorly in another in which the days are longer or shorter during the growing season. Only when, in the 1960s, Rockefeller Foundation research scientists developed strains of photoinsensitive rice and wheat did this problem decline in importance. But the other types of problems remain. And photosensitivity has been found advantageous in some conditions.

One costly change may not yield an increase in output unless it is accompanied by several other changes that are carefully tuned to one another. In the words of the report of a conference of experts on agricultural change:

> The interdependencies among the factors are so strong that the effects of a package of factors are likely to be very different from the sum of the effects of each one applied by itself. . . . Additional fertilizer without water control may have little result, and the consequences of more water may be very modest if additional nutrients are not supplied. If both are supplied together, existing varieties that do as well as any others in the absence of water and fertilizer may not benefit as much from these new inputs as new varieties, specifically tailored to water and nutient availability; yield on existing varieties may even be reduced by added water or fertilizer. Insects and diseases that are unimportant under existing practices may multiply

---

[10] Pranab K. Bardhan, "Chinese and Indian Agriculture: A Broad Comparison of Recent Policy and Performance," unpublished draft manuscript, Center for International Studies, Massachusetts Institute of Technology, 1964.

dangerously under irrigated and fertilized conditions and require new measures of disease and insect control.[11]

Moreover, with his traditional seed and methods of cultivation, the cultivator knows what adjustments to make in planting, manuring, or cultivation—or all three—if the year is unusually wet, or dry, or late, or hot, or cold. If he adopts a new variety, or uses commercial fertilizer, he does not. And the expert from the country of origin of the new variety or the fertilizer does not know either, for there is no way to be certain in the new climate and soil except by extensive trial and error in those different conditions.

The change, though advantageous in a technically advanced country, where yields are high, may not be economic in a "backward" country, where yields are low, for some new strains or techniques give no more than the same *percentage* increase in yield in the two countries, and they may cost more than the value of the absolute increase in yield in the backward country.[12]

A new method may have disadvantageous side effects not dreamed of in the area in which it was developed. In India high population density has caused much farmland to be denuded of trees and shrubs, and has made land too scarce to use any of it to grow crops for fodder. Wheat with long stalks has been developed over the generations; the straw is used for fodder. This wheat responded to an increase in fertilizer, but the heads became so heavy that the stalks often broke and the wheat failed to ripen. When a new short-stalk strain was introduced from Mexico in the mid-1960s, greatly increased yields were obtained with high-nitrogen fertilizer, but a fodder shortage resulted. The writer does not know how this difficulty was met.

Some machines do not require such adaptation. Many new machines have been developed in recent decades in Japan. Japan needed machines adapted to small-scale production, and devised them. However, the advantage of many of these depends on the cost of the labor they displace, being much smaller where farm incomes and labor costs are low. Some of the machines lack even this lesser advantage until the use of machinery in the economy as a whole has developed to the stage at which local maintenance and repair are available.

To conclude this litany of difficulties, it must be noted that in many types of change the peasant cannot act alone. Irrigation may not be possible for him alone. Interbreeding from close neighboring fields may destroy or greatly lessen the advantage of new seed. Where it is proposed to breed improved cattle strains, this may be possible only if inferior cattle from the

---

[11] Max F. Millikan and David Hapgood, *No Easy Harvest: The Dilemma of Agriculture in Underdeveloped Countries* (Boston: Little, Brown, 1967).

[12] Schultz, *Transforming Traditional Agriculture*, chap. 10.

village are prevented from breeding with the improved cattle and causing quick retrogression. In the Philippines, the use of seed brought to a certain community by a technical adviser promised an increased yield, but the plants would mature at a different time from the old variety. If a single peasant or a few peasants had adopted the new seed, the rats and birds would have converged on their fields and destroyed the crops.

And where a peasant's holdings are a half-dozen scattered bits of land, many of the problems of acting alone are compounded. Fragmentation of holdings results from demands for equity when ownership of land passes from one generation to the next. Each heir must get some of the richest land, some land that receives the early spring sun, part of the land with the best drainage, and so on. New methods cannot be used without consolidation, which is almost impossible unless the government can add land to enrich the deal.

The Necessary Measures

Once in successful local use, agricultural improvements have something of the "public good" quality of any nonpatentable technical advance whose success is visible and whose adoption is feasible. But there are a number of requirements for reaching that stage.

1. A basic requirement, if increase in productivity is to continue indefinitely, is continuing research. That requirement is being met effectively by nine international research institutions. These are financed by the World Bank, the United Nations Development Program, the U.S. Agency for International Development, other governments, and private American foundations. Their work is guided by a common International Consultative Group. The institutions (identified by their acronyms), their locations, and the matters on which they work are as follows. Where two or three are working on a common problem, their work is cooperative.

IRRI: The Philippines—rice.

CIMMYT: Mexico—maize and wheat.

IITA: Nigeria—rice, maize, cowpeas, pigeon peas, sweet potatoes, yams, cassava, cropping systems for the low humid tropics.

CIAT: Colombia—cassava, beef cattle, swine, beans, rice, and maize.

CID: Peru—potatoes.

ICRISAT: India—millets, sorghum, chick-peas, pigeon peas.

ILRAD: Kenya—East Coast fever, trypanosomiasis.

ICTA: Colombia—tropical agriculture.

ISTA: Nigeria—tropical agriculture.

The first and second of these, the International Rice Research Institute and the International Wheat Research Institute (Centro Internacional de

Mejoramiento de Maiz y Trigo), financed initially solely by the Rockefeller and Ford foundations, developed from earlier improved seeds the "miracle rice" and "miracle wheat" that have been the basis of the "green revolution."

2. The proposed methods must be carried to cultivators by demonstration farms, technically expert village demonstration teams, and the like. The experts must be expert. Often they are not. Farmers, Bardhan wrote concerning India, "have often refused to adopt new inputs and technology ... due to a better appreciation of their local unsuitability or technical complementarity than is to be found in the administrative officials pushing those programs."

3. The peasants must know that the inputs needed to prevent the failure of the new methods will be available when needed, and that the benefits, or a rewarding share of the benefits, will accrue to the cultivators and not to the landlord or the tax collector. In many countries, the governmental administration has been largely a mechanism for enforcing on the peasants the requisitions of landowners, moneylenders, and other economic elites, and for collecting taxes from whose expenditure the peasants perceive no benefit. Where this is true, there must be a broad change in the general tenor of administration if the cultivators are to be persuaded that the benefits of improved methods will accrue to them. Accomplishing such a change is like moving a mountain.

The transfer of landownership to cultivators, or as a minimum the institution by law of rental arrangements that give small-scale cultivators dependable assurance that they will receive the income from increased production may be necessary to lend the necessary conviction. But the countries in which such changes are most needed to lend conviction are the countries in which political influence is likely to block them or corrupt administration to foil them.

4. Literacy and elementary education presumably increase the ability of cultivators to receive information concerning improved methods and improved opportunities.

5. The capital market is not likely to function so smoothly that private benefit and social benefit will be identical in amount. If the other bases for successful technical advances in agriculture have been laid, the government intervention will probably be needed to provide cultivators with the credit that they will require to adopt the changes. But credit is scarce; there are other important demands for it; and, moreover, there may be other parties who have far more influence with government administrators than do peasants. The result may be, not that technical advances will not go forward, but that government benefits will be received and technical advances carried out more by wealthier farmers than by poorer ones.

Denmark, the United States, and Japan are the showcases of successful agricultural marketing and credit cooperatives. It is noteworthy that in all three countries much of the initiative for establishment of the cooperatives came from the farmers themselves. In a number of other countries, in which govermments have attempted to confer (or impose) cooperative organizations on the cultivators from above, the results have not been outstanding. In some of these cases, the administration of the attempt has been half-hearted, inept, and corrupt.

In Israel, the completely collective communities, the kibbutzim, and the communities organized for collective production, the moshavim, have been highly successful in solving new problems of production and in raising per capita agricultural income with great speed. But the motivation, the experience, and the problem-solving propensities of their members are so untypical that no deductions applicable anywhere else are justified.

The report of the conference of experts in agricultural change summarized the common opinion of those experts: "Sustained growth in agricultural output requires technical, economic, attitudinal, and political transformations of the whole structure of rural society that cannot be brought about quickly."

In some countries, where such changes have not been made and peasants and farm workers bemused by the hope of urban employment and by the attractions of urban life have flooded to cities, agricultural production has declined progressively during the past decade. This has been notably true in South American countries. In Asia, however, agricultural production in the aggregate and per hectare of cultivated land has risen progressively, and it gives indication of continuing to do so. Though governmental administration of pertinent programs has been less than perfect, it has on the whole been facilitating. By their nature, recent advances (the "green revolution") have increased employment and income for landless rural laborers, though they may have benefited small landowners less than large.

THE GREEN REVOLUTION

The most important single technical advance in agriculture in recent decades has been the "green revolution," the breeding of high-yield varieties of wheat and rice and their introduction into the agriculture of low-income countries. The "miracle rice" was developed by IRRI during the 1950s, the "miracle wheat" by CIMMYT between 1955 and 1970. The new rice has been the more important advance, since rice is much more important than wheat as a foodstuff in tropical countries.

Popular accounts have exaggerated the effects. The green revolution has been a revolution for only 10% to 15% of Asia.[13] Some areas grow cereals other than rice as well as other food crops. In some areas the irrigation

---

[13] Walter P. Falcon, "The Green Revolution: Second Generation Problems," *American Journal of Agricultural Economics*, 52 (December 1970), 701-9.

needed for the new rice is not available. When research workers from IRRI visited China, they found that the Chinese had bred high-fertilizer, high-irrigation, high-yield rice long before them. Moreover, locally bred varieties do better than the new rice in some areas of Java and in a few other places.

Yet the increases in production made possible by the green revolution have been very important. India and Colombia illustrate. India's production of food grains was 82 million tons in 1961 and 89 million tons in the bumper crop year of 1965, which made India self-sufficient in food grains for the first time in many years. Production fell back to 72 million tons and 78 million tons in the poor years of 1966 and 1967, respectively. Then in 1968 it reached 100 million tons, and in 1978, another good crop year, as the green revolution continued to spread, it reached 125 million tons. Since food reserves now exist and production will undoubtedly continue to trend upward, food-grain imports will be necessary only in an extremely poor crop year or two less extreme poor years in succession. The increases have removed the fear of expanding the demand for food as a constraint on development policy, and thus have permitted a more expansionary fiscal-monetary policy, even with falling foreign aid. (This in turn increases the demand for food and lessens the fall in the price of rice.) Rice production in Colombia, which had been only 680,000 tons in 1967, was 1,632,000 tons in 1975. The country had been a rice importer. It is now a significant rice exporter. Rice production in India is on small peasant holdings; in Colombia, on large "industrialized" farms.

The green revolution illustrates the complexity of both the means and the results that may characterize technical advance in agriculture.

Since growing the new strains requires greatly increased use of water, hence irrigation, expensive seeds, and greatly increased application of fertilizer, and makes more advantageous than previously the use of machinery for harvesting, threshing, and so on, it increases the capital cost of running a farm, hence makes the availability of credit important. However, the gain in yield is so great that even if the government does not arrange credit facilities and loans from the local moneylender are required, use of the new seeds is advantageous.

The advantageousness of the new methods has stimulated increased governmental expenditures for irrigation facilities. The new crops have also required improved milling, grading, transport, and storage facilities. As noted, the new methods encourage some mechanization.

Yet the new technology is "highly divisible," usable on small peasant plots as readily as on large ones. It is a yield-increasing rather than an acreage-expanding, that is, laborsaving, change. To obtain the needed water, where water from large irrigation projects has been unavailable or undependable, many thousands of Indian farmers have installed tube wells. Some of the larger tube wells have been installed by engineers, but many peasant farmers have devised such wells locally, using bamboo tubes wrapped with wire rather than steel tubing. These wells cost less than one fifth as much as the others, and in spite of their shorter life they are certainly cheaper per year of use when the interest cost on the investment is included in the calculation. Very small machines have been adopted—some of them hand-powered—machines devised mainly by Japanese for use on Japan's very small farms. Some have also been developed by IRRI.

When the green revolution began, many observers feared that it would cause disemployment of landless agricultural workers and the ousting of tenants to consolidate holdings into larger mechanized farms. Because of the efficiency of small-scale production of the HYV (high-yielding variety) rice, little ousting has occurred. The new seeds have a shorter growing season, and, especially with some mechanization to speed harvesting and threshing and preparation for planting, it is possible to grow two crops a year in some areas where only one was possible previously. Mechanization has lessened the peak demand for labor per crop at harvesting and planting time, but the new methods require more labor during the growing season, the demand for labor is spread more evenly throughout the year, and the number of worker-days demanded per hectare has apparently increased. Increased local employment has been generated in milling, transport, and storage. Altogether, the new technology has increased the income of all income classes of the rural population.[14]

Quite apart from the green revolution, there has been a small amount of consolidation of tenancy holdings into single larger farms by Indian landlords who fear the possible enforcement of land reform laws directed at absentee landlords that have been on the lawbooks for some years. The advantage of mechanization for the cultivation of the HYV rice has probably encouraged this tendency. Thus far there has been little of this, but the process may continue gradually, with the substitution of capital for labor and the loss of farm tenancies. In the past this tendency has been encouraged by the favorable exchange rates made available for capital imports and the subsidizing, in effect, of interest rates. Economists urge that India end the discriminatory exchange rates, let interest rates rise, and instead levy a heavy tax on large tractors.

LAND REFORM

Land reform may mean merely a transfer of ownership of parcels already under peasant cultivation from absentee landowner to peasant; a regrouping of scattered parcels into coherent units; or the subdivision of large estates, haciendas, or ranches into small holdings and the transfer of title to peasant cultivators. Usually, the transfer is by government compensation of

---

[14] See discussion of its effects in Gotsch, "Economics, Institutions, and Employment Generation in Rural Areas."

the former owners on such basis as seems equitable and is feasible, and then sale to peasants on easy terms.

The second type is important in countries in which fragmentation of holdings has occurred. Success may require that the government have or acquire lands of its own with which to enrich the exchanges, so that each peasant's unified holding is enough larger than before to assure him that it is superior even in spite of his fondness for those bits of especially choice land that he gave up.

The third type, division of large estates, is what is usually envisaged when land reform is referred to in non-Communist countries. The inequality of landholdings in the low-income countries is proverbial, and the proverbial picture is not greatly exaggerated. There are many large estates in some areas of India, in Java, and in Sri Lanka. In the Caribbean and Central America other than El Salvador and Costa Rica, agricultural holdings are also dominated by large estates. This was also true in East Africa before the colonies of that area gained their independence. In every country along the western half of South America, the conquistadores of the 16th century seized large estates for themselves. The land they took has remained in estate form—the *latifundia*—to the present time, while elsewhere in the same countries tiny farms—the *minifundia*—were formed as Indian villages disintegrated. The later creation of large holdings in the populated areas of Brazil followed somewhat the same pattern. In Argentina, in the 19th century, the government drove Indians off the land and distributed it in very large units to settlers who established the wheat farms of today (raising some cattle also). In Mexico feudal estates were distributed after the revolution of 1910–20, and in Cuba estates were divided and distributed by Castro. Today, in Latin America as a whole, even including Mexico in the computation, holdings of more than 6,000 hectares (about 15,000 acres, or some 25 square miles) constitute about one half of the agricultural land but only 1.5% of all farmholdings. They do not form as large a part of the cultivable land, for much of this estate land is suitable only for grazing.[15]

Many of the large holdings in South American countries, especially those in the western half of the continent, are cattle ranches. Although some of these ranches are on infertile land, many are not. For example, at least until the early 1960s extensive grazing was practiced on land of market garden quality near Caracas while fresh vegetables were imported from abroad to the city.[16]

---

[15] The data are from a 1951 United Nations publication, *Land Reform: Defects in Agrarian Structure and Obstacles to Economic Development.* They refer to the situation about 1950, but it has not changed greatly since that date.

[16] In *Transforming Traditional Agriculture* (p. 161), Schultz expresses surprise that farmers who operate large enterprises in parts of South America have not found and adopted improved methods: "Why they have not done better on this score is a puzzle." The solution to the puzzle lies almost certainly in the elite attitudes toward manual labor in general and the grubby details of farming in particular. To be a landowner is one matter, highly valued;

In the Middle East, large holdings are commonly rented to peasants for peasant-scale cultivation. In other areas of the world, the large estates are typically plantations, run as large-scale units. They may produce sugar in the West Indies and Java; rubber in Malaysia; wheat in Argentina; sisal, sugar, tea, coffee, or tobacco in Africa; and various other commodities in all of these places. The plantations in eastern, central, and southern Africa are owned by European settlers; most of those elsewhere in the continent are indigenously owned. In Africa south of the Sahara, much land is still held in communal tenure. On much of this land, "shifting cultivation" is still practiced. Many of the European-owned estates, for example in Kenya, were formed by occupying lands under shifting cultivation while they were unoccupied. This was often done by purchase of the rights from the indigenous tribal groups, who sometimes did and sometimes did not understand that they were giving up the land permanently.

In a few cases the small holdings nourish high-yielding specialized crops. An example is the highland peasant coffee plots of Colombia, which yield a fair living by Colombian standards. But where the small holdings are grain lands, on which income from the crop is eked out with that from the sale of eggs from a few hens, the peasant may live at little above a subsistence level and little better than the serf on the hacienda.

Land reform is said to release incentive and energy, to promote education and community development in general, and to have other socially desirable side effects. The United Nations is more or less officially in favor of land reform, and the Alliance for Progress made land reform one of its yardsticks of whether a country is socially progressive and would therefore use economic assistance to social advantage. But the problems and the economic advantage or disadvantage of land reform differ with these different types of large-scale ownership and operation.

Where land reform is simply a transfer of title from the absentee owner of a peasant plot to the peasant cultivating it, it can hardly have any but a highly favorable effect on productivity, provided that where the owners had furnished seeds and equipment these were furnished after land reform by someone else. Marketings would fall, and they might later rise to and above their former level only if production rose progressively and substantially, for the peasants become owners would eat better. A marked loss of marketings occurred after such land reform in Eastern Europe, and it would have occurred in the Soviet Union if the government had not used force to collect the grain from the peasants. The percentage of food-grain produc-

---

to be interested in the plebeian details of farming is another. Effective innovation on large farms is almost invariably carried out first by *industrial* innovators who are expanding the range of their operations. The relative advance of these innovators in social position may later goad traditional landowners to action. It is reported that in the Middle East, the landlord class has itself initiated changes that include entering into the modern processing of some agricultural crops.

tion in China that was marketed fell from above 35% during the first half of the 1950s to below 31% in 1956 and 1957. This was undoubtedly one reason for the formation of communes in 1958.

Where the peasants have been workers in the landlords' large fields, division of the fields into small plots owned by peasants is almost certain to reduce productivity greatly. Productivity will also almost certainly fall greatly even if the fields are left as a unified area under cooperative ownership and operation. Productivity will be restored only if there is highly skillful administration of the provision of capital and technical advice, and under cooperative operation it may not be restored even then unless the peasants are given incentives to individual diligence. The experience of China, discussed briefly in Chapter 14, is informative.

Where cultivation on a plantation was of plantation crops, a shift to peasant ownership typically causes a sharp and permanent decline in production, because large-scale operation is the more efficient form. There are exceptions to this rule: with respect to some tree crops in some conditions of cultivation, smallholder cultivation is efficient. The fall in sugar production in Castro's Cuba was due partly to the loss of the capital and management formerly provided by the owners of the sugar plantation and partly to loss of the incentive to diligent work.

On many haciendas of Latin America, the land is not in cultivation at all. It is held because landowning is a way of life. Much is idle; or because cattle ranching is more esteemed than agriculture, as noted, cattle roam fertile acres. With capable administration of land redistribution to peasants who would convert the land to cultivation, production would presumably rise quickly and markedly.

The problems of effecting the transfer of landownership to peasants are political as well as economic. The present owners are economically powerful, and they are able to call upon the conservative sentiments of traditional societies. The low-cost way of accomplishing transfer of ownership is to compensate the present owners with long-term low-interest bonds (which in effect is partial confiscation, and is a greater degree of confiscation if inflation occurs), but the political resistance is intense. Fiscal measures to penalize unproductive use of land are a less drastic means of change, but these run into severe administrative problems, especially in the mountainous areas of western South America, for which no good cadastral surveys exist and it is extremely difficult to make them.

Warriner's Summary

Land reform is as land reform does. It increased production in Egypt and Japan, reduced it in Iraq, Bolivia, and Chile. In a 1969 book, Doreen Warriner presents the most authoritative survey of the execution and degree of success of land reform in 13 countries (Denmark, Italy, Yugoslavia, Bolivia,

Brazil, Chile, Cuba, Mexico, Venezuela, Egypt, Iraq, Iran, and India).[17] She comments on the relationship between the provisions and administration of land reform and the effect of land reform on production, which

> ... may or may not be favorable depending on the conjunction of factors which influence incentive. ...
>
> On the basis of this range of experience, it appears that the more revolutionary the method of redistribution, the greater is the likelihood of reducing production; the more compromising the method, however, the greater is the likelihood of incurring high costs of expropriation. Yet this is too neat an antithesis, since in fact several reforms have increased production without incurring high costs, notably in Egypt and Japan, while in Mexico the reform indirectly stimulated investment in agriculture by private landowners. But of the countries observed, only Iran seems to have succeeded, up to a point, in avoiding both dangers. ... In Iraq, Bolivia and Venezuela, the laws were framed to provide for an integrated organization to support the farmers, and Cuba had a rational policy aim of diversification. Yet in practice the political impetus which drove through expropriation—communism in Iraq and Cuba, left-wing syndicates in Bolivia and Venezuela—could not work on these lines; success does not follow the prescriptions. The revolution brings sudden and violent change, but agriculture demands continuity; the kind of people who make revolutions are not, as a rule, the kind who can organize for increased production. ...
>
> If there is one lesson of universal validity that emerges from all this experience, it is the need for putting more practical intelligence to work.

LAND AS MINERAL RESOURCE

The earth is not only a farm; it is also a store of minerals. The role of the lower income countries as suppliers of minerals is of importance to them. Before it is considered, a prior question may be considered: whether economic growth in the world as a whole must soon come to an end because of exhaustion of the world's mineral stock. If it does, growth in the low-income countries will surely come to an end also. (The following chapter discusses whether the world will be unable to feed its growing population.)

DOES DOOM PORTEND?

The world's population in the year 1650 has been estimated at 550 million. Gross world product of that year may be estimated at $55 billion in U.S. prices of 1975. There is a wide margin of error in the estimate, but it gives us an order of magnitude.

A world population of 550 million with an average per capita income of $100 created little pressure on the land or its resources. But since 1650 the

---

[17] Doreen Warriner, *Land Reform in Principle and Practice* (Oxford: Clarendon Press, 1969). The passage quoted is from pages 375 and 436.

world's population has multiplied by about eight times. In addition, income per capita has risen, and with increasing speed. As it rose, the consumption of manufactured goods per capita rose in much greater proportion. Between 1750 and 1900, the world's population grew to 2.2 times its 1750 size and per capita consumption of minerals to 4.5 times, so that the world's aggregate annual consumption of minerals increased tenfold (2.2 × 4.5 = 9.9). And between 1900 and 1970, a period less than half as long, mineral consumption grew further by a factor of 12.7, for population increased by a factor of 2.4 and per capita mineral consumption by a factor of 5.3. In 1970, then, the world's aggregate mineral consumption was more than 125 times that of 1750. By 1980 that multiple will have risen to not far from 150.

The increase has been exponential. The effect of exponential rates of increase, if projected into the future, is great. For example, at the 1970 rate of coal consumption, the then "known" or "proven" world reserve (equivalent geologic terms) will be exhausted in 2,300 years; with consumption projected at the recent growth rate of 4.1% per year, the exhaustion period is 111 years. For copper, with a 4.6% rate of growth in consumption, the exhaustion period shrinks from 36 years to 21 years—exhaustion of world supply by 1991.

Repeatedly, observers noting exponential rates of resource use in an apparently finite world have expressed fears of impending calamity as people exhausted the world's natural resource supplies. One of the first United Nations conferences, in 1949, was on the Conservation and Utilization of Resources. A 1972 book by Donella and Dennis Meadows (with other authors), *The Limits to Growth*, presented to the world by the Club of Rome, warns anew.[18] Even though between 1949 and 1970 more lead, zinc, and copper had been mined than the known or proven world reserves in 1949, and aluminum and tin almost equal to the 1949 known world reserves had been extracted, in 1970 the known reserves of all these metals were much larger than they had been at the earlier date.[19] However, the Club of Rome book took the 1970 data as reflecting true total world supply and, averaging anticipated exhaustion periods for various metals, projected exhaustion of the world's mineral supplies, and calamitous collapse of industrial civilization, rather abruptly, between 2030 and 2050.

The forecast must be rejected.

Before the confusion about the world's total mineral supplies is discussed, another aspect of the forecast may be noted. There is no economics in it—no prices or relative costs. If impoverishment of the world through exhaustion of its mineral supplies ever occurs, it will not occur abruptly. The prices of materials becoming increasingly scarce will rise relative to other prices. The price rises will have three results.

---

[18] New York: Universe Books, 1972.

[19] Colin Clark recalls this history in *Population and Depopulation*, the 11th Monash Economics Lecture (Monash University, Clayton, Victoria, October 3, 1977).

First, lower grade ore bodies will be exploited. Because more productive resources will be required in mining, per unit of mineral output and in the aggregate, fewer will be available for other production. As a result, the secular rise in the world's aggregate and per capita output, hence in its level of living, will be slowed gradually, other things being equal. Second, manufacturers will economize on the use in production of the more costly materials; the ratio of capital to labor in production will rise more slowly than it would have risen otherwise. And consumers will economize on use of the more costly products; the share of services in GDP will increase.

Third, technical progress will be turned toward alleviating the effects of the growing scarcity of minerals. Since 1850 petroleum, aluminum, electrical power (more recently, nuclear electrical power), "artificial" fertilizer, and a whole array of plastics and synthetic materials have been "invented." Aluminum was "invented" by discovering how to extract the metal from bauxite. Petroleum was "invented" by discovering how to extract useful products from it. Other such inventions will no doubt occur in the future.

Figure 8-1 shows one example of such technical change. Energy consumption per unit of GNP in the United States, which rose very rapidly from 1880 to about 1920, fell almost as rapidly from 1920 to 1945 and has been falling gradually since that time. (The initial rapid fall was due largely to the efficiency gained in manufacturing by substituting electric motors for power carried from a prime mover by shafts, wheels, and belting.)

The condition for a continuing future rise in world per capita income, if the world should enter a period of increasing minerals scarcity, is that technical progress shall be more than sufficient to offset the need to devote an increasing share of productive resources to minerals extraction and processing. If resource costs rise progressively relative to technical progress, there will be no sudden catastrophe, but the rise in world per capita income will gradually slow down and may become zero and then negative. The

FIGURE 8-1   U.S. energy consumption per unit of GNP has fallen progressively during the past 60 years

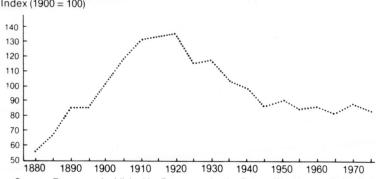

Index (1900 = 100)

Source: *Resources* (published by Resources for the Future, Washington, D.C.), Fall 1976.

question becomes: Is the world about to experience this progressively increasing scarcity?

The Question of World Reserves

Concerning this also, the doomsayers are mistaken.

One of the difficulties stems from misunderstanding of the term *known world reserves*. This and an alternative term, *proven world reserves*, are technical geologic terms. They refer to mineral deposits which have been fairly well identified and are of sufficiently high grade and sufficiently accessible to be worked profitably at currently metal prices and with present technology. They are reserves, that is, which have been sufficiently explored to determine this. The magnitude of "known reserves," then, depends on the amount of exploration that has been done.

Now, in general, mining companies do not prospect for additional mineral deposits so long as they have known reserves equal to some relatively short period, say two decades, of anticipated consumption—perhaps because the interest cost of developing properties this long in advance of need would be prohibitive and because they are confident that supplies can be found when needed. Thus, almost by definition, and not by virtue of world shortage, "known world reserves" of many minerals at any given time are less than 20 years' anticipated consumption. Important exceptions are coal, of which huge U.S. reserves are known; iron, of which a few individual deposits are very large; nickel, of which Canada's large deposits have been explored; bauxite, for which one company has explored throughout the world; and some metals used in small quantities and found in combination with others.

Because companies first explore close to home, in the industrial countries other than Australia, Canada, and the USSR mineral resources have been explored exhaustively and the total mineral potential is pretty well known and has been gradually depleted. However, most lower income countries contain areas in which there has been no minerals exploration whatever. Even in traditional mineral-exporting countries such as Peru and Indonesia, only a small proportion of the total area that geologists believe may contain valuable mineral deposits has been explored. Large areas of Saudi Arabia that "look promising" have not yet been explored for oil. It is thought that under the land surface of Mexico there may be oil deposits as large as the present known reserves of Saudi Arabia. Probably every geologist believes that there are large as yet unknown world reserves of important minerals. The recovery and processing of the manganese nodules that lie in large quantities on the deep ocean floor will probably be in full tilt before the end of this century. These nodules contain quantities of nickel, copper, and cobalt that are important even on the scale of total world supply.

In addition to known or proven reserves, geologists refer to "identified resources," by which they mean proven reserves plus deposits that are reasonably well known as to location, extent, and grade, and may be exploited profitably if the price rises or technology improves.[20] Two examples will illustrate. The search for oil is going on feverishly throughout much of the world in areas that were not worth considering at pre-1973 prices. Even within the continental United States many deposits too small to have been exploited at previous prices are now being tapped. Aluminum exists not only in bauxite but also in dawsonite, alunite, aluminum phosphate rock, and certain clays. A process to extract it profitably from alunite at present aluminum prices has been reported. At higher aluminum prices the world's aluminum reserves are virtually unlimited.

If minerals were becoming scarce, one would expect their prices to be rising. In fact, apart from lumber prices the U.S. prices of industrial raw materials were lower in 1970 relative to the prices of finished products than they were 100 years earlier.[21] The quadrupling of petroleum prices in 1973 and 1974 caused the index of industrial raw materials to rise sharply, but that rise, of course, was not caused by a natural resource shortage.

No academic observer of the natural resource situation is shrewder than the market practitioners. They understand well the discounting of future prices to the present. Far future prices do not affect present discounted values greatly, but if growing scarcities within, say, the next two decades were anticipated, one would expect a constant stir of excitement on the minerals markets and a significant steady rise in the prices of mining stocks relative to others. There is neither.

Edward S. Mason, a judicious student of natural resource supply and demand, wrote in 1977, ". . . we are not facing scarcities of industrial materials. So far as I can see, we do not even confront a danger of rising costs of these materials for the next century at least, and probably longer."[22]

MINERALS AND THE LDCs

Mining comprises a large share of total production in a number of LDCs, and minerals exports comprise an even larger share of the total exports of

---

[20] They also refer to "hypothetical resources," undiscovered deposits that are predictable from topography, geologic formation, and so on. Estimated hypothetical reserves do not include reserves in areas of the world that are quite unexplored.

[21] Evidence for the period 1870–1957 is presented in H. J. Barnett and Chandler Morse, *Scarcity and Growth—The Economics of Natural Resource Availability* (Baltimore: Johns Hopkins Press for Resources for the Future, 1963).

[22] Charles J. Hitch, ed., *Resources for an Uncertain Future* (Baltimore: Johns Hopkins University Press for Resources for the Future, 1978), p. 13.

The world level of energy costs, from which governmental action has temporarily shielded the United States, will probably remain permanently above its 1970 level. The level would have risen, though much less precipitately, even in the absence of OPEC action. Increasing scarcity of such convenient energy sources as oil and gas is very likely. But there are no practical limits to alternative sources, the most obvious of which are coal and nuclear power, that can perhaps be made available at no considerable further increase in real costs.

these countries. Petroleum is virtually the only export of the countries of the Arabian Peninsula. Although metallic minerals do not comprise as large a share of total exports of any country, the percentages are large in some countries, as Table 8-1 shows.

TABLE 8-1   In value, exports of major minerals comprise a large share of the total exports of some countries

	1960	1972–1974
Bolivia	83%	80%
Chile	77	78
Peru	49	57
Zaire	23	74
Zambia	98	96

Source: World Bank, *Commodity Trade and Price Trends*, 1973 and 1976 editions.

Minerals exports from the LDCs are also an important part of international trade in minerals. In 1972–74, the LDCs' share of internationally traded minerals supplies amounted to 37% for iron ore, 59% for copper, 60% for manganese ore, 65% for bauxite, and 85% for tin.[23] As geologic exploration goes on and new deposits are developed, the LDCs' share of world production and world exports of minerals will increase.

Increase in the Income Share: Processing

Mining in LDCs is predominantly by foreign firms. Since about 1960, LDC governments have extracted a progressively increasing share of the rent—in the economists' use of that term—from the mining ventures, by increased taxation, renegotiation of royalties, and, more recently, expropriation.

Moreover, these governments are pressing mining firms to process the ores at the mining site rather than in the consuming country. Precious metal, copper, and tin ores usually have a metal content of less than 1% of the weight of the ore. Large shares of the concentration of these are already done where they are mined, to save shipping cost. Bauxite, copper, and iron ores, with metal contents of 15% to 50%, have commonly been shipped to the consuming countries for processing, partly because the necessary infrastructure already exists there, partly because succeeding stages of fabrication are then sometimes combined with ore processing, and partly because the companies feel more secure there. The extracting companies

[23] Marian Radetzki, "Where Should Developing Countries' Minerals Be Processed?," *World Development*, 5, no. 4 (April 1977), pp. 325–34. The underlying data are from the World Bank. Tables 8-1 and 8-2, based on World Bank data, are also from Radetzki's article.

resist the pressure to process where they mine, in part for these reasons, but also because the processing plants, often very expensive, already exist and because expansion of capacity is often by partial replacement and expansion of an existing plant rather than by new construction. However, the pressure persists, and the percentage of processing done in the LDCs in which the ore is mined is increasing. Table 8–2 shows the increase from 1960 to 1970. Although data for the subsequent decade are not yet available, the increase has continued.

TABLE 8–2   Minerals processed in developing countries as a percentage of the total amount of the minerals mined in developing countries*

Increasingly minerals are being processed in the LDCs in which they are mined.

	1960	1970
Bauxite	3%	10%
Copper	75	78
Iron ore	23	25
Lead	57	69
Tin	66	79
Zinc	29	42

* Computed at the value produced by mining and processing operations as a percentage of the total value that would have been produced had all ore mined been processed to metal ingots (or pelletized in the case of iron ore).
Source: World Bank.

Increase in Income: Cartels

Many LDCs that produce minerals and some that produce agricultural products have contemplated increasing their incomes from such production in another way: by forming agreements to elevate export prices. These agreements are discussed in Chapter 19.

LAND AS A PLACE TO STAND

Except possibly for a few cases of land that has extremely high temporary value as minerals are being removed from beneath it, the most valuable land in the world is that which provides a choice location for doing business. The world's most valuable land is that of the financial centers of New York, London, and, recently, the central area of Tokyo. These cities developed as funnels through which trade passed and then as centers from which financial services were provided. It became increasingly advantageous for traders or financiers to be close to others with whom trade or financial matters were arranged. For that closeness they paid dear rent. Recently, as the elaboration of electronic communication has provided closeness without physical contiguity, some corporations have moved their headquarters to the suburbs of New York City, to the exurbs, or even to other urban centers. Those engaged in finance still find the center the most advantageous locale, but rents in the New York and London financial districts have probably peaked.

The pattern of land values in the lower income countries has been following that of the advanced countries. Saudi Arabia provides the extreme example. In Riyadh, for a time in 1975 and 1976, as governmental administration expanded and as representatives of foreign firms flooded the city to offer their firms' services in exchange for the fabulous amounts of oil money that had become available, and while houses and office buildings were being constructed laboriously by quasi-traditional methods, the demand for land became so great that land in the city center was held for prices that were probably exceeded only in the New York and Tokyo financial districts. It is not clear whether transactions were consummated at those prices, but it is clear that sales prices were such that men who had been only modestly well-to-do became millionaires (millions of U.S. dollars) in a few months. Then the construction of many buildings approached completion at about the same time, and the bubble burst. But land values remained at multiples of the highest previously known values.

During the generations before World War II, the governmental center in lower income countries, which might or might not also be a trading center, was likely to become the largest city. Since World War II, flight from the countryside has added to the agglomerations, as has been noted in Chapter 4.

FOR FURTHER READING

Agriculture and Economic Development:

Y. Hayami and V. W. Ruttan, *Agricultural Development: An International Perspective* (Baltimore: Johns Hopkins Press, 1971).

Bruce F. Johnston and Peter Kilby, *Agriculture and Structural Transformation* (New York: Oxford University Press, 1975).

Two older books of well-selected essays: Carl Eicher and L. Witt, eds., *Agriculture in Economic Development* (New York: McGraw-Hill, 1964); and H. M. Southworth and B. F. Johnston, eds., *Agricultural Development and Economic Growth* (Ithaca: Cornell University Press, 1967).

John W. Mellor, *The New Economics of Growth: A Strategy for India and the Developing World* (Ithaca: Cornell University Press for the Twentieth Century Fund, 1976), spells out an argument for major agricultural expansion and the development of small-scale manufacturing of consumer goods by labor-intensive methods.

Agricultural Productivity:

Theodore W. Schultz, *Transforming Traditional Agriculture* (New Haven: Yale University Press, 1964).

Theodore W. Schultz, ed., *Distortions of Agricultural Incentives* (Bloomington, Indiana: Indiana University Press, 1978).

Max F. Millikan and David Hapgood, *No Easy Harvest: The Dilemma of Agriculture in Underdeveloped Countries* (Boston: Little, Brown, 1967).

Thomas T. Poleman and Donald K. Freebairn, eds., *Food, Population, and Employment: The Impact of the Green Revolution* (New York: Praeger, 1973). See also the essays by Gotsch and Falcon cited in notes 8 and 9 of this chapter.

Gerald M. Meier, ed., *Leading Issues in Development Economics*, 3d ed., chap. 9.

Partap C. Aggarwal, "Green Revolution and Employment in Ludhiana, Punjab, India," in *Employment in Developing Nations*, ed. Edgar O. Edwards.

Land Reform:

Doreen Warriner, *Land Reform in Principle and Practice* (Oxford: Clarendon Press, 1969).

Concerning potential natural resource scarcity, see the book by Barnett and Morse and that edited by Charles J. Hitch, cited in notes 21 and 22, and see also the writings recommended in Chapter 9.

Robert S. Manthy, *Natural Resource Commodities, 1870–1973* (Baltimore: Johns Hopkins University Press for Resources for the Future, 1978), presents comprehensive data for the United States.

9

Labor. Will There Be
Enough Food?

THE SUPPLY CURVE OF LABOR

Capital, entrepreneurship, and in some countries land are the scarce factors in economic growth in LDCs, and labor is the plentiful factor. So it might have been said, without admitting any exceptions, 25 years ago. It was in 1954 that W. Arthur Lewis wrote about economic development with unlimited supplies of labor. Since that time, the oil-rich countries have provided instances of unlimited supplies of capital, and in those instances even "raw" labor has become a scarce factor, along with entrepreneurship-management. In all the high-income countries of Western Europe, and in the United States, labor to do the dirty, unskilled, low-income jobs has become scarce, and these countries import workers from lower income countries, to whom such jobs provide high incomes relative to those available at home. In Europe workers are imported legally, in the United States, both legally and illegally. In Europe they are termed "guest workers." When there is recession and jobs become scarce, the guests find themselves no longer welcome.

However, in LDCs other than those rich with oil, Lewis's conception continues to apply.

Lewis's conception related to untrained labor, not to specialized trained workers. In simple economic models, homogeneous labor interacts with homogeneous land and homogeneous capital. The assumption is as unrealistic for labor as for the other factors. An individual's qualities as a worker vary with his innate abilities, the motivations inculcated in him by his early nurturance—mostly unwittingly, and resistant to deliberate coaching—and the amount and the nature of the "investment in human capital" that he has

149

obtained by observation, formal (including vocational) education, training in the plant, and "learning by doing."

In growth theory it is implicitly assumed that there are no differences among countries in the innate abilities of the labor force. The assumption is justified. Very few scholars now believe that there is evidence of differences in inherited ability among national or ethnic groups. Prudent scholars also admit that there is no conclusive evidence differences in inherited intelligence do not exist among national, ethnic, or racial groups. Intelligence tests are culture-bound and cannot settle the question. However, there is a fairly strong presumption that the differences, if any, are not great.

Yet by the time of adulthood or even of adolescence there are differences among peoples in values and motivations, differences that must be due to the home atmosphere during the earliest years of life. The most plausible explanation for instances of unusual national economic achievement not explainable by economic circumstances is that these instances occurred "because they are Japanese" (or Swiss, or Swedes) or, at the other extreme, "because they are Burmese," and that the national differences are in motivations. However, economists, like shoemakers, stick to their lasts. Economic growth theory in the main ignores motivational differences among low-income peoples.

The conception that low-income peoples as a group have motivations different from those of Westerners is reflected in the saying that "East is East and West is West, and never the twain shall meet," and in the Dutch colonial administrator (in Indonesia) J. H. Boeke's view of the dual society, one social system being indigenous and the other imported.[1] Some anthropologists suggest that traditional peoples follow the "doctrine of the limited good."[2] Such peoples act as though they believe that the total amount of good—or goods—in the society is fixed. In the terminology of game theory, they view life, or at least economic life, as a zero-sum game. A person can get more only if he has a patron who will intervene for him or, at higher levels of the society, only by scheming. What one person gains, another must lose. This conception of society, which is to be thought of as an unconscious set of mind rather than a conscious bit of philosophy, is consistent with an absence of belief in the possibility of technical progress and expansion of the economy as a whole.

The Backward-Bending Supply Curve

The doctrine of limited good is to be distinguished from the economic conception that some LDC workers have limited wants. The one relates to

---

[1] J. H. Boeke, *Economics and Economic Policy of Dual Societies* (New York: Institute of Pacific Relations, 1953).

[2] The notion that peasants live in a mental world of "limited good" was advanced by Richard P. Adams.

supply, the other to demand. The notion of limited wants is associated with the conception of the "backward-bending supply curve" of labor. In a sense the labor supply curve of almost every individual is backward bending. All except a very few compulsive individuals choose to take part of higher income in leisure. The aggregate supply curve of labor is forward sloping in spite of this backward bend in individual curves. As applied to LDCs, however, the conception is more specific. Western managers of mining or other ventures in sub-Sahara Africa noticed that when native workers had accumulated a certain amount of pay, they disappeared into their villages in the bush, and that the higher wages were, the sooner the workers vanished. (The response of the colonial administration was to require the payment of head taxes in money and to pay lower wages, so that workers would be forced to work longer.) The Westerners concluded that the indigenous workers were not "economic men"—that they had limited wants and that they quit working when these were satisfied.

Anthropological investigation dispelled the notion. The "natives," like all people, merely had other wants in addition to economic ones. For religious and other cultural reasons, it was of great importance to them to be present in their villages for participation with their families in various ceremonies, rituals, and community activities. When they had earned enough money to buy certain necessities that were available only for money and to pay the enforced tax, no other economic goods equaled in importance the psychic goods that they could obtain only by being present in their villages, so they returned to the villages. A Western worker will similarly sacrifice money income to attend his daughter's marriage or his mother's funeral, or even, perhaps, to see a football game.

The Income Level and the Labor Supply Curve

In simple models it is common to treat the rate of increase in the labor force as identical with the rate of increase in labor inputs and in the population. This is justifiable in some models, but it is far from realistic. Economic development causes divergences among the three rates in two ways. As income rises, hours of work decrease. More important, the participation rate changes in a U-shaped fashion. In low-income agriculture husband, wife, and children all form part of the work force, at least seasonally. As income rises, children go to school, or go to school longer, and wives withdraw from the field to the home. Then, as income rises still further, the materialism of the culture perhaps increases, and the attraction of increased family income exceeds that of motherhood and, especially, of child care. Wives return to the labor force in increasing numbers. In the United States the percentage of women who are members of the labor force will have reached 50 soon after 1980, and a large percentage of mothers with children under six years of age are gainfully employed. The flow of young adults from country to city in low-income countries after World War II has caused changes in the nature and rate of labor force participation even in the short run.

LABOR UNIONS IN LDCs

Labor unions appear in developing countries as urbanization and industrialization proceed. They appear in the largest industrial enterprises, where, indeed, they are also most prevalent in industrial societies. These firms typically pay the highest wages in the economy. They do so in order to get the best workers and perhaps also because it is expected of them. They do not thus avoid labor troubles; strikes in lower income countries, if they occur at all, are likely in precisely these highest paying firms. The strikes occur there for two reasons. One is that the high wages attract the most self-assertive workers, who are also the most aggressive. The other is that industrial enterprises, and especially those owned by foreign firms, are regarded as affluent and able to pay high wages, and are therefore seen as appropriate targets for demands for "more."

To a greater extent than in industrial countries, the workers in these enterprises have weapons other than collective bargaining and strikes. They have political weapons. It is easy for the legislatures of countries beginning the industrialization process to pass laws requiring that large employers provide certain minimum wages, vacations, a "13th month's pay" as a year-end bonus, and generous severance pay; that they dismiss no one except by a complicated bureaucratic process that is subject to governmental supervision; and the like.

The high wages, the fringe benefits, and perhaps especially the near-impossibility of dismissing workers in some low-income countries have encouraged the adoption of capital-intensive and laborsaving methods. Although these methods have probably decreased income inequality within the top half of income receivers (who include the workers in the largest industrial enterprises), they have increased inequality in the economy as a whole by decreasing the number of industrial workers. The resulting increase in the prices of the products also increases income inequality, insofar as the products are bought by the mass of the people.

INVESTMENT IN HUMAN CAPITAL

Education via training courses on the job or via "learning by doing" prepares workers for specific productive jobs; schooling provides more general training. Education of all three types, but especially in educational institutions, is partly consumption, partly preparation for future production. Expenditure to produce physical equipment for future production is termed investment. In ordinary usage, expenditure to prepare human beings similarly is not. There are at least two reasons. Capital is usually thought of as a market commodity, and except where slavery is still practiced, human beings cannot be bought and sold. In addition, it is difficult to distinguish the investment aspects of education from the consumption aspects; the two are joint products. Yet in other respects investment in education is parallel economically to investment in physical capital.

A constant level of education per student, from generation to generation, in a population that is constant in size, is precisely analogous to the replacement of depreciated capital. The provision of the same quality and quantity of education per person to an expanding population is precisely analogous to capital widening. If, on the average, individuals are given more training than before by means of increased educational expenditures per person, then, insofar as the increase is to prepare them to produce, rather than to give them satisfaction as consumers, the increase in educational expenditure is analogous to capital deepening. (The terms "capital maintenance," "capital widening," and "capital deepening" are defined in Chapter 10.) The devising of new knowledge to be taught or of new teaching methods is analogous to technical progress. The advanced techniques may be introduced with or without net investment (increase in educational expenditure per student). And increased expenditure per student may mean a greater "investment" per student, or may only mean that with a rise in average income in the society, teachers are being paid better. Hence an analysis of educational expenditures per student gives only a general and uncertain indicator of the contribution of education to the training of workers. Yet it is often the only indication available.

Writing in 1966, F. Edding presented data for selected industrial countries showing that the percentage of national income or gross national product spent on education in educational institutions had been rising steadily during the 20th century, except when war intervened.[3] He also presented data showing the ratio of educational expenditures to national income for high- and low-income countries in about 1950. Although there is a high degree of correlation between per capita income and educational expenditures, the percentages spent by the low-income countries at that time were as high as those spent by the advanced countries early in the 20th century at much higher income levels. It seems that the course of history has shifted national tastes toward much increased expenditures for education. One may guess that the demand in higher income countries has to a considerable extent been for education as a consumer good, whereas in lower income countries, to a greater degree than in higher income countries, the demand has been for education to increase earning power. In both cases it is fre-

---

[3] F. Edding, "Expenditure on Education: Statistics and Comments," in *The Economics of Education*, E. A. G. Robinson and J. E. Vaisey, eds. (New York: St. Martin's Press, 1966).

quently the educational certificate, rather than education, that is desired and obtained.

The Social Return to Education

A child with higher native intelligence is likely to obtain more education than one with less. An individual with greater motivation to work effectively is likely to obtain more education than one with less. Examples of the latter: An individual brought up in a slum home and a community environment that suggest to him that neither his father nor the society outside his family group has respect for him or concern for his welfare will be a poorer worker than will an individual brought up, in a community that accepts him, by dependable parents whose behavior and attitudes toward him convey to him a sense of his worth. A peasant child who learns from his earliest observations of his parents' attitudes and behavior onward that life offers only limited good to an individual will be less resourceful than will a child whose parents' interests and attitudes give him belief in his capability and a wide range of interests. Of children from the same social class or even the same family, one is likely to have greater motivation to achieve than another. In each of these instances the child with greater motivation is highly likely to obtain more education than the other.

So-called calculations of the "rate of return to investment in education" relate differences in lifetime earnings to the cost of differences in number of years of education. But the differences in lifetime earnings are in fact due to differences in innate ability, motivation, and education (and, of course, differences in physical condition) in combination. Some studies make allowance for differences in social class. A few apply Denison's guess, made for a quite different and less exacting purpose, that 35% of differences in earnings are due to differences in ability, 65% to differences in education.[4] These are not adequate adjustments for the factors other than education. It would be very difficult to make adequate adjustments, even if one had measures of intelligence that one trusted and if plausible measures of differences in relevant motivation could be derived, since the relationships among the three factors may be multiplicative rather than additive, so that each intensifies the effects of others.[5]

---

[4] Edward F. Denison, *The Sources of Economic Growth in the U.S. and the Alternatives before Us* (New York: Committee for Economic Development, 1962).

[5] The method of calculating a "rate of return to investment in education" is as follows: (1) the year-by-year incomes throughout life of individuals with different levels of education are estimated by noting the incomes of persons at progressive ages during the year covered by a questionnaire or interview survey; (2) the year-by-year excess or deficiency of income of the higher educated individuals over the lower educated individuals is computed; (3) the year-by-year costs of obtaining the added education are noted; and (4) the rate of discount at which the excesses of income equal the cost of the added education is computed.

Hence these calculations are of little use either to test the benefits of education or to test whether greater lifetime output (income) is due merely to increased quantity of input. But comparisons among countries in these "rates of return," are illuminating. From work by Carnoy and by Psacharopoulos, Jeffrey Nugent and P. A. Yotopoulos present estimates of "social" rates of return to secondary education and both "social" and "private" rates for university-level education for 12 higher income countries and 14 LDCs.[6] The "social" rates of return do not purport to measure the social benefits of education not reflected in individual income; they merely reflect the costs of education borne by the state as well as those borne by the individual. Comparative percentage rates of return in lower and higher income countries are as follows:

	Lower Income	Higher Income
Social rate of return:		
To secondary education	18%	10%
To university-level education	13	8
Private rate of return to university-level education	22	11

The private rates of return shown omit countries in which they were calculated by arbitrarily adding 3% to the calculated social rates. The rates

---

An estimate by Gary S. Becker of the "rate of return to investment in education" for native-born white urban American males in 1939 will illustrate the pitfalls (Gary S. Becker, "Investment in Human Capital: A Theoretical Analysis," *Journal of Political Economy*, 70, supplement, October 1962). Becker found the rate of return to secondary school education to be 16% and that to college-level education to be between 13% and 15.5%. Becker tried to allow for differences in innate ability and motivation as much as possible, by matching intelligence test scores and ranks in high school class. But for lack of data he was forced to lump together all students in the lowest 60% of their high school class and all students in the lowest 45% of scores on an intelligence test (which in any case is a treacherous measure in comparing individuals with different informational background and interests). He thought that he had eliminated differences in motivation by matching brothers, thus making both social and family background comparable. However, this is naive psychology. Psychologists interested in personality development know that the most pronounced differences in motivations may include those among brothers, both because of differences in parental attitudes toward a first child and later children and because if there is rivalry between two brothers, the younger one, unable to compete in the area in which the older brother tries to be attractive to his parents, differentiates himself in ways that last throughout his life. If one of two brothers goes to college and the other does not, differences in motivation would be suspected immediately, though financial difference may also be the cause.

Concerning motivation, Becker argues that estimated effects of education on income that do not differ greatly from other estimates are arrived at in a study by J. Morgan, M. H. David, and others ("Education and Income," *Quarterly Journal of Education*, 77 [August 1963], 423–37) that attempts to "partial out" the effects of "achievement motivation." However, their measure of achievement motivation is an indirect one which, as their own comments indicate, will hardly bear this weight.

[6] *The Economics of Development: Empirical Investigations* (New York: Harper & Row, © 1976).

shown for university education are presumably marginal rates. These data are plausible evidence of the greater financial and social value of that scarce commodity education—or, at least, diplomas—in countries where education is scarcer. They also suggest the especially high scarcity value of university-level education in those countries.

Interestingly, a careful study in Thailand (which allowed for differences in social class and in type of school attended) showed results strikingly different from those for the LDCs in the Nugent-Yotopoulos list. In this study Mark Blaug found that the marginal "social rate of return to education" in Thailand was 17% for the 1st year of schooling, rose to 27% for the 4th year, then fell abruptly to 14% for the 5th and 6th years, to 10% for the 8th through 12th years, and to 7% or 8% for each added year.[7] An interpretation that makes the two sets of data consistent is that in Thailand, where the ferment of economic development is less present than in many other LDCs, there is little market demand for workers with education beyond the amount taken as evidence of elementary literacy. But this may be quite incorrect.

These data suggest that a "true" measure of the rate of return to education in the higher income countries, and perhaps also in the lower income countries, would show it to be less than that on investment in physical capital. This conclusion would be consistent with the thesis that, especially in the higher income countries, education is in considerable part a consumer good rather than investment for economic return. Yet the "true" measure would be misleading if, as suggested above, the relationship among the three factors is multiplicative. And in any event education has great externalities. Everyone gains, as a citizen and as a producer, from everyone else's education. The social value of education, in the usual meaning of the term *social value*, is much above the private value. For this reason, as well as because of the demand of their citizenry, providing the appropriate education is of concern to developing countries.

Learning on the Job

Productivity is of course increased not only by formal education but also by informal education. Much training in manual skills is on-the-job training, and even at the level of management training some U.S. corporations say, "We do not care much whether a prospective employee is a graduate of a liberal arts, management, or technical course. If his college career and personal qualities make him seem a good prospect, we will give him a training course after we hire him." Some apprenticeship programs do not even in-

---

[7] Mark Blaug, "The Rate of Return on Investment in Education in Thailand," *Journal of Development Studies*, 12 (January 1976), 270–83.

volve formal on-the-job training: rather, the training is pure watching and learning by doing. Sheer continuing industrial experience brings improvements not only in skills but also, in many instances, in work attitudes, regularity of attendance, and so on. This factor is no doubt also important at the level of top management.

PLANNING AN EDUCATION PROGRAM

In planning a development program, or even without a development plan, any less developed country must decide how great its expenditures for education should be. Two methods of estimating the most advantageous total of education expenditures and the relative emphasis that should be given to education at various levels have been proposed.

The Fixed-Input Coefficients Approach

One method is to estimate the rate of development of the country; on the basis of this estimate to estimate the country's needs for persons with various levels and types of training at various future times (say 1 year, 5 years, 10 years, 20 years in the future); then to plan the educational program that will meet those needs; and lastly to plan the training of teachers so that they will be available in time to do the teaching in time to produce the needed trained persons. Requirements may exist that it is impossible to fulfill by the target dates by use of the supply of indigenous teachers that can be trained in time. The problem can be met in part by importing teachers for a period and by sending students abroad for advanced education. Nevertheless, it may not be possible even if enough persons with appropriate talents and interests have been found to give those persons the needed number of years of education and experience by the time the persons are required. This is one reason why it may be necessary to import experts.

This method of forecasting assumes fixed coefficients of inputs of trained labor in production. That is, it assumes that certain numbers of persons with various degrees and types of education will be needed, absolutely, for a given basket of production—that no adjustments can be made for the scarcity of some types of trained persons. The cost of obtaining the persons does not enter into the calculation; no comparison is made between the return to investment in their education and the return to alternative uses of the funds.

The margin of error in the calculations of future requirements is of course great. It is assumed that if no calculations are made the error in educational planning will be greater, and that the spillover of capability from each type of job to closely related ones will compensate for errors in the estimates for each type.

The Infinite Price Elasticity of Demand Approach

An alternative approach is as follows:

1. To assume that the income earned by persons attaining each level of education indicates the economic value of education to that level, and that this economic value will not change as development proceeds.
2. To determine the income at each level.
3. To calculate the cost per student of providing each level of education, including the earnings forgone by the student.
4. By comparison of costs and future incomes, to calculate the education per student that will yield the highest return.
5. To stress education to that level. In principle, the method would indicate that all children should be educated up to that level and none beyond it, for the method includes no calculation of diminishing returns to education up to each level, but of course it is not proposed in practice to ignore those diminishing returns.

This model avoids the hazardous estimation of future demand for various types of workers. But it does so only at the cost of simplifying assumptions that make it reasonable only for moderate increases in the numbers of individuals to be educated rather than for larger increases, and only for fairly short term planning rather than for longer term planning.[8]

More Complex Models

The truth, of course, is somewhere between the assumptions underlying the first of these models and those underlying the second. Professor Adelman has applied to Argentina a linear programming model that combines some of the qualities of both approaches.[9] She divided the Argentinian economy into nine "sectors" of work, and from empirical data she derived an assumption of which of six levels of education was needed in each sector.

---

[8] Samuel Bowles presents this method, and applies it to northern Nigeria, in "The Efficient Allocation of Resources in Education," *Quarterly Journal of Economics*, 81 (May 1967), 189–219. His model yields the conclusion that educational expenditures should be concentrated on primary education, since the net yield of primary education per student is higher than that of advanced education (because of the zero opportunity cost of the student's years in school, and the very small opportunity cost of providing teachers, relative to the cost of providing university graduates to teach in high schools); and that a temporary reduction in primary school enrollment, to give teachers further training, would be advantageous. Bowles's model would provide the indicated level of education for every child in the society.

[9] Irma Adelman, "A Linear Programming Model of Educational Planning: A Case Study of Argentina. With Comment by Samuel Bowles," chap. 14 of *The Theory and Design of Economic Development*, ed. Irma Adelman and Eric Thorbecke (Baltimore: Johns Hopkins Press, 1966).

She also estimated (or guessed at) the marginal productivity of workers with each level of education in each sector. Previously, she had done a projection of Argentinian production, and had proposed a development program for a 20-year future period (in units of 5 years each). Taking this projection, and her estimates of educational needs and productivity, she was able by mathematical manipulations and the use of a high-speed calculator to do a projection which yielded both shifts in the amount of education of each level to be provided in order to increase the marginal productivity of labor and shifts in the pattern of production, because of the relative availability of workers with the various levels of education.

In principle, this sort of computation is superior to either of the two pure approaches. However, so many additional hazardous estimates and assumptions must be made that this model too has great uncertainties.

Concluding Comments

Educational planning requires forecasting work force needs one and even two decades in the future. The actual needs will be determined by the types of production, and the methods advantageous in each type, that emerge during that time. These will be affected not only by the country's innovational successes and rate of investment during that time, but also by changes in world demand and by technical progress. The uncertainties are such that only broad judgments about educational programs are likely to have great significance: the emphasis to be given to primary education, secondary education, technical education and so on. This may be true in principle because knowledge of the future is inherently uncertain, and not merely because we have not yet accumulated enough information to feed into models or because we have not yet developed sufficiently sophisticated models.

The Educated Discontented

It is sometimes suggested that by overemphasizing humanistic education, and thereby turning out graduates for whom there are no jobs in the society, an LDC may create a corps of frustrated and alienated individuals who may be a source of social instability. The argument assumes both that individuals make relatively little choice of type of education, but rather become humanists, social scientists, or engineers, depending on what their colleges happen to be teaching, and that the emotional attitudes and reactions of individuals are altered basically by their college career.

The argument may put the cart before the horse. Investigation of a small sample of individuals by the writer suggests that it does. Inquiry concerning five such frustrated intellectuals in Burma indicated that they had been emotionally unstable and socially rebellious while or before they were in secondary school, and suggested strongly that they had chosen to become humanistic intellectuals because they were insecure and anxious to become elite, and regarded such grubby subjects as engineering with distaste. One would not wish to generalize from such a small sample, but it does suggest careful scrutiny of the generalization that the provision of education is the cause of the social alienation of the educated unemployed, or even of their unemployment.

Reforming LDC Education

Because of the scarcity of university-educated individuals implied by the high rates of lifetime income associated with university-level education, an economist might conclude that LDCs should emphasize the expansion of facilities for higher education. The opposite is argued by Edgar Edwards and Michael Todaro, two experienced students of development who are especially concerned with the role of education.[10] They assert that pressures by elite groups seeking higher education have caused the development in LDCs of facilities for secondary and higher education much beyond those useful for purposes of economic development.

Among the possible causes are attitudes such as those of the Burmese intellectuals discussed in the preceding subsection and the very high level of civil service salaries. In colonial regimes these salaries were scaled to home country levels of income; the colonial scales still prevail in many ex-colonial countries; and success in higher education is a prerequisite for obtaining the positions.

The results, it is argued, include both the creation of a class of highly educated unemployed and the use of resources to provide secondary and higher education that would be used more productively elsewhere. There has been no empirical survey of the number of educated unemployed. That they are numerous seems inconsistent with the high lifetime incomes of the highly educated shown in the "rate of return" studies, except on the assumption that the samples surveyed in those studies did not adequately include the unemployed. This may be the case, since the phenomenon of "brain drain" also testifies to the existence of surplus educated in at least some low-income countries.

"Unfortunately," wrote a third judicious observer, Ronald P. Dore, "not all schooling is education. Much of it is more qualification earning. And more and more of it becomes so."[11] He was referring to both high-income and low-income countries, but perhaps especially to the latter.

---

[10] E. O. Edwards and Michael Todaro, "Education, Society, and Development: Some Main Themes and Suggested Strategies for International Assistance," *World Development*, 3 (January 1974), 25–30. See also E. O. Edwards, "Investment in Education in Developing Nations: Policy Responses when Private and Social Signals Conflict," *World Development*, 31 (January 1975), 41–45.

[11] Ronald P. Dore, "The Future of Formal Education in Developing Countries," *Development Digest*, 1975, no. 2, pp. 7–11.

A 1974 ECAFE report on education and employment deplored the existing situation and recommended that LDCs adopt either a "marginal incrementalist package" or a "structural reform package" of educational change.[12] The former would include:

Reducing salary differentials.

Increasing the cost of secondary and higher education to the students.

Substituting loans for subsidies to higher education students.

Encouraging the civil service to base promotions more largely on job performance.

Shifting educational expenditures as fast as politically possible from secondary and higher education to primary education.

Making primary curricula and secondary-level vocational training more relevant to farming and other traditional forms of self-employment.

The structural reform package would abolish school and university test results as bases for recruitment, partly substitute apprenticeship for formal precareer courses as training for occupations, and use aptitude tests and short-term teaching-and-testing courses as means of selection for highly desired positions.

There is little evidence that either set of recommended changes is being made.

THE BRAIN DRAIN

The market for technically or professionally trained persons is an international one. Because it is, many such persons have fled from the lower income countries, to seek higher incomes and perhaps greater amenities in the high-income countries. Rounding numbers to the nearest 1,000, between 1964 and 1972 inclusive more than 60,000 individuals with scientific, professional, or engineering training migrated into the United Kingdom from countries classed as "less developed." Between 1963 and 1972, 40,000 such persons entered Canada. Between 1962 and 1971, more than 200,000 entered the United States.[13]

By one economic analysis, the countries losing these workers have no cause to be concerned, for in a competitive economy a worker receives income equal to his marginal product. When he emigrates, output equal to that marginal product would be lost, along with his income. Other persons in the country will receive the same income, at least in the aggregate, as before.[14]

---

[12] Economic Commission for Asia and the Far East, *Economic Survey of Asia and the Far East, 1973,* part 1: "Education and Employment," cited in ibid.

[13] These data are from papers in the October, 1975 issue of *World Development,* vol. 3, no. 10, a special issue on the brain drain.

[14] Harry Grubel and Anthony Scott, "The International Flow of Human Capital," *American Economic Review,* 56 (May 1966), 268–83.

However, this model is often not applicable. First, the worker may not have paid the full cost of his education; the government may have subsidized it. If so, the country is losing "human capital" which cost income to someone in the past. (This is the argument by which the USSR forbids some emigration.)

Second, if the worker was working for the government, say in the public health service, the monopsonically set salary may not have been equal to his marginal product. A number of Canadian physicians are migrating to the United States because physicians' incomes in the United States are much higher than salaries in the socialized medical service of Canadian provinces. It may be argued, of course, that American physicians' fees under Medicare are set not only monopolistically but with no demand constraint, since almost any fee set by the physicians of a community is accepted by the government. If so, the international comparison does not measure relative social marginal utility.

Third because of the indivisibility of a single individual's services, if the loss of technical, professional, or scientific personnel exceeds a certain number, the loss to the economy may be greater than the marginal product of the persons who emigrated. If as many persons as remaining physicians can serve receive adequate medical care while others receive none, or if some structures receive adequate engineering design and others none, the loss is more than the conceptual marginal loss of spreading the services more thinly. Imperfect knowledge of alternatives, and demonstration effects, add to distortions.

One economist lost to India through the "brain drain," Jagdish Bhagwati of the Massachusetts Institute of Technology, has proposed that a tax be levied on the incomes of such migrants, the proceeds to be given to, say, all LDCs. The proposal has received elaborate analysis.[15] Bhagwati has estimated that for the world as a whole a 10% tax on post-income-tax incomes would have yielded $500 million in 1976 and would yield, say, $1 billion in 1985 (see note 15). Legal analysts conclude that in the United States the tax would be unconstitutional. Morally, the obligation of such émigrés is perhaps to their countries of origin. Some émigrés satisfy that obligation in full or in part by remittances to those countries.

It has been argued that the migration is not a brain drain but an "overflow" of an excess supply of personnel who would be frustrated and of low productivity in their home countries.[16]

---

[15] See J. N. Bhagwati and M. Partington, eds., *Taxing the Brain Drain: A Proposal* (Amsterdam: North Holland Publishing Co., 1976); and J. N. Bhagwati, ed., *The Brain Drain and Taxation: Theory and Empirical Analysis* (Amsterdam: North Holland Publishing Co., 1976).

[16] George B. Baldwin, "Brain Drain or Overflow?," *Foreign Affairs*, 48 (January 1970) 358–72.

WORLD POPULATION

The world's labor force is growing, and that of the lower income countries is growing the fastest. Before we ask what effects this growth may have on economic development, we must consider these workers and their dependents as consumers and we must ask: Can the earth's growing population, and especially the growing population of the LDCs, be fed?

World Population History

Between the beginning of the Christian era and A.D. 1650, the average rate of increase in the world's population was little more than one twentieth of 1% per year. In 1650, the world's population was about 550 million. Its rate of growth was rising. Between 1650 and 1750, using Carr-Saunders's world population estimates, the growth rate was 0.3% per year, and during the four succeeding 50-year periods it was, successively, 0.4%, 0.5%, 0.6%, and 0.8%. A spectacularly fast rise then began in about 1950, caused largely by technical aid to LDCs from the U.S. Public Health Service and the World Health Organization that greatly reduced deaths from infant diseases and the "big killers": tuberculosis, malaria, smallpox, and typhoid fever. By 1960 the annual rate of world population growth was about 1.8%. By 1970 it was probably 2.0%, but the rate was no longer rising. Table 9–1 shows an estimated growth rate of 1.8–1.9% in 1976, but the U.S. Bureau of the Census publication *World Population, 1977*, from which the table is drawn, presents a range of estimates of 1.7% to 2.0%. The data for many areas of the less developed world are so uncertain that the true world rate for 1975–77 may be as low as 1.7% or as high as 2.0%. In any event the speed of world population growth has crested and it may have begun to decline. To understand these historical changes and probable future trends, it is necessary to understand the "demographic revolution."

THE DEMOGRAPHIC REVOLUTION

Before the industrial revolution, crude birth and death rates per year (the total number of births and of deaths divided by total population) were at or a little above 35 per thousand in Western European countries, and birth rates were a little above death rates. Life expectancy at birth was below 30 years ($1,000/35 = 28$). During the second half of the 18-century, death rates began to fall slowly in France and England, and they began to fall elsewhere in Western Europe a little later. Birth rates began to fall only after a long lag—a century or so in France and England, 75 to 50 years elsewhere—but because the fall in death rates was so gradual, nowhere in Europe did the rate of natural increase rise much above 1% per year for long.

The population growth rates of the United States, Canada, Australia, and New Zealand were much higher because of immigration, and their rates of natural increase were probably also higher for some decades. While these changes were occurring in the West, population elsewhere in the world was increasing very little, except for the 18-century increase in China as the introduction of early-ripening rice and other foods needing only a short growing season made geographic expansion northward possible. The total effect on the population growth rate of the world as a whole was the gradual increase between 1650 and 1950 that has been mentioned.

By 1950 population growth had begun to slow down in the high-income areas mentioned above, and by the present time the growth rates in the entire "developed" world, including Japan, have declined to the very low rates shown in Table 9–1. In these countries the "demographic revolution," the transition from high birth and death rates and low population growth, through rapid population growth, to low birth and death rates and a low rate of population growth, is complete.

The birth and death rates of non-Western countries were much higher

TABLE 9–1   Demographically, the earth is "a world divided"

Region	Estimated Population, July 1, 1977 (millions)	1976 Births per 1,000 Population	Deaths per 1,000 Population	Rate of Population Growth (%)*
World	4,200	31–32	12–13	1.8–1.9
More developed	1,150	16	9	0.7
Less developed	3,050	36–38	13–14	2.2–2.3
More developed				
Asia	160	21	7–8	1.3–1.4
Oceania	17	16	8	0.9
Northern America	240	15	9	0.8
Europe and USSR	740	16	10	0.6
Less developed				
Asia	2,270	34–37	12–14	2.1–2.2
Of which:				
China†	930	30–33	12–13	1.8–2.0
Other	1,340	37–40	12–15	2.4–2.5
Africa	430	46–47	18–20	2.6–2.8
Oceania	5	40–41	12–13	2.3–2.5
Latin America	340	34–37	9	2.4–2.7

* Includes the effect of migration.
† Excluding Taiwan.

Source: U.S. Bureau of the Census, *World Population, 1977* (Washington, D.C., 1978), modified in three respects: (1) Population data except for Oceania have been rounded to the nearest 10 million. (2) For the Census Bureau's estimate of China's population, 983 million, an estimate of 930 million had been substituted. (3) Narrower ranges of estimate of birth rates and rates of population growth have been substituted for the Census Bureau's wider ranges for the following: less developed world, China, less developed Asia, and Africa. As a result, the estimates presented here have wider margins of error, but are in a sense more useful, than the more cautious estimates presented by the Bureau of the Census.

up until World War II than birth and death rates had been in the West in 1650. In many countries birth rates were 45 per thousand or even more, and death rates only a little lower. Soon after World War II the first stage of the demographic revolution was introduced "artificially" into the countries of the non-Western world. The introduction of Western preventive medical practices rapidly reduced death rates. Though the death rates of the non-Western countries are still much above present Western levels, nevertheless a large gap between their birth and death rates was created, and most of these countries reached population growth rates never known in the West. Those high growth rates, shown in Figure 9–1, will continue until birth

FIGURE 9–1   A population growth rate of 2% per year is a divide which the demographic revolution in many LDCs has not crossed

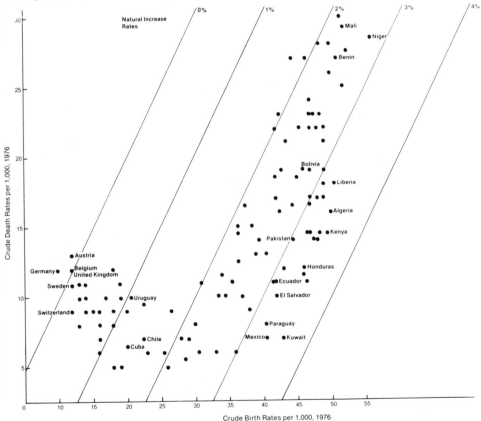

Note: Of the 21 countries with rates of natural increase above 3% per year, 11 are in Africa (10 below the Sahara plus Algeria); 6 in Latin America, including Mexico; and 4 in Asia (Jordan, Kuwait, North Korea, and Pakistan).

Source: U.S. Bureau of Census, *World Population, 1977* (Washington, D.C., 1978). A range of estimate of birth or death rates as wide as four per thousand is given for some countries. The midpoint was used.

rates have fallen greatly. Because the population of the "Third World" is very large in total, its high growth rate has raised the rate of world population growth to a rate more rapid than ever before.

Between 1965 and 1970, persons concerned about world population growth began to breathe a little more easily. Death rates had been reduced in the 1930s in four Asian countries—Ceylon, Malaya, Singapore, and Taiwan. Birth rates began to fall in those countries by about 1950, and in many of the countries in which death rates had not been reduced appreciably until after World War II, birth rates began to fall in the mid-1960s. It seemed that the demographic revolution was going to be completed rapidly. But the fall in birth rates did not occur everywhere—almost not at all in low-income Africa—and by 1975 it began to seem that the decline in birth rates in many LDCs in which they had fallen was tapering off at a level at which the population growth rate remained high—about 2% per year. Their trend is still uncertain today.

THE FUTURE

The world's population in 1978 was some 4.3 billion (It may have been 200 million more or 200 million less; there is a considerable margin of uncertainty about the population of China and of a number of African countries.) By the year 2000 it will have increased to perhaps 5.7 or 5.8 billion, plus or minus that same margin of uncertainty in the data.[17] What of the longer future? To provide even a speculative answer to that question, it is necessary to ask what factors will determine the decline in birth rates.

Fertility Theories

Three main types of theories are advanced concerning the determinants of birth rates. One type is economic. In peasant agriculture, the labor performed by even young children is useful. Children, it is suggested, are a good investment. The suggestion is challenged, on the ground that that "investment" involves the risk of unrequited loss if the children die young. Yet the suggestion is plausible, since the marginal cost of rearing an added child is small. Moreover, children provide economic security in old age. As urbanization proceeds and children become less useful, birth rates fall. However, children are then wanted as consumer goods, not merely as producer goods. Hence, along with the negative relationship with urbanization there may be a positive relationship with income level, except as affluent families

---

[17] In the early 1970s, when the world's population was about 4 billion, it was sometimes said that it would double by the end of the century. Sober demographic projections have dispelled that fear, at least in the minds of informed persons. Even in the 1960s, the median projection of the Population Division of the United Nations indicated a world population in the year 2000 of only 6.1 billion.

spend more on a smaller number of children—"substitute quality for quantity." So runs the theory.

The second type of theory argues that birth rates are high in traditional rural life because of the desire to ensure perpetuation of the family through the male line (or, in a very few societies, through the female line—the argument is parallel). Since any given child born is approximately as likely to be a girl as a boy, and since death rates are high, this desire leads to a high number of births. Birth rates will follow death rates down, but only after a lag long enough so that families feel that family perpetuation is sure with few births. The apparent leveling off of the decline in birth rates in many developing countries in the 1970s, it is argued, is due to a judgment of the number of births that is still needed.

The third type of theory may be called cultural, though of course the second is also cultural. The family perpetuation theory, it is argued, is too narrow an explanation of the noneconomic factors. Various complex and not well-understood attitudes toward the role of women, the family, and the community influence the number of births. Psychoanalysts, to whose judgment in this field one must give serious attention, state that the procreation of children is influenced by unconscious attitudes having to do with, for example, "manliness" and mastery on the part of the man, fear as well as love of children, the desire of the woman to relieve the emptiness of life, and many factors in the complex tensions between husband and wife. Perhaps the surge of births that follows major wars—a surge throughout the population, not merely in families that have lost sons—is evidence of the importance of unconscious attitudes.

Knowledge of birth control devices, and their availability, will also affect birth rates, if those rates are higher than wanted, though contraception was achieved long before the "modern" devices were invented.

The three types of theory are of course complementary, not mutually exclusive. Some observations concerning them can be made on the basis of casual empiricism. Decline in birth rates has rarely occurred except after a decline in death rates. The recent decline in birth rates in many countries testifies to the operation of "cultural" factors; economic factors offer little explanation of it. It is not possible to measure something called "culture," but empirical research has measured change in factors that are thought to affect "culture." Early in the 1960s Irma Adelman presented a regression analysis among 37 countries, ranging in income level from Morocco to the United States, of the relationship between age-specific birth rates and four factors that may influence them.[18] She found that birth rates tend to be positively associated with the level of per capita income and negatively associated with the share of the labor force engaged in nonagricultural

---

[18] "An Econometric Analysis of Population Growth," *American Economic Review*, 53 (June 1963), 314–39.

employment, the level of education, and the density of population per square kilometer. In research in Taiwan and Puerto Rico in which individual families rather than nations were the units of observation, T. Paul Schultz found relationships consistent with these.[19] Many other studies of the 1960s and 1970s have made similar findings.[20]

Rise in income level, increase in education, urbanization, and decline in death rates occur together. In a statistical association any of them may be a surrogate for the others, and even statistically, and much more so causally, partial correlation coefficients are therefore highly suspect. If education increases, how much effect on birth rates will it have without increase in income, urbanization, and decline in mortality? This is not known. Similarly for each of the others. The studies thus provide only an uncertain guide to public policy, except for the not very encouraging suggestion: Achieve all of these. The studies do, however, indicate fairly certainly that decline in birth rates until they are little above death rates will be gradual, for except for increase in education the desired changes necessarily occur only gradually.

A fourth factor affects birth rates in some African countries. Several tribes compete within one country. High birth rates are maintained because large tribal population is thought to be crucially important.

Age Distribution and Population Increase

Before considering world population projections, we must consider one other factor. Population trends are much affected by the age distribution of the population. Population growth rates have fallen to 0.7% to 0.9% in the West. Yet in Western countries the number of children born per mother during the entire childbearing age of women (the "total fertility rate") is already down to 2.1, the number necessary to just replace the population, or less. The population is growing because from past higher birth rates and decline in infant mortality the number of women of childbearing age comprise an unusually high percentage of the population, and therefore the total number of children being born is high. As these mothers grow older, the crude birth rate will fall even though there is no change in the total fertility rate. But in time the children of these mothers, and then in turn *their* children, will bear enough children to create population bulges a generation and then two generations from now, and population in some of the present high-income countries will not cease to grow until the year 2050 or

---

[19] *A Family Planning Hypothesis: Some Empirical Evidence from Puerto Rico* (Santa Monica, Calif.: Rand Corp., 1967); and "Explanation of Birth Rate Changes over Space and Time: A Study of Taiwan," *Journal of Political Economy*, 81, no. 2, part 2 (1973). Schultz's research did not test the association between birth rates and population density.

[20] A comprehensive survey is presented in Robert H. Cassen, "Population and Development: A Survey," *World Development*, 4 (October–November 1976), 785–830.

later, even if the total fertility rate remains at only the population replacement level from now on.[21] The population of the present high-income countries, now some 1.15 billion, will then be 1.6 billion or 1.7 billion.[22]

World Population Projections

In 1973 the demographer Tomas Frejka made a minimum estimate of the world's maximum future population.[23] He based it on one assumption and one fact. The assumption was that in the countries with high population growth rates total fertility rates would fall rapidly to the population replacement rate of slightly more than two children per family. The fact was the continuing population growth that would occur thereafter because of the age distribution effect just described. Frejka calculated that even if this assumption held true, population growth in the non-Western world would continue until at least the year 2150. By the time it had ceased, non-Western countries would have a population of 6.5 billion, some 2.6 times their 1970 population. World population would then total some 8.2 billion or 8.3 billion.

This of course is a minimum projection, not a forecast. Birth rate trends in non-Western countries since 1970 already belie it. *World Development Report, 1979* presents a more recent speculative (and not minimum) projection for the 125 countries with which it deals. It shows population in those countries of 6.0 billion in the year 2000, population continuing to grow in some countries until late in the 22d century, and total population of 9.8 billion when stationary population is reached. Another 100 million or 200 million might be added by the smaller countries not included in the projection.

The total figure is considerably more than double the world's 1980 population of 4.4 or 4.5 billion, but it is far below the "standing room only" figure that persons fearing for the world's food supply forecast a decade ago.

WORLD POPULATION GROWTH: ENOUGH FOOD?

Such projections always have an implicit caveat: "provided that the world's inability to feed its growing population does not bring mass starva-

---

[21] The age distribution greatly affects crude death rates also. A death rate of ten per thousand would seem to indicate a life expectancy at birth of 100 years, and a death rate of seven per thousand an average life expectancy at birth of 143 years ($1,000/10 = 100$; $1,000/7 = 143$). However, this is true only in an "age-balanced" population. Western countries now have crude death rates this low because they contain a high proportion of people of the young ages at which death rates are low. As these people grow older, the crude death rate will rise.

[22] These countries, which not so long ago contained 30% of the world's population, would then have 20%.

[23] "Prospects for a Stationary World Population," *Scientific American*, 228 (March 1973), 15–23.

tion." Forecasts of a world food shortage in the short run (10 or 20 years) or the long run (a century or more) have been common. All are based, implicitly or explicitly, on the assumption that technical progress in food production will not continue its past pace.

However, the present upward trend in the world's capacity to produce food is faster than the upward trend in population. As Figure 9–2 shows, productivity per hectare and also per worker is continually increasing in the more developed grain-producing countries. The United States, Canada, and Australia can and do produce far more grain than they consume, and have the problems of curtailing their production and of storing their surpluses when the world market will not take them. There is no reason to expect any specific limit to the productivity of the advanced countries. Moreover, the improvements can be transferred, with adaptation, to the present less productive countries, and new seed strains and cultivation methods especially adapted to the conditions of the less productive countries can be developed. As noted in the preceding chapter, nine agricultural research centers are busily engaged in the process.

For the longer run Roger Revelle, director emeritus of the Harvard University Center for Population Studies, has estimated that the earth could feed between 38 and 48 billion people on a European diet, if the unused but cultivable land around the world were put into cultivation and if the methods and technology practiced in Iowa today were used throughout the world. As Nick Eberstadt, research associate at the same center, comments, "If this estimate's range seems too precise, its order of magnitude is certainly correct."[24] The estimate makes no allowance for the potential of tropical soils.

There is, then, no problem of either short-run or long-run shortage of world food production capacity, unless one assumes that in agriculture technical progress *de novo* or the ability to adapt new seeds and cultivation methods from one geographic area to another will come to an end or fail badly. By present methods, very large increases in the use of artifical fertilizers would be required in countries now using relatively little. The fertilizers are made from the hydrocarbons found in petroleum and natural gas. Yet in spite of the large increases in oil prices the cost is not prohibitive. The Tennessee Valley Authority has calculated that the cost of producing nitrogen fertilizer from natural gas, at the 1974 U.S. natural gas price of $1.80 per thousand cubic feet and with 1974 technology, was not greater than the cost with free natural gas and 1960 technology.[25] There has been a subsequent increase in real terms. Further increase may occur, and food

---

[24] Nick Eberstadt, "Myths of the Food Crisis," *New York Review of Books*, February 19, 1976, p. 32. Eberstadt quotes Revelle.

[25] Cited by Cassen, "Population and Development," from D. G. Johnson, "Food for the Future: A Perspective," *Population and Development Review*, 2 (March 1976), 1–19.

FIGURE 9–2 Agricultural productivity continually increases in the developed countries

In land-poor countries, innovation has increased productivity both per hectare and per worker; in the land-rich United States and Canada, mainly per worker.

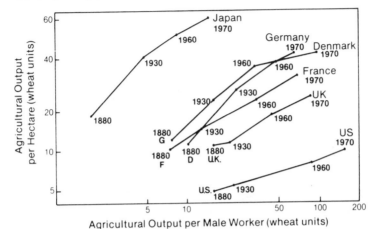

Source: Hans P. Binswanger and Vernon W. Ruttan, *Induced Innovation: Technology, Institutions, and Development* (Baltimore: Johns Hopkins University Press, 1978), fig. 3.7. © 1978 by The Johns Hopkins University Press.

costs may rise, but no absolute shortage seems in prospect. Moreover, the need for fertilizer may decrease. Experimentation is now being conducted to breed into certain tropical food plants the ability to fixate nitrogen from the air.

The persons and organizations that worry about the world's future capacity to feed its people thus seem to be misguided. However, problems may be caused by the present failure of some countries to produce enough food for their needs. Presumably, except in years of extremely unfavorable weather, India will hereafter be comfortably self-sufficient in food. Brazil, Pakistan, and Indonesia may soon join it. In 1978 Bangladesh grew 88 percent of the food it needed, had cut its import requirements in half in five years, and hoped to achieve self-sufficiency in food by 1985. The OPEC countries and such high-growth food-deficit countries as South Korea, Taiwan, and Singapore can readily pay for needed imports. However, the sub-Sahara countries of Africa and some Central American, Caribbean, and South American countries in which food production deficits are increasing will probably not have the exports to pay for needed food imports. Meeting the financial burden of providing all of them with needed food may be politically very difficult, and in any event economic aid for this purpose might deprive them of economic aid for development. The problem is compounded by their need to pay greatly increased prices for the petroleum that they must import. For many—almost certainly most—of them feasible increases in their food production would remedy the problem. With improvements in techniques that are now readily feasible, even densely populated Bangladesh has ample land for ample food production.

Providing the lower income groups in lower income countries with enough income to buy enough food is a problem of income distribution, not food production.

Yet a serious problem must be faced in the very long run. The cost of fertilizer in real terms has increased greatly since 1978 because the price of petroleum has increased more than have prices in general. Petroleum is likely to become increasingly scarce relative to demand, and hence, increasingly costly. Some presently known petroleum deposits are being exhausted, and new ones will not be discovered indefinitely. No decisive steps to reduce demand are being taken in the United States, the world's greatest petroleum user.

To make ample food available in the future, one sober school argues that its production will have to become increasingly energy-intensive and its price will therefore have to rise more than do energy prices.[26] In the long run, costly nuclear and solar energy will have to be resorted to increasingly in the LDCs. The changed price relationships will create a social problem that will not be handled without great hardship unless the government of LDCs show greater concern for their poor than many of them have shown to date.

Certain possible developments may lessen the problem. One is the conversion of organic materials to a gas usable as a fuel or as raw material from which to make fertilizer. A study done for the Ford Foundation concludes that even in India crop residues not now used are ample to provide large amounts of fuel and fertilizers. Moreover, the amount of crop residues will increase as agriculture becomes more productive.[27]

The Question of Famine

There were calamitous crop failures in the Soviet Union and some areas of China and India in 1972. These crop failures were followed by a poor harvest in some of the same areas in 1973. Had there not been very large purchases by the Soviet Union and China of wheat from the United States and other major producing countries and also large wheat shipments to India, there would have been mass deaths from starvation. Imports by the stricken countries almost exhausted world grain reserves. The world wheat

---

[26] C. Peter Timmes, "Interaction of Energy and Food Prices in Developing Countries," *American Journal of Agricultural Economics*, 57 (May 1975), 219–24.

[27] Arjun Makhijani, "Fuel for Agriculture in the Third World," in *Energy and Agriculture in the Third World*, a report prepared for the Ford Foundation with the collaboration of Alan Poole (Cambridge, Mass.: Ballinger Publishing Co., 1975), chapter 4.

price rose to triple the previous U.S. price, and prices of other grains also rose sharply.

The event demonstrated both the need for large world grain reserves and the enormous productive capacity of the world's three major grain-exporting countries, the United States, Canada, and Australia. In response to the high prices, such increases in grain production occurred in those three countries that in two years world grain reserves were again at a comfortable level and by 1978 the U.S. and Canadian problem was again how to curb production and what to do with the large accumulating surplus. At the end of the 1978–79 crop year world grain reserves were at an all-time record level. In 1979–80, following another very poor harvest, the USSR is again making large purchases of foodgrains. But though these will reduce the world's foodgrain reserve, they will not deplete it.

To forestall a recurrence of the threat of famine, international organization of a world grain reserve would seem desirable. But though the idea has received academic discussion, nothing has been done. Some American farm organizations are opposed for the shortsighted reason that they do not want to deprive their members of the chance for a "killing" if extreme shortages should occur elsewhere. A delicate political compromise concerning wheat production and prices in wheat-surplus France and wheat-deficit Germany is a part of the EEC structure; this would make it difficult for the EEC to negotiate a world reserve arrangement. The main reason, however, is that the rest of the world knows that for their own domestic political reasons the United States and Canada will in any event hold large surpluses, even though somewhat smaller ones in total than would provide complete world insurance. The rest of the world is content to leave the burden to those two countries.

In the 1970s famine occurred in some of the "Sahelian" countries—the countries just south of the Sahara. It occurred, however, merely because of bad administration and corruption in some of those countries and because of the desire of at last one ruler to let his people die rather than admit to the world that his country had a problem.

POPULATION GROWTH AND INCOME GROWTH IN THE LDCs

Even though there need be no food shortage, the question remains whether population growth in the lower income countries may not create an insurmountable barrier to progressive increase in their income levels. The answer seems obvious from the data presented in Chapter 2. Though the populations of many LDCs are increasing rapidly, except in a very few countries per capita income is rising. But because this may conceivably be temporary and because the "population question" has long been an important one in economics, it is worthwhile to consider it briefly.

Theories of a "Low-Level Equilibrium Trap"

The thesis about the effects of population growth which Malthus stated in 1798 and restated with modifications throughout the next two decades had been felt by some analysts to be applicable to the lower income countries today. Briefly, Malthus argued:

> That as the income of people rises above the subsistence level, population will tend to increase because death rates will fall and the sexual urge will cause birth rates to remain at the biological maximum.
>
> That because diminishing returns to land will set in, the supply of food per capita will decrease and income will be forced back to the subsistence level unless men and women check population increase by restraining their sexual desires.

Recent restatements of Malthus have allowed for technical progress. In 1954 Harvey Leibenstein developed a model of economic development in which a low-income country will tend to be caught in the Malthusian trap and will then be able to enter upon a continuing rise in per capita income only if some powerful quick-acting force (a great and rapid rise in the rate of investment, a great technical surge, etc.) rapidly raises the growth rate of aggregate income above the biological maximum rate of population increase. A rapid ensuing rise in per capita income may then cause birth rates to fall.[28]

Two years later Richard Nelson developed a somewhat similar theory, giving the conditions in which a low-income country might be held from increasing its income. He supplied the term "low-level equilibrium trap."[29]

Model and Reality

The model has been entirely irrelevant in the West. Population growth has simply not responded to rising per capita income in the way postulated by Malthus, Leibenstein, and Nelson.

There are 17 countries in the world in which a moderate or faster rate of aggregate output (1.5% per year or more) began before the end of the 19th century, and thus has gone on long enough so that it might be expected to have brought the Malthusian mechanism into play. Kuznets has analyzed population and national product data from about 1860 or later to about 1954 for 13 of them.[30] Data are not available for the other four.

1. Per capita income rose steadily in all of the 13 countries.

---

[28] A Theory of Economic-Demographic Development (Princeton: Princeton University Press, 1954).

[29] R. R. Nelson, "A Theory of the Low-Level Equilibrium Trap," American Economic Review, 66 (December 1956), 894–908.

[30] S. S. Kuznets, "Quantitative Aspects of the Economic Growth of Nations," no. 1, Economic Development and Cultural Change, 5, no. 1 (October 1956).

2. In none of the 13 did the rate of natural increase remotely approach the biologically possible maximum rate. Though birth rates were well below the possible maximum rate, they did not rise. Only in Canada and the United States, with their rapid immigration, did population growth, including that from immigration, exceed 17.5% per decade for even a single decade of the 80–90-year period analyzed.

Four years after Nelson presented his model, he published an article in which he tested its applicability to the case of Japan. His conclusion: The model is not applicable.[31]

The model also fails in that the future in which diminishing returns will dominate life has never arrived. Though diminishing returns to land become a reality as the quantities of capital and labor applied to land are increased, those diminishing returns are more than offset by technical progress.

In the absence of technical progress Malthusian effects would occur. The distress of the sub-Sahara countries of Africa may appropriately be termed Malthusian, even though drought was the immediate cause of starvation there in the mid-1970s. China of the early modern period also apparently presents a true Malthusian example.

As noted in the preceding chapter, the introduction of sweet potatoes, peanuts, and early-ripening rice into China made possible the habitation of areas in which the growing season had previously been too short or the soil had not been suited to the previous crops. The level of living of many persons, and average income in the country as a whole, presumably rose as people moved to new lands, lessening population pressure on the old. But the rate of population increase probably also rose. When the new lands were filled with people, the level of per capita income apparently was no higher than it had been before the introduction of the new crops began. This account is somewhat speculative because information concerning population and income in China before recent decades is scanty, but this seems to be what happened. If they had had no contacts with the outside world, and specifically no technical aid from it, the countries in which there have recently been food deficits might have been Malthusian cases, and some of the countries in which food deficits now persist may become such. However, the available evidence indicates that where the ferment of technical progress appears, the Malthusian specter disappears.

Population Growth and Income Growth

Rapid population growth may nevertheless be lessening the rate of per capita income growth in lower income countries. However, the empirical evidence is that rapid population growth seems to be no hindrance.

---

[31] "Growth Models and the Escape from the Low-Level Equilibrium Trap: The Case of Japan," *Economic Development and Cultural Change*, 9 (July 1960), 378–88.

Kuznets has shown that among 19 countries in which economic growth was occurring in the first half of the 20th century, and among a smaller group for which data are available back into the 19th century, there is a positive correlation between the rate of population growth and the rate of growth in income per capita.[32] He ranked the countries and various groups of them in each of the two respects, then calculated the rank correlation. The correlation was positive in every grouping. In only one of the eight groupings was the correlation significant at even the 5% level, but that it was positive in every case is significant.

Kuznets reached similar results in a study of lower income countries for the period 1950–64, when population growth spurted. He found a positive rank correlation between population growth and economic growth among 21 countries of Asia and Africa (excluding Israel and South Africa), among 19 countries of Latin America, and among the 40 countries treated as a single group. Again, the correlations were not statistically significant, but that there was no negative correlation, much less a statistically significant negative correlation, is significant.[33]

The association appears even though the statistical sample includes land-poor as well as land-rich countries. It appears so consistently that its appearance is probably not coincidence. However, the causal flow may not run from differences in population growth rates to differences in economic growth rates. The latter may be the cause, the former the result. But at least population growth creates no important barrier to economic growth. It may even facilitate economic growth. Consider its favorable and its unfavorable effects.[34]

Favorable: Less social overhead per capita is needed if the population density is greater. Population growth absolves entrepreneurs of some of their investment errors by providing an expanding market for the many products whose market size is influenced more by population size than by the level of per capita income. In these products larger population permits larger scale of production. Population growth forces bottlenecks to the attention of entrepreneurs and thus makes innovational decisions easier, in the way that Albert Hirschman suggested. A rapidly growing population is a young population and the quality of the labor force may therefore be better. Lastly, vigor in procreation may be associated psychologically with in-

---

[32] S. S. Kuznets, "Quantitative Aspects," no. 1, table 7, p. 29.

[33] S. S. Kuznets, "Population and Economic Growth," *Proceedings of the American Philosophical Society*, 3 (June 1967), 170–93. Kuznets found negative correlations among 23 developed countries and among the 63 less and more developed countries as a single group. The latter was significant at the 5% level. Both results were no doubt due to the rapid postwar economic growth and the low rate of population growth of the more developed countries. Both were so clearly due to special factors that the statistical association hardly implies any causal relationship between them.

[34] Keith B. Griffin and John L. Enos discuss favorable and unfavorable factors in their *Planning Development* (Reading, Mass.: Addison-Wesley, 1971).

novational vigor; this common factor may be the cause of high rates of both.

Unfavorable: Increase in family size reduces the capacity to save. Moreover, rapid population growth diverts capital from innovation to the production of housing and other "consumers' capital." It also brings diminishing returns into play more sharply.

As between the two sets of influences, it is possible that the balance of the effects of population growth on growth in per capita income is favorable or at least neutral.

FOR FURTHER READING

Labor and Development

Wilbert Moore and Arnold Feldman, eds., *Labor Commitment and Social Change in Developing Areas* (New York: Social Science Research Council, 1960).

Manning Nash, "Work, Incentives, and Rural Society and Culture in Developing Nations," in *Employment in Developing Nations*, ed. Edgar O. Edwards.

Henry J. Bruton, "Economic Development and Labor Use: A Review," *Employment in Developing Nations*, ed. Edgar O. Edwards. An excellent comprehensive survey.

Clark Kerr, J. T. Dunlop, F. H. Harbison, and C. A. Myers, *Industrialism and Industrial Man* (New York: Oxford University Press, 1964). This paperback edition is slightly revised, with bibliography augmented, from the 1961 edition.

Clark Kerr, J. T. Dunlop, F. H. Harbison, and C. A. Myers, "Postscript to 'Industrialism and Industrial Man,'" *International Labor Review*, 103 (June 1971).

Education

Gary S. Becker, *Human Capital*, 2d ed. (New York: Columbia University Press, 1975).

Theodore W. Schultz, *The Economic Value of Education* (New York: Columbia University Press, 1963).

F. H. Harbison and C. A. Myers, *Education, Manpower, and Economic Growth* (New York: McGraw-Hill, 1964).

C. A. Anderson and M. J. Bowman, eds., *Education and Economic Development* (Chicago: Aldine, 1965). Useful collection of essays.

E. A. G. Robinson and J. E. Vaizey, eds., *The Economics of Education* (New York: St. Martin's Press, 1966). Proceedings of a conference held by the International Economic Association.

Richard S. Eckaus, "Economic Criteria for Education and Training," *Review of Economics and Statistics*, 46 (May 1964), 181–90.

The essays on the subject by Bowles and Adelman are cited in notes 8 and 9 of this chapter.

G. S. Fields, "The Private Demand for Education in Relation to Labour Market Conditions in Less Developed Countries," *Economic Journal*, 84 (December 1974), 906–24.

Future World Food Supply

Nick Eberstadt, "Myths of the Food Crisis," *New York Review of Books*, February 19, 1976.

Donella H. Meadows, Dennis L. Meadows, and others, *The Limits to Growth* (New York: Universe Books, 1972).

Robert Heilbroner, *An Inquiry into the Human Prospect* (New York: Norton, 1974). Takes a gloomy view of almost all aspects of the future.

Robert M. Solow, "Is the End of the World at Hand?" *Challenge*, 16, no. 1 (March–April 1973), 39–50. The best brief critique of the Meadows methodology.

William Nordhaus, "World Dynamics: Measurement without Data," *Economic Journal*, 83 (December 1973), 1156–83.

Mancur Olson and Hans H. Landsberg, eds., *The No-Growth Society* (New York: Norton, 1973). Reprint of the Fall 1973 issue of *Daedalus*.

J. N. Bhagwati, ed., *The New International Economic Order* (Cambridge, Mass.: MIT Press, 1977), chaps. 10 and 11.

U.S. Bureau of the Census, *World Population, 1977* (Washington, D.C.: U.S. Bureau of Census, 1978).

The Low-Level Equilibrium Trap

See the volume by Leibenstein and the articles by Nelson cited in notes 26, 27, and 29 of this chapter.

The Brain Drain

J. N. Bhagwati, ed., *The New International Order*, introduction and chap. 5.

World Development, 3, no. 10 (October 1975). Entire issue, edited by J. N. Bhagwati, on the brain drain.

10

Physical Capital

Few countries are blessed—or perhaps, if it occurs suddenly, cursed—by the augmentation of their supply of "land" through the discovery and exploitation of rich deposits of natural resources that were previously unknown or unvalued. For all other countries, increase in productivity and income per worker must depend on the formation of physical capital, increase in the capability of labor, and innovation. Capital formation is a necessary member of the trio. Increase in output per unit of labor input is possible without capital formation—by managerial improvement, by improvement in labor skills, by technical inventions that require no added capital, in the production of many products by increase in scale, and in other ways—but there is no recorded case in which these have been sufficient to obviate the need for physical capital formation if there is to be sustained economic growth in the economy as a whole.

Capital formation, technical innovation, and cost-reducing increase in the scale of production occur together. (Increase in scale can usefully be considered separately from other innovation.) Most technical progress is embodied in new productive instruments. Chapter 12 discusses the intricate question of separating out the effects on productivity of these joint means of achieving it. Here only physical capital and its formation are discussed.

Physical capital is any man-made object that is useful in production. Strictly speaking, all production is the production of services, and any man-made object that provides services to anyone—a toothpick, a toaster, a slice of bread—is capital. In practice, in discussing physical capital we think only of fairly durable capital designed for use by producers, plus very durable consumers' capital, namely houses, other consumer structures, and the land development associated with them. Resources ready to be used for the

179

construction of physical capital—generalized capital, the other name for ongoing saving—are also capital. In Chapters 15 through 18 this generalized capital is discussed, but at this point the discussion will deal almost wholly with physical capital.

Though I shall largely ignore financial capital at this point, any business-person ignores it only at great risk. A study of U.S. businesses made several decades ago showed that nine out of ten new business ventures failed within one year of their formation, and that the single most frequent immediate cause of failure was inadequacy of capital, caused by failure to recognize the amount of "working capital" that would be needed to maintain inventories and pay wages and other expenses before the receipt of revenues from sales.

Capital is sometimes said to be scarce in low-income countries in the sense of "scarcer than other factors in production." Thus used, the term *scarce* has no clear meaning. However, if the term *scarce* is used with the meaning: "In country X there is less of this factor, relative to the amount of other factors, than in country Y," then the term has meaning. In this sense, in all but a few low-income countries capital is scarce and labor plentiful relative to the high-income countries.

HOW MUCH CAPITAL FORMATION?

How much capital formation does a country need if its income per capita is to rise? Consider the three functions of capital formation.

Capital formation replaces capital that wears out, provides capital equipment for an increasing labor force, and increases the amount of capital per worker (strictly, per unit of labor input). These three effects are termed capital replacement, capital widening, and capital deepening, respectively. Conceptually, it is possible to distinguish among the three types of capital formation. For example, if it is estimated that the annual depreciation on a country's capital stock equals, say, 5% of GDP, then capital formation in that amount is merely replacement. If the labor force is increasing by 1.5% per year, then an annual increase in the capital stock of 1.5%, which may require investment equal to, say, 4% or 5% of GDP, is capital widening. Capital formation in excess of these two amounts is capital deepening. The amount of capital formation, including that for replacement of depreciation, is gross capital formation; excluding this, net capital formation.

If replacement and widening require capital formation equal to 10% of GDP, then in a simple analysis it would be concluded that capital formation must equal more than this percentage of GDP if per capita incomes are to rise. However, this is not correct, for capital formation for any of the three purposes may embody improved techniques. Even if the amount of capital per worker, measured by its cost at constant prices, remains constant, GDP per capita may be increasing because of the increase in the productivity of the capital. For this reason, in considering the amount of capital needed for rising output per worker we usually lump together capital replacement, widening, and deepening.

THE ICOR

Lumping them together, it may require gross capital formation equal to say only 2% of GDP in one country, but in another country 6% or 7% of GDP, or even more, to increase by 1% the volume of goods that the country can produce. The ratio between the value of the added capital and that of the resulting increase in output per year—ranging from 2 to 7 in the figures just given—is termed the incremental capital-output ratio, or ICOR. The ICOR is not a refined theoretical concept but a crude empirical one, for it reflects the effect not only of capital formation but also of the technical progress embodied in it, changes in the scale of production, improvements in management, and any other factor that affects the increase in productivity in the country.

The magnitude of a country's ICOR depends in part on its climate, which affects both the expenditures required for housing and the nature of the country's production. It also depends on the country's natural resources, which also affect the nature of its production. Norway's ICOR is high, for example, both because it needs warm housing and, especially, because of the importance in its economic activity of shipping and hydroelectric production, both very capital-intensive. A country's geographic size and its population density both probably affect its ICOR by affecting its need for infrastructure per capita and per unit of GDP. The higher its rate of capital formation, the lower its ICOR will tend to be. One reason presumably is that a lesser share of the capital formation will be to replace depreciation and to equip added workers, and a greater share will be to introduce improved techniques in production by existing workers. Also, where the rate of capital formation is high, effective innovation by business firms is probably also high; this is why they are constructing much new capital.

A country's ICOR will be affected by whether its government adopts policies favoring the use of much capital with little labor or policies encouraging the use of much labor per unit of capital. This complex question of the capital-labor ratio is discussed in Chapters 20 and 21.

A visitor to a very low income country may think of it as having very little capital, and that will be correct if he comes from a high-income country and is comparing the low-income country with his own. Yet the low-income country will have capital—houses, other structures, infrastructure, tools, simple machines—equal in value to several times the value of the country's production per year, for the latter is also low. The ratio of the value of the capital stock to that of a year's GDP will neither increase nor decrease tremendously as economic growth proceeds, for as additional capital is constructed, productive capacity is increased, and though the two will not necessarily be in the same proportion, there is a rough correspondence. A given country's ICOR may change from one decade or one generation to another because of a gradual shift from agriculture to other production. For a reason mentioned a few paragraphs farther on, this will decrease the inventories needed in the country, and hence the ICOR, but the other effects of this shift are so complex that it is difficult to know in which direction they will change the ICOR. The ICOR will tend to change over time if the respective shares of the country's heavy and light manufacturing industry change. It will increase if newly discovered mineral deposits that loom large among the country's total resources are exploited. Except possibly in the latter case in a little-developed country, the ICOR will not change abruptly.

The data for a country's capital formation and change in GDP during any given period will falsely indicate a low ICOR if GDP rises during the period through the employment of productive capacity that existed at the beginning of the period but was idle then, and will falsely show a high ICOR if unemployment of productive capacity increases during the period.

The following six country ICORs for the period 1960–70 show the possible range of variation: Uruguay, 11.0; Iceland, 8.9; Thailand, 4.5; Taiwan, 2.2; Nigeria, 1.9; Mozambique, 1.6. Uruguay's ICOR may have been high because of the sluggishness of innovation by its entrepreneurs, Iceland's because its economic activity involves much use of ships. That of Taiwan was probably low because of the effectiveness of its innovation; those of Nigeria and Mozambique, more largely because idle capacity was put to use. Differences in climate no doubt affected all six.

If now we return to the question: How much capital formation must there be if there is to be rise in output and income per capita?, the answer must be, That depends on the country. However, an illustrative answer may be given here. For illustrative purposes we may take four as a typical ICOR at low rates of capital formation and three as typical at higher rates. With that ICOR, capital formation of 5% of GNP would increase productive capacity by 1¼% per year, no more than the slowest rate of population growth in low-income countries (except for a very few). Per capita GNP would not be increasing. If GNP is to grow at 5% per year, ensuring rising income since this is considerably faster than the fastest rate of population increase, then with an ICOR of three capital formation would have to equal 15% of GNP.

INVESTMENT IN WHAT?

That 15% may and should be put into different types of capital goods in one country than in another. Tropical countries and Norway have been cited. An agricultural country will have a high ratio of inventories to total capital because holding agricultural crops for consumption requires holding average stocks equal to one half of a year's production, if there is only one crop per year, and in addition requires a carry-over to allow for possible variation in yields. In an industrial country the ratio of inventories to GDP, and their share within total capital formation, depends on the way in which production is organized. During the period 1961–64, the ratio of increase in inventories to increase in GDP was 50% in Japan, 24% in Western Europe on the average, and 21% in the United States.[1]

Japan's large inventory requirements are caused by its system of producing components in many small plants and its very poor transportation system. The national income accounts of Japan indicate that inventory increases were 79% of the increase in GNP during 1931–39, 87% during the reconstruction years 1947–52, and 80% during 1953–55. It is doubtful that the figure of 50% for 1961–64 is comparable with these earlier data; so abrupt a decline is highly unlikely. But whichever figures are correct (probably the later ones), Japan's ratio is very high.

The share of a country's investment to be allocated to housing, the degree of congestion to be permitted in the use of transportation, communication, and other infrastructure facilities in order to minimize investment in them, and the risk to be run that the power supply will be inadequate at times of peak demand or if equipment breaks down are all subject to variation if investment is controlled by government decision. Such power shortages may occur in the United States because of the objection of environmentalists to the construction of nuclear power plants. Such minimizing of these types of investment may increase rather than lower the ICOR, because of the inefficiency in production that it may cause.

Although there are differences among countries in the types of capital in which investment is made, there is a certain degree of uniformity in the trend over time in the share of different types. Table 10–1 shows the more or less typical or average share of different types of investment in low- and high-income countries respectively in recent decades. Investment in structures was a little more than half of total investment, and investment in producers' durable equipment plus inventories was a little less than half, at both low and high levels of income. But note the differences within each half.

Investment in Inventories

The most commonly overlooked component of capital formation is the increase in stocks of goods. Perhaps investment needs (of firms or countries)

---

[1] The data for Western Europe and the 1961–64 data for Japan are from the United Nations *World Economic Surveys,* 1963 and 1965. Those for the United States are from the *Economic Report of the President,* January 1967.

TABLE 10-1 The forms of capital formation in modern times
Construction takes, very roughly, about one half of investment at both low and high income levels, and investment in equipment plus increase in inventories the other half. Infrastructure requires a fairly constant fraction of total investment. The share needed for other nonresidential structures is small. Producers in high-income countries stress investment in improved equipment more than do producers in low-income countries.

	Income Level	
	Low	High
Housing	Less than $^1/_5$	More than $^1/_5$
Infrastructure	25–30%	25–30%
Other construction	Less than 10%	Less than 10%
Producers' durables	35% or so	More than 40%
Increase in inventories	12% or so	5%

Source: Distilled from various data sources.

have been underestimated more often through neglect of the inventory requirement than through any other error. But in Table 10-1, note the decline as income rises in the share of investment that goes into inventory increases. As GDP rises during economic growth, the volume of goods in inventories—raw materials, goods in process, and finished products, in the entire chain of production from raw materials to sale at retail—must also rise, but because of the change in the nature and organization of production, a smaller proportionate increase is needed in inventories than in the volume of production.

The large inventories of agricultural products that a country requires have been mentioned. The reduction in the share of inventory increase in total investment as income rises is accounted for partly by reduction in the share of agriculture in GDP. The ratio of inventories to output in industrial countries also depends on the arrangement of production, the speed of freight transportation, and the efficiency of inventory control. In recent years the physical volume of the inventories that are required to handle a given physical volume of total production has been falling by reason of improvement in the last two of these three factors. Increased transportation by truck and computerized control of inventories have been important contributors. During the period 1935–40 the value of the increase in stocks in the United States was 27% of the increase in GNP; during the years 1958–63, 23%; during 1961–64, 21%; and during 1971–76, less than 20%.

Investment in Housing

Both data comparing countries at various income levels and historical data for the United States and the United Kingdom indicate that the share of investment going into dwellings increases as income rises. Historical data for eight countries for the 19th and 20th centuries do not indicate this; the average percentage in the eight countries has been about the same in the 20th century as it was in the 19th.[2]

FOR FURTHER READING

See reading suggestions for Chapter 12. Concerning investment in manufacturing, see reading suggestions for Chapter 20.

---

[2] Data for the United States are from S. S. Kuznets, "Quantitative Aspects of the Economic Growth of Nations," no. 5, *Economic Development and Cultural Change*, 8, part 2 (July 1960); those for other countries are from the same, no. 6, *Economic Development and Cultural Change*, 9, no. 4, part 2 (July 1961).

Scale

From Adam Smith onward, economists have been intrigued by the theory of economies of scale. Economies of scale are important in economic growth.

As a primitive country turns from traditional methods of producing handicrafts to more advanced methods, its entrepreneurs are at first capable of managing only small plants efficiently. Before long, however, they are ready to manage somewhat larger plants. As they do so, they find that in most manufacturing production, even by rather simple methods, the unit cost of production decreases. Only up to a certain point, however, does increase in the scale of production decrease costs per unit of output. Usually, there is then a range of size within which cost per unit (i.e., the number of units of input required per unit of output) is roughly constant. At still larger sizes of plant, unit cost rises again (diseconomies of scale). A curve showing the relationship of unit cost to plant size is about as in Figure 11–1 for most manufacturing production.

There are also economies of scale for the size of a firm, of an industry, and of an economy.

THE SOURCES OF ECONOMIES AND DISECONOMIES OF SCALE

Economies of scale are due to indivisibilities of persons or material objects. A larger size of plant permits the advantages of division of labor sketched by Adam Smith. A large or complex machine may be possible which will do more than four times as much work as any that can be devised with one fourth the depreciation and interest cost. To achieve the potential economy the volume of production must be great enough to use the large

FIGURE 11-1   Unit cost varies with plant size

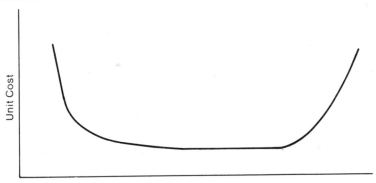

Plant Capacity (in units of output)

machine full time. If one person has the ability to manage a plant employing 3,000 persons, part of his ability is wasted and unit costs are increased if there is only a 1,000-person-plant for him to manage. By a sort of law of large numbers, the volume of inventories that must be maintained rises less than the volume of production and sales, for one need not expect that many buyers will unexpectedly reorder at once or many flows of supply fail at once.

The diseconomies of plant size arise largely from the increase in the complexity of administration and/or physical organization of the plant as the size grows, and from increases in the transportation cost of inputs if they must be brought from farther away and of finished products as they must be shipped to more distant customers.[1]

The lowest-unit-cost size of plant may be one at which many components are made in a volume below lowest unit cost because increasing the plant size (or the firm size) to the size at which these components are produced most cheaply would be uneconomic in other respects and would increase total unit costs. In this event, if the market being served is large enough to include several plants that use one of these components (they may not be in the same industry), jointly they may use enough of it so that a separate firm producing it and selling it to more than one of them can produce it more cheaply than any one plant making a product that incorporates it. In this case there are economies of scale of the industry or group of industries. Insofar as there are no international barriers to the flow of goods, these economies through specialization may be obtained through international sale of the component if transportation costs are not too great.

Economies of firm size arise largely from spreading superior manage-

[1] Or diseconomies may arise from congestion if the needed resources are obtainable in only one place.

ment talent over several plants of minimum-cost size. This is part of the rationale underlying the formation of huge conglomerate corporations—corporations producing many unrelated types of products. "A superior person at the top can increase the efficiency of almost any number of types of production." In a dispassionate view the theory has its limitations. Another purpose is to average out cyclical swings or secular trends, so that the corporation as a whole will continue to do well even if one division does not. Sometimes the motive is merely a none too rational quest for bigness.

Discussion of minimum-cost plant size or firm size implies the existence of a market large enough to permit one or more plants or firms of that size. If the market is smaller, the maximum-profit size of a plant is smaller than the minimum-cost size. This situation occasions the existence of an oil refinery much below minimum unit cost size in many a small country. Diseconomies of scale of an industry exist when its volume of production causes it to have demand for natural resources so great that diminishing returns, and hence increasing unit costs in their production, set in. This is usually a result of worldwide, not local, demand.

Economies of scale are especially conspicuous in manufacturing, mining, power, transportation, and communications industries, but up to some size of plant they exist in any type of production. Even in primitive production, an enterprise so small that it does not require the full-time work of one worker is in general uneconomically small, and unit cost will fall as the scale increases up to the capacity of one worker (or one family). Where draft power is animal power, peasant farms smaller than the size that can be cultivated with one yoke of oxen or water buffalo are uneconomically small. For "wet cultivation," a size of 15 to 20 acres, the maximum one yoke–one family size, seems to be the minimum-cost size. For "dry farming" the minimum-cost size may be much larger. In the Plains states of the United States, there was a time when 40 acres was the minimum-cost size for grain farms. Three generations ago, 160 acres may have been the minimum size in many localities. Today, with the development of power machinery and large-scale plowing, cultivating, harvesting, and threshing equipment, minimum cost is achieved only at several thousand acres in wheat farming. But beyond some size of farm, unit costs rise because the economies of the use of the indivisible large machines so far invented have already been achieved and costs of management rise.

MARKET SIZE AND SCALE ECONOMIES: SUMMARY COMMENTS

1. In most manufacturing industries, most technical economies that are gained by increasing the size of the plant or firm are very largely exhausted by plants and firms of moderate size. Beyond this size there is a plateau of roughly constant unit costs, then rising unit costs with larger size. However,

for industries producing complex or heavy machinery that is susceptible to mass production—automobiles and aircraft are examples—the minimum-cost size is larger.

2. Even small countries with per capita incomes of, say, $1,000 or more can support most manufacturing industries, but the minimum-size market required to sustain production of complex and heavy machinery is one of 10–15 million people with at least a middle-income level of income. Australia does so with smaller population because of its higher per capita income. The automobile industry of Sweden is not an exception, for its market is not Sweden but the Western world and its production facilities are scattered throughout Europe. Aggregate national income is not a sufficient measure of market size. An indefinitely large number of persons with annual incomes of $100 each will not create a market large enough to support an automobile industry. The same principle applies to other products that are used only at a fairly high level of personal income.

3. With larger markets there is a greater degree of specialization. The comment applies to the production of both goods and services. The typical firm in a large country produces a narrower range of products or services than does a corresponding firm in a smaller country. Differences in this respect are noticeable through the entire range of population of the higher income countries, from the smallest ones to France and the United Kingdom to the United States.

4. The size of plant that is minimum-cost in a country is not merely an objective engineering datum. It depends not only on engineering facts but also on the level of the country's managerial capability.

5. Techniques also importantly influence minimum-unit-cost plant size. With simple techniques the most economic plant size is small. As techniques advance, the size of plant needed to use the improved techniques efficiently almost always increases, though there are exceptions.

6. The principle just stated applies throughout the entire range of techniques from the simplest to the most advanced that the world now knows—though this is an empirical fact, not an obvious matter of principle. As the world's technical margin moves outward, some new products possible at the margin require larger industries, hence larger economies to support them, than the largest industries that were previously required. Recent examples are high-speed computer systems, supersonic airplanes, and interplanetary space vehicles. The enterprises of most European countries do not regard themselves as large enough to attempt the production of high-speed computers. France and Great Britain think it necessary to combine to attain the size of productive complex necessary for the production of supersonic airplanes. And only the Soviet Union and the United States deem themselves large enough, at the late 20th century point of technical progress, and—even with the government being the organizing unit—to undertake the production of interplanetary space vehicles. As techniques and humanity's vi-

sion advance, it may be hypothesized that neither of these countries alone will have sufficient resources or a sufficient market for some technically feasible and perhaps attractive ventures, even with the government summoning up the necessary resources. And still later some technically feasible and attractive venture may be beyond the economic scope of the entire world at that time. Some ventures in the exploration of space may be illustrative of each of these cases.

SCALE AND DEVELOPMENT

It follows from the facts just stated that the smaller a country is, the sooner in its technical advance will the size of its market hamper its further development.

To begin at the very beginning. In traditional agricultural societies production and trade are largely local. Only items such as salt, gold, spices, and jewelry are transported long distances. The first industries to develop beyond production in the home were mentioned in Chapter 6: textiles, sugar and sugar products, leather and leather products, and other such commonly used staples.

As the production of a number of staple items moves from early shops to somewhat larger plants and somewhat more capital-using methods, the bar to more rapid development is not, or not significantly, the size of the market. There is a theory that if only modern low-cost transportation were introduced into such economies, there would be a surge of growth. The theory is as distorted as is any single-key theory of development. As noted earlier, Hla Myint has put it well: "economies of experience" must exist before economies of scale can be attained. The gaining of experience at somewhat more complex production and at production on a somewhat larger scale, a slight degree of standardization of items, the emergence of attitudes by which more "modern" items are desired by some people, improvement in transportation facilities, slowly emerging impersonality in trade relationships, a shift from haggling in the purchase and sale of handmade items to the fixed-price sale of more standardized items; all of these changes, and many others, proceed together. Economies of scale are of only marginal relevance until these processes have proceeded a long distance.

Chenery and Syrquin, analyzing country data for 1950–70, found that at per capita income levels between $200 and $800 in prices of the late 1960s, the share of manufacturing in total production was 5 to 6 percentage points higher in countries with large populations than in countries with small populations.[2] The added manufacturing was mainly in basic metals, paper, chemicals, and rubber products, all of which have important economies of

---

[2] Hollis B. Chenery and Moises Syrquin with the assistance of Hazel Elkington, *Patterns of Development, 1950–1970* (London: Oxford University Press for the World Bank, 1975). Other findings of this study are summarized in Table 3–1.

scale, and was no doubt due to those economies. However, at income levels above $800, the smaller countries began to catch up, and at income levels well above $1,000, manufacturing constituted as large a share of total GDP in small as in large countries.[3] Presumably this result occurred both because at higher income levels the domestic market was larger and because at the level of technical proficiency which higher income levels implies, the smaller countries were able to compete in the world market, and exported some of their manufactured goods.

A country that has fostered production for the home market and now faces the problem of market size may do one of two things to prevent stagnation. It may alter its policies in ways that will both permit and induce its producers to export to the world market. Those changes in policy will hurt some producers. The country may be so wedded to production for a protected market that it is not ready to believe that competition in the world market is possible. The choice, a complex one, depends on matters not analyzed until later chapters. It is discussed in Chapter 21.

The other alternative is to form a customs union or a free trade area with neighboring nations.

CUSTOMS UNIONS AND FREE TRADE AREAS

A customs union is an arrangement among countries which, in the ideal version, makes them a single integrated economic area. Such a complete customs union involves the elimination of all tariff and trade barriers among the member countries and of all governmental regulations or aids which provide differential advantages in production costs; the establishment of a common tariff against the outside world; and the elimination of all restrictions on the movement of labor or capital among the member countries. A free trade area, on the other hand, involves only the elimination of tariff and trade barriers with respect to specified products, without harmonization of the member countries' tariffs and without other types of economic integration. Since a free trade area is usually a weak substitute for a customs union among countries that find it inexpedient to go the whole way, the emphasis here will be on customs unions.

The potential advantages of a customs union are two. It permits indus-

---

[3] In an earler study relating to the early 1950s, Chenery had applied a quadratic multiple regression equation (population and income the independent variable, size of each of 15 manufacturing sectors the dependent variable) to countries at all income levels, and had concluded that the size of 9 of the 15 manufacturing sectors was significantly positively affected by population size at all income levels—that the reversal mentioned in the text did not occur. Alfred Maizels, using data for only middle-income countries (and dividing manufacturing into only 6 groups) had found little relationship. It turns out that Maizels was correct. Chenery's analysis had not caught the difference in relationship at different income levels. See Hollis B. Chenery, "Patterns of Industrial Growth," *American Economic Review*, 50 (September 1960), 124–54, and A. Maizels, *Industrial Growth and World Trade* (Cambridge: Cambridge University Press, 1963).

tries to achieve the economies of scale that are attainable in production for the larger market, and it provides competition in the larger market, thus reducing the opportunities for monopoly. The advantages apply almost exclusively to industrial production; there are few economies of scale in other production. In general, the two advantages do not apply with respect to the same industrial establishments. If a national market is too small for a single plant, then at best there will be oligopolistic competition among two or three firms in a customs union.

Among the requirements for the success of a customs union are: that the physical circumstances of the union be such that transportation costs do not bar economical trade; that the members have something to trade with each other; and that the technical productive capacities of the members be reasonably equal, so that union does not condemn one of them to a prolonged period of producing primary products or low-technology manufactures while the others proceed with advanced manufacturing. In principle, an adjustment of exchange rates when the customs union is formed would place countries at different technical levels on an even basis, but in practice the necessary adjustments are seen as too great.

The great model of a customs union is the European Economic Community, formed during the crisis of post-World War II reconstruction, when at an advanced economic and technical stage even the large countries of Western Europe found their national markets too small. The EEC approaches but does not quite reach the ideal defined above. From its formation in 1958 through 1972 the EEC consisted of France, West Germany, Italy, and the Benelux countries. On January 1, 1973, England and Denmark entered the community. Later, Ireland joined. In 1968 the EEC completed the elimination of tariffs among its members, subsidies to any industrial production, and almost all governmental or private measures which directly or indirectly gave any advantage to the producers of one member country over those of another in trade within the community. Subsidies on major agricultural products continue. The movement of labor is entirely free. Individual members still maintain barriers against free entry by other members of their capital markets, and during the currency upheavals that began in 1971 it was not possible to maintain fixity of exchange rates among the currencies of member countries. "The snake" broke down. This was an arrangement by which a member country's exchange rate could move a limited distance on either side of the agreed-upon rates among members (like a snake weaving across the ground). The member countries made larger changes. In 1979 the members other than England moved again to fixed exchange rates among themselves (with a "snake" arrangement), and as this is being written the Conservative government of Britain is considering whether to join in fixed rates. The EEC countries are also discussing, as they did earlier, the adoption of a common currency. With this step the Western European countries would become virtually a single country economically. There are many difficulties; the odds are against the step in the near future.

In 1979 the ECC and Greece had agreed on steps by which Greece will become a member by 1983.

The EEC has been highly successful. However, there is no parallel between the economic circumstances which produced it and those which face LDCs.

International trade is largely among industrial countries, or between them and countries producing primary products. Within modern industry there is a large degree of specialization. This also holds true among primary producers, but—except for minerals—in products that are substitutes for each other rather than complements to each other. The trade is between such countries and industrial countries, not with one another. Of the foreign trade of the industrial countries of the West in the period since World War II, about three fourths has been with one another. Of the foreign trade of the LDCs of the world, only about one tenth is with one another.

There is no advantage in the availability of a large market for products which the producers of an area are not yet technically competent to produce. It may nevertheless be true that trade among LDCs in which the less complex types of industrial production have been established or are beginning to be established may be advantageous. That trade in these products forms a small percentage of total trade is not highly relevant. But early industrialization raises in acute form the question of relative industrial capability.

Consider the Central American countries and the countries of South America. Per capita income can be taken as a rough first-approximation measure of technical capability. In 1965, the highest income country of the European Economic Community, West Germany, had a per capita income only about 80% greater than that of the lowest income country, Italy. And the technical capacity of the industrial area of Italy was much more nearly equal to that of the other members than the per capita comparison would suggest. In Central America the per capita GDP of the highest income country, Costa Rica, was also less than twice that of the lowest income country, Honduras, and the industrial capabilities of the five Central American countries were not too much unlike. Hence a common market was possible. On the other hand, the per capita income of Bolivia was only one fourth, and that of Paraguay only one third, of that of Argentina. (That of Venezuela was still higher, but only because of its oil.) The industrial capacity of these two low-income countries was not remotely comparable to that of São Paulo (Brazil) or even that of Córdoba (Argentina). The differences are even greater today, especially those between Brazil and the backward countries Bolivia and Paraguay, for Brazil has advanced rapidly, whereas they have not. It would be extremely awkward politically to form a customs union or free trade area that omitted Paraguay and Bolivia (or other Latin American countries), yet the formation of a Latin American free trade area with fairly comprehensive product coverage would require special measures to prevent dooming Paraguay, Bolivia, and in lesser degree some other countries to being agricultural hinterlands for a long time. For this reason, some Latin American economists have declared that a customs union must not merely facilitate the expansion of industry, but must promote it in the more backward countries. (That principle is not readily given effect unless a fair degree of entrepreneurial vigor is present in the latter countries.)

As an aspect of such promotion, it is suggested that the establishment of new industrial enterprises be allocated among the member countries, rather than left to private initiative and the inducements of the market. The extreme proposal is that industrial establishments of each given type be barred by law except in the country or countries selected as their sites. The more usual proposal is that when an allocation of industrial establishments among the member countries has been decided upon, an establishment in the preferred country shall be given technical aid, financial aid from a development bank, and exemption from profit or other taxes and from internal customs duties for, say, 10 to 15 years, whereas any competitor from another member country would receive none of these benefits.

The members of the EEC occupy a compact area within which there is excellent and cheap transportation. The Central American countries also occupy a compact area, within which there is reasonably good transportation. On the other hand, the transport costs between the industrial area of Brazil and that of Chile or Colombia are probably greater than those between New York and any of these three points. Though an increase in the volume of traffic would reduce the intra–Latin American costs, for many products it would not do so enough to make this trade economic for various points in Latin America relative to trade with the United States or Europe.

These circumstances point to the greater likelihood of success of a Central American common market than of a broader Latin American one. In 1958 a series of bilateral agreements and then a multilateral agreement among the five Central American countries were signed, announcing general intentions to proceed to internal tariff removal and establishment of a common external tariff on all products except a specified list. Then in 1960 the three countries of El Salvador, Guatemala, and Honduras agreed to free trade by 1965 except on a specified list of items, and by 1962 a similar five-party treaty had been put into effect. Free trade was in effect for almost the entire list by 1966 or 1967. A common external tariff, low on raw materials not produced in Central America and on capital goods, and high on consumer goods, was put into effect simultaneously.

It was recognized that Honduras and to a lesser degree Nicaragua would need special help. The agreements of 1958 provided that a firm given "integration-industry status" in return for an agreement to establish itself in a designated country should like other firms be exempt from tariffs in its trade within the common market, but that competitors should not. These were not to be barred, but initially they would have to pay the external tariff on their intra–common market sales. They would receive a reduction of 10% of the original tariff rate each year.

A number of new firms, many of which were foreign firms, established themselves, and other firms expanded their facilities, when the common market arrangement had been completed. Many of the new firms were "trade creating," that is, they achieved economies of scale that reduced costs markedly, and that stimulated increased demand (and also raised the level of living) through reduced prices.

After the establishment of the CACM it was provided that new industries might be granted increased tariffs against external producers if they agreed to produce at least half of the requirements of the common market, with the qualification that the Executive Council might eliminate the excess tariff if it saw fit. The Executive Council, eager for the creation of added manufacturing industry, then behaved as irrationally as a typical country that sets up tariff walls to promote industry. The council granted the favor to a number of firms for products that could not be produced economically in Central America—by reason of the absence of raw materials, the absence of complementary industry, the small size of the total market, or other circumstances. Five products of which this was notably true were galvanized sheets, rayon cloth, tires, cardboard boxes, and electric wire and cable. The prices of these products increased above the previous imported prices. Their production within the common market was merely "trade diverting." Such production, however, did not loom large within the CACM total.

During 1962–66, the CACM as a whole boomed, though Nicaragua had its troubles. In 1950, about 3% of the foreign trade of the five Central American republics was among themselves. In 1966, this was true for 20% of their trade, though this figure is somewhat misleading, since much of the intracountry trade was in imports which arrived at the most convenient port and were then transshipped.

But even the entire CACM provides a market that is large enough for only some types of manufacturing production, largely so-called low-technology manufacturing—of textiles, shoes, clothing, and the like. The total population of the area in 1970 was some 15 million, and the total GDP some $5 billion. By 1968 import substitution seemed to have run its course. During the 1970s the CACM faced the problem that many individual low-income countries face: the need to be able to export if it was to continue its industrial expansion.

A declaration for the creation of a Latin American free trade area was set forth in the Treaty of Montevideo in 1960. Like CACM, LAFTA was stimulated largely by the example of the EEC. The South American countries faced a problem that had been present in Central America in much lesser degree, namely, that factories making products that might have been candidates for trade within the free trade area already existed behind tariff walls in almost all of the countries. No country was willing to sacrifice its producers. Negotiations within LAFTA from 1960 to the present have been largely frustrated by the almost complete inability of the governments to find any products for which they could agree to remove intra–Latin American customs.

The automobile industries of Brazil and Chile agreed in 1962 or 1963 that Chile would import partial automobile assemblies from Brazil and in return would ship components to Brazil, both without tariffs. At about the same time, the industries in a number of countries producing electronic tubes, "statistical machines," and glassware agreed to free trade in these types of goods except on listed items. Later, Chile and Argentina reached an agreement for the barter of automobile parts similar to that between Brazil and Chile. In both agreements, Chile largely makes upholstery and receives metallic parts in return. The governments concerned ratified the several agreements, and they are in effect. Beyond these and some recent discussions for very limited similar moves, LAFTA is a concept which has not yet attained much reality.

In September 1967, four coastal countries along the Andes—Chile, Peru, Ecuador, and Colombia—formed the Andean Development Corporation. Venezuela joined later. This is not actually a development corporation, but rather an arrangement among the five countries for a trading group within LAFTA. The Andean countries visualize a common market, at least for certain products, and the provision of incentives to investment. This movement has made more progress than has free trade in Latin America as a whole, but it is still very far from being a customs union. Foreign firms have been offered the free trade arrangement only if they would agree to "divestment," that is, to sell a majority ownership in their subsidiary to local investors within a period of 15 years. None has done so.

Customs unions in Africa have failed within a few years of their establishment. One existed between Rhodesia and Nyasaland when the two were federated. When the federation broke up, the customs union did so also. Even aside from the political difficulties, it would probably have been doomed to failure by the great disparity in industrial capability. Five countries of equatorial West Africa that had been French colonies formed a pact for a customs union, but the union did not emerge. When the three countries of Kenya, Uganda, and Tanzania (minus Zanzibar) were British colonies, the colonial authorities had instituted a customs union, the East African Community, among them. Some 20% of their foreign trade was among themselves. But at independence, 70% of the manufacturing in the community was in Kenya, and the trade balances of the other two countries with Kenya showed a continuing deficit. Gradually, the belief of Uganda and Tanzania that the benefits of the union were unequal had its effects. Presently, the common currency and the common tourist services of the three countries were broken up, then other common services—notably the railroads and telecommunications. Restrictions were imposed on trade. In an earnest attempt to salvage the customs union, the three countries signed a treaty that took effect on December 1, 1967. The treaty provided for a Community Development Bank and a new arrangement concerning trade. Kenya contributed one third of the capital of the bank, but it was to receive a maximum of 22% of the bank's loans. When any trade deficit country (in practice, Uganda and Tanzania) was offered a factory which would produce a traded industrial product, it might levy a transfer tax of up to 50% of the common external tariff on the product and use the funds to subsidize the infant enterprise. The tax might be continued in effect for a period of not more than eight years. This piece of economic statesmanship offered some uncertain promise, but that promise was not allowed to be tested; the union foundered on political differences. After Idi Amin was ousted as dictator of Uganda, the three countries again discussed a limited customs union. Possibly a new one will be formed.

MULTINATIONAL CORPORATIONS

The unindustrialized or less industrialized countries may welcome or fear multinationals, or both. Welcome them because they bring their own capital when they first establish a plant, import high technology, and create employment. Fear them because it is believed that they do not contribute enough, because they are thought to be too big to deal with effectively, and because they are suspected of extorting exorbitant profits and of evading national regulation through their international operations. These fears have varying degrees of justification or lack of justification. These questions are discussed in Chapter 18. The multinationals are mentioned here only to show the extreme limit of growth in firm size.

A financial summary concerning an American corporation of any considerable size, even one fairly well down *Fortune's* list of the largest 400, will read: "30% (or 40% or 50%) of annual revenues from foreign operations."

Table 11–1 shows that by 1970 American, European, and Japanese firms together had well over 3,000 manufacturing subsidiaries abroad (assuming that U.S. firms had at least 1,000). By 1980 the number may be more than 5,000. Corporations with such widespread operations are known as international, transnational, or multinational corporations (MNCs). Table 11–1 also shows that by the mid-1960s U.S. firms had ceased to have more such subsidiaries than the other industrial countries combined. Most of these subsidiaries are in other industrial countries, but a significant number are in lower income countries. In a few instances, notably some of the oil companies, it is misleading to refer to the home country of the multinationals. Though each of these multinationals has a head office somewhere, they are

TABLE 11–1   The number of foreign manufacturing subsidiaries has risen rapidly

	Nationality of Parent Firms			
	United States	United Kingdom	Continental Europe	Japan
1953–55	283	55	117	5
1956–58	439	94	131	14
1959–61	901	333	232	93
1962–64	959	319	229	160
1965–67	889	459	532	235
1968–70	n.a.	729	1,032	532

Source: Y. Tsurumi, "Multinational Spread of Japanese Firms and Asian Neighbors' Reactions," unpublished paper presented to the conference on the Multinational Corporations as an Instrument of Development—Political Considerations, Yale University, 1974. Cited by Constantine V. Vaitsos, in *A World Divided*, ed. G. K. Helleiner (London: Cambridge University Press, 1976), p. 16.

world corporations, no longer based in any very important sense in any one country.

There are few manufactured products for which a plant of minimum-unit-cost size located in one of the larger industrial countries would not find the national market ample. There are many instances, however, in which the producing corporation feels that its talents would be wasted if it were not reaching beyond the national boundaries for a share of the world market. The implication is not that the firm can produce more cheaply if it serves this larger market. It may merely be that the complexity of organization required to expand to international size does not raise unit costs, or raises them so little that production of a differentiated and branded product in and for the international market will greatly increase corporate profits.

The multinational corporations make products whose production involves "high technology." These are branded products. The competition in their sale is of the sort termed monopolistic. The term should not be taken to imply that there is not keen competition; there may be. There is less opportunity for profitable competition with national firms in the production of "low technology" products. But such competition is possible: Nestle and Unilever produce such products.

FOR FURTHER READING

The article by Chenery and the book by Chenery and Syrquin cited in note 2 of this chapter.

Hla Myint, *The Economics of the Developing Countries* (New York: Praeger, 1965).

The discussion in Chapter 6 of vicious circles, the "big push," and balanced growth is also pertinent.

12

Advance in Technology
in LDCs

If a country's advance in technology continues long enough, it will probably reach a stage at which here and there, in one field or another, it develops techniques beyond those known in the most advanced countries. Until it reaches this stage, its technical advance will consist in large part of the adaptation of techniques already in use in the technically advanced countries. The process is described as the "transfer" or "transmission" of technology from the advanced countries. Both words fail to reflect the degree of creative adaptation that is always necessary, but the words do denote an essential aspect of the process. This chapter will be concerned with the "transmission" of technology, but before this is discussed, some relevant aspects of the course of technical advance anywhere will be noted.

IS THERE UNPRODUCED INCREASE IN PRODUCTIVITY?

To some economists the notion that there is an element in rising output that is unexplainable by economic calculus seems bizarre. All increase in output, they say, results from increase in inputs. Technical advance is wholly the product of investment—investment in education and research if not in physical capital. Output increases no faster than inputs properly measured.

Professor Theodore W. Schultz has written:[1]

> Advance in knowledge and useful new factors based on such knowledge are all too frequently put aside as if they were not produced means of produc-

[1] *Transforming Traditional Agriculture* (New Haven: Yale University Press, 1964), pp. 136–39.

199

tion but instead simply happened to occur over time. This view is as a rule implicit in the notion of technological change. . . . What is concealed under technological change . . . are particular (new) factors of production that are adopted and employed because it is profitable for firms to do so. . . . These new factors are produced means of production.

Professor Schultz and his associates have cited as illustrations a number of cases of the high rate of return on the expenditures for various pieces of research into improved agricultural methods. These are examples of produced technical advance.

An extreme example of this view is found in a 1967 article by Dale W. Jorgenson and Zvi Griliches. They try to show that estimates for the United States presented in a 1962 book by Edward F. Denison grossly understated increases in labor and capital inputs, and that if these were appropriately measured there was very little greater increase in outputs than in inputs. However, careful criticism by Denison of their adjustments (the most important of which he termed, with convincing demonstration, "magnificent in its implausibility") brought somewhat reluctant acknowledgment of errors by the two authors.[2]

Jorgenson has withdrawn from this extreme view. In a 1975 publication with two coauthors, he finds annual increases in total factor productivity (that is, increases in output beyond the increases in all inputs combined) in nine countries from 1960 to 1973, ranging from 1.1% in the United States and 1.8% in Canada to 4.0% in Korea and 4.5% in Japan.[3]

The Significance of the Controversy

The controversy is more or less ended, but it is worthwhile to note its significance. The issue is whether technical advance is produced mechanically by investment in education and in research, as automobiles or suits of clothes are produced, so that if, for example, the Japanese rate of investment (gross investment between 30% and 40% of GNP) were somehow imposed on another nation that had as good an educational system as Japan's, Japan's rate of economic growth would be duplicated. (It would be necessary, presumably, to believe that the differences in economic performance of, say, the Singaporeans, the Taiwanese, and the Koreans, on the one hand, and of the Burmese and the Malays, on the other hand, are explainable without reference to differences in the peoples themselves.) Or whether, on the other hand, there are differences in innovational performance among

---

[2] The Jorgenson-Griliches and Denison articles are reproduced and a rejoinder by Jorgenson-Griliches added in the 1972 Brookings Institution publication *The Measurement of Productivity.*

[3] L. R. Christensen, D. Cummings, and D. W. Jorgenson, "Economic Growth, 1947–1973: An International Comparison," mimeographed (Madison: University of Wisconsin Social Systems Research Institute, December 1976).

nations and between different eras in time that are not explainable by a calculus of investment. Put in another way, the issue is whether economists must yield to other disciplines (and to the future) part of the explanation of differences among people in economic behavior. Economists need hardly feel threatened at the thought that they must do so.

The notion that there is no increase in output beyond increases in inputs sits strangely beside the notion of the transmission of technology from one country to another.

Economic Theories of Innovation

A few economists have striven to explain innovation by economic factors. There are many economic factors that constrain innovation in various ways. These factors are discussed at various points in this book. The reference here is to factors other than the desire for "more" that are positive causes of innovation. In a balanced survey of neoclassical and evolutionary growth theory Richard R. Nelson and Sidney G. Winter view economic growth as "a moving equilibrium driven by changes in product demand, factor supply, and technological conditions," but all they have to say about the search for new methods is that the "major considerations" are "market prices, information concerning the decision rules of other firms (the basis for imitative behavior), and *exogenous changes in relevant knowledge*" (my italics).[4] They might well have added "and exogenous differences in human values and motivations."

CAPITAL FORMATION AND TECHNICAL PROGRESS: HOW MUCH FROM EACH?

How important is technical progress? Increase in output per worker hour is due either to increase in the quantity of inputs, primarily capital, cooperating with labor, or to increase in output per unit of total inputs, that is, in total factor productivity. In principle it is easy to distinguish between the two statistically. The first attempts at attribution, in the 1950s and 1960s, dealt with output in the United States. They treated all increase in output per worker-hour not attributable to increased capital inputs as attributable to a single other variable termed "technical progress." The findings are presented in Table 12–1.

Both of Abramovitz's estimates and the higher estimate of the share attributable to technical progress in the Solow and Massell studies used as a final step the "remainder" method. The rate of increase in output per worker or worker-hour attributable to capital inputs was first estimated.

---

[4] "Neoclassical vs. Evolutionary Theories of Economic Growth: Critique and Prospects," *Economic Journal*, 84 (December 1974), 886–905.

TABLE 12–1 Most increase in productivity is due to something other than capital formation

Author and Scope of Study	Share Attributed to Technical Progress
Abramovitz: *NNP* per capita, 1869–78 to 1944–53	.80–.95
Solow, with correction by Hogan of an arithmetic error, and definition of lower limit by Levine: Private nonagricultural output per worker-hour, 1909–49	.81–.90
Massell: Manufacturing output per worker-hour, apparently 1919–55	.67–.90
Massell: Same, by different method	.87

Sources: M. Abramovitz—*Resource and Output Trends in the United States since 1870*, Occasional Paper 52 (New York: National Bureau of Economic Research, 1956). Both estimates treat "technical progress" as the remainder. The higher estimate uses 1929 weights in computing indexes of net national product, and capital and labor inputs; the lower estimate computes the inputs with 1869–78 weights.

R. M. Solow—"Technical Change and the Aggregate Production Function," *Review of Economics and Statistics*, 39 (August 1957), 312–20. "Note" by W. P. Hogan and "Reply" by Solow in ibid., 49 (1958), 407–13. Both use technical progress as the residual. H. S. Levine, in ibid., 42 (1960), uses Solow's data but treats capital formation as the residual.

B. F. Massell—"Another Small Problem in the Analysis of Growth," ibid., 44 (August 1962), 330–35. The pair of estimates by Massell first cited above treat first capital formation, then technical progress, as the residual. The alternative estimate avoids the remainder problem by assuming that rates of increase in output and technical progress are exponential through time, an assumption that happens to fit this period fairly well but is not usable in general.

The remaining increase in output per worker or worker-hour was then assigned to technical progress. This method contains an error. Assignment of the "remainder" to technical progress is overattribution.

Consider Figure 12–1. The original rectangle is *ABCD*. It is increased in length to *AE* and in width to *AF*. If the increase in area *BCGE* is attributed to the increase in height *BE*, and all of the remaining increase in area, *DFJG*, is attributed to the increase in width, all of the shaded area, actually due to the interaction between length and width, will be attributed to the increased width. Similarly, the statistical method used in these estimates understates the share of increase in output that is attributable to capital, and overstates the share of technical progress. Or, more precisely, there should be three attributions, to increase in capital, to technical progress, and to their interaction, but though this last can be measured in the case of the rectangle, separating it out in the case of increase in productivity is hardly possible except as a matter of subjective judgment.

The lower of the Solow estimates (actually by Levine, using Solow's data) and the lower of the Massell estimates define the magnitude of error due to this cause, for in these estimates the contribution not attributable to increase in capital inputs was calculated first and the contribution of capital inputs treated as the remainder. The "true" estimate of productivity increase per unit of input is therefore between the lower and higher estimates (assuming no other sources of error).

These limiting estimates show a very striking result. Of the entire in-

FIGURE 12-1   The attribution problem

When the length and width of the original rectangle *ABCD* are increased, is the shaded segment of the increase in area due to increase in length or to increase in width?

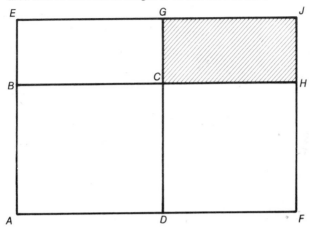

crease in output per worker or worker-hour, as a maximum less than one third is attributed to capital formation, and the data suggest that the best estimate is less than one fifth. The rest is due to increase in factor productivity.

The estimates must not be misinterpreted. Many technical advances can be put into use quickly only because a goodly amount of capital widening and deepening which incorporates improved techniques is going on. Technical progress could not have been introduced at the same rate without the capital formation. The converse is also true; capital formation would not continue to make the indicated contribution if technical advance were slower. The statistical analysis does not capture these constraints. However, some technical advance is "disembodied," and could proceed without capital formation.

Studies of Norway, Finland, and Great Britain have confirmed the importance of increase in factor productivity.[5] The highest attribution to capital formation is in two studies of Israel, one for the period 1950–59, the other for the period 1953–64.[6] In these studies it is estimated that capital formation accounts for some 50% to 60% of the increase in output per capita.

---

[5] The sources are cited in Charles Kennedy and A. T. Thirlwall, "Surveys in Applied Economics: Technical Progress," *Economic Journal*, 82 (March 1972), 11–72.

[6] A. L. Gaathon, *Capital Stock, Employment, and Output in Israel, 1950–1959* (Jerusalem: Bank of Israel, 1961); and Michael Bruno, *Interdependence, Resource Use, and Structural Change in Israel* (Jerusalem: Bank of Israel, 1962).

Learning by Doing

A consideration of a quite different sort indicates further the impossibility of neat attribution between capital formation and technical progress. Numerous examples have been cited in the literature of continuing increase in labor productivity without capital formation and even without the overt introduction of changes in method. The matter is an important practical one, not merely an analytical curiosity. One example will illustrate the point.[7]

In a 1972 article, Emile Benoit summarizes an elaborate study of the effects of growth in defense expenditures in developing countries. The main finding that interested him was that the burden of defense expenditures seemed to be positively, not negatively, correlated with growth rates in nondefense GNP. Benoit analyzed data for 44 lower income countries for the period 1960–65 and for a lesser number of countries for the period 1950–65—in each case, all of the countries for which he could get data.

Robert Dorfman commented on that article.[8] In a multiple regression for the period 1960–65, Benoit had found a significant positive correlation of the defense burden (defense expenditures not contributed from abroad) with nondefense growth. Dorfman performed additional regressions. He found that in an analysis for the five-year period, differences in the rates of domestic investment and the inflow of external resources together accounted for only 22% of the differences among countries in growth rates (R^2 = 0.22), whereas with defense expenditures added, R^2 rose to 0.41. But if the 15-year period 1950–65 was used, domestic investment and inflow of resources accounted for 63% of differences in growth rates, and defense expenditures added nothing to the explanation. "The hypothesis comes to mind," Dorfman wrote (p. 11), "that investment and foreign resources are indeed the effective variables that determine the growth of the civilian economy,[9] within this simple model, *but that their influence . . . is subject to considerable lags*" (my italics).

---

[7] Kenneth Arrow's 1962 article "The Economic Implications of Learning by Doing," *Review of Economic Statistics,* 29 (June 1962), 154–94, presents an elegant exposition of the implications of the assumption that each act of capital formation is more productive than the one before it because the advances made in learning by doing are embodied in successive acts of investment. Arrow cites three examples of continuing increase in labor productivity without capital formation. The Kennedy and Thirlwall article cited in note 5 adds several. P. A. David, *Technical Choice, Innovation, and Economic Growth: Essays on American and British Experience in the Nineteenth Century* (London: Cambridge University Press, 1975), discusses learning by doing in the American cotton textile industry, and concludes that elapsed time rather than cumulated output (suggested by Arrow) is the best index.

[8] Benoit's article, Dorfman's comment, and a rejoinder by Benoit appear in *International Development Review,* 14, no. 1 (1972). See also E. Benoit, "Growth and Defense in Developing Countries," *Economic Development and Cultural Change,* 26 (January 1978), 271–80.

[9] The growth rate data excluding defense GDP.

The deduction one may draw is that working with new capital equipment effectively requires a learning period much longer than has usually been assumed. If long lags are introduced, statistical studies may attribute to capital formation a considerably higher share of increase in output than has been attributed in studies not assuming such lags.

Or should the delayed increases in productivity be regarded as adjustments not to new capital equipment but to the new methods incorporated in that equipment, that is, to innovation? The question is a rhetorical one. The question is unanswerable. What the findings of the analysis seem to indicate is rather that the processes of capital formation and innovation are so related that insistence on too rigid attribution of increase in output per worker-hour to one or the other obscures understanding of the process of growth.

Capital Formation or Innovation: Which Leads?

Even apart from learning by doing, the estimates discussed above do not fully answer the question of whether innovation has an influence entirely separate from that of capital formation. Perhaps innovation occurs only when it is induced by capital formation. Or perhaps the degree of technical progress, explained by noneconomic influences, largely determines the rate of capital formation. Can one country accomplish more with given additions to capital than another because it is more innovational? In contrasts among countries and among industries, there is some pertinent evidence.

Two students of the Japanese economy studied the relationship between investment and growth in Japan from 1890 to 1931. With few exceptions, when the growth rate rose, the amount of investment needed to yield a given increase in capacity declined.[10]

Using a regression method devised earlier by W. E. G. Salter and data by Salter, Leif Johansen analyzed the increase in productivity in 28 groups of British industries from 1924 to 1950. As among industry groups, he found that the faster the increase, the greater was the share of the increase in productivity attributable to technical progress (i.e., not accounted for by capital formation).[11] It is a reasonable deduction that in both the Japanese and British cases the rate of technical progress was in the main the autonomous factor and the rate of capital formation the induced factor.

Some nonstatistical evidence concerning the United States supports this conclusion. During the late 1960s the author had systematic discussions with groups of executives of large U.S. corporations, a total of more than 100 executives. These executives were unanimous in stating that up until

---

[10] Kazushi Ohkawa and Henry Rosovsky, "Economic Fluctuations in Prewar Japan," *Hitotsubashi Journal of Economics,* 3 (October 1962), 10–33.

[11] Leif Johansen, "A Method for Separating the Effects of Capital Accumulation and Shifts in Production Functions upon Growth in Labor Productivity," *Economic Journal,* 17 (December 1961), 775–82.

the monetary stringency of 1965–66, the level of capital formation of their corporations had been determined by their needs for expansion and by the number of new products and processes that they had evolved that seemed worth investing in. They had had available from the company's "cash flow," or had readily obtained, all of the capital that they found it worthwhile to invest. When asked what they would have done if given, say, 25% more capital to invest, they answered almost unanimously that they would not have been able to make added productive investments; the capital would have been wasted. Except for executives from telephone or railroad companies, they felt that even a 1% reduction in interest rates (which is a rather large reduction) would not have altered their plans appreciably. In short, they felt that the rate of capital formation in their industries was wholly determined by the flow of innovation; the flow of innovation induced a flow of capital formation appropriate to introduce it.

In LDCs the "borrowing" and adaptation of techniques is more important relative to innovation *de novo* than in the technically more advanced countries. Yet this difference hardly alters the logic. There seems to be no reason why ability to adapt should not play the same determining role that innovation "from scratch" does.

The implication is that where ability to innovate in techniques of production and interest in doing so are lacking, the availability of capital will not bring economic growth. However, it is unwarranted to say that ability to innovate and interest in innovating are determining for even where these qualities are present, lack of capital may prevent the innovation.

FACTORS IN PRODUCTIVITY INCREASE: DENISON'S ESTIMATES

Although it was legitimate to contrast technical progress with capital formation in the above discussion, the term *technical progress* is a misnomer for the total increase in factor productivity. Among other factors at work are economies of scale, improved education and training of workers, shifts of workers or capital from one sector to another (mainly from agriculture to elsewhere), organizational improvements, and the effects of a shortened workweek on efficiency. For a time, economists wrote of increases in total factor productivity as *the residual,* in order to avoid applying the term *technical progress* to these various factors as a group. A more neutral term would be simply *other* since these factors are not a residual except statistically in some calculations.

Denison, making use of such clues to the importance of various factors in productivity increase as were suggested by bits of research, and necessarily making generous use of his own judgment, has presented estimates of the residual as a whole and of the contribution of the various factors within it, during the period 1950–62 in nine Western countries and during 1953–72 in

TABLE 12-2   Sources of growth of national income per person employed, 1950-1962 (contributions to growth rate per year in percentage points, and index)

Sources of Growth	United States		Northwestern Europe		Japan, 1953-1972	
	Percent	Index	Percent	Index	Percent	Index
National income per person employed	2.15	100	3.80	100	7.17	100
Total factor input	0.79	37	0.73	19	2.38	33
Capital	0.60	28	0.65	17	1.73	24
Land	−0.03	−1	−0.04	−1	−0.06	−1
Labor						
Hours of work	−0.17	−12	−0.14	−3	0.21	3
Age-sex composition	−0.10	−12	0.03	1	0.14	2
Education	0.49	23	0.23	6	0.34	5
Output per unit of input ..	1.36	63	3.07	80	4.79	67
Advances of knowledge.................	0.75	35	0.76	20	1.95*	27
Changes in the lag in the application of knowledge, in general efficiency, and errors and omissions	—		0.56	15	0.95	13
Improved allocation of resources	0.29	13	0.68	18	1.93	27
Economies of scale	0.36	17	0.93	24	−0.09	−1
Irregularities in pressure of demand .	−0.04	−2	−0.01	−0	0.05†	1
Other			0.15	4		

* Includes n.e.c.
† Effect of weather on farming.
Sources: For Japan—Edward F. Denison and William K. Chung, *How Japan's Economy Grew So Fast: The Sources of Postwar Expansion* (Washington, D.C.: Brookings Institution, 1976), table 5-1, index computed. Copyright © 1976 by the Brookings Institution, Washington, D.C.; for the United States and northwestern Europe—Edward F. Denison, *Why Growth Rates Differ: Postwar Experience in Nine Western Countries* (Washington, D.C.: Brookings Institution, 1967), tables 21-1 and 21-3. Copyright © 1967 by the Brookings Institution, Washington, D.C.

Japan.[12] His estimates are useful, even though they are subject to wide margins of error, because of their indication of plausible magnitudes and of the complexity of the residual. Table 12-2 summarizes the estimates for the United States and for eight countries of northwestern Europe as a group. Only the estimates of land and capital inputs are results of fairly precise

---

[12] Edward F. Denison, *Why Growth Rates Differ: Postwar Experience in Nine Western Countries* (Washington, D.C.: Brookings Institution, 1967), presents the estimates for the United States and the western European countries. In a 1974 book he presents estimates for the United States for 1929-69. The estimates for Japan are given in Edward F. Denison and William K. Chung, *How Japan's Economy Grew So Fast: The Sources of Postwar Expansion* (Washington, D.C.: Brookings Institution, 1976).

statistical procedures. Denison *assumes* that about two thirds of the decrease in hours was compensated for by a resulting increase in output per worker-hour. He derives his estimate of the contribution of increased education on the *assumption* that of the income differentials that appear when workers of the same age are classed by educational levels, three fifths are the result of the education. He lays down the quite arbitrary judgment of the increase that growth in the size of the national market added to the increase in output that would otherwise have been caused by all other forces. And so on. The estimates should be given only the credence which careful evaluation of the partially (or wholly) subjective reasoning underlying them suggests to the reader of Denison's thoughtful study. But with due qualification on this account, the estimates indicate two things clearly: the approximate share of increase in output per worker attributable to factors other than inputs, and the general order of magnitude of the factors included. Even though increase in education, with a generous estimate of its effects, is included in factor inputs, 63% of the increase in output per worker-hour in the United States and 80% of the increase in Europe are attributed to other factors. But among those other factors, in the United States variables other than technical progress yield almost as large a contribution in the estimates as does technical progress; and in the special conditions of postwar Europe, three times as large a contribution. These other variables are not added ones thrown in from the outside; rather, apart from the postwar reconstruction process, they are resultants of the growth process itself. Change in the allocation of resources and economies of scale are, generally speaking, effects of the increases in per capita income and the changes in techniques that result from capital formation and technical progress. Capital formation and technical progress remain the important originating factors in increases in output and in per capita income.

THE TRANSMISSION OF TECHNOLOGY

The discussion turns now to the advance in technology in the LDCs. To many persons this seems to occur simply by the transmission of knowledge from the technically advanced countries. The reader has been warned in Chapter 6 how inadequate a conception of the total process of technical advance in the LDCs this is.

The transmission of techniques that increase productivity in agriculture has been discussed in Chapter 8. The discussion here relates to industry or, more broadly, to the process of industrialization throughout an economy. It is a little explored subject. "It is a striking historiographical fact," wrote one scholar in 1972, "that the serious study of the diffusion of new techniques is an activity no more than fifteen years old."[13] Nor have methods of diffusion

---

[13] Nathan Rosenberg, "Factors Affecting the Diffusion of Technology," *Explorations in Economic History*, 10 (Fall 1972).

advanced much more than the study of them. Another student of the subject writes that "the [method of] diffusion of technology in the modern world has been largely limited to techniques not unfamiliar to St. Paul or Mohammed: the movement of persons and the transmittal of written documents."[14] It is difficult to think of other means.

Scientific knowledge is transmitted freely among scholars through the scientific journals. Techniques of production are a commercial product, transmitted for a price, except as they can be acquired by observation. The techniques are protected by patents, or exist in the practices of a firm, in which there is also a proprietary interest, or are embodied in capital equipment, or, in their simpler versions, are embedded in the skills of laborers.

The modes of transfer are many: migration; travel abroad by individuals from low-income countries; popular magazines; technical journals; trade journals; catalogues; machinery salespeople; the follow-up service of machinery sellers; staff engineers; consulting engineers; management consultants. Formal education; vocational, technical, scientific; training programs; technical assistance flowing from voluntary associations, governments, and international organizations; research, development, and engineering processes; research institutes and laboratories, in the contributing countries and in the recipient countries. Direct private investment from abroad; via a subsidiary or a joint venture; licensing agreements; management contracts; the sale of equipment; the construction of a plant for a government or a private party. And even as a summary listing, this list is surely not complete.

None of these methods of transmitting technical knowledge is likely to be fully effective. Any of them is of very limited usefulness without personal contact. No written material conveys full information, especially since adaptation is virtually always necessary and the written material is unlikely to provide the needed information about adaptation. But human contacts too are fallible. Information often passes as if through a series of relays (W. Paul Strassmann's phrase), at each of which it is filtered and something may be lost, since the agent at the relay does not know fully what it is important to transmit.

In the insightful second chapter of his book *Technological Change and Economic Development*, Strassmann reminds readers of the complexity of the process of "transferring" technology:

> The bulk of activity today in technological transfer is diffusion of routine advice about standard processes. ... A harder transfer occurs when new equipment is not to be installed or used according to standard foreign or local practice. If the equipment is to be redesigned, even more knowledge

---

[14] William Parker, "Economic Development in Historical Perspective," in *The Economics of Technological Change*, ed. N. Rosenberg (Harmondsworth, Middlesex: Penguin Books, 1971).

is needed; and information flows must increase, especially if redesign first calls for scientific exploration. An interesting order of flows is the diffusion of knowledge about information channels themselves.

Information about manufacturing processes is immensely complex and heterogeneous, and it is sent only sporadically to widely separated places in poor countries. If enormous libraries were shipped abroad, the knowledge would get there physically but with no effect on productivity. The books would need readers who require training, and therefore schools; the schools need teachers—and, in any case, not all is clear from books, for not enough combinations of circumstances can ever be covered. Books must be complemented by experience, and experience in operating modern industry is precisely what underdeveloped countries lack and seek. . . . Experience is embedded as "judgement" in the human tissues of those who have long participated in a species of events.[15]

There is a paradox in the demand for and flow of information which the market cannot solve. For no one can know how much to bid for information unless he already has the information. Learning pays, but how much? As Strassmann puts it, the entrepreneur cannot "simply keep spending until marginal gains vanish, for discoveries never pass in review prearranged according to merit like the nobility at a coronation." The would-be recipient, or the country's planning minister, needs an adviser who is already immersed in the technology, but then he faces the problem once removed: How shall he know that he has a capable and unbiased adviser?

Sociologists have found that in the reception of professional knowledge, for example in medicine, there is often a "gatekeeper" in any community, the person who reads the journals most thoroughly, maintains professional contacts, and adopts new knowledge and methods, and from whom these spread to the rest of the community. Whether a parallel holds in industrial technology we do not know.

Casual empiricism suggests that travel—travel abroad by an entrepreneur of a nonindustrialized country, or (no longer frequent) migration into that country by a person who intends to establish a business and thereafter live there—is a typically important ingredient at the very first stage of industrialization; and that licensing agreements and formal research are of major usefulness only at a very advanced stage. But other channels or flows surely complement these.

There are now institutions that have been established for the purpose of aiding in the transmission of technology, or that have assumed this function as one of their activities. The United Nations Industrial Development Organization is an example of the former, the U.S. National Academy of Sciences and National Academy of Engineering are examples of the latter. Their advice, unsystematic evidence indicates, often suffers from lack of contact

---

[15] W. Paul Strassman, *Technological Change and Economic Development* (Ithaca: Cornell University Press, 1968), pp. 24–25.

with detailed reality. UNIDO is bureaucratic, and even brilliant men in the U.S. academies, more versed in science and engineering than in economics or the need to adapt methods, may rather woodenly recommend the adoption of their home country's practices.

Formal education in less developed countries is likely to be by instructors with a longing for the modern, disdain for practice, and inadequate knowledge of it; and in industrial countries, by instructors who are also primarily interested in the modern and the "advanced"and are without knowledge of the problems relevant to less industrialized countries. In any event, instructors in schools are not likely to understand fully processes that are are not yet in use in the country.

Technical assistance is likely to be limited by advisers' lack of knowledge of the framework within which the process must operate and sometimes by their uncreative assumption that things can best be done just as they are done in their home country.

The governments of some LDCs have established research organizations, presumably to help their industrial producers modernize production, but workers in these organizations have shown a craving to be "modern" that has made their work "academic" in the sense of having little practical relevance. In the 1960s the director of Pakistan's Council for Scientific and Industrial Research proudly presented visitors with small slabs of a marblelike material that the council had succeeded in making. The materal had no discernible use that much cheaper stone would not serve as well, and it was probably made by means that even on a commercial scale would have cost many times as much as marble. Argentina's National Council for Scientific and Technological Investigations spends less than 3% of its funds on applied projects. UNESCO estimated in 1963 that only 71 of Africa's 3,428 research workers were engaged in industrial research.[16] An exception is South Korea's Korean Institute for Science and Technology, which has done some highly successful research on contract for Korean firms.

Detached research has been of little use because of the unreadiness of firms to accept it and because of the unreadiness of detached institutes to give it. In the early stages of industrialization, production itself is the research; research is done on the shop floor. Only when industrial firms have reached the stage of quality control and standardization and have complex organization do they become fully able to benefit from separately organized research. As a U.S. National Academy of Sciences committee observed:

> Industry must go through certain evolutionary phases before it is ready to make commercial use of R&D efforts. As in the United States, so in the

---

[16] Frances Stewart gives the information concerning Africa and Argentina on pp. 114 and 121, respectively, of her article "Technology and Employment in LDCs," in *Employment in Developing Nations*, ed. Edgar O. Edwards (New York: Columbia University Press, 1974).

LDCs, the development of basic engineering capabilities—the ability to manage quality-control systems, introduce materials specifications and standards, maintain tool shops, and establish other production-support activities— normally must precede more ambitious developmental and applied research on product design, new materials, equipment design, and other changes in production or processing techniques.[17]

At this time firms are about ready to enter upon separately organized research themselves, but detached national research institutes and laboratories may then also become useful.

Intermediate Technology

Some students of economic development have recently become aware of the virtues of intermediate technology, just as others have recently become aware of the "informal urban sector." "Virtually unknown until very recently" are the opening words of an article in the May–June 1975 issue of the *OECD Observer* reporting on a conference on intermediate technology.

One is tempted to say that these students have "rediscovered the wheel," and indeed the comment is fair, for small-scale producers in LDCs knew that capital-intensive methods were inappropriate long before Western students of development knew it. As the *OECD Observer* article recognizes a few paragraphs later, the Chinese speak of "walking on two legs" (using both modern and traditional technology) and Indian social reformers before 1900 were urging the use of intermediate technology as a means of countering British-introduced employment-destroying technology—though their efforts were unsuccessful because the intermediate technology they urged was often inefficient and inappropriate.

Yet if the early exponents of intermediate technology were somewhat naive in thinking that they had made a great discovery, their preachments did enlighten some economic aid administrators in DCs and even elites in LDCs who had thought that the path to development was the adoption unchanged of advanced Western "know-how." Only too many still do. Though economic theorists had long argued that where labor is cheap and capital expensive, relative to their costs in more affluent countries, methods using much labor and little capital are most economic, their argument had had little practical impact. Even some economists in LDCs, and many other persons in those countries, have thought that this economic doctrine was preached as part of a Western conspiracy to keep the non-Western countries nonmodern and oppressed.

The conversion in Vietnam of outboard motors brought in by Americans into water pumps for irrigation, improved hand rice-pounding methods in

---

[17] National Academy of Sciences, *U.S. International Firms and R, D, & E in Developing Countries* (Washington, D.C.: National Academy of Sciences, 1973).

India, water purification in Thailand using rice and coconut husks as a filter, small-scale agricultural machines devised in Japan (and at the International Rice Research Institute in the Philippines)—these are recent examples of intermediate technology. A primitive intermediate-technology movement, which emerged in the 1950s, was the urging of the transfer to LDCs of machinery, obsolete in the West, that was less capital-intensive than the machinery that displaced it. The idea is a crude one, only occasionally appropriate. Much of this machinery is not "intermediate," but only marginally less capital-intensive than the latest machinery, and is in poor condition.

The first leader of the new movement for the development of intermediate technologies was the Briton E. F. Schumacher, whose 1973 book *Small is Beautiful* expounds ideas that he had been urging for several years. Schumacher was instrumental in the establishment of the Intermediate Technology Development Group Ltd. Other such centers then emerged. The *OECD Observer* article lists three in India, two in the United States, and one each in Canada, the Netherlands, Pakistan, and Ghana, and IRRI in the Philippines. Not only IRRI but also most of the other international agricultural research centers mentioned in Chapter 8 conduct such research in greater or lesser degree.

THE DEMAND FOR LEGAL CHANGE

UNCTAD and the Group of 77 (the latter now representing 125 LDCs) have demanded the adoption by the technically advanced countries of a legally binding code of conduct for technology transfers. The code would include, among other matters, the establishment of "fair" terms and prices; guarantees that the technology provided is "complete"; limits on royalty payments; time limits on licensing agreements; and the prohibition of various practices, among them limitation of the area within which products made under license may be sold, limitation on the types of production in which the techniques licensed may be used, prohibition of the acquisition of competing technologies, tied purchase of raw materials, and the obligation of the licensee to furnish the licensor with any future improvements in the technology. Western businesspersons, observing that they agree to license a technique only if doing so is advantageous to them, reply that if these restrictions were in force they would either charge much higher prices for the granting of licenses or would not grant them at all. "What the developing countries forget," said one of them, "is that you can't decree technology transfer, you can only encourage it." No doubt, however, by judicious bargaining, as a group or individually, LDCs can narrow the scope and shorten the duration of the patent rights held by companies that wish to enter the LDCs, without materially reducing the inflow of technology. Emphasis must be on the word *judicious.*

FOR FURTHER READING

Brookings Institution, *The Measurement of Productivity* (Washington, D.C.: Brookings Institution, 1972).

Edward F. Denison, *Why Growth Rates Differ: Postwar Experience in Nine Western Countries* (1967), *Accounting for United States Economic Growth, 1929–1969* (1974), and, with William K. Chung, *How Japan's Economy Grew So Fast: The Sources of Postwar Expansion* (1976), all published by the Brookings Institution, Washington, D.C.

Charles Kennedy and A. P. Thirlwall, "Technical Progress: A Survey," *Economic Journal*, 82 (March 1972).

J. N. Bhagwati, ed., *The New International Order*, chap. 10 and 11.

Richard R. Nelson, "Less Developed Countries—Technology Transfer and Adaptation: The Role of the Indigenous Science Community," *Economic Development and Cultural Change*, 23 (October 1974), 61–78.

Nathan Rosenberg, "Factors Affecting the Diffusion of Technology," *Explorations in Economic History*, 10 (Fall 1972).

Nathan Rosenberg, ed., *The Economics of Technological Change* (London: Penguin Books, 1971).

Amir U. Khan, "Appropriate Technologies: Do We Transfer, Adapt, or Develop?," in *Employment in Developing Countries*, ed. Edgar O. Edwards.

Richard P. Suttmeier, *Research and Development: Scientific, Political, and Societal Change in China* (Lexington, Mass.: Heath, 1974).

Gerald M. Meier, ed. *Leading Issues in Development Economics*, 3d ed., chap. 6, sec. D.

13

Entrepreneurship

The discussion to this point has been like presenting the drama *Hamlet* without the prince. The prince among factors in growth is entrepreneurship. Entrepreneurship has been lurking in the wings, entering into the theory of unbalanced growth discussed in Chapter 7, bringing about the growth process described in Chapter 6 and the technical advance discussed in Chapter 12, and affecting the use of each of the factors of production discussed in this part of the book. In this chapter entrepreneurship is examined. A good deal of attention is paid to non-economic determinants, to indicate how complex the causation of innovation is.

Entrepreneurship is to be distinguished from management, though the difference is only one of degree. Large corporations know the distinction. In virtually every large American corporation, a chief executive officer (CEO) provides entrepreneurship, a chief operating officer, under the CEO, management.

The function of management is to run the firm with as few units of input, including inputs of management, as possible per unit of output, and thereby to maximize profits or, perhaps, to maximize a weighted balance of profits, enlarging the firm, and gaining an increased share of the industry's market. Management has a place in the theory of production coordinate with that of each of the other factors in production: land, labor, and capital. A little of any of the four can be substituted for a little of any other. Like any other factor, management can be economized on. The relationships among management and the other inputs are symmetrical.

Entrepreneurship achieves innovation, the introduction of methods or products unprecedented within the knowledge of the entrepreneur, intended to increase output per unit of input even after output has been maximized within known technologies. There is no symmetry and no substitutability between entrepreneurship and the factors of production, for innovation, the product of entrepreneurship, accomplishes a change in the relationship between all of the other inputs as a group and output.

As noted, the difference between management and entrepreneurship is only a difference of degree. A manager who orders a machine raised six inches for easier operation or rearranges the stacking of supplies in a warehouse to save steps in removing them is innovating. Few would call conceiving of and executing these changes entrepreneurship, yet an element of entrepreneurship is present. There are no fully known technologies; in some degree any manager creates a unique technology within his or her plant. This is why even in the static theory of production some economists give management a special place.

Since innovation is the stuff of economic growth, we are interested here in entrepreneurship, not merely management. And we are more interested in early entrepreneurship, the entrepreneurship that gets growth started, than in entrepreneurship in technically advanced societies. The theory of entrepreneurship is a theory of the role, the nature, and the origins of the entrepreneur, and of the conditions in which he or she functions best. Entrepreneurial behavior, like other behavior, is a joint product of personal qualities and external circumstances. This chapter considers both.

THE NATURE OF THE FUNCTION

Entrepreneurship is not a single function, but all entrepreneurship has certain common qualities. The entrepreneur conceives of the more productive idea (or evaluates and accepts it when it is presented to him), faces the problems, and takes the risks.[1] When Yusif Sayigh listed entrepreneurial functions and asked 207 heads of Lebanese business firms which four on his list, or which others, they regarded as their most important contributions to their firms, the two most often ranked high in their replies were conceiving

---

[1] In the modern corporation, the executives who make the risky decisions risk their positions and their income but not their capital. The shareholders, who risk their capital, have no direct voice in the entrepreneurship.

In India, as the British introduced fairly large and fairly complex business organizations into a society in which the attitudes of industrial Britain did not yet exist, they created the device of the "managing agency." British or other investors not resident in India could have the direction of a venture there undertaken by a managing agency of Britons who were resident there. The somewhat peculiar phenomenon emerged of a company operating in India (or Burma) with all the usual organization of an industrial company except that it was run by a quite separate company. The same managing agency often directed enterprises in several different industries. Before the British left India, managing agencies of competent Indian industrialists had emerged. These are still prominent in India, though apparently the formation of new managing-agency contracts is now uncommon. This type of organization does not seem to have developed elsewhere. Its introduction into India met a problem of the time but perhaps at the cost of retarding the evolutionary process of economic growth.

the idea and designing the organization, that is, converting the idea into a functioning organization. It is surprising that they did not give high rank to obtaining the resources.[2]

AND OF THE ENTREPRENEUR

Joseph Schumpeter wrote that the entrepreneur acts "to found a private kingdom. . . . Then there is the will to conquer: the impulse to fight, to prove oneself superior to others, to succeed for the sake, not of the fruits of success, but of success itself. . . . Finally, there is the joy of creating, of getting things done, or simply of exercising one's energy and ingenuity."[3]

It is possible to sketch more fully the qualities which in combination the business entrepreneur has in greater degree than other persons. The sketch is drawn from studies of innovational businesspersons and from personality theory.

The entrepreneur's central satisfaction is in solving problems—material problems, and problems of relationships with other persons. This problem solving, whether or not he recognizes the fact, is an end in itself, not merely a means to an end. He wants recognition of his success. His "reference group"—the group whose approval gives him satisfaction—is not, like that of the intellectual, some set of thinkers living, dead, or not yet born, but people around him. He wants a position that gives him recognition within his organization and his business world. The position he gains is satisfying evidence that he has been a good problem-handler. He wants money, too, as evidence of his success. If his desire for position and money exist too greatly for their own sake, rather than as evidence of achievement, he is likely to become the manipulative innovator of whom Erich Fromm writes.[4] He will then be not innovative but only cunning.

In common with all effective entrepreneurs, the business entrepreneur trusts himself. That is, he feels that the world is amenable to his manage-

---

[2] Yusif A. Sayigh, *Entrepreneurs of Lebanon* (Cambridge, Mass.: Harvard University Press, 1962).

In his *Entrepreneurship and Economic Development* (New York: Free Press, 1971), Peter Kilby lists 13 aspects of the entrepreneurial task. Four deal with technical innovation in production, three with purchasing and marketing, and three with personnel, financial, and production management. The others are perceiving opportunities, obtaining resources, and dealing with the public bureaucracy. The students of economic development whom he cites identify technology and production managements as the areas in which indigenous entrepreneurial performance is least satisfactory in lower income countries. Kilby and the scholars he cites drew their conclusions from enterprises already in operation—when in the minds of the Lebanese entrepreneurs the most important functions of entrepreneurship had already been completed.

[3] J. A. Schumpeter, *The Theory of Economic Dvelopment* (Cambridge, Mass.: Harvard University Press, 1934; first German edition, 1912).

[4] Erich Fromm, *Man for Himself* (New York: Rinehart, 1947).

ment, that if he tackles a problem with energy and thought, the result will be good. Facing a problem may raise tensions within him, but not tensions that deter him; he is drawn to problems.

In these respects, he is like all innovators. In other respects, he differs from the intellectual innovator, the conceiver of new, more satisfying explanations of things (in physical or other sciences). Unlike the intellectual, he finds only incomplete satisfaction in working with ideas. The resolution of an intellectual inconsistency does not excite him, as it does an intellectual. He derives his satisfaction from tangible, not merely mental, results. He has no sense (the traditional person has, and the intellectual may have) that working with material things—with engines and materials, clean or dirty— is grubby and demeaning. Directly or vicariously, he works with his hands most of his life.

He is flexible and pragmatic. If one method of operation or one structure of relationships does not solve his problem, he is ready to try another. He does not mind friction with others, or he does not mind it so much that it inhibits him. But he is not overtly aggressive, since he needs to work with people. He likes the sense that he can operate with them in such a way that they will help him to achieve his goals. (This varies to pleasure in dominating people, an attitude that is effective in only certain types of entrepreneurship.)

Entrepreneurial talent in at least moderate degree is not highly uncommon. There are only a few James Wattses, Thomas Edisons, or Henry Fords, but there are many persons who innovate in the small.

WHENCE INNOVATORS COME

Entrepreneurial talent is probably not distributed randomly throughout the population in any country. At any rate, in every case that has been studied, entrepreneurs have sprung disproportionately from some one social group that has been distinguished fairly sharply from other groups of the society. Some social or psychological theorists have tried to explain what groups produce entrepreneurs, and why.

Personality Theory: Weber and the Protestant Ethic

Though the German sociologist Max Weber would have denied vehemently that he was a personality theorist, he was the first of the group. In 1904–5 he wrote *The Protestant Ethic and the Spirit of Capitalism*. He argued that the Protestant Dissenters in England brought about the industrial revolution there, and that they did so because their religion taught them that the duty of human beings to God is to glorify Him by making the earth fruitful. Each member of the Dissenting sects worked systematically and feverishly, for if he brought forth "good fruit" he could reassure himself that he was a "good tree" and was destined for eternal salvation.

Weber was correct in thinking that the Protestant Dissenters were leaders in the industrial revolution in numbers out of all proportion to their number in the population, but he was wrong in asserting that their religion was uniquely the cause of their ability and zeal.[5] For, as is noted in this chapter, in Russia the Old Believers were innovators; in Japan, Buddhists; in Germany, Lutherans; and at earlier stages of development, in India, Parsis; in Pakistan, Muslims; in Colombia, pious Catholics. The literature of each of these groups places the same value on frugality and zeal that Weber found (and exaggerated) in Protestant literature. One would be hard put to find the origins of this attitude in each of these greatly differing religions. The religions are hardly the cause.

McClelland. David C. McClelland concluded, on the basis of research presented in a 1953 book, that "achievement motivation" is inculcated in early childhood.[6] "Achievement motivation" or "need (for) achievement" is not an urge to get ahead, as the term might seem to imply, but satisfaction in achievement—in solving problems. McClelland suggested that one of the influences that inculcates need achievement is reward for independent action early in childhood (but not so early for any given type of action that the child tries and fails) and emotional reward, not candy or "goodies." McClelland argued that the Protestant Dissenters were "high achievers" not as a direct result of their religious beliefs but because the concern that a child prove to be an effective person and thus destined for salvation caused parents to insist on early independent action. McClelland argued that high need achievement necessarily finds expression in economic achievement, since this is the field in which there is overt evidence of having done well.

In later books and articles, McClelland elaborated and somewhat modified his theory of the conditions of early childhood that foster need achievement and guide it into economic prowess, but he also cited research which proved, he thought, that where countries had forged ahead economically a high degree of concern for achievement could be found manifested in their literature a few years—or perhaps 50 years—or perhaps 200 years—previously. McClelland's willingness to accept almost any time lag, and some of his statistical methods, leave something to be desired, but all or almost all psychologists concerned with personality formation agree that differences among individuals in achievement motivation are real, important, and associated with achievement, though not necessarily economic achievement.

---

[5] Kurt Samuelsson, *Religion and Economic Action* (New York: Harper and Row, 1961), demolishes Weber's evidence concerning the supposed uniqueness of the "Protestant ethic" piece by piece. However, Samuelsson errs in estimating that English Protestants did not contribute disproportionately to the industrial revolution. He estimates that the Dissenters constituted half of the English population of their time. A better estimate is 7%. See E. E. Hagen, *On the Theory of Social Change* (Homewood, Ill.: Dorsey Press, 1962), p. 309.

[6] D. C. McClelland, *The Achievement Motive* (New York: Appleton-Century-Crofts, 1953); *The Achieving Society* (Princeton, N.J.: Van Nostrand, 1961); McClelland and David G. Winter, *Motivating Economic Achievement* (New York: Free Press, 1969).

Hagen. In a 1962 book, the present writer noted the historical developments in seven countries that will be summarized in this chapter, and sketched a broad historical argument that the sense within any social group that leading groups in its society of the same blood and general culture look down on it will tend to create within the group a home atmosphere—a concern that children be capable, so that they can overcome or discount the derogation, and a corresponding joy in their little achievements—that will inculcate need achievement. Thus the derogation, it is argued, is a source of the talents that lead to innovation.[7]

At least a moderate degree of innovational ability, directed toward technical achievement, is now manifesting itself in many societies. If that innovational ability is manifesting itself widely within many societies, and not merely within some derogated group or groups, then clearly social derogation is not a necessary condition. It is not known that this is true. Research may show that in almost every society there is social derogation of some important group or groups, and that technical progress is being led by these groups and is then spreading to the general society in the way suggested in this chapter. No entirely sure statement can be made without further knowledge.

The logic of the theory of differential personality as an explanation of differential rates of growth is a psychological logic. This economics text is not the place to spell it out or to evaluate it. To say of a country in which growth is proceeding more rapidly than in other countries (say, Japan, Switzerland, or Sweden) that its people must be more effective is tautologous, but if there is independent evidence of the presence of greater creativity within its people, then the theory has an attractive quality: it explains differences in growth rates for which economic analysis alone sometimes provides only a lame and halting explanation.

Economic Background: Occupational Origins

In all but the most primitive societies there are many small craftsman-traders (who sell their own products) and a smaller number of larger trader-financiers. It is to be expected that entrepreneurs in developing countries would come largely from these groups, probably mainly from the latter. Few relevant studies have been done. Just over one third of the fathers of the industrialists surveyed in Sayigh's study in Lebanon were themselves industrialists; 31% had been in trade and 35% in other occupations. Though farmers or their sons became industrial entrepreneurs in a lesser proportion than their proportion in the population, the proportion was somewhat surprising. A survey of 63 industrialists of the Aegean region of

---

[7] *On the Theory of Social Change* (Homewood, Ill.: Dorsey Press, 1962).

Turkey determined their preceding occupation.[8] Only 8% had inherited their industrial position from their fathers; 43% had been in trade before moving to industry; 19% had been farmers; 17% had been craftsmen or skilled workers; and 12% had other occupational backgrounds. A study of the 47 British innovators in manufacturing mentioned in Ashton's *The Industrial Revolution* (1948) for whom information concerning their fathers' occupation was available showed that 17 of the fathers had themselves been manufacturing proprietors, 10 artisans or laborers in industry, 12 cultivators, 4 professionals, and only 4 in trade.[9] However, Ashton's study deals mainly with heavy industry and the textile industry. It is possible that entrepreneurs in other consumer goods industries had different occupational origins.

From this scattered evidence it is clear that trade is an important source, but that no simple generalizations concerning other occupational origins of industrial entrepreneurs are warranted. And concerning trade as a source, the statistics are ambiguous; the category may include craftsmen. A "trading family" from which an industrial innovator emerges may be either a family of "great traders" who had never worked on materials with their hands or a family whose head two or three generations earlier was a craftsman-trader, a son and perhaps a grandson expanding the scope of activity, and a member of the next generation innovating as an industrialist. The route in England was often the latter over a period of two or three generations. By steady expansion of activity in an energetic family, the son or grandson of an artisan or small craftsman-trader had become a large merchant in London or one of the other cities who obtained his goods by "putting out," that is, supplying materials and capital to craftsmen who made the products he sold, and he or his son established a true factory. It seems likely that a more or less similar route, with a craftsman origin, would be revealed in many instances in other countries in which the family origin is listed simply as "trade."

Social Origins

However this may be, in any country that has been studied, innovators came disproportionately from some one social group that was distinguishable from other groups quite apart from its innovativeness. In some instances, the group was no more prominent among craftsmen and traders than were other social groups, but more of its members than other craftsmen or traders had become innovators. More commonly, a disproportionate

---

[8] A. P. Alexander, "Industrial Entrepreneurship in Turkey: Origins and Growth," *Economic Development and Cultural Change*, 8 (July 1960), 349–65.

[9] Hagen, *On the Theory of Social Change*, pp. 302–9. Information could not be obtained concerning the occupations of the fathers of 25 other innovators in manufacturing.

number of the members of some social group had entered into crafts production and trade in earlier generations and then had moved on to innovation. The social groups concerned have interesting common characteristics.

In 17th- and 18th-century France, economic innovation was clearly correlated with Huguenot religious belief. The Huguenots were middle- and upper-class townspeople, but they were barred by their religion and perhaps also by their bourgeois attributes from membership in or close association with the king's court.

In Russia, when in 1667, for diplomatic reasons, church ritual was revised to accord with Greek practice, the revision included the use of three fingers rather than two in making the sign of the cross. This implied equality of Christ with God the Father and God the Holy Ghost, in a trinity, an implication that was sacrilegious to millions of Russians. These "Old Believers" seceded from the church, were condemned as schismatics, and from then until the Bolshevik Revolution of 1917 were persecuted now and again with varying degrees of severity. The Old Believers were prominent in the accelerating economic growth that occurred in Russia during the last half of the 19th century.

In 19th-century India, the community known as the Parsis—the name derives from their origin in Persia ten centuries earlier—was prominent far out of proportion to its numbers in industrial innovation in western India.[10]

In none of these cases has a statistical study been made that would quantify the relative participation of the group in innovation, but it seems clear from less precise evidence that each played a disproportionate part within its society. In other cases, the participation of a select group has been quantified.

A study by the present writer found that in the English industrial revolution the Protestant Dissenters provided some ten times as many innovating entrepreneurs between 1760 and 1830, in proportion to their numbers, as did the Anglicans.[11]

In a Javanese village, Clifford Geertz found that apart from some Chinese-owned enterprises, the firms in which the transition to manufacturing was occurring were owned and operated predominantly by Reform Muslims.[12] In Lebanon, the shares of various religious groups in the population and among the innovating entrepreneurs were as shown in Table 13–1. In

---

[10] Ashok V. Desai, "The Origins of Parsi Enterprise," *Indian Economic and Social History Review*, 5 (December 1968).

[11] Hagen, *On the Theory of Social Change*, pp. 294–309. There is an arithmetic error in the text. The Nonconformists (Dissenters), who numbered some 7% of the population, contributed 43%, not 41%, of the English and Welsh entrepreneurs in the sample studied, and thus about ten, not nine, times as many as the rest of the population in proportion to their numbers.

[12] C. Geertz, *Peddlers and Princes* (Chicago: University of Chicago Press, 1963).

TABLE 13-1 In Lebanon, disproportionate numbers of Christians and Jews become entrepreneurs

Group	Percent of Population	Percent of Innovating Entrepreneurs
Christian	50.0	80.2
Jewish	0.4	1.9
Moslem	44.0	16.4
Druse	5.6	1.5

Source: Yusif A. Sayigh, *Entrepreneurs of Lebanon* (Cambridge, Mass.: Harvard University Press, 1952), p. 69.

proportion to their number, Christians provided 4.5 times as many innovators as did Moslems, and Jews 13 times as many.

In West Pakistan, in 1959, two "communities" (quasi-castes) constituting less than 0.2% of the population controlled more than 44% of the private Pakistani-owned industrial capital surveyed by Gustav Papanek.[13]

George B. Sansom, a standard historian of Japan, states that "the organization of Japan at and following the Restoration of 1868 was in great measure the work of samurai of the lower grades." A survey of 196 corporate executives and individual business entrepreneurs of the period between 1868 and the early 20th century shows that a very large percentage came from the "outer" clans—those whom the Tokugawa had held in a socially inferior position for 2½ centuries—and investigation of a smaller sample shows that among those whose fathers' social rank could be determined, lower rank samurai of the outer clans and "wealthy peasants" were common. These formed only a small proportion of the population. (During the Tokugawa era some "ordinary" peasants became relatively wealthy. The reference to a special class of "wealthy peasants" is not to these, but to the rural samurai of the previous period, who became classed as peasants by the Tokugawa, and who were local community leaders.)

The major settled areas of Colombia are divided into three regions, Cundinamarca, also known as the Sabana (the area around Bogota), Antioquia, and the Valley of the (Upper) Cauca. These regions are separated by rugged mountain ranges over which until after World War II there was only poor transportation except by air. Historically, the Bogota area has had much the most and the closest contact with Europe. The Bogotanos, who formed the political and social elite, did—and still do—look down upon the Antioqueños as rustic and somewhat crude, yet the Antioqueños, like the business people of the other regions, claimed to be of Spanish stock little tainted by mixture with Indian blood. Hence they too were "elite." A gradual acceleration of economic growth occurred in Colombia at the turn of the 20th

---

[13] G. F. Papanek, *Pakistan's Development: Social Goals and Private Incentives* (Cambridge, Mass.: Harvard University Press, 1967).

century until shortly after World War II. The writer surveyed the history of all nonfinancial private business concerns in the three regions shown in a 1956 census of industry as employing more than 100 workers. Of the 141 entreprises for which information was obtained, 110 were founded by "Old Colombians" (a term that excludes both foreign forms and those founded by recent immigrants or not so recent immigrants regarded as still "foreign"). Of the 110, 75, or 68%, were founded by Antioqueños, who in 1905 constituted about 40% of the population. In proportion to population, then, more than three times as many Antioqueños became entrepreneurs as did Old Colombians of other stock.[14]

There are, then, nine cases (or eight if we omit Java, where the innovation was petty and was in trade rather than in production in the layperson's sense of that word). As against these instances in England, France, Russia, India, Lebanon, Japan, Colombia, and Pakistan, there are no studies known to the writer showing a more or less random distribution of early innovating entrepreneurs among the population.

Common Qualities

If one asks why these groups had turned to crafts or crafts-cum-trading, gradually became established in it, and then burst out at a later period in industrial innovation, certain qualities that are common to all of them provide an answer.

First, they were native. This is worth mentioning because there is a thesis that innovators will be "outsiders," aliens in the society. This was not true in these societies. As will be noted a few paragraphs farther on, these groups were outsiders in a sense, somewhat estranged from the leaders of their societies, but in race, residence, and culture they were flesh of the flesh, bone of the bone, of their societies.

Second, with slight qualification the innovating groups were groups whose members were used to working with their hands or to supervising workers who did. These groups did not object to "getting their hands dirty." That is, they did not have the disdain of traditional elites for manual labor. This was directly and obviously true in France, Russia, Colombia, England, and probably India. It may seem to have been untrue of Japan, insofar as the innovators were samurai, but in fact they were lesser samurai (of the outer class), whose duty it had been to supervise the estates of their lords. In Pakistan, this familiarity with hand labor may have been less prevalent, but

---

[14] Hagen, *On the Theory of Social Change,* pp. 364–65. The total sample included 161 firms. Seven of these were elsewhere than in the three main regions. No information was obtained about 13. Of the 141, 9 were subsidiaries of foreign companies and 29 had been founded by persons regarded as of foreign origin. Since there is a tendency in Colombia to term a person an Antioqueño if *either* of his or her parents is Antioqueño, the figures given in the text somewhat overstate Antioqueño participation, but the correction on this account would not be great.

at least the innovators in industry—many or most of them in jute production—were working with materials with which they were familiar and with whose processing they had been concerned even if they themselves had not worked at the processing. A firm statement concerning Lebanon is not possible.

This may seem to be a sufficient explanation: the innovators were persons doing things that were extensions of what they had been accustomed to doing. But though their familiarity with hand labor may have been almost a necessary condition for their later industrial innovation, it was not a sufficient one. For it is necessary to explain why these groups had earlier gone "into business" (as we would say today) in much greater numbers, proportionately, than other groups in the population, and why out of the groups that were in business these groups disproportionately became innovators. Both seem to have been true. There were many other members of the same societies with this same "business" background who did not become early innovators or far fewer of whom became early innovators: non-Huguenots in France and non-Dissenters in England, Tokugawa samurai in Japan, producers on the Sabana and in the Valley in Colombia, Pakistani not of the two tiny business "communities," probably non–Old Believers in Russia, and so on. And in other countries groups with about the same experience in production did not. Other forces must have also been at work.

Third, then, every one of the eight groups we are considering had for generations been derogated in its own society—looked down upon unjustly and unreasonably, in its own eyes—by the social leaders of the society. The innovating groups were, in a sense, "outsiders," but they were native outsiders. They were all protestant dissenters, though they were not all Protestant Dissenters. This is the most striking common quality apart from their work experience. In England, the groups who had adopted new faiths, in part out of protest at abuses and immorality in the church, were ridiculed, "harried," and persecuted by the elites of the society whom they, the Protestants, thought ungodly. In France, the Huguenots were persecuted and ultimately destroyed by force of arms. In Russia, from the 17th century on, the persons who clung to what they believed the true faith, the only faith that would bring them salvation, had been belittled and often harshly persecuted. In Japan, the traditional rights of the outer clans had been denied them from the time of the ascendancy of the Tokugawa soon after 1600; they were subjected to regulations and constraints that were undignified and humiliating. In Colombia, the Bogotanos expressed their contempt for their crude and crass countrymen, the Antioqueños, who were in fact of the same Spanish stock that was the Bogotanos' claim to eliteness.

In India, the Parsis, who fled from persecution in Persia at the end of the 7th century, were uprooted again in the 14th by Muslim invaders of northwest India, and in the 15th century they are found in a different region, where they were uneasy intruders who made their living increasingly in "tax farming, shipbuilding, shipping, and trading." A "tax farmer" reaches an agreement with the government by which he pays a lump sum in settlement of all the taxes of a given area, and in return he has the right to collect any amount he can from the cultivators of the area. Undoubtedly the Parsis felt the condescension and contempt with which the landed elite looked upon the first and last of these occupations. The Pakistan innovators were survivors of an uneasy history in Hindu communities in India, in which they had felt the derogation of the larger community.

Groups whose members had historically worked with their hands were looked upon with some disdain by traditional elites because they had engaged in distasteful work. Or, members of such groups had worked at distasteful occupations because, since they had been looked down upon, they had not been admitted to the traditional channels of social advance. The causation is reciprocal. Research to determine which came first, for example in England after the Norman Conquest, would be hopelessly intricate. But it is clear in history that the two often go together.

That innovation is associated with a sense of social derogation explains an aspect of innovation in England early in the industrial revolution that might otherwise be puzzling. A number of large and titled landed proprietors were early innovators, though not in industry. They innovated in agriculture, and at least one, later, innovated in mining. On examination of these cases it turns out that these individuals, though members of the titled country elite, were not a part of the inner titled group associated with the king's court, and were looked down upon by the court elite. They too suffered from a sense of derogation.

These groups had less wealth available for investment. In the recent cases, they had less opportunity to be acquainted with technical advances in other countries than did the economic and social leaders in their societies. This was true of the innovating groups in Russia, Japan, and Colombia, and possibly also of those in India and Pakistan, though the facts in these two countries are not clear. In Russia the industrialists to whom the tsar had granted monopolies, in Japan the Tokugawa, in Colombia the Bogotanos (and in Java the wealthier elites)—all of these had much more contact with foreign countries than did the groups who became the innovators. And in all nine countries except perhaps for India, the top economic and social groups were better placed to provide or obtain capital for investment if they had wished. Yet with these disadvantages it was the derogated groups who were, disproportionately, the innovators.

A fourth quality is common to seven and perhaps eight, if not to all nine, of the cases. The cultural differences between the groups that produced innovators and other groups in their societies included religious differences. The innovators were Huguenots in France, Dissenters in England, Old Believers in Russia, Parsis in India, Muslims in Pakistan whose history was in Hindu India. There appears to be nothing unique and common in the substance of these religions; the only common feature lies in the relationship of their adherents to the dominant religion: dissent. In Colombia, the Antioqueño innovators were as piously Catholic as other Colombians. However, it seemed to the writer and a fellow research worker that there was a subtle difference in religious attitude. It was symbolized by the plaques or pictures of Christ on the cross on the walls of their offices. Without exception, each Colombian executive in 1958 had such a representation hanging on the wall behind his desk. Many of those in Bogota were subdued in style. The color tones were muted. In Medellín, the central city of Antioquia, in more cases the flesh was stark white, the blood that flowed from Christ's wounds bright red. The pronouncement of the religion was, so to speak, more garish. Perhaps it was simply less self-conscious, and without "art."[15]

THE SOCIAL SETTING

The Innovating Group and the Larger Society

If a native group, too deeply rooted in the culture to be regarded as alien—too like the other members of the society in history, dress, manners, traditions, even if deviant in some respects—if such a group forges ahead economically in fields that have traditionally been distasteful, a problem is created for the rest of the society. The derogators have now become inferior in an important respect—economically. A familiar principle of sociology comes into play, the principle that it is relative status, not absolute position, that moves people. The erstwhile superior majority presumably now chafes; some of its members will see the newer sort of activity as not so demeaning after all; and the society as a whole may follow its minority into economic growth. To follow in a new field is not so difficult as to enter upon it, and the less innovative majority may readily join the process.

An illustrative instance of the importance of relative status is cited by T. Scarlett Epstein.[16] When one of two companion Indian villages received irrigation in the 1930s, while the other, on somewhat higher ground, did not, because the water would not flow up to it, little change occurred in the

---

[15] An unpublished study indicates a statistically significant correlation between the percentage of non-Catholic population in Latin American countries in 1960 and the level of per capita income. The study was first suggested and done by Eduardo Garcia, with data for the late 1950s. It was later done more elaborately by the writer. The elaboration consisted of doing a multiple regression between population, number of non-Catholics, and aggregate GNP, to avoid the remote possibility of spurious correlation because for each country the same denominator, population, appears both in per capita GNP and percentage of non-Catholics. One should not take this study alone as strong evidence of the causal importance for economic growth of either the religion or dissent. Protestantism is associated with urbanism. Urbanism may conceivably be the cause of both Protestantism and growth.

[16] *Economic Development and Social Change in South India* (New York: Humanities Press, 1962).

fortunate village during the next two decades except multiple cropping and considerable increase in income. But the residents of the "dry" village acted as though the relative reduction in their status had goaded them to at least limited innovational fury. Family members sought jobs outside the village. Two rice mills were established in the village. Organized rice smuggling was undertaken during a period of rice rationing and prohibition of the interstate shipment of rice. These actions were within the bounds of previously known behavior. They were not creatively innovational. But they show the stress of relative reduction in status bursting the bounds of traditional behavior.

Innovational activity because of threat to a previously satisfying relative status may explain the movement of Iranian landed groups directly into industrial activity (mainly, the processing of agricultural products), a move that has been rare elsewhere.[17] Agricultural innovation by the German Junkers after the middle of the 19th century may have a similar explanation.

Aliens versus Natives: The Great Traders

Why have alien groups nowhere led a society into continuing technical progress? Why have the great traders nowhere done so, except perhaps in the case of Pakistan? The two circumstances are related.

Aliens entering a new society have usually been traders, partly because it is easier to set oneself up in trade in a new country than to fit into the complex of social relationships involved in industry or agriculture, perhaps also because trading and finance are more congenial to the attitudes of persons who pull up their roots in their home culture and set out to make a life for themselves within an established alien culture. Perhaps they did not enter industry because of those attitudes. But in any event a sufficient reason may be that they feared to. Aliens are often fair game. Aliens who are becoming well-to-do are uniformly regarded as exploiters. Capital embodied in fixed equipment can readily be levied on or destroyed by a dominant majority that turns against the aliens. If a group that is culturally alien does forge ahead in industry, the native majority is not likely to emulate the alien group. It is likely to crush it.

The great traders have usually been members of an alien group. Examples are provided by Chinese in Southeast Asia, Marwaris here and there throughout India, Marwaris and other Indians in Southeast Asia and East Africa, individuals from the Middle East in many Latin American and Afri-

---

[17] The Iranian change is discussed briefly in A. J. Meyer, *Middle Eastern Capitalism: Nine Essays* (Cambridge, Mass.: Harvard University Press, 1959), chap. 3. Meyer suggests that it occurred because the threat of land and tax reform made insecure the traditional landed haven, and because the oil consortium agreement of 1954 and the Iranian seven-year plan gave promise of expanding markets for Iranian industry. The general pressure of the outside world on the Middle East, with its resulting psychological unease, may also be mentioned.

can countries, and Jews in many countries throughout history. (Many studies by anthropologists testify that even where they were native, as in China and Japan, the great traders were a group apart.)

Papanek notes that the two tiny Pakistani business "communities" that had become owners of 44% of the country's industrial capital by 1959 were trading communities. The economic achievement in the 1960s and 1970s of Brazilians of Middle Eastern origin in the state of São Paulo, and of Chinese in Hong Kong and Singapore, demonstrates that alien groups will not everywhere fail to innovate. These cases demonstrate that where the aliens gain dominance in a new area and need not fear political suppression, they may innovate effectively. The Hong Kong and Singaporean Chinese, incidentally, should not be regarded as typical Chinese. These are Chinese who, under economic stress, chose to pull up roots and migrate to a new land, and these Chinese surely had values, motives, and a view of life different from those held by their fellows under economic stress who did not choose to migrate. So also the Brazilian Middle Easterners.

Groups, Not Individuals

Economic growth requires innovation by many individuals, not isolated persons, for no more complex reason than that if an isolated person becomes an economic innovator, this in itself will not be enough to lead to growth. However, there is an added reason. A single individual who does things that are looked upon as gauche will be squashed by the social disapprobation. The individual needs the protection of a group. Hence, turning away from old ways of behavior to economic innovation in "grubby" fields occurs within such groups as the Protestant Dissenters, the Old Believers, and the Antioqueños. An occasional individual outside these groups was also an early innovator. The existence of the group active in the new field may have provided psychic support to these other deviant individuals.

Social Mobility and Social Blockage

It has often been stated that the availability of upward social mobility is conducive to economic prowess. The generalization is incomplete. The blockage of traditional channels is also required. If traditional ways of gaining increased social status (e.g., landedness) are not open, because the derogated group is not accepted into them or is not accepted socially even if it succeeds in entering them, and if in addition there is no institutional bar to gaining wealth, which gives at least one sort of social status, by a new route, then the blockage plus the opportunity is conducive to economic prowess.

There was a good deal of upward mobility through traditional channels in England in the later medieval and early modern period. Yeomen became larger landowners; larger landowners became titled; service of the court might bring recognition; and so on. The names of land registers show considerable "circulation of the elite." But the Protestant Dissenters were at such odds with the top elites that such channels brought little reward to them.

Old Ruts or New Actions

Lastly, it has often been noted that people often innovate with great effectiveness when their old ways of behaving are no longer possible—when, as the older anthropologists say, the "crust of custom" is broken. If a person cannot tread along in an old rut, or if doing so no longer yields the former satisfying results, then if the person has a certain degree of self-reliance, he will consider how to act more effectively.

A. J. Meyer attributes the rise in entrepreneurial activity in the Middle East during the three decades following 1930 in part to the depression in Europe, the expulsion of individuals from various countries, and the Arab-Israeli war.[18] In Colombia, a major shift of capital and entrepreneurship from commerce to industry occurred in Antioquia between 1905 and 1915, when the opening of roads and the Panama Canal greatly reduced the profit opportunities in commerce.[19]

That migrants to America moved to an area in which the social structure and economic facilities of their homelands were entirely lacking may account in part for their innovative vigor in American colonial history and in U.S. history. (The bountiful natural resources waiting for them must also be given their due.) The Hindu refugees from Pakistan and the Muslim refugees from India, whose old lives were destroyed, have both been exceptionally effective business innovators. The innovational vigor of immigrants, other than immigrants of low economic classes, has been noted in various other places as well. It has been argued that the physical destruction by bombing in Germany and Japan, and the demonstrated nonviability of a previous way of life in Germany, France, Italy, and Japan, may be important causes of the rapid rate of technical progress in those countries since World War II. The achievement of the three European countries may be contrasted with the relatively poor rate of rise in productivity in Britain during the same period. The British social system scored well during the war, so that old ruts seemed satisfying after the war.

Education and Entrepreneurship

The formal content of education is likely to do little to make an individual more self-reliant or less anxious when he faces new problems—in tech-

---

[18] Ibid.

[19] On the broad plain of the Sabana, the erstwhile traders turned to a landed life; in the Valley (around Cali), for reasons that are not immediately obvious, they sank into relative obscurity.

nical terms, to increase his "need achievement." Teaching students inductive or deductive or syllogistic reasoning apparently has little effect on their logical abilities. However, the individual's tendencies are reinforced and elaborated or, on the other hand, confused, contradicted, and blunted by the models of behavior set by instructors and other seniors during his school years, by his sense of his success or lack of it in relationships of various types with his school fellows, and by various other relationships with other persons.

And education, perhaps especially college education, gives the individual more knowledge pertinent to later entrepreneurship and acquaints him with a wider range of career alternatives. In these ways an increase in education of pertinent types increases his ability to conceive of and establish new productive ventures or widens the range of ventures which he is well fitted to conceive of and establish.

FOR WHOM DO THEY INNOVATE?

No doubt an individual with innovational motivation and energy will be innovational in almost any circumstances in which he finds himself. Yet few persons would claim that the individual will innovate equally well, no matter for whom or in what circumstances he works. The question of the institutional loyalties that best draw out innovational talent is discussed in the following chapter.

FOR FURTHER READING

Schumpeter's *The Theory of Economic Development* (note 3) is a classic.

No summary can take the place of reading Max Weber's *The Protestant Ethic and the Spirit of Capitalism* (New York: Scribner, 1930; German original, 1904–5). Read also Kurt Samuelsson's critique of Weber's evidence, remembering the crucial error of Samuelsson in estimating the number of English Dissenters.

Concerning the personality theories of entrepreneurship, read the books by McClelland and Hagen cited in notes 6 and 7 of this chapter.

Clark Kerr, J. T. Dunlop, F. H. Harbison, and C. A. Myers, *Industrialism and Industrial Man* (New York: Oxford University Press, 1964; paperback). Slightly revised from the hardcover 1961 edition.

Irma Adelman and Cynthia T. Morris, *Society, Politics, and Economic Growth* (Baltimore: Johns Hopkins University Press, 1967). Deals with sociological and political determinants of economic growth rather than specifically with entrepreneurship, but is relevant here.

14

Institutions

The word *institution* refers to an organization that has been established for a particular purpose, such as a church or a bank, or to practices that have become an established part of the behavior of a society, such as primogeniture—inheritance by the oldest son—or marriage.

The term is used here in both senses. Economic development, like other economic activity, proceeds not in a void but within the framework of institutions in the second sense and through institutions in the first sense. Many of these institutions are not economically exogenous in a historical sense: they may have arisen out of economic imperatives in the past; but in the current era they constrain, channel, or motivate much economic activity. Selected institutions are considered here.

LAND TENURE

Where primogeniture rules, as in England, agricultural holdings remain intact and relatively large, and they may increase with acquisitions. Where equal division among heirs is mandated by law or custom, as in France, southern Italy, Sri Lanka, and some areas of India, agricultural holdings not only shrink, they fragment, for as noted in Chapter 8, each heir must get some of the land that is the richest, some with the best drainage, and so on. T. Scarlett Epstein cites a case in Sri Lanka, where the birth rate is high and daughters as well as sons inherit, in which in three generations an estate was divided into 384 parts.[1]

---

[1] Scarlett Epstein and Darrell Jackson, eds., *The Paradox of Poverty: Socio-Economic Aspects of Population Growth* (London: Macmillan, 1976, for the Institute of Development Studies, University of Sussex).

A. K. Sen argues that the choice of technique in production—the main variation of interest here is that between more labor-intensive and more capital-intensive technique—is determined in considerable part by whether production is within a nuclear family, an extended family, by means of wage employment, or by a cooperative association.[2] The cost advantage of different techniques, he argues, varies among these modes of organization because of differences in labor costs and in the cost of finance, and techniques vary not only because of these differences in cost elements but also because of differences in the share of output going to the decision-maker and because of differences in his concern for the other persons associated in the enterprise.

The meaning of ownership varies among societies. Landownership may be a perpetual right or one for a limited term; it may include or not include water rights, or rights to minerals beneath the land, and these differences may exist not by legislation or contract but by established usage. "Use ownership" of land prevails, or has prevailed, in some societies. One has the right to use the land throughout one's lifetime, for the benefit of one's extended family, after which the right passes to the next generation. But if one chooses to leave the community, the right passes to the other members of one's family, or if the entire family leaves, it is assumed by some other member of the community. One does not have the right to sell the land. The land is therefore not available as security for a mortgage. It is said that when the British came to Burma and, unknown to the Burmese, brought strange institutions of property with them, some Burmese lost their land because they did not understand the concept of the alienation of land and eagerly accepted the money that moneylenders offered them in return for their signatures on what turned out to be mortgages which British-established courts enforced.

BUSINESS ORGANIZATION

Economic needs have molded various forms of business organization: the sole proprietorship, in which all the property that the individual owns is security for his business (or other) debts; the ordinary partnership, in which every partner has unlimited liability for debts incurred by any; the partnership which must have "general partners" with unlimited liability but may increase its capital by having "limited partners" who risk only what they invested; the ordinary corporation, accepted in law as the "person" who has unlimited liability, so that the shareholders risk only their investment; banks with "double liability," meaning that each shareholder may not only lose his investment but to meet obligations of the bank is liable for an addi-

---

[2] A. K. Sen, *Employment, Technology, and Development* (Oxford: Clarendon Press, 1975).

tional amount equal to the par value of the shares he owns. Without the corporate form of organization, which can attract thousands of shareholders and will continue to live as shareholders die, modern large-scale production would hardly have been possible. Before the days of governmental deposit insurance, double liability for bank shareholders provided better protection for the funds of depositors than did single liability, and thereby aided banks in attracting depositions.

In Antioquia, a region of Colombia, a special form of business association arose, permitted for a mining venture but for no other type of business operation. When a prospector had filed a claim, he might organize a company with 24 shares and invite participation. As the company needed added funds, by a majority vote of the shareholders each shareholder could be required to contribute identical added amounts, without limit. A shareholder was unable to do so, he dropped out, and reorganization followed. Legal liability to creditors was limited, as in the modern corporation, but in practice it was compulsory for shareholders to contribute equally sums needed to pay the debts of a venture that failed. Without the Antioqueño mining corporation the exploitation of the mineral wealth of the region would probably have proceeded far more slowly.

BANKS

The obligations of commercial banks—demand deposits, savings accounts, or 6- or 12-month certificates of deposit—are payable on demand or in the short run. Banks incur these obligations to attract funds which they in turn lend out at long term. By American law their function is limited to this "intermediation," and their extension of credit to corporations or the government is limited to the acquisition of debt, not equity, claims. An American bank interferes with the management of a corporate debtor only when the security of the debt comes into question; the bank may then agree to extend or renegotiate the debt only in exchange for a voice in the management or for the institution of new management approved by the bank. In European countries, however, commercial banks have acted as entrepreneurs: identifying business opportunities, indicating the management that they will approve and finance, guiding all the steps in the establishment of the firm, and buying not only the bonds or the intermediate-term notes of the firm but also shares of its stock, or receiving the shares in return for their services. Especially in France, beginning with the Credit Mobilier in 1852, and then in Germany and in the smaller countries to the east and south of these, private joint-stock banks sprang up which often were the entrepreneurs as well as financers of new ventures. In the aggregate they played a quantitatively important role in the development of large-scale industry in their countries. These private investments have continued to be important in Germany. In France, they abandoned their entrepreneurial role in considerable degree as time passed.

A somewhat different relationship between bank and corporation exists in Japan. A major bank is the sponsor, so to speak, of each major corporation. A bank official is prominent among the corporation's directors. If the corporation needs added funds for expansion, that bank provides them. If the corporation passes through hard times, so that it needs more cash to keep afloat, the bank provides that too. If the corporation fails, the bank is disgraced with it. No relationship between bank and corporation in any Western country quite parallels this one.

One economic historian, Alexander Gerschenkron, has argued that the industrial development of Italy proceeded slowly while that in France and Germany was booming because Italy lacked the institution of aggressive investment banking. The argument has been challenged. Other causes have also been adduced.

Gerschenkron has also suggested that when economic growth began in an advanced country (his definition of a country that is "advanced" but has not yet had economic growth is not clear), the leaders in economic advance were private manufacturing corporations; that when it began in areas of moderate backwardness, the leaders were banks; and that when it began in very backward countries, the government took the lead.[3] The generalization is fragile; too many instances that violate the supposed rule have occurred; but entrepreneurial banks certainly played an important role in the economic growth of a number of European countries.

In the United States, during the decades before the Civil War "wildcat banks" sprang up in frontier states. Chartered by those states under the loosest of requirements, the banks came into existence with tiny capital bases. When recession occurred and some of their loans turned sour, many of them failed, at cruel cost to large numbers of their depositors. Meanwhile, however, the banks extended credit freely to new enterprises arising overnight in the new areas, and surely hastened the development of the country.

Since World War II, governmentally owned or internationally financed "development banks" have evolved. Some of them, within a country, have the purpose of aiding the development of one industry—agriculture or manufacturing—or one geographic region. Thus in Brazil there is the "Bank of the Northeast." Others are nationwide in scope. And in Chapter 18, international development banks, each for one region of the world, will be discussed. The financial aid of development banks within a nation may be via loans only or also via stock purchases. In the latter case there is usually legal provision of the circumstances in which the bank will divest itself of the stock.

The International Finance Corporation of the World Bank provides funds to private corporations in LDCs through the purchase of the pre-

---

[3] Concerning Italy, see A. Gerschenkron, "Social Attitudes, Entrepreneurship, and Economic Development," *Explorations in Entrepreneurial History*, 6 (October 1953), 1–19. Concerning leadership in growth, see his *Economic Backwardness in Historical Perspective* (Cambridge, Mass.: Harvard University Press, 1962).

ferred stock. A borrowing corporation must agree that IFC may sell its stock on the open market if the corporation becomes successful enough to make such sale possible. At the apex of the world set of development banks is the International Bank for Reconstruction and Development, out of which the two other "windows" of the World Bank evolved: the International Development Association, which makes "soft" loans to low-income countries, and the IFC. The financial solidity of the IBRD has enabled it to borrow readily on the financial markets through bond issues at rates as favorable as those granted to the U.S. government. The IBRD's prominence has enabled it under untimid management to blunt some types of political pressure and thus extend loans on dispassionate economic development grounds to countries to which on political grounds prominent national members of the bank would have wished to refuse the loans. The history of the IBRD since its establishment in 1946 demonstrates how an institution may acquire a life of its own, different from that which its founders envisaged.

GOVERNMENT

Adam Smith judged in 1776 that economic progress was more rapid in Britain than elsewhere because of the superiority of Britain's social institutions. Other economists have seen other causes for Britain's primacy in the Industrial Revolution. Today few observers would make generalizations as sweeping as that by Smith.

Under centralized control, the Soviet Union made remarkably rapid technical and economic advance during the half century that followed the Bolshevik Revolution. With the heavy hand of Soviet control upon them, the satellite Communist countries of eastern Europe have been among the world's leaders in the rate of increase in per capita income during the 1960s and 1970s. Under socially repressive governments, South Korea, Taiwan, and Brazil have surged forward economically. On the other hand, both in the long run and in the short run, the democracies of western Europe and western European colonization have been world leaders economically.

Hence, facile generalizations concerning the relationship of national political institutions to economic prowess are not warranted, but some observations may be made briefly.

Forms of government range from authoritarian through democratic and from forms that rely heavily on private enterprise to carry out economic functions to Communist forms. Communist governments are authoritarian. Like rightist authoritarian governments, they suppress individual freedom of expression, whereas if such suppression occurs in democracies it occurs mainly through the weight of public opinion rather than through governmental force. Rightist authoritarian governments and democracies are similar in their reliance on private enterprise, though the extent of that reliance varies so greatly among democratic nations that this comparison is true only in a very general sense.

The U.S. government is extreme in its degree of reliance on private enterprise to carry on economic functions. No other Western government leaves in private hands so many of the types of services known as public utilities. Many other democratic governments carry on as public enterprises types of production which they define in some sense as "basic," in addition to public utilities. The Italian government owns and operates a large international oil company. The French government owns, among other companies, an automobile manufacturer and an airplane manufacturer. The British government has taken over a string of companies that were in danger of going bankrupt. These range from coal mines, steel mills, and a shipbuilding firm to several manufacturing corporations. And so on.

Nor are the economic institutions of all Communist governments alike. They vary from the still heavy-handed central direction of the Soviet Union, seen also on a smaller scale in Cuba and North Korea, to the economic decentralization of Yugoslavia, and the mixture of centralization and decentralization, ideology and pragmatism, of China.

Yugoslav reforms in 1965 created a full market system with "laissez-faire socialism." Each factory was allowed to set the prices of its products, to determine the distribution of the proceeds among wages, investment, and other uses, and to plan its own investments. Not all of the effects of thus creating a large number of monopolies were anticipated. Those effects included accelerating price increases and declining investment.

Between 1968 and 1974, the system was dismantled. A large element of control over the planning of investment was returned to the central government. Production units were persuaded to enter into "social compacts" which limit their decision-making powers. Yet each local production unit still has an important voice in the planning process.

Chinese institutions are discussed in a later section of this chapter.

The range of commercial operations that Western governments conduct is not the only economic dimension on which these governments differ. Japan and France provide examples of different sorts of variance.

In Japan, especially since World War II but probably also earlier, the government and the major corporations have jointly planned the major outlines of the nation's economic advance and then taken joint steps to execute the plans. This occurred, for example, when it was decided that Japan must enter the synthetic textiles field. One may guess (the discussions are not public) that officials of the Ministry of Trade and Industry, of the Japanese National Mortgage Bank, of main commercial banks, and of the major textile firms jointly decided which corporations would do what. The sources of financing were then arranged, and also the measures that the government would take to protect Japanese production while it was developing and the measures that it would take to facilitate exports. "Japan, Inc." then got into action, and presently Japan emerged as a highly successful producer of the new textiles. More recently, the same procedure has been followed with regard to large-capacity high-speed computers. Four firms merged into three, and these three later into two, and as this is written in 1979, the two are busy with the research and development which are intended to foster a major advance in Japan's ability to produce the largest computers competitively, beginning in, say, 1982 or 1983.

These instances do not stand alone. There was a burst of such "emergency" planning soon after the end of the American occupation of Japan after World War II, then, apparently, a lull, and in the last few years renewed activity of this sort.

Napoleon, who saw a need to create entrepreneurs to counteract French "bureaucratic" tendencies, founded the École Polytechnique. Subsequently, the other Grandes Écoles sprang up. These schools have attracted able young men with managerial and entrepreneurial talent. Their graduates, technically trained, have ever since moved easily from private business to government and back again, as the occasion demanded, and acted ably in either. When in government they have taken it for granted that they could make business decisions more capably than the private business executives directly concerned, and they have often done so, and through the elaborate French system of regulatory commissions and governmental and quasi-governmental investment banks, they have persuaded or coerced private executives to adopt the policies they prescribed. In Andrew Shonfield's words, "These are men who take pride in assuming personal responsibility; their habit is to assume the initiative, and to think up formal justifications for their actions afterwards."[4]

In some of the LDCs, especially those of Asia but also others, governments themselves have established many industrial and mining enterprises even though the governments do not espouse socialist ideologies. The colonial histories of these countries created antipathy in them to large private enterprises, especially foreign-owned ones. Government officials thought that large enterprises would advance their countries rapidly toward "modernity," but only governmentally owned large-scale enterprise seemed to be in the public interest. It was also asserted that governmental operation was needed because no private executives were available. Officials of the new governments eagerly organized governmentally owned corporations and placed themselves at their head. But if a person is not a competent manager he or she does not become one by being given an official title. In some of these countries a traditional aversion toward concerning oneself with the grubby details of industrial activity, managerial incompetence, or a readiness to use the government corporation as a vehicle for personal en-

---

[4]A. Shonfield, *Modern Capitalism* (London: Oxford University Press, 1965).

richment, or all of these, have caused public operation of enterprises to be disastrously wasteful.

FOR WHOM DO ENTREPRENEURS INNOVATE?

Another way of approaching the question of the importance of institutions is to ask whom entrepreneurs feel loyalty to—what institutional framework evokes their innovational energies.

The conception commonly expressed in Western writings of half a century ago, that an individual will function efficiently in economic endeavors only if he is working in a private enterprise to further his own economic interests, has been proved overly simple by history. Depending on his view of the world and the circumstances of his life, the entrepreneur may act effectively on behalf of himself, his family, his community, his country, some one social group, or the business organization to which he is attached.

The extended-family firm is ubiquitous in nonindustrial societies. The phrase refers to a firm that is managed by (usually) the senior family member, that depends on relatives for its capital, and that draws its managerial members only from among relatives. Extended-family ownership and management of a firm has been attacked as inimical to entrepreneurship. The most important criticisms are that obligations to relatives force the extended family firm to dissipate its capital in loans or gifts to them when these are requested and to employ incompetents as managers. Associated drawbacks, it is suggested, are a refusal to delegate authority, hence neglect of foremanship, and a stress on economic security that causes excessive caution in evaluating even small risks. E. Wayne Nafziger concluded from a study of Nigerian entrepreneurs that the support of the extended family helped a would-be entrepreneur to obtain apprenticeship training and to establish a firm, but that the family's demands upon him hindered his use of the capital he accumulated to expand the firm.[5]

The inability of extended-family firms to refuse requests that dissipate their capital has been commonly observed. Yet the criticisms are misplaced if they imply that development would proceed faster if extended-family firms were somehow outlawed. Among the attitudes common in traditional cultures is the importance of the moral duty to care for one's kin. Correlatively, persons outside one's kin or "pseudokin" group are likely to serve one's interests badly if doing so will benefit their own group. Where such values prevail, patrimonial management in the family firm is not an obstacle to the innovational conduct of business but a necessary condition for it. Where one can neither trust a stranger or an acquaintance as a business associate, nor persuade him to lend one money, then the extended family may

---

[5] E. Wayne Nafziger, "The Effect of the Nigerian Extended Family on Entrepreneurial Activity," *Economic Development and Cultural Change*, 18 (October 1969), 25–31.

be a necessary source of capital and a necessary bond among business associates. Its abolition would not modernize the society; in the circumstances it would merely paralyze business activity.[6]

United States corporations demand a high degree of loyalty to the organization as such. This does not mean that every corporate officer must suppress his or her individuality. In recruiting and promoting executives, American corporations, and presumably corporations elsewhere, stress nothing so much as the ability to make competent judgments. They will put up with a considerable degree of idiosyncrasy in a person with great ability, within the limits of his being able to work with others. But U.S. business life attracts and puts a premium on persons to whom the interests of the company become their interests, so that, among other results, in the allocation of their time between their business careers and their families, their families sometimes come out second best. However, this loyalty is to the concept of a career in a corporation, rather than an indissoluble tie to a given corporation. It does not prevent the individual from accepting a position in another firm, and operating with full zeal there, if the transfer promises him more income or, perhaps more important, a wider scope of managerial activity.

In the United States, as well as in other countries that stress private enterprise, individuals have nevertheless seen opportunities to exercise their abilities in public corporations, and have managed them with distinction. Examples are Lilienthal in the Tessessee Valley Authority, Mattei in Italy's ENI (Ente Nazionale Idrocarburi), and Bermudez of Pemex (Petroleo Mexicano). Government employees in the Soviet Union have innovated so effectively as to give that country one of the world's higher rates of economic development during a period that included two destructive wars.

Like the U.S convictions of the effectiveness of private enterprise, governmental operation of virtually all economically productive activity in the Soviet Union is probably the result of historical experience, but experience contrasting with that of the United States. In tsarist Russia, agriculture was feudal or (even after the freeing of the serfs in 1861) quasi-feudal, and industrial enterprises were owned by nobles, often with monopolistic franchises from the tsar. The Russian nobles were self-centered, callous, and contemptuous in their treatment of the classes beneath them. The Russian lower and middle classes and intellectuals so bitterly hated and distrusted the nobles, who would naturally be the owners and managers if there were private enterprise in Russia, that they could not conceive of business operation by

---

[6] S. Khalaf and E. Shwayri, "Family Firms and Industrial Development: The Lebanese Case," *Economic Development and Cultural Change*, 15 (October 1966), 59–69. Khalaf and Shwayri, noting the importance of the family-oriented firm in Lebanon, argue this side of the case persuasively. In Lebanon, they state, property and kinship create a sense of responsibility and loyalty, necessary for the efficient conduct of business, that would not otherwise exist.

private firms as being in the public interest. I do not mean to imply a conscious decision by this chain of reasoning, but rather a deep-seated emotional attitude. As a consequence, the operation of economic activity by the state "automatically" and "inevitably" seemed to them the necessarily best form of economic organization, and aroused their emotional support sufficiently so that they have innovated with effectiveness and satisfaction in government enterprises. It seems highly likely that in the Soviet Union economic growth during the past 60 years would have been slower under a mixed enterprise system, just as it seems certain that in the United States it would have been slower under a socialist system. What form of operation of productive enterprises is most efficient at any given historical period depends on the national temper, a factor which is not notably easy to evaluate. (There were non-noble business entrepreneurs in tsarist Russia, but they were too few to affect the attitudes noted here.)

There is some evidence that Soviet bureaucracy has generated business managers of decreasing innovativeness. While European economies have shown remarkable vigor during the postwar period, the growth rate of the Soviet economy seems to be running down. The very long run verdict may be in favor of private enterprise within a social welfare political framework. However, this conclusion may result from Western bias. The U.S. economy, like the Soviet economy, has done none too well during the postwar period, especially relative to the European economies.

Japan during the Tokugawa era (1600–1868) and France up to the present day provide examples of economic loyalties and energies different from either those of the Soviet Union or those of the United States. France has been discussed.

During the Tokugawa era there was a great deal of economic innovation in Japan. For many a samurai effective in conceiving and promoting technical progress in agriculture or crafts, service to his feudal lord took precedence over his own interests or those of his natural family. The formal rule of inheritance was that the family property passed to the first born son. However, if that son was incompetent, for the sake of the enterprise over coming generations a father sometimes created a new firstborn son by adopting a capable young man, who then inherited the property, the position as head of the family, and the family responsibilities.

THE INDUSTRIAL CORPORATION IN JAPAN

Japanese industrial management, at least up to the present time, provides an example of extremely successful factory management that grossly violates principles believed in the United States to be essential to effective management. The rate of increase in productivity in Japan from the 1880s to the 1970s has been the highest in the world.

The relationships between employees and their corporations described here have probably not prevailed in every Japanese corporation at any time since World War II. Moreover, during recent years they seem to have been breaking down to some degree. Yet they are still very common. They are described here in the present tense; this is more appropriate than a past tense that would imply that they have ended.

Major features of the pattern are as follows. Companies hire young men and women for worker class jobs ("those who work") as they leave school, and for managerial positions ("those who direct") as they leave college, after fairly intensive investigation of the individual's background and reliability and in the case of managerial positions of his general ability. The company will not seek workers from among individuals already employed in industrial jobs elsewhere, for (after a probationary period, in the case of the worker class) there is a lifetime commitment between an individual and his company. He will not move to accept a better job, and the company is committed to retaining him until retirement except in instances of the most extreme provocation, such as several unexplained absences for periods of weeks. During such absences, until the man is discharged, his family receives his wages, for he continues to be an employee. Economic slack, causing a downturn in sales, is not sufficient justification for discharging or laying off workers. Similarly, an executive, once he has become attached to a given corporation after his graduation from college, owes and honors loyalty to that corporation throughout his business career, and the corporation has a converse obligation to him. He would no more think of moving to any position whatever in another corporation than he would of stealing from the company's till.[7]

The obligation not to lay off employees does not work hardship on employers as often as might appear, for a company may succeed in a voluntary appeal to some of its employees to return to their family village for a time, to aid the company, or to retire early in return for a bonus in addition to regular retirement pay; and the turnover among women employees is sufficient so that their number may be reduced rather rapidly by attrition. However, the obligation to retain workers has typically been recognized even when it imposed a heavy financial cost on the company.[8] The decision of a

---

[7] The simplest exposition of the relevant aspects of Japanese factory organization is that by James C. Abegglen (*The Japanese Factory* [Glencoe, Ill.: Free Press, 1958]; and *Management and Worker: The Japanese Solution* [Tokyo: Sophia University, 1973]). Jean Stoetzel, in his *Without the Chrysanthemum and the Sword: A Study of the Attitudes of Youth in Post-War Japan* (New York: Columbia University Press, 1955), reports some variations. In the 1960s, in Japan's persisting extremely tight labor market, this loyalty broke in some degree. As early as 1963, Ezra Vogel presented evidence that the loyalty of Japanese workers to employers is much less than absolute; the evidence has been increasing since that time. The account given in the text is also based on conversations of the writer with a considerable number of Japanese executives in 1956, 1960, and 1974.

[8] The security thus afforded the workers has been somewhat reduced by the high bankruptcy rate among Japanese companies in recent years, associated with the displacement of the less progressive by the more progressive. However, the firms going bankrupt have typically been small firms employing relatively few workers.

mining corporation in the 1950s to discharge some workers, after the offer of bonuses for early retirement had not brought a sufficient reduction in the work force, caused a long and bitter strike.

Within both the worker ranks and the management staff, the members of one "class" (one year's recruits) are almost never promoted over those of another. Yet within this limitation, superiors seek out ability among the employees under them, and promote the ablest, with as close a search for the best employees as is conducted anywhere in the world. Advancement of workers in pay is on the basis of seniority and size of family, with a very small variation based on function and deficiency.

In managerial positions, overt assignment of responsibility for a function, and thereby of credit for successful performance or blame for failure, is avoided. Though executives must in fact know who among them are capable and effective, formal assignment of responsibility or credit is avoided through the use of management committees on whose ambiguous shoulders responsibility falls. Indeed, extreme care is taken to avoid any formal or public imputation that one executive or one worker has not performed as well as another.

In principle, suggestions for innovations start with a memorandum by a managerial employee of low rank and work their way up to the top with notations by executives of each superior rank as the memorandum ascends. But often, it is said, there is a quiet discussion between an executive of top rank and one of low rank before the process begins. And there is provision to short-circuit the procedure when quick action is needed.

To a person acquainted with Japanese history, the origins of this form of personnel relationships in Japanese factories are clear. It is a direct transference to the factory of the former reciprocal obligations between an individual and his lord. The personality traits that made the former bond so compellingly necessary still exist.

The success of the system is probably explained by one positive and one negative element of those persisting traits. The positive element is the great need of a subordinate to perform his obligations to his superior loyally in return for the fulfillment by the superior of his obligations to the subordinate. This has been as effective an inducement to Japanese workers and executives to labor diligently and competently as other incentives have been to Western workers. The negative element is the extreme shame felt in the Japanese culture at being exposed as having failed at formal fulfillment of the responsibility of one's position. Perhaps a Japanese executive whose superiors or peers said openly to him, "You have failed to perform the duties of your station," would feel such shame that he could not continue to function. Apparently also, workers who gained such a perception through the fact that fellow workers of equal seniority had been promoted above them in rank or salary would be affected in a similar way. To avoid this, invidious distinctions are avoided. That everyone may know the true facts of relative ability is unimportant if the facts are not formally signaled. Yet Japanese industrial success is surely also due in large degree to a factor quite separate from these structural arrangements, namely, the high innovational abilities of Japanese. The structural arrangements are the ones in which Japanese are freest and most motivated to exercise those abilities.

Since this deep mutual sense of comprehensive obligations exists (or has existed), there is a corresponding intense sense of treachery or abandonment if either side seems not to fulfill its obligations. This is probably an important factor in the radicalism of one segment of the Japanese labor movement and in the bitterness and intransigence that are seen in some Japanese labor disputes.

With the growth in scale of Japanese factories, it has been impossible to preserve the full paternalistic employer-employee relationship. A corporation is not a samurai or a lord. This is no doubt one of the reasons why relationships within Japanese corporations are changing—probably to the detriment of Japan's future rate of technical progress.

INSTITUTIONS AND MOTIVATION IN CHINA

No more than capitalist societies do socialist ones closely resemble one another. "We do not regard the Soviet Union as a socialist country," a Chinese guide recently told an American visitor. This section discusses briefly the institutions within which the Chinese economy has functioned and the development of the Chinese economy since the accession of the Communist leaders to governmental power in 1949.

Certain facets of China's economic development during the three decades since 1949 parallel those of Japan's development during the half century following the overthrow of the Tokugawa in 1868:

1. *The capture for the government of the share of the national income that in Japan had gone to the feudal lords and in China to landlords, the wealthy gentry, moneylenders, and others.* The channeling of the income stream into capital formation was quite different in the two countries. Governmental capital formation in Japan was by the central government, except for local community infrastructure, and was mainly for infrastructure. Only a few early factories were built by the government, and when operating successfully these were sold on extremely generous terms to influential members of the "outer clans" that had overthrown the Tokugawa. In China, the only private capital formation has been for the development of the small agricultural plots that individuals have been permitted to retain alongside the communal land. All other capital formation has been by communes or by the county or provincial governments or the national government, not merely or predominantly the last.

2. *Emphasis on agricultural development.* Neither Japan nor China had the surplus agricultural production which the government of the Soviet Union was able to seize for the cities during the 1920s while it destroyed the kulaks ("rich" peasants) and devoted its energy to industrialization.

3. *Emphasis on rural agriculture-based industry.* In Japan small local factories developed which supplied components to larger urban factories. In China the communes have been permitted to retain funds to develop self-standing local factories to make items needed in agriculture or in rural life.

At least until 1977, economic activity in China was carried on so far as might be within three rules of behavior dictated by the chairman of the Communist Party, Mao Zedong. The last two stated below are closely related to a belief deeply seated in Mao's mind that society must repeatedly be purged by a surging from below. His view has seemed to evoke a favorable emotional response from many, probably most, of the Chinese people.

The three rules have been described by a number of writers. Paragraph (i) below is paraphrased from an article by Lloyd Reynolds. Paragraphs (ii) and (iii) are quoted *verbatim* from him.[9] Writing in 1975, he put in the present tense descriptive remarks for which the past tense might now be more appropriate.

(i) *Emphasis on non-material incentives.* Individuals to work to promote the social good, the laggards prompted by pressure from their fellows, rather than for personal economic gain. Monetary reward, at least in each broad segment of the economy, to be almost identical regardless of position or economic or technical contribution.

(ii) *Antibureaucratization.* In any industrial society, capitalist or socialist, there is a tendency for government officials, industrial managers, and professional experts to crystallize into an elite—Djilas' "ruling class," or Galbraith's "techno-structure." Chinese leaders are determined to maintain social fluidity to prevent the emergence of marked distinctions, either of prestige or income. This underlies, for example, the new policy of requiring high school graduates to work for at least two years before they can be considered for university admission, and of giving preference in admission to children of workers and farmers. This is intended to prevent hereditary transmission of status through the educational system.

(iii) *Mass participation in decision making.* This is evidenced in worker membership in the "Revolutionary Committees" which now govern all organizations in China; in the rapid promotion of factory workers to leadership positions during and since the Cultural Revolution; in the establishment of "three-in-one teams," including managers, technicians, and workers, as the responsible groups for industrial research and development. The opposite side of the coin is the downgrading of the expert, the specialist, the technician, who is urged to "learn from the workers," and to spend frequent periods of time in manual labor.

In the first of these rules the Chinese ideology coincided with the Russian, though observance of the egalitarian principle soon faltered in the Soviet Union. The second and third rules were uniquely Chinese, and diametrically opposed to both Soviet principle and Soviet practice.

---

[9] "China as a Less Developed Economy," *American Economic Review,* 65 (June 1975), 418–28.

In 1966 (or beginning at the very end of 1965) there began the great surging from below (stimulated and led by Mao from above in order to destroy the power of the "pragmatist" leaders within the Communist Party) that became known as the Cultural Revolution. Whatever Mao may have intended, the movement became anti-intellectual as well as antielitist and antibourgeois. Colleges were closed; professors thought to be anti-Maoist were sent to distant provinces to do menial labor; the requirements for university admission and graduation were ended; through the disruption of laboratories and offices, technical and scientific research was brought almost to an end, to be replaced by the energy of the workers, which, if it followed Mao's principles, would make research and technical instruction unnecessary. As is now known, the discipline of factories was upset and production fell for a time. After three years order was restored, largely by the army, but technical advance was not resumed, or was resumed only falteringly. "We lost a decade," Chinese intellectuals said in 1978.

But even before the reversal of practice in 1977 under Deng Xiaoping[10] ideology had been modified here and there by pragmatism. This had been especially true in rural life. In 1958–59 the "Great Leap Forward" had occurred. It was based on faith in decentralization and in the ability of working zeal to substitute for technical expertise. The notorious example of its excesses were its efforts to increase rice production at a bound by planting the rice plants closer together (output fell) and to have backyard steel furnaces provide each rural community with the material that it needed for its tools and implements. The furnaces were built and produced steel, but it was of such high sulfur content that even crude shovels made from it were brittle and broke. But it is noteworthy that the Great Leap Forward had some successes and that, since its failures were quickly apparent, its excesses, unlike those of the later Cultural Revolution, were promptly abandoned.

The Communes

The formation of communes to replace private agricultural production was of course decreed by Communist ideology. First, cultivators were organized into work brigades, which cultivated larger areas than the individual peasant plots; then these areas were organized into small communes; then the small communes were consolidated into larger and larger communes. But when the larger communes proved too large for efficient management, pragmatism asserted itself and they were divided into smaller communes. The ideology of nonmaterial incentives dictated that material rewards should be equal, and for a time all workers on a commune were given virtually identical pay, regardless of position, technical contribution, or, for

---

[10] Or, in the old transliteration, Teng Hsiao-ping, just as present Mao Zedong was Mao Tse-tung.

that matter, diligence. In accordance with the principle of decentralization, which followed from the antibureaucratic rule, the commune itself determined the rate of pay; the balance of the proceeds went into a fund for the replacement of depreciating capital and for capital investment. The national government obtained its share by determining the buying price of the produce that it obtained from the commune, and the resale price of the produce in the cities. By the principle of decentralization communes were allowed to sell nearby cities their surplus of produce above the amount contracted for by the national government, at a premium price negotiated between the communes and the cities. But the practice of equal pay did not work well, and so, again with peasant pragmatism but with national guidance rather than commune autonomy, it was abandoned in favor of payment according to work units—skilled labor, management, and the like, being awarded more work units than common labor.

Principle was bent in another way. For a time peasant families were permitted only a tiny amount of private production for their own use. A family might have its own pig, or its own vegetable garden. But the virtuous results of permitting a greater amount of private production soon suggested themselves, and after a reversal of permitted practice, according to a very careful and nonideological student of Chinese agriculture, the 5% of China's cropland allowed to remain in private hands produces about one fifth of China's food output.[11]

Food Production

China has greatly increased the amount of machinery in use in agriculture, has expanded and improved its irrigation facilities, and has reclaimed or almost literally constructed some land by diligent toil. For some years Western scholars have thought that Communist China has consistently increased its per capita food production. The facts turn out to be less impressive. One's conclusion of course depends on what year is taken as the base for calculation and on what estimate is made of the rate of population growth. In a very careful collation and analysis of available estimates, a careful scholar estimates that from the disorderly year of 1949 (the year of the Nationalist government's collapse) to 1976, food-grain production rose by about 3.3% per year; from the not very good crop year of 1952, 2.4%; and from the better year of 1957, 2.0%. Depending on which among alternative estimates of population growth one chooses, one concludes that from 1952 to 1976 food-grain production per capita increased annually by just over 0.5 percent, by about 0.3 percent, or by 0.1 percent. Two large-scale surveys

---

[11] Kenneth R. Walker, *Planning in Chinese Agriculture: Socialization and the Private Sector, 1956–62* (Chicago: Aldine, 1965), quoted in Nick Eberstadt, "Has China Failed?," *New York Review of Books*, April 5, 1979, p. 39.

gave estimates of China's food-grain production in the early 1930s. Even if these estimates are adjusted downward for probable overestimate, comparison with estimates for recent years suggests that (depending on one's population growth estimate) per capita food-grain production in the late 1970s was, at best, no greater than in the early 1930s, and may have been appreciably less.[12]

In one sense the explanation is obvious. The pressure of population on the land during the past 45 years has brought diminishing returns which have been just offset by an increase in the amount of capital per worker and by technical advance. (The technical advance has not been merely in capital. Visitors to China from the International Rice Research Institute, where the high-yielding rice of the "Green Revolution" was developed, found that China had bred high-yielding rice before them.) Yet the failure of the intense efforts of the past quarter century to increase per capita yields greatly suggests that some aspects of the agricultural campaign may have been grossly mismanaged.

The failure to achieve a great increase in per capita food-grain production (even while proclaiming the increase) may explain a phenomenon that puzzled Reynolds: the continued import of considerable amounts of grain.

Yet infant mortality in China has decreased greatly—by two thirds or three quarters, Eberstadt estimates—during the Communist period. Hence infant nutrition must have improved greatly. One may reasonably assume that the incidence of starvation and near-starvation in the population in general has decreased correspondingly, for it is only starving mothers who have starving babies. This must be the result of such increase in per capita agricultural production, not merely in the production of food grains, as has occurred, plus increased concern for the public welfare and reasonably efficient management of the distribution of the nation's food supply.

The Revolution of 1977

With the death of Mao and the ending of the influence of his wife Chiang Ching, a virtual revolution in Chinese policy has occurred. Full authority in factory management has been restored or is to be restored to technically competent persons. Examinations again determine advancement in schools and colleges. Technical and scientific research has been resumed. Above all, technical progress is to be achieved, not by the efforts of uninformed workers made capable by being imbued with the proper ideology in a China cut off from the West, but by contact with the West. One may assume that many among the masses of Chinese people still feel the emotional attractiveness of surging from below. Indeed, that surging, reasonably restrained,

---

[12] Eberstadt, "Has China Failed?" All of the data concerning food-grain production are from Eberstadt.

has its economic virtues; the efforts and talents of every worker, not merely of technologists, contribute to increase in productivity. Unrestrained, that surging may overwhelm the new pragmatism. It remains to be seen what policies will prevail in China over the shorter and the longer run, and what economic development will result.

FOR FURTHER READING

Tun Wai, "Interest Rates in the Organized Money Markets of Underdeveloped Countries" and "Interest Rates outside the Organized Money Markets of Underdeveloped Countries," International Monetary Fund *Staff Papers*, August 1956 and November 1957, respectively. Excerpts in G. M. Meier, ed., *Leading Issues in Economic Development*, 3d ed., pp. 299–305.

Concerning China:

Colin Clark, "Economic Development in Communist China," *Journal of Political Economy*, 84 (April 1976), 239–64. Reviews available statistics. Bibliography.

Christopher Howe, *China's Economy: A Basic Guide* (London: Paul Elek, 1978).

World Development, 3 (July–August 1976). Special issue on "China's Road to Development."

Lloyd G. Reynolds, "China as a Less Developed Economy," *American Economic Review*, 65 (June 1975), 418–28.

"China and India: Development during the Last 25 Years," Proceedings of the American Economic Association, 1974. *American Economic Review*, 65 (May 1975), 345–71. Two papers with discussion.

Richard P. Suttmeier, *Research and Development: Scientific, Political, and Societal Change in China* (Lexington, Mass.: Heath 1974).

IV

Resources for Growth

15

Domestic Saving:
Private Sector Sources

In this and the following four chapters the possible sources of resources for capital formation are considered.

THE NEED TO SAVE

Unless there is either saving within a country or an inflow of capital from abroad, there can be no capital formation in the country. The elementary economics of saving and investment are reviewed briefly here by way of introduction. If at full employment all of the income of a country is spent for consumption goods, then (ignoring capital inflow for a moment) all of the country's productive capacity will be occupied producing them. Saving will be necessary if there is to be capital formation. The saving may be by the investing entrepreneur himself, but it need not be. Suppose, for example, that the saver hoards the funds saved, and that a bank creates credit which the investing entrepreneur uses to divert resources from the production of consumer goods to the constructionof capital goods. There will be no excess demand for consumer goods; the effect will be the same as if the entrepreneur himself had done the saving.

The investing may cause the saving. The investor may finance his capital formation with bank-created credit without the simultaneous saving of an equal amount by anyone. Then, when he has bid resources away from the production of consumer goods to the production of capital goods (assuming full employment, so that no idle resources were available), there will be demand for more consumer goods than can be supplied at previous prices, and out of the higher prices that they have been able to charge, dealers will find that they have extra unspent funds on hand—savings.

Low-income economies are open economies. There will be exports and imports. Exports can exceed the imports of consumer goods if there is saving within the country. The excess can be used to import capital goods. In the familiar national accounts equation,

$$Y = C + I + X = C + S + M,$$

where Y = national income or product, C = consumption, I = domestic capital formation, X = exports, S = saving, and M = imports. Therefore,

$$I + X = S + M.$$

Lastly, capital formation may exceed domestic saving by the amount of a capital import. The relevant flows of funds in this case are traced in Chapter 17. The limit to a country's rate of capital formation, then, is its domestic saving plus the amount of capital that the country can attract from abroad.

HOW MUCH SAVING?

The neoclassical economists thought that they knew how to define the optimum rate of saving, and they were willing to accept as sufficient whatever rate of growth resulted from it. The rate of interest, they said, brings to equality the supply of saving and the demand for it for investment. People prefer present goods to an equal amount of future goods. The higher the rate of interest, the more present consumption people will be willing to forgo in order to gain a greater amount of future goods — $(1 + r)^n$ times the value of present goods forgone, where r is the rate of interest per year and n is the number of years for which consumption is postponed. The higher the rate of interest, the smaller the flow that will be borrowed for investment. The rate of interest balances saving and investment, or balances the present and the future. The flow of saving evoked by that rate of interest is the optimum rate, no matter how little economic growth it brings about.

However, many economists now agree with Keynes that a determinant of the interest rate is the desire for liquidity, part of which has nothing to do with balancing present and future, so that the supposed present-future balance function of the interest rate is a myth. In any event, they say, individuals may prefer goods now to goods in the future, but at any future moment their children and even they themselves will prefer a given amount of goods then to an equal amount at the past moment that is now the present. These economists see no reason why in evaluating the welfare of the society as a whole—future welfare as well as present welfare—the present should be given more weight than the future. They argue that this would be true even if the neoclassical conception that the rate of interest reflects the society's present time preference were accepted.

Hence to many economists the concept of an unambiguously defined optimum rate of saving and investment seems to be a will-o'-the-wisp.[1]

However, it is possible to indicate the rate of saving that will be necessary if there is to be economic growth. If capital formation equal to $x\%$ of the gross national product is necessary if there is to be rising per capita income, then saving plus capital inflow equal to $x\%$ of the gross national product must occur. This calculation provides a backdrop against which to appreciate the opening sentence of W. Arthur Lewis's celebrated article, "Economic Development with Unlimited Supplies of Labor":

> "The central problem in the theory of economic development is to understand the process by which a community which was previously saving and investing 4 or 5 percent of its national income or less converts itself into an economy where voluntary saving is running at about 12 to 15 percent of national income or more."[2]

EARLY SOURCES OF SAVINGS

Broadly speaking, there are five and only five possible domestic sources of savings in a nonindustrial low-income economy. Savings may be obtained from (1) agriculture (cultivators or landlords), (2) trader-financiers, or (3) consumers. (4) The saving rate may rise through the increasing plowing back of profits by innovators. (5) In the few fortunate countries rich in petroleum or other mineral resources, the exploitation of those resources will not create saving within the country, but the foreign exchange proceeds from their exploitation may be used in ways precisely parallel to a capital inflow. The broad early bases in all but these few fortunate countries are the first and third. Any of the first three flows may be obtained through private thrift or govermental coercion. In a socialist economy the government may also create the fourth, by setting a wide margin between its production costs and the sales prices of its products.

If a large flow of savings is to be obtained quickly in a traditional economy, part of the value of agricultural production must be siphoned off for investment, since no other sector is large enough to provide a large flow. This may be done by reducing the income of the peasants, the landlords, or the consumers, many of whom will of course be peasants. In a private enterprise economy, this siphoning off will presumably be done by the government by interposing a tax between the cost of production and the retail

---

[1] A. K. Sen discusses these and other considerations in his "On Optimizing the Rate of Saving," *Economic Journal*, 71 (September 1961), 479–95.

[2] "Economic Development with Unlimited Supplies of Labor," *Manchester School*, 22 (May 1954), 139–91. See also Lewis's article in the January 1958 issue of the *Manchester School* (vol. 26, pp. 1–32), "Unlimited Supplies of Labor: Further Notes." Lewis referred to net saving, but his statement is also reasonable if it is applied to gross saving.

price of mass-consumed goods; in a socialist economy, it may be done by interposing a markup on the price of the goods as they pass through the hands of the state. Japan financed rapid industrialization by siphoning off the large stream of income that had previously gone to the feudal lords. The Soviet Union did so by imposing forced levies on the peasants and by imposing a large markup, only part of which was a substitute for the "rent" previously taken by feudal landlords. However, except after a revolution that changes the political structure drastically, as occurred in Japan and the Soviet Union, apart from the mineral resource cases the financing of early growth is virtually always by private initiative and from private sources. Virtually no government still controlled by traditionally powerful groups is ready to take the actions needed to divert energies from traditionally satisfying activities to the management of development, and to divert resources from traditional uses to investment. Only after a corps of private individuals in the country has entered upon growth may that new group provide the political demand and support for effective government action.

Since early investment is largely by the savers themselves, we may consider together each type of investment and the source of saving for it.

Landlord Entrepreneurship

In at least three historical cases, landowners have been contributors in important amounts to investment and progress in agriculture. In England, nobles and members of the landed gentry carried out the enclosures, and later, in the 18th century, both groups conceived of new projects connected with the land and invested large amounts of money in them: new methods of cultivation, toll roads, and canals. They were the entrepreneurs as well as the investors. In Germany, the Junkers carried out changes in agricultural methods that required both their personal involvement and, in some cases, sizable investments. And in Japan, which in this respect as in so many others is a special case, landlords and peasants have cooperated, with initiative from both, in technical progress. There are records of increases in agricultural yields during the Ashikaga period, 1336–1582.[3] It is not clear whether landlord-peasant cooperation, with dual initiative, was the vehicle at this early period, but it clearly was the vehicle from the early Tokugawa period until the end of landlordism after World War II.

The Expansion of Peasant Production

Peasants have occasionally flooded onto empty lands (and produced crops by traditional methods) when world markets were opened to them.

---

[3] These are discussed in E. O. Reischauer and J. K. Fairbank, *East Asia: The Great Tradition* (Boston: Houghton Mifflin, 1958), p. 557.

This development required investment to clear the new lands and plant the crops, and a "wages fund" to sustain the peasants while they carried out the investment. In both Southeast Asia and West Africa idle land was available, needing only to be cleared and planted. The nation's moneylenders provided the "wages fund" on which the peasants lived for a year, and the peasants cleared the land and planted the crop. Since the increase in the value of the land was more than the amount of the year's subsistence, the peasants should be regarded as having contributed saving, in kind, by their labor. The moneylenders were glad, even eager, to lend additional sums against the security of the land,and many peasants, living extravagantly for the time being, could not repay out of their annual harvests and soon lost their land. "The "subsistence fund" which the moneylenders had advanced was recouped with a large capital gain. By this process large areas were opened up, production was greatly expanded, and the peasants' income level was, on the average, undoubtedly raised.

Shopkeepers also made advances to peasants against the next harvest. The loans by moneylenders, for either production or consumption, were (and are) at very high interest rates, justified in the moneylender's eyes by the alternatives open to him, the cost of making small loans, and the risk, and paid by the peasant for lack of alternative sources of funds.

Trade and Commerce

Early innovation in trade and commerce has usually been financed by the traders themselves, who came into the business from other countries with resources previously accumulated, or plowed back profits from local trading.

Industry: Plowing Back Profits—The Lewis Model

The contribution of the landed class to savings to finance industrial ventures has not been large in any country until growth was far advanced. In the Middle East some large landowners have since 1950 established manufacturing plants to process the products of their lands. Neither has the financing come in any large flow from merchant-financiers as a group, because of the mentality sketched in Chapter 13 in discussing entrepreneurship. Nor from small craftsmen as a group. But some craftsmen-traders whose small businesses had prospered through their capability became industrial innovators, and some merchants whose larger businesses had prospered through their capability became industrial innovators. They themselves or their families or friends financed their start in industry. Of the initial funds of 486 industrial enterprises in Nigeria surveyed in 1965, more than two thirds (68%) were financed from the entrepreneur's own savings, loans or gifts from his family, or loans or gifts from his friends. The banks provided 6% of the funds; moneylenders, 2%; and suppliers, 7%. The remaining 17% were loans from Nigerian investors, loans from the government, loans from or investment by foreigners resident in Nigeria, and in one case investment by the government.[4]

Once such persons had established small industrial enterprises, if the enterprises were successful, the entrepreneurs financed expansion by plowing back profits. A small producer devised an improvement which increased quality or reduced costs. A profit margin appeared. He lived frugally, expanded his business from his earnings, and in, say, 25 years he became a major industrialist. A reader of the biographies of early industrialists in the West is impressed by the frequency of this route to industrial success. It is, wrote W. Arthur Lewis in the 1954 article that has been mentioned, not only the source of funds for industry but the major source of increase in savings in a low-income country as a whole. "A country's saving rate is low," Lewis wrote, "not because the country is poor but because its capitalist class is small." As those of the country's businesspersons who have capitalist temperaments invest, profit, save, and invest, the saving rate and the investment rate rise and growth proceeds.

Lewis's model accounts not only for funds for industrial investment but also for the availability of labor. In his model, there are many workers with "zero or negligible" productivity in agriculture or employed as retainers, but they are not available to industrial employers at a wage equal to their productivity, for as family members or retainers they are provided a subsistence income on peasant farms or by their patrons. But this labor is available in "unlimited" quantites at a wage equal to the subsistence level of living plus a margin sufficient to overcome the friction of moving from the "subsistence sector" to the "capitalist sector." I shall term this wage the "subsistence-plus" wage.

Central aspects of the model are presented in Figure 15–1. In this figure, the quantity of labor employed in the capitalist sector is measured on the horizontal axis, and output and real income are measured on the vertical axis. OS is the subsistence level of earnings, OW the subsistence-plus wage of the capitalist sector, and the curve N_1O_1 represents the marginal productivity of the labor being employed with a given quantity of capital. The capitalist-employer will add labor until its marginal productivity has fallen to equality with the wage. The area N_1O_1W represents his "profits," using that term to refer to return on capital as well as profits above that amount.

The capitalist is a saver and investor. By plowing back those profits into more capital, he will raise the marginal productivity of labor to the curve N_2 and increase his employment to the amount Q_2. And on to N_3Q_3, N_4Q_4,

[4] J. R. Harris, "The Development of Industrial Entrepreneurship in Nigeria," unpublished doctoral dissertation, Department of Economics, Northwestern University, 1967. Harris's survey included all sources from which one fourth or more of the capital had been obtained.

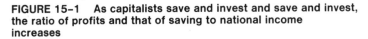

FIGURE 15-1   As capitalists save and invest and save and invest, the ratio of profits and that of saving to national income increases

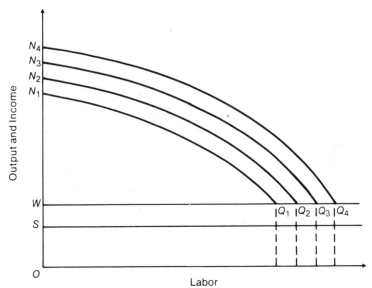

and so on. The many "little islands" of which the capitalist sector consists will grow, the ratio of profits to national income will grow, and because capitalists are high savers, the ratio of saving to national income will grow.

Industry: Dualistic Models—Fei-Ranis

Lewis's model is of course a two-sector model. His sectors are the subsistence and capitalistic sectors. John Fei and Gustav Ranis have presented a model based on the idea that since agriculture is the only preindustrial sector with large aggregate income the use of an agricultural surplus in industry must be financed by saving in the agricultural sector.[5] In their model the sectors are agriculture and industry.

The two writers explicitly make the marginal productivity of a considerable share of agricultural labor zero. Workers can therefore leave the agricultural sector without reduction in agricultural production. The consumption per capita of remaining cultivators in the model remains constant. The food previously consumed by the workers who transfer to industry is therefore available to be sold to the industrial sector, where the new

---

[5] *Development of the Labor Surplus Economy* (Homewood, Ill.: Richard D. Irwin, 1964). In an article in the September 1961 *American Economic Review* (vol. 51, pp. 533–65), they present the core of the argument.

industrial workers buy it out of their wages. All of these workers can be employed in producing capital goods, for there is no increase in the aggregate demand for consumer goods, since (in the model) all of the income received by agriculture from the sale of this food is saved. The savers become owners of industrial capital. The model is thus consistent; there is a flow of workers into industry and a flow of saving from agriculture to permit their use in capital formation rather than in the production of consumer goods.

The assumptions underlying the model have some peculiar implications, however. Who would give workers with zero marginal productivity employment in agriculture? Not the landlords, except for the tiny number of family retainers. The realistic explanation is that these workers are members of peasant families, which will not turn away members to starve. However, there is ample evidence that peasants whose income rises increase their consumption. Thus if redundant peasant family members shifted to industry, in this way increasing the per capita income of the families they left, those families would provide none or only a share (probably a small share) of the saving needed to support the migrant workers in capital formation. If the workers were agricultural wage workers, they would presumably have been contributing to production an amount equal to their wages. With their departure, their erstwhile agricutural employers presumably would not increase their consumption, but agricultural production would decrease, so that in this case too there would be no surplus to transfer.

The model is unrealistic in three important respects. (1) The transfer of savings from agriculture is not necessary for the establishment of industry. (2) Surplus workers in agriculture do not carry their consumer bundle with them. (3) If taxation or other governmental coercion is used to extract the savings, then there is no need for the elaborate model. By reducing consumption, the governmental measures will free labor somewhere for use in capital formation.

Lewis's model, in which the saving occurs within nascent industry itself, is more realistic and more useful.

LATER STAGES OF DEVELOPMENT

Marginal Saving Rates

An increased flow of saving and investment by entrepreneurs (or, in Lewis's term, capitalists) brings a rising level of income and is associated with it. As income rises, an increasing flow of individual savings is invested in savings institutions and is thus made available to investors. Government captures an increasing share of the national income in taxes, and an increasing share of government expenditures can, if desired, be devoted to public capital formation. The question arises: Can the percentage of private income saved, plus the willingness of citizens to bear increasing taxes and of the government to hold down its consumption expenditures, be expected to rise sufficiently with rising income to finance an expanding development program?

Many persons hoping for the rapid development of the less developed countries have placed high hope on the marginal saving ratio. If a country begins to develop so that its per capita income begins to rise, then out of the higher income surely private individuals, and the government through taxation, can be expected to save a larger share of income. If they do, the average saving ratio will rise steadily and the country will become increasingly capable of financing its own domestic investment (though not necessarily the foreign exchange cost of that investment). If a country with per capita national income of $100 saves 8% of it, and if it saves one fifth of increments in income, then when income has risen to $150 per capita the average saving ratio will have risen to 12%.

However, the Duesenberry study of saving in the United States[6] makes it seem very unlikely that average private saving rates will rise cumulatively as income rises. Duesenberry's study indicates that the share of an unanticipated increment of income saved is larger than the average ratio of saving to income, but that people's consumption habits soon "catch up" with their income; people consume as large a share of higher income as of lower income, as soon as they become used to higher income. If a succession of annual increases in income occur, only out of the last increment would an increased share be saved. For the same reason, proposals for heavy taxation of increases in income would meet strong opposition. In any event, it is very difficult to administer a tax levied specifically on increases in income rather than the level of income.

The empirical evidence is contradictory.

Careful and complex research concerning Latin American countries indicates that in the 1950s and part of the 1960s the percentage of income saved did not rise as income rose. Raymond V. Mikesell and J. E. Zinser, in a survey of studies of saving-income relationships in LDCs, presented a study for almost all Latin American countries for periods between 1953 and 1968.[7] Hollis Chenery and Peter Eckstein calculated coefficients of saving on income for each of 16 Latin American countries for the period 1950–64, or about that.[8] Both studies analyzed the change in individual countries over time. In both studies the median and average ratios of saving to national product were between 10% and 15%, and in neither study was the marginal ratio consistently above the average ratio. Between 1951 and

---

[6] James S. Duesenberry, *Income, Saving, and the Theory of Consumer Behavior* (Cambridge, Mass.: Harvard University Press, 1949).

[7] "The Nature of the Savings Function in Developing Countries: A Survey of the Theoretical and Empirical Literature," *Journal of Economic Literature*, 11 (March 1973), 1–26.

[8] "Development Alternatives for Latin America," *Journal of Political Economy*, 78 (July 1970), 966–1006.

1964, per capita income in the 16 Latin American countries rose markedly, on the average—probably by 20% or more. Chenery and Eckstein note that during that period on average saving rate rose only from 16.3% to 16.9%. This very small rise is well within the probable error of the estimates.

On the other hand, in a cross-national study of 20 Latin American countries, Luis Landau found a statistically significant association between the percentage of national income saved and the level of per capita income.[9] S. K. Singh found the same relationship in a cross-national study of 70 countries for 1960–65.[10]

These studies seem to contradict the Mikesell-Zinser and Chenery-Eckstein analyses. In fact they may not. The following alternative explanation is possible. The percentage of income saved was not higher in higher income countries because of their higher level of income. The higher income countries are higher income countries because from the time when they were lower income countries they were higher savers and investors, and presumably also more effective innovators. What Landau and Singh found was differences among countries, not differences in saving propensities as income rose.[11]

But now there is further evidence. Of 18 countries with per capita incomes of $250 or less in 1976 in which per capita income rose between 1960 and 1976, the ratio of gross domestic saving to gross domestic product fell in 10 and rose in only 8. But of 44 higher-income "developing" countries in which per capita income rose, the saving ratio rose in 33 and fell in only 12.[12]

One cannot draw firm conclusions concerning the present causal saving-income relationship from these several sets of data. The only sure conclusion one can draw is that the middle-income countries, in which per capita

---

[9] "Differences in Saving Ratios among Latin American Countries," unpublished doctoral dissertation, Department of Economics, Harvard University, 1969. A condensed version is presented in *Studies in Development Planning*, ed. H. Chenery (Cambridge, Mass.: Harvard University Press, 1971).

[10] *Development Economics: Theory and Findings* (Lexington, Mass., Heath, 1972).

[11] Because the income level–saving rate relationship in his data holds in short-run time series as well as in cross-national analysis, Landau concludes that the income level is causal. The evidence of the other analysts, which justifies the opposite conclusion, is more broadly based.

Mikesell and Zinser calculated estimates of the elasticity of saving with respect to income, an indication of whether savings were rising more rapidly than income. For only 6 of the 18 countries was the elasticity above unity.

[12] The data are from annex table 5, *World Development Report, 1978*, p. 84. In the text of that *Report* (p. 6), a table is presented which states that in 1960 and 1975 the ratios of gross domestic saving to gross domestic product for the two country groups were:

	1960	1976
Low-income countries	11.6%	15.6%
Middle-income countries	17.8	22.1

The apparent discrepancy between this tabulation and annex table 5 is not explained. In any event, the data for individual countries are pertinent here.

FIGURE 15-2 Savings as percent of GDP are loosely related to per capita rate of growth (less developed countries)

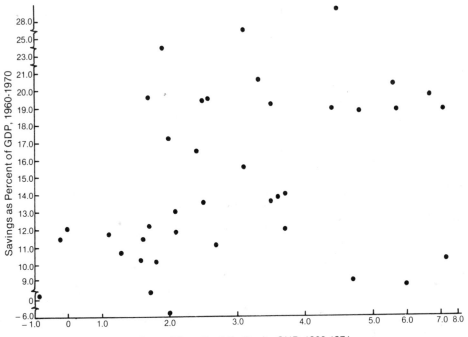

Rate of Growth of Per Capita GNP, 1960-1971

Source: Per capita rates of growth, *World Bank Atlas, 1973*; Savings, Economic Analyses and Projections Department, World Bank.

income was rising faster than in the low-income countries, were in fact saving a higher share of their incomes in 1976 than they had been saving in 1960.

Figure 15-2 presents data showing the relationship between the rate of growth of per capita income and the saving rate. The scatter is very wide, but there is a diffuse positive relationship. This may be interpreted as indicating that a high saving rate, permitting a high investment rate, causes a high growth rate. The converse causal interpretation is also possible. When income is rising rapidly, the increase in consumption lags behind it; hence the saving rate is high. Rapid growth provides nourishment for itself. This is a plausible explanation not only of such extreme phenomena as the extremely high Japanese saving rate but also of moderate differences in saving rates associated with more moderate differences in growth rates.

Interest Rates and Saving Rates

Growth in South Korea and Taiwan during the 1960s is discussed briefly in Chapter 21. Edward S. Shaw and Ronald McKinnon claim that the high interest rates that then prevailed in these countries stimulated very large flows of savings and accumulations of financial assets. The rates of interest on one-year deposits exceeded the rate of change in the wholesale price index by 18.6% at the peak in Taiwan, and by 22.1% in South Korea.[13]

These interest rates must have significantly stimulated saving. That the high saving and accumulation resulted primarily from the high interest rates is uncertain. The two countries were growing very rapidly, partly because of governmental policies favorable to growth, probably partly because of national characteristics of the people, and partly because high American military demand for exports during part of the period gave innovational entrepreneurs handsome opportunities that they took advantage of—as well as because high saving rates and capital inflow made possible high rates of investment. McKinnon himself unwittingly illustrates the effect of the high growth rates on saving when he quotes the following conversation (p. 123): Economist: "Why do the Japanese save so much?" Man on a Tokyo street: "Because our income grows so fast." For Tokyo, substitute Seoul or Taipeh.

Institutional Supports

The discussion thus far in this chapter has ignored the channels through which savings flow from the saver to the investor, if these are not the same person. Such channels, when the country has developed sufficiently for them to function well, not only improve the allocation of resources; they probably also increase the aggregate flow of saving.

Direct lending by the owner of money to the user is as old as human specialization. Traders, whose principle of business is to operate to as large an extent as possible with someone else's capital, early develop the practices of obtaining or extending commercial credit, borrowing or lending on the security of goods, and transmitting funds via commercial banks or their equivalent. Moneylenders lend to peasants on the security of a forthcoming crop, or, where land is alienable, on the security of land. Pawnshops flourish in probably every low-income country. In many parts of Africa, Latin America, the Middle East, and East and Southeast Asia, peasants and other villagers form rotating credit associations, in which every member contributes regularly to a fund, the whole of which is given to each member in turn. Thus each month, say, one member will have at his command a fairly large sum which he would not have had the willpower to accumulate by himself.[14] Producers' cooperatives or cooperative marketing associations are much less common and less viable. Often fostered by the government, they often wither and die.

---

[13] For references to the work of Shaw and McKinnon, see Chapter 21.

[14] F. J. A. Bouman, "Indigenous Savings and Credit Societies in the Third World," *Development Digest*, 16 (July 1978), 36–47, analyzes the functioning of these societies.

Apart from saving through rotating credit associations, where they exist, the first regular saving by the members of low-income societies is usually in anticipation of death—saving to cover at least burial expenses. An early sign of economic development is the appearance of insurance companies whose business includes so-called industrial life insurance (which has nothing to do with industry). The agent appears at the door weekly to collect the petty premium.

Savings banks and savings and loan associations first come into their own in cities, and after development is under way. Large capital market intermediaries—investment banks and securities markets—appear much later. Capital markets cannot be created by fiat, or by erecting on paper a set of institutions that would be capital markets if only people used them. Before they can function effectively, a number of concepts alien to traditional societies must become accepted and embedded in institutions.These include the concepts of: that impersonal legal person, the corporation; the dependability of impersonal contractual obligations, because of the attitudes of the business community (more than through action in the courts); the security of paper claims; the anticipation of future production as wealth.

By the criteria used by U Tun Wai, a staff member of the International Monetary Fund, in the mid-1950s capital market transactions in Latin America were significant in scope only in Chile, Colombia, Cuba, and Peru; and in Asia, only in Japan and in limited degree in India, where securities markets played some role in the accumulation of capital by large corporations. Shares of stock were marketed as early as the 1880s in Japan, when industrialization was in its infancy, but even after World War II there was no public market for government bonds. The government sells its bonds through a process of allocation of quotas to the commercial banks, which the banks by convention are obliged to accept.

In 1973, 16 years after U Tun Wai's first survey, he and Hugh Patrick surveyed capital markets again. They found little further development. They wrote:

> With only a few exceptions (for example, in Brazil, India, Malaysia, and Singapore), markets are thin, with little or no trading and with relatively few and insignificant amounts of new public issues by private corporations. With a somewhat larger amount of issue, the market for government debt may appear to be more developed, but its sales are mainly to captive buyers. Information is poor and manipulation is substantial, especially for private issues.[15]

---

[15] See Tun Wai, "Interest Rates outside the organized Money Markets of Underdeveloped Countries," *International Monetary Fund Staff Papers,* 5 (November 1957) 249–78 (excerpts reprinted in *Leading Issues in Development Economics,* 3d ed., ed. G. M. Meier [New York: Oxford University Press, 1976]), pp. 299–305; and Tun Wai and H. T. Patrick, *Stock and Bond Issues and Capital Markets in Less Developed Countries,* Paper no. 200 (New Haven: Yale University Center for Quantitative Studies in Growth, 1973).

The role of "wildcat banks" in the United States during the several decades before the Civil War and that of private joint-stock banks in France and Germany and neighboring countries beginning in the 19th century have been discussed in Chapter 14.

The existence in the United States of a very active market for equity and debt securities has relieved U.S. corporations of the necessity for sponsorship by such financial institutions. The U.S. capital market is the freest in the world, the only one in which foreign securities may be floated without any government sanction except to ensure the validity of the issues and the accuracy of the information provided concerning them.[16] In some countries, for example Japan, sponsorship by a large bank is a necessary aspect of the life of a large corporation. The corporation receives all of its capital, throughout its life, from that bank.

In the less developed countries, there has been a great vogue of formation of government development banks or development corporations. These, however, have commonly served more as merely financing agencies than as entrepreneurial agencies.

LABOR-INTENSIVE CAPITAL PROJECTS

In both low- and middle-income economies there may be either rural underemployment or potential rural underemployment that causes the flight of workers to the cities. It has been suggested by various writers that the "hidden rural savings" (Nurkse's term) embodied in the underused labor of low-productivity agricultural workers can be captured directly, by drawing those workers into labor-intensive rural capital projects. If those workers have zero productivity, the social cost—loss of other output—is zero, it is said; if they have positive but low productivity, the cost is low. Dams, irrigation or drainage channels, wells, roads, village water reservoirs, rude village schools, riverbank improvements to contain rivers in floodtime—all these and other rural public works call out to be constructed. Government action to mobilize such labor in the construction of such projects has been urged. Even if the notion that the marginal productivity of labor is zero is quite incorrect, the low productivity of the rapidly growing or disemployed labor force would make such employment appropriate.

The cost to society of the projects would of course not be zero. In the first place, workers cannot build projects by labor-intensive methods with their bare hands. There must be some cooperating capital equipment, even if not large modern bulldozers, trucks, and the like. In addition to equip-

---

[16] At the height of the U.S. balance of payments crisis in the late 1950s, the U.S. government levied a 15% tax on the purchase of foreign securities not already owned within the United States, and the transfer of funds abroad by American operations was regulated by the U.S. government.

ment used directly in the project, if the project is a large one, a community must be constructed in which the workers can live.

There are also other costs. For large projects the greatest may be the cost of management. There are few models of labor-intensive projects. A partly original engineering design may be required. Innovational engineers and capable administrators are in general among the scarcest resources of LDCs. If management of the needed quality is diverted from other work important in economic development, the cost may be high.

These considerations suggest that the labor-intensive projects that promise the greatest benefit may be small rural ones that are simple enough to make elaborate engineering design unnecessary and that are near the homes of the workers who will be employed, to minimize food transport and the provision of housing. There are certainly many of these that can be done advantageously, and even if the financial cost is as great as it would be with capital-intensive methods, the social cost is low, for the labor is, in social terms, costless, and such works increase productivity and real income as truly as does more conventional capital formation.

Increased goods will have to be provided for consumption, for two reasons: because the erstwhile underemployed or unemployed workers will eat more and probably purchase more clothes, and because the cultivator families from which they were drawn, having higher income per remaining member, will consume more. Insofar as the country itself can produce these items which constitute the increase in real income of the workers, everyone should rejoice. If some of the goods, for example food, must be imported, then a government that does not rate the welfare of its rural families high relative to its "modernization aims" may be concerned about the drain on its foreign exchange. The United States has tried to alleviate this problem and at the same time alleviate its own farm produce surplus by offering surplus commodities on concessional terms.

One of the best-known successful programs for the use of underemployed labor to construct labor-intensive public works is the program executed in Bangladesh, then East Pakistan, between the years 1962 and 1968. During those years the local councils of East Pakistan spent the equivalent of $149 million for rural projects. The U.S. government provided surplus agricultural commodities, financed by a loan payable in rupees, in a much larger amount, part being precisely in consideration of this rural works program. The $149 million expenditure was financed from the sale of these commodities. After 1965, because world demand during a period of poor harvests drained U.S. food reserves, fewer surplus commodities could be made available. The Pakistani government reduced the size of the program accordingly, and it apparently had dwindled to nonexistence some time before the Bangladesh war for independence disrupted the society. It had been opposed, and where possible obstructed, by landlords because of the lessened dependence of peasants and the increased cost of agricultural wage labor that occurred even though the work was performed mainly in the off-season. That increase testifies that the labor employed had not been entirely unproductive previously.[17]

FOR FURTHER READING

W. Arthur Lewis's articles cited in note 2 are basic theoretical papers.

The reader interested in marginal saving rates may wish to read in their entirety the works by Mikesell and Zinser, Chenery and Eckstein, Landau, and Singh cited in notes 7–10 of this chapter.

Dualistic Models

A somewhat ponderous presention of dualistic theory in relation to saving and capital formation is the volume by John C. H. Fei and Gustav Ranis cited in note 5 of this chapter. Two articles by Dale W. Jorgenson, "The Development of a Dual Economy," *Economic Journal*, 71 (June 1961), 309–34, and "Surplus Agricultural Labor and the Development of a Dual Economy," *Oxford Economic Papers*, n.s. 19 (1967), 288–312, are indispensable in the advanced theory of the subject. Douglas Paauw and John Fei relate theory to Southeast Asian experience in an illuminating way in *The Transition in Open Dualistic Societies* (New Haven: Yale University Press, 1973). G. M. Meier, *Leading Issues in Development Theory*, 3d ed., chap. 3, excerpts other papers on dualism and the labor surplus economy.

---

[17] See John W. Thomas, "Rural Public Works and East Pakistan's Development," Development Advisory Service Economic Development Report no. 112, mimeographed (Cambridge, Mass.: Harvard University, 1968); or, for a brief account, of the initiation of the program, R. V. Gilbert, "The Works Programme in East Pakistan," *International Labor Review*, 39 (March 1964), 213–26.

16

Monetary, Tax, and Fiscal Policy; Inflation

MONETARY POLICY'S LIMITED ROLE

The very important question of the effects of legal limits on interest rates is discussed in Chapter 21. Apart from the decision of whether to impose the limits, monetary policy can do much less in the LDCs than in the MDCs to influence the flow of resources into investment, because the institutions by which monetary influence can be wielded are rudimentary or at least less developed in the LDCs. Virtually all of the LDCs have monetary agencies if not central banks, but the commercial banks depend very little on these for their loanable funds, and the central banks or the monetary agencies therefore have no levers by which to influence the availability of funds to borrowers. Much commercial banking is by branches of foreign banks, which have their own sources of funds: their head offices. Open-market operations by the central bank are not possible, because open markets—large impersonal markets for securities—do not exist.

TAX STRUCTURE AND TAX POLICY

In the lowest income countries, the traditional sources of governmental revenue are traditional types of direct taxes. In Asia, land taxes were most important; in Africa, head taxes; and in some countries, taxes on livestock.

Taxes on land are only roughly equitable. Yet in less developed countries they have much to recommend them. They obtain revenue. If landownership is concentrated, their incidence is on a high-income group. If landowners were collecting approximately the maximum feasible rent before the land tax was imposed, they cannot pass any great share of the tax back to renters.

In few of the LDCs is it feasible to levy the types of direct taxes that are levied in economically advanced countries. An income tax can be collected from the affluent only if the administrative honesty and the efficiency of government employees are at a high level, if business institutions have become sufficiently complex to require the keeping of fairly complex financial records, and if political and social attitudes are such that it is possible to levy an income tax on economically powerful and socially eminent individuals, and to collect it if levied. In all or almost all of the lowest income countries none of these conditions exists. A proposal in Guatemala in 1966–67 for a personal income tax rising to 4% at high incomes was blocked by a group of politically powerful high-income individuals who denounced it as communistic. Similarly, inheritance taxes cannot be collected.

When the stir of economic development has begun and more widespread education and better infrastructure are wanted, government expenditures increase faster than GNP does. The government turns to export taxes, tariffs on imports, and taxes on goods—and also begins to spend more than its revenues. H. H. Hinrichs has shown that the governments of the lowest income countries depend on traditional direct taxes; that even counting export taxes as direct taxes, the governments of middle-income countries obtain more than one half of their revenues from indirect taxes; and that in advanced countries direct taxes are again made the main source of revenue. Also, the budgets of the lowest income countries are balanced, deficits grow as income rises, and deficits shrink again as countries reach high-income levels.[1]

Even apart from the countries that are able to form cartels or cartellike agreements, export taxes will be the greatest source of revenues in countries in which a single basic commodity looms large among exports. Since the tax will rarely affect the world price appreciably, it is borne by the producers within the country, whether large mineral-extracting firms or small low-income producers. A margin extracted by a government marketing board has the same incidence.

In other countries import duties will usually loom large among indirect taxes. Hinrichs showed that a good rule of thumb estimator of the ratio of government revenues to national product in LDCs is the formula: 5% plus one half of the percentage of imports to national product.

The canons of tax theory suggest that indirect taxes should be collected at the final point of sale to prevent "pyramiding." However, in less developed countries an indirect tax on a commodity may be more equitable if it is collected at the point of manufacture or import, for with tax administration considerably less than perfectly efficient, the prospect of actual col-

---

[1] H. H. Hinrichs, *A General Theory of Tax Structure Change during Economic Development* (Cambridge, Mass.: Harvard Law School, 1966).

lection at the point of manufacture or import is better than when the commodity has entered the channels of trade. Selective excises or customs duties, on items consumed mainly by the well-to-do, may have a higher degree of progressivity than any other taxes, even though their incidence is uneven among persons of the same income level.

FISCAL POLICY

As incomes rise, consumer demand for services increases more rapidly than do other consumer expenditures, and more rapidly than consumer incomes. This tendency extends to government services, whether voted by legislatures or decreed by authoritarian rulers to meet public demand. One would therefore expect to find general (or "final") government consumption expenditures a higher percentage of GDP in high-income than in low-income countries, as Figure 16–1 indicates, though the wide scatter in that table indicates that many specific circumstances affect individual countries. ("General government consumption expenditures" exclude capital expenditures, transfer payments, interest on the public debt, and the expenditures of commercial government corporations, as well as minor items not for the purchase of goods or services.)

When Alison Martin and W. Arthur Lewis separated "basic" government expenditures from those for defense, public debt, and agricultural subsidies, for six high-income countries and ten low-income countries, for years shortly after World War II, they found very little difference in the percentages of national income spent for the "basic" purposes.[2] Yet there is a difference for total general government expenditures. A trend line drawn or computed to fit the data of Figure 16–1 would trend significantly upward.

But the percentage for the low-income countries is certainly much more than it was for the present high-income countries in the past, when they had low incomes. There has been a secular change in the role that government is expected to play. In view of present attitudes, if the present LDCs rise to present high-income levels they will probably devote a significantly higher share of their GNPs to government consumption expenditures than the high-income countries now do.

The major cause of increased government consumption expenditures in the lower income countries is the demand for services such as education, health care, and medical care. Meeting that demand may have been facilitated since World War II by the extension of economic aid, which by financing some governmental expenditures for infrastructure and other development purposes made it easier for LDC governments to spend their

---

[2] A. Martin and W. A. Lewis, "Patterns of Public Revenue and Expenditure," *Manchester School*, 24 (September 1956), 203–44.

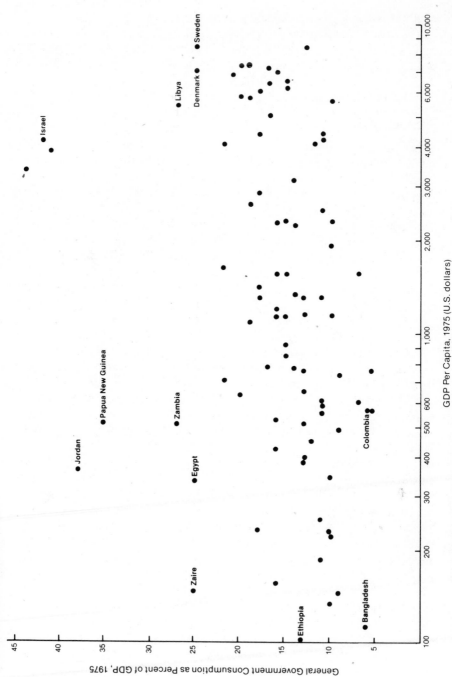

FIGURE 16–1 High-income countries use a larger proportion of GNP to provide government services than do low-income countries, but the scatter is wide

General Government Consumption as Percent of GDP, 1975

GDP Per Capita, 1975 (U.S. dollars)

Source: United Nations Yearbook of National Accounts Statistics, 1977.

own funds for social services. However, as noted, the governments of many LDCs also resort to deficit financing.

NONINFLATIONARY DEFICIT FINANCE

Deficit financing is noninflationary if it is merely the spending abroad, to purchase capital or other goods for import, of funds which the government has previously accumulated abroad or can borrow abroad. The deficit financing of expenditures within the country is also noninflationary if it merely meets the need or desire of individuals and firms to hold more money.

As GDP rises, individuals and firms hold more money. As farmers shift from subsistence farming to production for the market, they tend to increase the amount of money they hold on hand by a larger ratio than the

FIGURE 16-2   Does the money/GDP ratio rise as the level of per capita GDP rises?

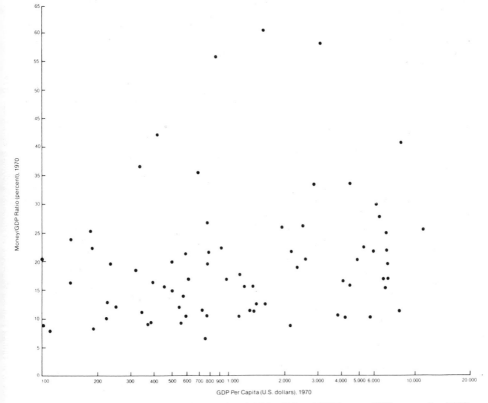

Sources: Money/GDP ratio—*International Financial Statistics*, 1972 issues; GDP per capita, 1970— United Nations *Yearbook of National Accounts Statistics*, 1972, vol. 3.

increase in their incomes. This is also true, though presumably to a lesser degree, of other individuals as their incomes rise. This tendency, however, largely is offset by improvements in transportation and communication and in bank check clearing systems which permit business to be handled with smaller cash balances. The money-GDP ratio varies so greatly among countries with differing financial institutions that it is difficult to judge whether it varies with the level of income, but perhaps Figure 16–2 shows a slight tendency for the ratio to rise as per capita GDP rises.

In a typical LDC, the money supply is some 10% to 20% of GDP—for easy computation, say 15%. If GDP is rising at 5% per year, the money supply must be expanded annually by 0.75% of GDP to hold the ratio to GDP constant, and by a slightly larger amount if the need or the desire to hold money is increasing faster than GDP. This is a significant amount. The expansion in money supply is much less likely in LDCs than in MDCs to occur by the expansion of commercial bank credit, since commercial banking is not well developed in LDCs. The expansion may occur if private firms are able to borrow abroad for expenditure within the country, and obtain the local currency by selling their foreign exchange to the monetary authority. Where this does not occur in sufficient amount, the government should run a deficit to provide the monetary expansion.

Lastly, deficit financing may be noninflationary if it counters unemployment. The danger of inflation from the resulting increase in demand is like that from any increase in demand not associated with an increase in supply, for example, one caused by increased investment. The prices of some goods whose supply cannot be increased quickly will be bid up. The increased demand for imports may cause foreign exchange difficulties.

INFLATION AND ECONOMIC GROWTH: DEMAND-PULL INFLATION

If government deficit expenditure or private investment occurs in a magnitude that causes inflation, does the inflation accelerate or retard economic growth? Does economic growth necessarily cause inflation ultimately? These questions divide theorists and economic growth practitioners alike.

Inflation may be due to the upward pull of excessive aggregate demand or the upward push of costs. Consider demand-pull inflation first.

The governments of less developed countries may engage in deficit financing to the point of inflation, even rather rapid inflation, not to increase aggregate demand for its own sake, but to divert resources to investment, for example the construction of infrastructure, by creating new money and hiring the resources with it. The immediate result is to increase the share of capital formation in the GDP. However, inflationary spending cannot achieve and maintain more than a minor increase in the share of capital formation, for the added money incomes created by inflation increase the demand for consumer goods and may draw workers and materials back into their production. Investment gains only if it "keeps ahead of the multiplier." The policy questions are whether, if a significant degree of inflation results, the aggregate level of productive investment will be larger in the somewhat longer run, and, if it is larger, whether the other effects of the inflation constitute a cost too great to justify the benefit.

Growth-Stimulating Effects

One basic argument in favor of the policy is that the developmental projects are executed. Resources are diverted, and idle resources are drawn into use. It may have been impossible to levy or collect the necessary taxes, but inflation requires no administrative skill.

Second, it is argued that mild inflation diverts income to the mercantile and industrial classes, who are the saving and investing classes. This redistribution of income in itself increases the share of the nation's product that will be used for developmental purposes. The argument is sound, provided that entrepreneurial spirit exists among these classes, that the inflation continues to be mild, and that effective countermeasures to prevent the redistribution of income to higher income groups are not adopted by other groups. A country must be both wise and lucky to meet these requirements.

It is argued that inflation need be neither extreme nor prolonged. The investment projects being carried on in a country may include some that will permit the expansion of production in a short time: the import of fertilizer, the digging of tube wells, the construction of factories that will quickly begin the production of goods much in demand. If the investment consists of such projects and the supply of goods soon increases, the inflation may end. But limiting government deficit-financed investment to such a carefully calculated level and nature is "fine tuning" that is not likely to be achieved in practice if the urge to spend in order to develop exists.

It is suggested that the country may be more certain of a quick end to the inflation if the government either operates the projects, so that increased profits flow to the government or siphons off a share of the increased profits in taxes. If the government can operate the projects efficiently—an important qualification—it will receive the profits, but the question remains whether the government itself can or will wish to resist the temptation to respend the increased income. Whether the tax system will act in an anti-inflationary manner depends on its nature. Where the corporate profits tax and the graduated personal income tax are absent, or not collected, inflation is likely to increase a government's cost more rapidly than its revenues. On balance, inflation may feed the deficit and become chronic.

Evils

A major argument against the inflationary finance of development projects is that the inflation will become chronic or perhaps even accelerating. One element of this argument has just been stated. Another is the assertion that once inflation has begun, a cost-push process is likely to keep it going, in the way discussed later in this chapter.

Moreover, inflation, by raising domestic prices relative to foreign prices, tends both to divert to the domestic market some output formerly exported and to encourage imports. Thus it worsens the balance of payments. This imbalance may be corrected by devaluation or increased protectionism. Either increases the cost of goods formerly imported, and contributes to the cost-push element in inflation. Devaluation, by increasing the amount of domestic currency received from exports, also adds to the demand-pull element.

Moreover, the threat of devaluation both repels foreign capital and causes a flight of domestic capital to foreign havens. If the holders are confident that there will be only one devaluation, they will bring their money home after devaluation has occurred, but if they fear successive devaluations they are likely to leave it abroad.

Continuing inflation diverts investment from projects expected to produce income into channels expected to give protection against the inflation by yielding a capital gain. One of these is inventory accumulation, in anticipation of profits on price rises. Moreover, the groups whom inflation benefits are likely to include not only high savers but also luxurious spenders. For this reason there will be increased demand for the services of luxurious urban apartment houses, resort hotels, nightclubs, and the like. This demand increases the likelihood of capital gains from their construction, and on both counts resources tend to flow into such projects, which do little to further economic growth. Inflation seems always to accelerate the development of cities. Hence in urban areas land itself is purchased for a price rise, and the circulation of money from landowner to landowner may also keep it diverted from productive investment. Insofar as the individuals investing in these luxury construction ventures or land speculation are persons who are attracted by "a quick buck" and would not enter upon industrial or agricultural ventures in any case, little has been lost, so that this excrescence is less damaging than it appears to be, but these opportunities created by inflation attract more sober entrepreneurs also, and there is always some loss.

Empirical Evidence

The theoretical argument without quantities attached is inconclusive.

That within a fairly wide range of each, any rate of inflation is consistent with any rate of growth is indicated by the association of price stability with no growth or slow growth in Burma and India; of price stability with rapid growth in Japan and in Pakistan before the separation of Bangladesh; of rapid inflation with a low rate of growth in Indonesia, Argentina, and Chile; and of very rapid inflation with rapid growth in Brazil.

Somewhat more systematic evidence is provided by more comprehensive data for Asian and African countries and for Latin American countries, though like the episodic evidence above this does not discriminate between demand-full and cost-push inflation. The two groups of countries should be considered separately, since Latin American countries, on the average, are so much more advanced technically than Asian and African countries that they might be expected to have higher rates of growth quite apart from any effect of their inflation rates. Figures 16–3 and 16–4 present data for the period 1960–71. Both scatters are wide. Neither shows much indication of a relationship between inflation and growth. Perhaps a modest positive one can be seen in Asia-Africa.

Henry Wallich has presented a more elaborate analysis.[3] He did a multiple regression, using data for 43 countries, with aggregate growth rates from the average GNP for 1956–60 to that for 1961–65 as the dependent variable, and the rate of inflation, the rate of population growth, the ratio of investment to GNP, and per capita GNP as independent variables. He found that an increase in the rate of inflation of 1% per year was associated with a reduction in the rate of growth of 0.03 percent. This is a very small effect except where very high rates of inflation are present.

On the basis of these data, it is impossible to make a strong statement about the effects of inflation on growth, except that whatever that effect is, it is not large.

Curbing Demand-Pull Inflation

The means of curbing inflation that is due merely to excessive money demand is simple: eliminate the excessive rate of creation of money income.

The curbing of income creation has been the formal recommendation of the International Monetary Fund concerning inflation anywhere. Apparently without exception, its agreements to support the currency of a country have required stringent fiscal-monetary policy. The position that virtue requires monetary restraint sufficient to prevent inflation is a necessary one for the fund. It is difficult to see how an agency whose purpose for existence is the treatment of monetary problems could formally adopt any other viewpoint. That the IMF at times recognizes the unvirtuous necessity of relaxing monetary restraint is indicated by the fact that in a number of

---

[3] H. C. Wallich, *Money and Growth—A Country Cross-Section Analysis*, Center Paper no. 141 (New Haven: Yale University Economic Growth Center, 1970).

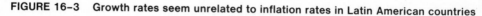

FIGURE 16-3   Growth rates seem unrelated to inflation rates in Latin American countries

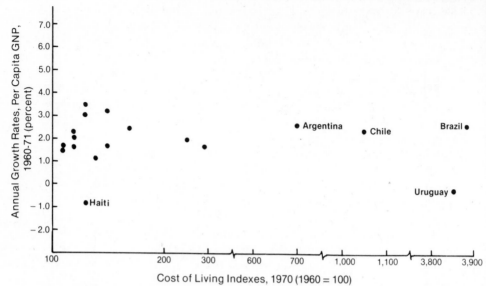

Cost of Living Indexes, 1970 (1960 = 100)

Sources: Per capita growth rates—*World Bank Atlas, 1973*; cost-of-living indexes—calculated from data in *International Financial Statistics*, various issues.

instances, among them that of Argentina (discussed later in this chapter), it has not withdrawn its support of the currency when a country has perforce broken the restrictive agreement.

Even if one accepted wholeheartedly the desirability of ending demand-pull inflation, the question would remain: How abruptly should the remedy be applied?

One danger of the abrupt application of monetary policy so stringent that it is inconsistent with the continuation of rising prices is that a quick reduction of the excessive rate of expansion of the money supply is likely to cause a temporary depression. The reason is that projects are likely to be in existence that are profitable only during inflation. These projects are likely to be checked quickly by monetary stringency, and inventory accumulation even reversed, but there may be a considerable lag before other projects replace them.

However, if the undue creation of money income is tapered off only gradually, individuals are not likely to believe that the government will really end inflation. In this event, the expectation of continuing inflation will itself prolong the inflation.

It is sometimes recommended that abrupt action be taken and a temporary depression be risked, but that to cushion it a program of public works be associated with the anti-inflationary fiscal-monetary policy, to offer employment to workers disemployed. McKinnon argues, but without

FIGURE 16-4 **Is there a positive association between inflation and growth in Asian and African countries?**

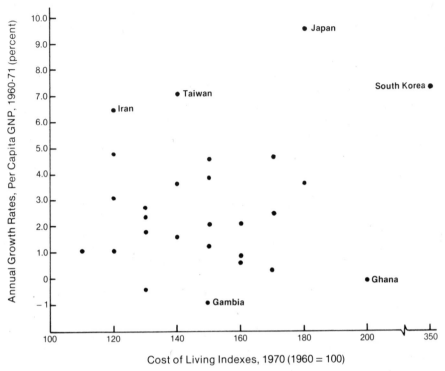

Cost of Living Indexes, 1970 (1960 = 100)

Sources: Per capita growth rates—table 1-1; cost-of-living indexes—calculated from data in *International Financial Statistics*, various issues.

empirical evidence, that if a ceiling on interest rates is carefully removed when counterinflationary measures are applied, deflation of the money supply can be prevented and recession prevented or lessened.

COST-PUSH INFLATION

A danger of the application, abrupt or gradual, of stringent monetary policy to check rising prices is that the inflation may be due, not to demand-pull occasioned by excessive increase in the money supply, but to a cost-push process. In that event checking the increase in the money supply will cause, not a cessation of price rises, but unemployment and depression. Consideration of cost-push inflation will indicate why this is true.

Cost-push inflation may begin with an increase in either prices or wages. Suppose that because of a rise in the price of imported foods, the real income of workers is reduced, or that for some reason many industrial workers feel that their employers are not treating them fairly. In either case, they organize, demand a wage increase, and are able to get it. Employers then raise their prices, to restore profit margins that have been squeezed. The rise in price reduces workers' real incomes again, and they demand and obtain a compensatory wage increase. But producers then raise prices again. And so on. If there is no relationship between prices and wages that is regarded as satisfactory by both workers and employers, and if both in turn have the economic power to get more for themselves when the situation from their viewpoint is unsatisfactory, inflation may continue forever—provided that the monetary and fiscal authorities permit the money supply to expand to finance the ever-increasing cost of the total turnover of goods and services.

Suppose that they do not. Suppose that the expansion of bank credit is checked. (The government would have to cooperate by reducing the rate of increase in its expenditures.) Employers seeking to borrow added funds to finance their increasing cost of inventories, accounts payable, and wages find that the banks do not have added funds to lend to them. The employers must then refuse wage increases and tolerate the strikes that follow, or reduce the volume of their production, laying off some workers and purchasing fewer materials. Because of the monetary stringency and because total demand will then rise less rapidly, other producers must reduce the volume of their production or refuse wage increases or both. If wages and prices are pushed still higher, the process will be repeated until unemployment is so high that workers, though still aggrieved, are unable to push up wages further and the market for goods is reduced so much that employers, even though they think their profit margins unsatisfactory, find that raising prices further is too costly in reduced sales. Wage and price equilibrium will be achieved by causing depression. In more than one country, monetary stringency has resulted in such a depression price and wage equilibrium, rather than merely in the cessation of inflation. So long as the attitudes of workers and employers toward each other and toward the market remain unchanged, price stability at full employment will be impossible unless wage and price controls are instituted.

LATIN AMERICAN INFLATION: THE STRUCTURALIST VIEW

The Latin American structuralist economists have argued that the cause of the exceedingly high inflation rates in Latin American countries has been neither demand-pull nor cost-push factors, but special circumstances that exist in low-income countries.[4] They say that (1) when increases in the demand for and therefore the prices of one or another type of goods have been induced by one or another *initiating factor*, (2) because of certain *basic factors* in the LDCs, suppliers do not respond to increased demand by increas-

---

[4] See the works cited in Chapter 6, note 9.

ing the supply of goods, and (3) the price rises then spread and become general inflation because of certain *propagating factors*.

The initiating factors cited are familiar ones: the growth of cities resulting in increasing demand for agricultural products that the country itself cannot meet; the growth of population, income, and demand for imports without a parallel increase in exports to finance them, resulting in shortages; and so on.

Among the "basic factors" cited as preventing production from increasing adequately in response to selective increases in prices are the supposed sluggishness of response the producers in low-income countries and the lack of manufacturing industry. The structuralists add two others. Monopolistic producers of industrial products, they say, raise prices rather than increase output when demand increases. And inequality of income distribution deters response. If the mass market were enlarged through income redistribution, production for that market would be established, would contribute to economic growth, and would also keep prices down.

The weakness of the argument concerning inequality of income distribution was indicated in Chapter 4. The argument concerning monopolists is also overstated, because monopolists produce only a small share of the total supply of consumer goods and also because, since the monopolists had already set their profit margins to maximize profits before inflation occurred, their profits are maximized by increasing production as well as prices when demand increases.

In the main, the "propagating factors" are simply familiar cost-push elements.

Little is left, then, of the supposed unique inflation-causing characteristics of low-income countries except the fact that if a country experiences an increase in income without an increase in its ability to export, and thus to finance added imports, increased demand will cause scarcity of imports, which will indeed be inflationary. The other conditions are common to advanced countries and LDCs—for cost-push elements and the inability to supply to respond are the causes of inflation in industrial countries as well as in LDCs.

To these familiar arguments a more complex and compelling one is added by Raúl Prebisch. When foreign exchange earnings are high, income and both investment and consumer spending in the country are high. When foreign exchange earnings and therefore domestic incomes fall because of a fall in the volume of exports or in their prices, the government is likely to encourage private credit expansion and to resort to deficit financing itself in order to maintain a high level of income and prevent depression. The demand for imported goods then remains high, but their supply on the domestic market falls for lack of foreign exchange with which to import them. This situation may be an important "initiating factor."

Moreover, if this event trips off a general price rise through a cost-push process, that price rise will make the country's exports less attractive to buyers and will increase the demand for imports. Thus the prices of imported goods will be bid up further. This is an added propagating factor.

"Aggression Inflation"

The structuralist arguments were advanced by Latin American economists seeking to explain the extremely high rates of inflation in their countries. One may suspect that the cause is a quite different and in a sense simpler condition unique to Latin American countries: a degree of distrust between workers and employers so great that the result may reasonably be termed "aggression inflation" rather than merely cost-push inflation. The distrust was and still is so great that any claim of the other party seems grossly unreasonable, because this is the sort of greed that one would expect from that party—unreasonable by a margin of, say 30% or 50% rather than the 2% or 3% or 4% that may separate unions and employers in industrial countries. Once previously submissive workers felt their power and savage social tensions were unloosed (as in Argentina under Perón after 1946 and in Chile much earlier), aggressive cost-push inflation began; thereafter the expectation of large price increases caused labor to increase its wage demands and the expectation of large wage demands caused employers to increase their price hikes. Other groups used their political influence to gain self-protective income increases, which contributed to the inflation.

But why should class tensions be uniquely great in some Latin American countries? One may speculate that two facts of Latin American history provide an answer. One is that the elites of Latin American countries are the descendants of European conquerors who looked upon the indigenous people with contempt, and abused them. (At least the elites think of themselves as descendants of Europeans; the racial intermixture is greater than they care to admit.) Racial memories are long. The other is the late 19th- and early 20th-century waves of immigration, especially into Argentina and Chile, of immigrants of lower-class European stock sharply different from that of the Spanish and Portuguese elites, who treated the immigrants, as they had the Indians, with contempt.

These suggestions are presented only as speculation. They provide a plausible explanation of a puzzling economic phenomenon.

Whatever may be their cause, the social attitudes which breed the extreme rates of inflation are not whims, but are deeply and solidly based. The callousness of the Latin American upper classes to the material welfare and the psychological needs of the peasants and the urban poor is a real fact of the social structure. The perception of those upper classes that the poor, if they could, would oust them from their position of traditional privilege, and perhaps dispossess them, is also only too solidly based. One must think of these class tensions as being alleviated in a generation or generations, not in years or a single decade—or perhaps as never being alleviated, but someday eventuating in radical political revolution unless the elites are able to maintain their positions forever by military force. In such upheavals the new successful and wealthy industrial elite are likely to be swept aside along with the traditional ruling class.

SUPPLY-COST INFLATION AND GROWTH

The structuralists do not say that ordinary cost-push, structural, or aggression inflation is conducive to growth. They say that it is a necessary evil, that curbing such inflation by limiting the money supply will also curb investment, the response of supply to new demands, and in general the forces for growth. The only remedial program that will not inhibit growth, they say, is one that will alleviate the "basic factors." This takes time. Meanwhile, if growth is not to be choked off, inflation must be tolerated. The structuralists do not deny that some moderate braking of inflation may be salutary. (They reject wage controls without price controls as inequitable, without considering their effect on growth.)

The remedies that many structuralists propose are to have the government (1) act to lessen the country's vulnerability to export fluctuations by promoting import substitution and by pressing for commodity price stabilization agreements; (2) redistribute income to the lower income groups; and (3) bring about increased responsiveness of supply to changes in demand, especially in agriculture, both by direct action and by the establishment of incentives for change. The measures would include improvement of the country's infrastructure, irrigation projects, land reform, and tax reform. One may doubt that these measures would moderate inflation, or that commodity price stabilization would much reduce fluctuations in foreign exchange earnings. Their effects on growth would be various. Import substitution might at first accelerate growth but at a later stage would certainly hamper it. Improvement in rural infrastructure would speed growth. The effects on growth of tax reform and income redistribution would depend on the specific measures. The effects of land reform were discussed in Chapter 9.

FOR FURTHER READING

Most of the major essays on both sides of the monetarist-structuralist controversy are presented in the following three volumes:

H. S. Ellis and H. C. Wallich, eds., *Economic Development for Latin America* (New York: St. Martin's Press, 1961.)

A. O. Hirschman, *Journeys toward Progress: Studies of Economic Policy-Making in Latin America* (New York: Twentieth Century Fund, 1963).

A. O. Hirschman, ed., *Latin American Issues: Essays and Comments* (New York: Twentieth Century Fund, 1961).

Among other essays, see especially Raúl Prebisch, "Economic Development or Monetary Stability: The False Dilemma," United Nations Economic Commission for Latin America's *Economic Bulletin for Latin America*, 6 (March 1961), 1–25.

Raymond F. Mikesell, *Survey of the Alliance for Progress: Inflation in Latin America* (90th Congress, 1st Session, Committee Print, September 25, 1967), is valuable for both facts and analysis.

In 1955, Martin Bronfenbrenner argued in "The Appeal of Confiscation in Economic Development" (*Economic Development and Cultural Change*, 3 [April 1955], 201–18) that confiscation of private property would be an advantageous way to finance economic development in many countries. His exceptions included Cuba (too close to the West) and the petroleum-producing countries (adequate revenues from private investment). In a 1963 sequel (*Economic Development and Cultural Change*, 11 [July 1963], 367–71), he acknowledged that he had erred in the earlier article in assuming that only the marginal, not the average, productivity of capital would fall under government management. His quantitative analysis is of interest.

Richard A. Musgrave, *Fiscal Systems* (New Haven: Yale University Press, 1969).

Alan R. Prest, *Public Finance in Underdeveloped Countries*, 2d ed. (New York: John Wiley, 1972).

H. H. Hinrichs's monograph cited in note 1 of this chapter presents an interesting analysis of fiscal system change during development.

17

The Inflow of Capital:
Overall Analysis

CAPITAL INFLOWS: FORMS, FUNCTIONS, AND HISTORY

By a capital inflow into a country is meant a loan or a grant from abroad to the government, enterprises, or people of the country, or direct investment in the country by a foreign firm or individual. Direct investment is the construction or purchase of an enterprise in the country. Some of these flows are on commercial terms: direct investment, and the purchase of securities or the extension of credit on terms set by supply and demand in the international market. In contrast are flows on "concessional terms," namely, grants and loans on easier than commercial terms. All private inflow except that from humanitarian organizations or an occasional philanthropic individual is on commercial terms. "Economic aid" or "foreign aid" is flows on concessional terms. Almost all flows from non-communist governments to LDCs are on concessional terms. Governments make their grants and loans both directly ("bilaterally") and through international organizations ("multilaterally").

Economic aid and private capital flows to LDCs (especially direct investment) will be examined separately in Chapter 18. In this chapter they will be lumped together, and the effects they have in common as capital inflows considered. All forms of either have one or more of three general effects: they may augment a country's capital formation; they may provide the country with foreign exchange; and they may carry with them technical knowledge or managerial expertise.

Consider direct investment. A foreign firm intending to build a factory or a warehouse in the country may ship in materials and components for the construction. The country's supply of capital goods is thus increased. The

285

firm may later not only receive dividends on its investment but may repatriate the capital, but at the time of the investment there is a net capital inflow. In order to pay the domestic costs of erecting the building, the firm may also buy domestic currency from the country's banks, paying for it with foreign funds. The banks then have an added supply of foreign currency (deposits) in foreign banks available for sale to the government, an enterprise, or an individual of the country for the purchase of goods or services abroad in addition to those for which the country's own exports will pay. This part of the investment transaction, unlike the shipment of capital goods into the country, was not a net addition to the country's productive resources, for the country's labor and materials were used in erecting the building. The transaction gave the country foreign resources in exchange for its domestic resources. It was an addition to the country's capital formation (unless there was no slack in the economy and the resources used were bid away from another investor). The firm may also send into the country persons who are experts in the technical field in which the firm is engaged. Thus its investment may have all of the three effects listed above. A private loan or economic aid may have the same three effects, or only one or two of the three. Either may provide the country with foreign exchange with or without occasioning the use of domestic resouces in exchange.

A BRIEF HISTORY

Every country's major source of resources for capital formation is its own saving, but only three countries have not also received a capital inflow in the early stages of their economic development. The economic rise of the Netherlands in the 16th and 17th centuries was financed from the earnings of the Dutch as seafarers. Japan neither received nor permitted any capital inflow until after 1900. England's early development was also almost entirely self-financed, though wealthy Netherlanders invested some fairly small amounts in England, and the Lombard merchants who settled along the street in London that became known as Lombard Street brought at least their stocks of goods. Beyond these fairly small amounts, which at the time may have exceeded England's investment abroad, England had no net capital inflow during the entire period of its economic growth until it sold off foreign assets to finance the purchase of munitions from the United States in World War I. And has the Netherlands ever had a net capital inflow? Perhaps through investment by MNC in recent decades.

Among the earliest developing nations, capital flowed from England into Germany and France, mainly to finance railroad building, after economic development was under way in those countries. Immigrants to the lands of English settlement brought capital on their backs, and later capital flowed from England into those countries in large amounts—into the United States, as into France and Germany, mainly for railroad construction; into Canada,

Australia, and New Zealand to develop "empty lands." As Table 17–1 shows, for a period of about four decades the capital flow to Australia and Canada exceeded 35% of gross domestic capital formation, which of course means an inflow more than half as large as domestic saving. Almost nowhere else in the world in modern times has a capital inflow been so large relative to domestic saving, though during the five-year period 1911–15 53% of Canada's gross private domestic investment appears to have been financed from abroad.[1] Even Japan, the exceptional case, began to receive an inflow of capital after 1900, when through its increasing self-confidence Japan had become willing to accept foreign loans and when its success in industrialization had made it an attractive candidate for them.

TABLE 17–1   Capital inflow ratios have been high at peak periods in some countries

Country and Period	Ratio to GDCF	Ratio to Imports	Approximate Ratio of GDCF to Imports
Australia, 1861–1900	0.37	0.25	0.7
Canada, 1870–1914	0.40	0.31	0.75
Norway, 1885–1914	0.29	0.11	0.4
1920–1929	0.31	0.14	0.45
Sweden, 1861–1910	0.11	0.13	1.2
United States, 1869–1898	0.02–0.03	0.07	3.0

Sources: Ratios to GDCF—S. S. Kuznets, "Quantitative Aspects of Economic Growth of Nations," no. 6, *Economic Development and Cultural Change*, 9, no. 4, part 2 (July 1961), appendix tables; ratios to imports—Kuznets, ibid., no. 10, *Economic Development and Cultural Change*, 15, no. 2, part 2 (January 1967), 62–63, table 13. Ratios of GDCF to imports calculated from the other two columns.

Capital inflow into the present lower income countries has financed typically between 5% and 20% of their gross domestic capital formation. The governments of imperialist countries expended some of their own resources in some of their colonies; colonial administrations were not always self-sufficient financially, especially in their early years. In the 1920s Latin American governments were able to sell bond issues (at high interest rates) to foreign buyers. They did so mainly in England and the United States. However, before World War II the flow of capital into LDCs was largely direct investment. In the 19th century the investment was often by companies formed for the purpose. When such companies were well established in the foreign country, and profitable, they might sell bonds to their countrymen at home to raise more capital. The investments except in Latin America

---

[1] " R. E. Caves, " 'Vent for Surplus' Models of Trade and Growth," in R. E. Baldwin, et al., ed., *Trade, Growth, and the Balance of Payments: Essays in Honor of Gotttfried Haberler* (Chicago and Amsterdam: Rand McNally and North Holland Publishing Co., 1965), p. 115, quoting K. A. H. Buckley.

were in countries on which European powers had imposed colonial rule. "Money followed the flag."

The early European investments in Latin American countries were often to construct public utilities. Elsewhere, they were largely for trade at first, and later for the purpose of extracting minerals or other raw materials. There was little fear of confiscation in Latin America. The Latin American rulers were men of European stock who "understood the sanctity of contracts" and were friendly, and in any event it was expected that international business contracts would be enforced by gunboats if necessary.

For a variety of reasons, from the beginning of the Great Depression in 1930 until the 1960s the flow of private investment to LDCs was small. That which occurred was largely investment to exploit mineral resources, including oil, in selected areas. And until 1970, private loans to LDCs were virtually zero. There are several reasons. Early in the depression Latin American governments defaulted on their bond issues of the 1920s. Since 1930, except for a short period after World War II, the international financial exchanges have been disturbed. Since World War II political district has made many types of foreign direct investment no longer welcome in LDCs. In any event, there have been many new governments, whose stability and policies have been unfamiliar to investors. It has no longer been possible for the governments of lenders to enforce payment of debts or to prevent the nationalization of business enterprises by "gunboat diplomacy," and diplomatic pressure of more subtle sorts has often been ineffective. In these circumstances direct investment and private lending have shrunk.

Post-World War II economic aid by governments, directly or through international organizations, was in a sense something new under the sun. Yet, as the account above shows, it was also merely a new form of a flow that has "always" been essential for the acceleration of economic growth.

Private investment in LDCs revived during the 1960s, and private lending to LDCs began again at about 1970. By 1970, as Table 17–2 illustrates (opposite page), private investment was almost as large in amount as "concessional" loans. By 1977, private investment plus private loans were more than twice as large as concessional loans. In 1978 and 1979 private lending soared further. However, the private loans went to selected countries, not to all LDCs.

There is a new element in the financial need of the non-oil-producing LDCs. It is foreign exchange deficits created by the quintupling in 1973 and 1974 of the price of the oil that they import. Those oil imports are a large element in the import bill of many LDCs. For a few countries, the need has been met by loans from OPEC countries. However, these loans have been made, not to the countries hit hardest by the oil price increases, but to the few countries with which the OPEC members have cultural ties. A rela-

TABLE 17-2   Total net resources receipts of LDCs from all sources ($ billions)
The private flow of resources into LDCs much exceeds the flow via Official Development Assistance.

	1970	1973	1977
ODA	8.04	11.57	19.54
Nonconcessional flows:			
Private:			
DAC bilateral, nonbanking sector (almost wholly private investment)	7.16	8.43	22.60
Commercial bank lending	0.60	8.47	17.60
Public			
Multilateral agencies	0.69	1.28	3.10
OPEC bilateral	0.10	0.14	0.86
Centrally planned economies	0.11	0.10	0.03
Subtotal, nonconcessional	8.66	18.42	44.39
Total	16.70	29.99	63.93

Note: By 1977, nonconcessional flows were more than double ODA. The increase in direct investment was for both natural resource exploitation and the construction of manufacturing facilities.
Source: *Development Cooperation: 1978 Review*, p. 189, table A-1.

tively small amount of aid has been extended by the two International Monetary Fund "oil facilities." A much larger total of loans has been made by commercial banks, loans especially of "Eurodollars"—explained later in this chapter—but those loans too have been made to selected LDC countries, in this case countries whose rapidly rising exports seem to presage ability to repay. But many of the lowest income countries who have neither received loans from Middle East OPEC countries nor been successful candidates for Eurodollar loans have depended heavily on loans from Western governments to meet the new problem.

USEFUL OR WASTEFUL?

Some persons skeptical concerning economic aid have asked whether it, or a capital inflow in general, does in fact augment the resources that are available for capital formation.

A Net Addition to Resources?

When foreign funds flow into a country, the national accounts of the country are likely to show a decrease in domestic saving. When this phenomenon was noticed, a few economists pointed to it as evidence that the ability to borrow abroad made people profligate. The charge is misplaced. The national income accounts will show any increase in capital formation that accompanies the capital inflow, but they will also show negative investment abroad by the country equal to the inflow of funds—for foreign claims on the country have increased by this amount. At best, therefore, the accounts will show no increase in investment. Moreover, if so much as a penny of the funds that flow in on loan is spent for consumption, the national income accounts will show net disinvestment in the transaction, and this will be interpreted as a reduction in aggregate saving, even though every person and organization in the country is saving as much as before and capital formation within the country has been increased. The recorded decrease in saving does indicate, of course, that some part of the capital inflow was spent for consumption.

A 1973 econometric analysis by Hollis Chenery and Nicholas Carter of the relationship of capital inflow to growth used data from 37 LDCs.[2] If the capital inflow was reduced, the two research workers concluded, "[recorded] savings would rise, but output, investment, and consumption would fall."

It is a quite separate fact that capital may flow out of a country, because its holders think savings abroad more secure than savings at home, even while economic aid or other capital is flowing in. If so, the inflow, by relieving the country's foreign exchange stringency, may make it easier for earners of foreign exchange to escape the grasp of a government that is seeking to gain control of it. In this case the net addition to the resources available for domestic capital formation is decreased.

Absorptive Capacity

A second question is whether a country can use added resources effectively. A premise of the worldwide program of economic aid that began soon after World War II was that with technical help the LDCs could make effective use of an inflow of capital in addition to their own saving. Some of the "least developed countries," which seem to have almost no entrepreneurial capacity whatever, or, more precisely, no motivation to use their managerial capabilities to increase their nations' productivity, may be exceptions. But even concerning other countries, one may ask: Can the government and entrepreneurs of the country use effectively for capital formation more resources than the country itself saves? How much more? Economists call this the question of absorptive capacity. A recipient country may think of absorptive capacity as a lower limit, and donors or lenders as an upper limit, to an appropriate flow of aid.

Every economist would agree that there is some limit. There are technical limitations: the size of the country's construction industry; the capacity of the ports and the transportation system to carry goods, of the communication system to carry messages, of the country's housing to house foreign

---

[2] "Foreign Assistance and Development Performance, 1960–1970," *American Economic Review*, 63 (May 1973), 459–68

workers, if workers and materials are imported to meet the shortages; the state of the existing productive complex into which or onto which the new enterprises must be fitted and on which their productivity will depend in part. There are other limitations as well: the number of individuals in the society with adequate managerial and technical capabilities, and the values and motivations of many groups in the society—of workers, which will affect their availability for new enterprises and their efficiency in working in them; of government officials, which will influence the efficiency of government investment and of the institutions that affect private investment, or on the other hand, the degree of waste, corruption, and misdirection of investment; and so on. Some of the human problems can be met by the importation of managers, engineers, and technicians, the only limit to this being their worldwide availability and the tolerance of the people of the LDC for such an invasion.

Morals from Saudi Arabia

The recent experience of Saudi Arabia illustrates what is possible if a country has virtually unlimited supplies of capital in the form of foreign exchange.[3] Before World War II Saudi Arabian economic arrangements were, from a Western viewpoint, primitive. Even today very few Saudi Arabians have great interest in technical activity at either the manual or the intellectual level. Until the 1960s they had almost no acquaintance with it. Yet when oil revenues began to be available in large amounts late in the 1960s, Saudis geared up with great rapidity—within a decade—and with great skill to manage their use. For a few years infrastructure and then especially port capacity and administration were bottlenecks. More recently it has been difficult to identify one. The Saudis brought in foreigners to do everything they did not know how to do or had no interest in doing. Foreign firms execute almost every development project. In the private nonagricultural sector the number of foreign workers much exceeds the number of native workers. Foreign corporations contract not only to execute projects, but in large projects they contract to bring in all needed workers and also, often, their housing. Where the workers have strong preferences for certain foreign foods, the corporation also brings in much of their food. There is, then, a development program managed at the very top by Saudis and below the very top managed by foreign managers and executed by foreign workers for the benefit of Saudis.

There has been a large increase in both the money and the real incomes of Saudis at all economic levels, in effect largely through a transfer of oil revenues from the government to the Saudis. However, at least to date

---

[3] The observations about Saudi Arabia are based on information gathered by the writer during trips to that country.

there has apparently not been a great increase in the productivity of Saudi workers apart from the considerable increase resulting from the shift from less productive to more productive occupations, notably from nomadic life and agriculture to urban pursuits. But this lag has not prevented a very rapid increase in the rate of capital formation.

Table 17–3 shows the estimated increase over a five-year period in construction activity, in absolute terms and relative to nonoil GDP. The data, from an understaffed and overworked Saudi Arabian government agency, are almost incredible, but in view of the extremely rapid rise in construction activity in the country they may be correct. The table should not be misunderstood; the data for construction activity include not only value added with Saudi Arabia but the total value put in place, including imported materials and components. If the value of imported capital goods components was one half of the value of total capital formation—a plausible estimate—then construction activity within the country in 1975–76 was 40 percent of nonoil GDP.

TABLE 17–3 The rate of construction activity in Saudi Arabia has increased very rapidly

Fiscal Year	(1) Nonoil GDP	(2) (billions of US $) Construction Activity	(3) Col. (2) as Percentage of Col. (1)
1971–72	2.6	0.9	35
1972–73	3.6	1.5	47
1973–74	4.4	2.4	55
1974–75	6.6	4.0	61
1975–76	11.0	8.0	81

Source: Kingdom of Saudi Arabia Central Department of Statistics, *National Accounts*, June 1977, but converted to U.S. dollars. Percentages calculated from unrounded data.

This account would seem to suggest that there is virtually no limit to the capacity of a country to absorb capital, or, more precisely, that the limits are short-lived—can fairly easily be pushed back. It does indicate that, with one important qualification. Beguiled by their dreams of the future, Saudi officials have not learned rapidly to limit government development expenditures to useful fields. Since this is likely to be the usual result of sudden entry into wealth, it too must be taken into account in generalizing from the Saudi Arabian experience. Much of the capital formation within Saudi Arabia will yield an extremely low, even a negative, social as well as financial return; much of the construction of infrastructure for industrial activity prepares for activity that will not take place. Apart from some (but not all possible) production using petroleum or natural gas as feedstock, very little industrial production for export will be possible except with large subsidies.

The Saudi Arabian experience, then, does not suggest the absence of any limit to absorptive capacity, but it does suggest that the limit is a vague and fuzzy band rather than a sharp line. It also suggests that economists have "more normal circumstances" in mind in applying the concept elsewhere.

Measuring the Limit

Hollis Chenery and Alan Strout proposed a method of estimating absorptive capacity that is plausible and objective.[4] They suggested that a country has the absorptive capacity (they used the term *skill limit* rather than the term *absorptive capacity limit*) to increase its volume of investment from year to year by the maximum percentage by which it has done so during any five-year period in the recent past. They applied this concept to each of 31 LDCs for which reasonably good data were available and, more roughly, to 19 others.

Their study was done in 1966. The recent previous periods of fastest investment growth varied from 1950–54 to 1960–64. "Sustained rates of increase in investment of 12–15 percent per year are common," the two writers noted. "The highest observed value . . . over any recent five-year period is about 20 percent per year, but few countries have sustained a growth of investment of over 10 percent for as long as ten years."

Chenery and Strout may have erred in thinking that they were merely measuring expanding "skill limits." Some of the five-year periods may have begun during times of economic depression and low investment levels, so that at least some of the increase in the investment rate may not have broken new ground. Or, the five-year spurt may have been made possible by the increased availability of foreign exchange, for within the 15-year intervals covered there were two periods of increasing demand for raw materials. Moreover, a country's entrepreneurs may have been capable of the investment rate achieved during the fifth year, or approximately that rate, at the beginning of the period, and may not have been increasing their capacity to manage investment at a rate that could be projected into the future. However, the exercise provides at least a rough tool by which to estimate what countries could do if the economic resources were available.

THE TWO GAPS

The gap to be filled, then, is the gap between a country's own provision of resources and its absorptive capacity. But there seem to be two gaps, and before we turn to estimates of the magnitude of useful capital inflow it is necessary to explain this conception.

---

[4] "Foreign Assistance and Economic Development," *American Economic Review,* 56 (September 1966), 680–733.

If at full employment a country is not saving as much as its private entre-preneurs and government could usefully invest, a "savings gap" exists. By augmenting the resources available, a capital inflow can then make possible a higher rate of capital formation.

However, the two-gap proponents argue, even if the country could save enough at full employment to finance all of the investment that its govern-ment and its private entrepreneurs could manage, they may not be able to carry out the investment projects because the country may not be earning enough foreign exchange to pay for materials and components that must be purchased abroad. If so, there will be less capital formation than the full-employment level of domestic saving would finance, and there will be un-employment within the country. This is the "foreign exchange gap" or "trade gap."

In the terms of national income accounting, the two gaps are explained as follows. The reader will remember that the following equation must al-ways hold true after the fact:

$$I + X = S + M,$$

where these symbols are used with the usual meaning (I = domestic capital formation, X = exports, S = saving, and M = imports). But S may be too small to permit the full amount of I for which the country otherwise has the capability (a savings gap), or X may be too small to permit the needed M, even though some resources are idle in the economy (a foreign exchange gap).

The conception of a foreign exchange gap, separate from the savings gap, did not enter the economic literature until the 1960s, because under the as-sumptions of neoclassical economics it could not exist, or it could exist for only a limited time. For neoclassical theory assumes that productive re-sources are adaptable and shiftable. Idle resources can be used to increase exports, whereupon the foreign exchange gap will disappear. Or, if the in-vesting entrepreneur can modify the project design to use capital goods that can be produced in the country in lieu of imported capital goods, he can carry out the project without having the foreign exchange needed to buy the imports. Neoclassical economists argue that a government can bring about either result: it can induce an increase in exports by permitting the value of the country's currency to fall, or it can itself put the idle resources to work at labor-intensive capital formation projects if the country's private entrepreneurs are not sufficiently imaginative. This question is discussed in Chapter 21.

However, Chenery argues that, whatever may be true in an ideal econ-omy, or might have been true if a government had adopted ideal policies in the past, rigidities do exist and will exist, and that they cannot be quickly remedied. Many governments will not think it desirable to do what neo-classical economists think they "ought" to do. Moreover, the "proper" action might not be effective. Whether it will be is controversial (see Chapter 21), but, in any event, in a perspective of, say, a decade or even two decades, in many LDCs, as in many economically advanced countries, there will in fact be two gaps.

The Gaps: How Large?

Two studies made in the 1960s estimated the rates at which LDCs would be able to grow from the time of the study to 1975 if neither savings limitations nor foreign exchange limitations constrained them, and estimated the size of the capital inflow that would be needed to prevent such constraints. The two studies make a useful platform from which to view actual developments in the 1960s and 1970s.

Chenery and Strout estimated maximum manageable investment rates for 50 countries during the period 1957–62 to 1975 by projecting the "skill limits." They then estimated savings from the trend in the relationship of savings to GNP, and from these two sets of data they estimated savings gaps. They estimated exports of goods and services by projecting past rates of increase, and they estimated import requirements from the trend in the relationship of imports to the national product. Thereby they derived estimates of foreign exchange gaps. On these bases they concluded that 19 of the 31 countries for which they had the most complete data would still need foreign aid in 1975 but that 12 would not. (They also made various alternative projections on more optimistic assumptions of possible rates of increase in investment. In general, in these projections the amount of foreign aid that would be needed in 1975 was greater than the amount that had been provided in 1962. The foreign exchange gap exceeded the savings gap in most of the projections.)[5]

A study by UNCTAD, directed by Robin Marris, was simpler than the Chenery-Strout study in some respects, more sophisticated in others.[6] The study projected to 1975 the trend rate of growth in national product from 1950 to 1965 in each of 40 countries, and alternatively a moderately accelerated rate of growth. Marris then estimated capital requirements through estimates of ICORs, and savings (except for countries for which there were not enough data) from their recent past relationship to the national product. He estimated exports by projecting the growth rates of the higher in-

---

[5] The conception is associated with Chenery. Although he uses it in earlier articles, it is expounded most clearly in Chenery and Strout, "Foreign Assistance and Economic Development," and in Chenery, "The Two-Gap Approach to Aid and Development: Reply to Bruton," *American Economic Review*, 59 (June 1969), 446–49.

[6] United Nations Commission for Trade and Development, *Trade Prospects and Capital Needs of Developing Countries* (New York: United Nations, 1968). See also Robin Marris, "Can We Measure the Need for Development Assistance?," *Economic Journal*, 80 (September 1970), 650–67.

come countries and estimating the imports of major commodities by those countries. On this basis Marris estimated that the foreign exchange shortage of the countries having one in 1975 would be $25 billion in 1965 prices, or $19 billion if the higher income countries opened their boundaries more widely to imports from the LDCs. The Marris study did not find that foreign exchange gaps predominated over savings gaps; both gaps were estimated to exist in many countries; but Marris concluded that the inclusion of savings gaps where they exceeded trade gaps would not have increased the total estimates of need greatly.

In a 1973 article, Chenery and Carter compared actual developments during the 1960s in 37 countries with the Chenery-Strout projections. The capital inflow during the decade had been below that calculated as required to permit the countries to invest up to their "skill limits." Yet for the group as a whole the actual growth was about that projected.[7] The explanation is that the exports of the countries surveyed increased faster than had been projected. That within limits this trade was an adequate substitute for aid is one of the significant facts of recent economic development. The subject is discussed further in Chapter 19.

PRIVATE FLOWS IN THE 1960S AND 1970S

Through a coincidence of five circumstances, loans to selected LDCs by large American and European banks increased at a very rapid rate during the 1970s. (1) LDCs, as always, were eager to obtain loans for development purposes and to increase their foreign exchange reserves whether or not they had balance of payment problems. (2) Imports of petroleum and petroleum products are important among the imports of a large majority of LDCs. The oil price increase of 1974 alone increased the import bill of LDCs by some $11 billion, and the price increase of 1979 by an additional sum of some $12 billion. The current account balance of payment deficit of LDCs as a group was $11 billion in 1973, $22 billion in 1977, and an estimated $35 billion in 1979, and this in spite of the fact that total exports of the countries usually classed as LDCs rose from $67 billion in 1973 to $151 billion in 1978. (Calculation of the balance of payment on current account excludes loans and other capital flows.) (3) The exports of manufactured goods of eight or ten LDCs were increasing rapidly. Notably among these countries were South Korea, Taiwan, Singapore, Brazil, Spain, and Israel. The exports of others, for example Mexico and Indonesia with their newly discovered oil deposits, held promise of future increases. Banks were eager to lend to such countries: loans to countries with rapidly increasing export revenues appear safe. (4) Inflation was reducing the burden of previous debts; while import revenues were increasing because of rising prices, a previous debt burden remained constant in amount. A country's debt bur-

---

[7] "Foreign Assistance and Development Performance, 1960–1970."

den that may have worried bankers in 1970 may have caused them no worry in 1977. (5) Lastly, commercial banks outside the United States, including foreign branches of American banks, were awash in a flood of "Eurocurrency" (see the final section of this chapter) for which they sought borrowers.

The ease with which fortunate LDCs borrowed is indicated by the increase in total LDC foreign exchange holdings from $26 billion at the end of 1973 to $61 billion at the end of 1978. A large part of the increase was through borrowing. There is an obverse to this coin. The debts of LDCs rose with their net borrowing—to $205 billion at the end of 1977 and an estimated $274 billion at the end of 1979. The amount of interest repayment of principal due in any one year rose from a few billion dollars in 1970 to $29 billion in 1977 and $40 billion in 1979.

None or very few of the low income countries experienced this increased ability to make private loans. Almost all of them still needed to depend on official development assistance if they were to pay their increased oil costs, to pay other increased net imports costs, or to avoid curtailment of their economic development expenditures. Of the nonconcessional financial flows to low income countries reflected in Table 17–4, almost all were private investment, not loans.

TABLE 17–4 Flows to nonoil LDCs grouped by per capita income levels (1975–1977 average)

Much aid has gone to countries with the lowest incomes, and much aid per capita to those with the highest.

	LDC Income Levels, 1976			
	$400 or Less	$401– 1,000	$1,001– 2,500	More Than $2,500
Official development assistance				
Dollars per capita	7.50	9.70	4.40	22.60
Percent of recipient's GNP	4.6	1.9	0.4	0.7
Percentage of total ODA flow	61.1	22.5	8.9	7.5
Nonconcessional resources flows, (loans plus private investment)				
Dollars per capita	3.20	21.10	35.70	104.80
Percent of total nonconcessional flow	31.1	25.4	28.4	15.4

Source: *Development Cooperation: 1978 Review*, p. 107. Per Capita data for nonconcessional resource flow calculated by subtracting ODA per capita from total per capita in the source. The classification of countries is that of Development Cooperation: all countries other than the industrialized members of PECD are included as LDCs. Aid flows not geographically allocated are not included.

CAPACITY TO REPAY

Foreigners' claims resulting from capital inflow must be either paid or repudiated. With respect to direct investment by a foreign firm, the government has no direct obligation, but if interest or dividends on this investment are to be paid, the government must sell the foreign firm the foreign exchange needed, or permit it to retain enough of its own foreign exchange earnings. With regard to the government's own borrowing, the obligation is more direct. Inability to pay or to provide foreign exchange makes it more difficult for a country to attract capital in the future, though in due time lenders looking for borrowers and investors seeking advantageous investment opportunities ignore past defaults if they think that the circumstances have changed.

In order to service foreign debt a country must both export and save. ("Debt service" refers to the amount of interest plus repayment of principal that is due year by year.) It must produce goods that it does not consume, but instead exports, and having exported them, it must not use all of the proceeds to finance consumer goods imports. The ability to export beyond the need to import is not necessarily high because the country's exports are high relative to its GDP, for the country may specialize in producing an export commodity and may import many of its consumer goods. This is especially likely to be true for a small country. Yet there is some presumption that a high-export country has a greater than average debt service capacity.

Many capital inflows neither increase a country's exports nor reduce its import requirements in the short run. Such inflows may therefore create a short-run debt service problem. This does not necessarily cause difficulty, for a country whose productivity and exports seem to be increasing will usually find it easy to obtain loans abroad to meet a problem that is seen as temporary.

Debt service is not necessarily burdensome because it is large relative to foreign exchange earnings. Suppose that foreign exchange earnings are 4 and debt service requirements 1. Suppose also that an added capital inflow increases debt service requirements to 2 but that by increasing exports it also increases foreign exchange earnings to 5½. Debt service requirements will then have risen from 25% to more than 36% of foreign exchange earnings, yet the burden of the debt service will have decreased.

There is some presumption that a country whose productivity has increased is better able to service debts than it was previously, but this is at best a weak presumption, for the ratio of saving to income does not necessarily increase with growth, as was noted in Chapter 15. There is a much stronger presumption that rapid growth enables a country to service debts more readily than it would be able to otherwise, for increase in consumption lags behind increase in income. The savings margin widens. However, in any of these cases the country must be able to export as well as to save.

The Debt Service Problem

A number of LDCs now have or recently had debt service problems of varying seriousness, because of cumulating debt service obligations on official aid; because development expenditures either failed to produce development or, though they increased productivity, did not increase ability to export; because for one reason or another their exports fell markedly; or because they squandered funds in ways that lenders had not anticipated. In 1970 India and Indonesia seemed headed for trouble.[8] It is testimony to the inscrutability of the future that neither experienced this particular sort of trouble. The "Green Revolution" eliminated India's need to import food, and increases in domestic production reduced some of its other import needs. Indonesia's prospective problem vanished temporarily as its anticipated oil exports increased (because with this anticipation it could easily attract added capital), then reappeared when the official in charge of its petroleum enterprise mortgaged future receipts recklessly to finance various schemes, then eased again when he was replaced by a more responsible administrator who is correcting his mistakes.

On the other hand, in 1978 Peru was almost "bankrupt" in the eyes of foreign creditors, and Zaire was in even worse shape. Both countries had been able to borrow freely up to 1975; in 1974 and 1975 the price of copper, their chief export, was at record highs. Both countries then spent all of their foreign exchange earnings plus added funds which they borrowed. A military government in Peru that preceded the present one spent an estimated $1 billion for tanks and military airplanes (both purchased from the USSR), and for the purpose of economic reform made changes that greatly reduced productivity in the copper mines in the short run. Zaire squandered money on grandiose transportation, power, and communications schemes symbolic of "modernism," while extreme corruption too ate into its loans. In 1978, when the price of copper plummeted, Peru's debt service obligations totaled more than 50% of its export earnings, and Zaire was earning too little foreign exchange to pay for essential materials or spare parts, much less make payments on its $3.5 billion of foreign debt.

A country in such difficulty may repudiate its debts, ask its creditors to reschedule them, or request new loans for the purpose of paying the old ones without rescheduling. Late in 1978 and early in 1979 both Peru and Zaire were negotiating rescheduling. In both cases the International Monetary Fund was making relatively small loans to provide foreign exchange reserves; the price paid by the countries was acceptance of IMF insistence on severe fiscal and monetary restrictions, which may bring economic stabilization at the cost of a temporary reduction in the level of living. Early in 1979, increased world demand caused copper prices to rise again to record levels; that should somewhat ease the problems of both countries.

Turkey provides the most dramatic example of a country in foreign ex-

---

[8] India and Indonesia were two of the four countries for which the most serious danger of trouble was foreseen by Charles R. Frank and William R. Cline in "Measurement of Debt Servicing Capacity: An Application of Discriminant Analysis," *Journal of International Economics,* 1 (1971), 340–42.

change trouble. Turkey had decided in the mid-1970s to try to continue its economic growth in spite of the 1973–74 increases in oil prices, the 1974–75 recession in the industrial countries (which reduced its exports), and the inflation which was increasing the cost of its imports. The country had a foreign exchange deficit of $4 billion in 1977 and of $2.3 billion in 1978. By the end of 1978 the large foreign banks had refused to make further loans to Turkey, some smaller institutions had continued to make loans, Turkey had attracted deposits by offering very high interest rates, some suppliers had continued to extend credits, and some Western governments had made loans to prevent economic collapse. At the end of 1978 Turkey's foreign debts totaled more than $12 billion. In mid-1979, many Turkish manufacturing plants closed for lack of foreign exchange to import needed oil or materials. It was impossible to obtain fertilizer imports. This, the most serious debt repayment problem of modern times, was being met in 1979 by forcing on Turkey an IMF directive for economic stringency, including drastic currency devaluation. In return, creditor governments were lengthening the terms of public and private loans, and, as part of the package, extending net governmental loans to meet immediate needs.

Debt Relief as Development Assistance

In 1976 UNCTAD proposed debt relief for all LDCs who desired it, as a form of development assistance. The greatest proportionate relief would go to the least developed countries, the "developing" landlocked countries, and the "developing" small island countries. Some middle-income countries oppose the recommendation; they do not wish to have their creditworthiness placed in jeopardy. There is no prospect that the proposal will be accepted, even by official creditors. (The forgiving of debt by the World Bank would place its own creditworthiness in jeopardy.) But some observers suggest that some countries should be allowed to simply default on private debts. These observers say that disciplining is needed by private banks and other lenders as well as the borrowing countries.

A Sea of Credit, a Sea of Trouble?

A Eurodollar is simply a dollar deposit held by a bank outside the United States. An American importer pays for his imports by a draft drawn on an American bank; the seller of the goods deposits the draft in his local bank; that bank sends it to an American bank for deposit. If Americans were exporting as much as they are importing, that deposit would be drawn on to pay for the American exports. However, during the 1960s and especially during the years since 1973 Americans have imported far more goods than they have exported. As a result, foreign banks have accumulated unprecedented dollar deposits. Moreover, one bank abroad may deposit a dollar draft in another bank abroad, thus obtaining a dollar deposit; the second bank may deposit the dollar draft in a third bank, and the third one in a fourth. Thus three or more dollar-denominated deposits may exist abroad and be used as a basis for making loans, on the basis of one dollar draft. Banks everywhere in the world and especially in Europe, including branches or subsidiaries of American banks, have used such deposits to make dollar loans to any creditworthy borrower they could find, and to some borrowers that were none too creditworthy. When the borrower (say an African, Asian, or Latin American government) spent the borrowed money, its check probably was deposited in one of the lending banks, and so there was little net drain on the dollar-denominated deposits.

The reader may remember from his Principles of Economics course that this relending is the process by which, within the United States, on the basis of an initial creation of bank credit through a loan, an increase in loans and bank deposits of four, five, or six times the amount of the initial loans may be created. This multiplication of credit is limited by the reserve which each bank is required by law to hold against its deposits. But since Eurodollars are *dollar* deposits, there is no reserve requirement against them in the country on which the bank holding them is located, and since they are held by banks abroad, American banking authorities cannot impose reserve requirements. There is, then, no legal limitation whatever on the amount of Eurodollars that can be created per initial one dollar of deposits. On the basis of initial Eurodollar deposits of some tens of billions of dollars, it is estimated that at the end of 1975 some $200 billion and at the end of 1978 some $400 billion of Eurodollar deposits had been created. (Only a minority of the loans that created them were made to LDCs.)

There are Euroyen, Euromarks, etc., but the great bulk of Eurocurrency is Eurodollars.

For the time being all is well, even though since 1974 the exports of LDCs as a group have been increasing more slowly than they did during the boom in the West that preceded the industrial country recession of 1974–75. But some bankers fear that a financial crisis might result if a number of LDCs should have serious debt service problems and as a result the condition of some of the lending banks comes into question. For Eurodollar deposits there is no "lender of last resort." In the United States, no matter how heavy the run on members of the Federal Reserve System, Federal Reserve banks can provide the money necessary to meet it. (If a bank in a basically unsound condition is closed by the banking authorities, the Federal Deposit Insurance Corporation will protect its depositors.) But if there is a run on Eurodollar deposits because some Eurodollar loans turn sour, will the central banks of the countries in which the threatened banks are situated feel an obligation to bail them out? Will American banks and through them the Federal Reserve System do so?

It is an anomaly of present-day world finance that such huge liabilities can have arisen quite unregulated and quite outside the cover of any financial umbrella. If financial catastrophe should occur in the Eurodollar system, the economic development of LDCs and probably that of Western countries would be hobbled for a short period. However, the danger has been eased and possibly largely eliminated (unless future excesses occur) by a development that is otherwise regarded as a curse: world inflation. For the amount of a loan remains unchanged during inflation, but the loan becomes progressively easier to repay as prices, including those of the goods one is selling, increase.

FOR FURTHER READING

Concerning two-gap analysis, see in addition to the articles by Chenery or Chenery and Strout cited in notes 4 and 5 of this chapter Henry J. Bruton, "The Two-Gap Approach to Aid and Development: Comment," *American Economic Review*, 59 (June 1969), 439–46.

Gerald K. Helleiner, *A World Divided*, parts 3 and 4, discusses issues in international finance and debt burden.

See also "For Further Reading," Chapter 18.

18

Economic Aid,
Private Lending,
Direct Investment

Economic aid and direct investment by private firms are alike in that both bring capital into LDCs. They differ greatly in most other respects. Intermediate in nature are private loans.

ECONOMIC AID: INSTITUTIONS AND PROBLEMS

As Point Four of a 1949 address to Congress, then President Harry Truman proposed an American program of bilaterial economic aid to low-income countries, that is, aid directly from the United States to recipient countries. Congress assented. Point Four proposed technical assistance— the provision of "American know-how," in Truman's unfelicitous but popular phrase. Emphasis on capital aid developed later. At about the same time, nations of Europe that had freed their colonies and saw an obligation or advantage in extending aid to the new nations established bilateral aid programs. Some European nations that had not had colonies followed suit. Japan, the USSR, and China also have their bilateral aid programs. In the 1970s, the oil-rich Middle East countries began to grant foreign aid, both bilaterally and through regional institutions which they established.

The International Bank for Reconstruction and Development and the International Monetary Fund had been formed in 1944. Their central purposes as visualized at that time were to promote the postwar reconstruction of the war-ravaged countries of Europe and stability in international monetary relationships. The last two words in the name of the bank were added as an afterthought. The bank's initial funds were from subscriptions by member governments, but it soon became able to borrow large sums from the financial markets at low rates of interest.

It began lending operations in 1946. Its loans were initially "bankers' loans," loans toward large industrial, transport, communication, and power projects, and covering only the foreign exchange costs of these projects. The loans were granted at a rate of interest one and a fraction percent above that at which the bank itself borrowed, 1% to reimburse the bank for its services and the added fraction to set up an insurance fund against losses. (No losses occurred.) The interest rate at which loans were granted to LDCs was still a concessional one.

The bank's position as a borrower in the financial markets presently became secure, because it was incurring no losses and because its income from interest on its loans was accumulating. It could therefore make loans on easier terms without endangering its borrowing power. Taking advantage of this financial security, the bank established two subsidiaries as the foreign exchange problems of LDCs, including their debt service obligations, worsened. One of the subsidiaries, the International Development Association (IDA), makes "soft" loans to governments (mainly for infrastructure projects)—loans with low interest rates, long maturities, and often a grace period before the repayment of the principal or even the interest begins. Because loans by IDA are not self-supporting, IDA must depend for its funds on subscriptions by governments plus a share of IBRD net income.

The other subsidiary, the International Finance Corporation (IFC), was established to provide funds directly to private business concerns in the LDCs. The funds typically consist of the purchase of preferred stock, with an agreement that IFC may sell the stock in the open market if the firm prospers and the stock becomes marketable.

The three institutions together are self-titled the World Bank Group, or merely the World Bank. A fourth organization, the International Center for Settlement of Investment Disputes, has become attached to the World Bank but is autonomous.

Countries of each region of the LDC world urged the formation of a lending agency specifically oriented toward that region, and successively the Inter-American, Asian, African, and Caribbean Development banks were set up. The countries of the European Economic Community also established their own multilateral agencies, the European Development Fund and the European Investment Bank. The funds of these various agencies are small relative to those of the World Bank. The richer oil-producing countries have also established several well-funded multilateral funds and banks.

Occasionally a consortium of a small number of governments or of governments plus the World Bank jointly make a development loan. The "Aid India Club," formed by ten countries and the World Bank after the Indian drought of 1966–67, is the largest of these.

The United Nations Organization was formed in 1945. It has spawned various specialized agencies, including the Food and Agriculture Organization (FAO), the World Health Organization (WHO), the United Nations

Economic, Social, and Cultural Organization (UNESCO), and the United Nations International Children's Emergency Fund (UNICEF), and it took over an older agency that had been fostered by the League of Nations, the International Labor Office. These agencies offered technical assistance in their special fields, and pretty much went their separate and uncoordinated ways in doing so, though in the 1970s a certain degree of coordination was achieved. The United Nations Organization also spawned the General Agreement on Tariffs and Trade (GATT—an organization, not an "agreement"), to negotiate trade agreements, and the United Nations Conference on Trade and Development (UNCTAD—also an organization) to be the voice of the LDCs for seeking trade concessions.

Changing Conceptions, Changing Programs

Foreign aid has taken four physical forms and one purely financial or generalized form: capital goods, agricultural commodities, technical assistance, military hardware, and on occasion the provision of foreign exchange, intended to aid a country's development program as a whole, which the recipient country is free to use at its discretion. These loans are called "program loans." Military aid is excluded in this chapter in the calculation of the amount of aid granted and in the discussion of economic aid.

Both bilateral and multilateral official economic aid have undergone successive changes in emphasis. In the first years of the American aid program, technical assistance was stressed. It was thought that if the lower income countries were shown the methods of the technically advanced countries, they could quickly adopt those methods and raise their incomes. When it became apparent that the transfer of technologies is not so simple a matter as had been assumed, emphasis on the provision of economic resources, especially capital goods, increased. Today the American aid program is an eclectic one. It is based on no ideology about "the key" to economic development. The provision of "surplus" American agricultural commodities on concessional terms has been fairly important in the aid program.

Especially in the IBRD, emphasis during the 1950s was on loans for large manufacturing projects and for transportation, communication, and power facilities. Such projects could be appraised more readily than others. They were "sound"; the IBRD could readily raise money by selling bonds if the funds were going to be used for such "solid" projects. The MDCs, like the LDCs, may have had the mistaken notion that since advanced countries had much manufacturing, the establishment of factories would quickly bring modernity.

Five subsequent changes of emphasis in loan policy merit comment. The first was a diversification of loans to other, including smaller, projects. Second, loans were made in increasing amounts for "social infrastructure"— schools, housing, health facilities, and the like. Third, in the 1960s the world "food problem" became appreciated, and contributors of development aid increased their stress on aid to agriculture. Recipient countries, bemused with the desirability of industry, were slower than donor countries to understand the importance of increasing productivity in agriculture; perhaps the Indian drought of 1966–67 was influential in changing their attitudes.

Fourth, as the relationships among the various components of the development process became better understood, and as the indirect ways in which investment increases foreign exchange needs also became better understood, there came a certain degree of willingness on the part of some aid-giving countries, as well as the IBRD, to grant loans to support the foreign exchange needs of a development program as a whole, rather than merely to finance imports for a given project. These loans are known as "program loans."

Lastly, as mentioned in Chapter 4, in the 1970s the World Bank emphasized loans aimed specifically at relieving the poverty of the lowest income groups in LDCs.

While its loan activities were evolving, the IBRD realized the need to give technical assistance to countries receiving loans in order to make the loans both more effective and more secure. Today, like the American government, other governments, and some specialized United Nations agencies, it has resident technical assistance staffs in a number of countries.

However closely a given loan or grant may be tied to a specific purpose, most loans are program loans in effect, for if a country has a development or current expenditure program containing five parts and a foreign government or institutions will finance any one of them, the government can use its own funds to finance the other four. If the recipient government wishes to buy military airplanes, and the lending institution refuses funds for these but will make a loan to finance the construction of schools, the government can and probably will then spend for airplanes the funds that it would otherwise have had to spend for schools. Only in two circumstances does the economic aid alter the government's overall program. If the country is not creditworthy on the private capital market, and if the lending government or institution makes a loan for a very large project that the government could not have financed out of current funds, then the loan augments the country's plans. And if a lender offers funds for a purpose which the LDC government has had no intention of pursuing, and if the lender is able to persuade the government to incur indebtedness for that purpose, then too the lender has altered the country's total program. This is probably true of some recent IBRD loans to aid the lowest income groups in LDCs.

The "fungibility" of aid—the ability of the recipient government to use aid to augment any type of expenditures it chooses—has given rise to political frictions. Because of aid fungibility, lending agencies—perhaps especially the U.S. Agency for International Development—have sometimes insisted on scrutinizing a recipient government's entire expenditure program before agreeing to extend aid, whereupon the government has denounced this interference with its internal affairs.

ECONOMIC AID: THE MAGNITUDE

Table 18-1 gives figures for Official Development Assistance (ODA) by the governments of Development Assistance Committee countries since 1962 (when programs of economic aid were already 13 years old). The table and data for the years not shown in the table indicate:

That the value of governmental economic aid, in constant dollars, seemed to be on a plateau during the 1960s, then shifted to a slightly higher plateau (about $450 million per year higher) in 1971.

That in current dollars the amount of economic aid has been rising fairly steadily.

But that as a percentage of the GNP of DAC countries it fell during the 1960s, between 1970 and 1976 fluctuated slightly above and below one third of 1%, and dropped in 1977 to a lower percentage. It may not recover from this low level.

TABLE 18-1   Net development assistance from DAC countries to less developed countries and multilateral agencies, 1962-1977

The amount of DAC official development assistance peaked in 1976. Its ratio to the GNP of DAC countries has been falling since 1962.

	1962	1965	1968	1971	1974	1975	1976	1977
Millions of U.S. dollars, in 1970 prices	6,481	6,768	6,806	7,418	6,855	7,781	7,414	7,296
Millions of U.S. dollars, in current values	5,438	5,895	6,309	7,759	11,317	13,585	13,665	14,695
Percent of GNP of aid-giving countries	0.52	0.44	0.37	0.35	0.33	0.35	0.33	0.31
U.S. aid as percent of U.S. GNP	0.56	0.49	0.37	0.32	0.24	0.26	0.25	0.22

Source: *Development Cooperation*, various annual issues.

The United States has done less well. In every year before 1968, the percentage of U.S. aid to its GNP exceeded the DAC average; in every year since 1968, the U.S. percentage has been below the DAC average. The U.S. percentage has not been as high as 0.3% since 1971, and in 1977 it fell to a new low of 0.22%, which drew the average pecentage for all DAC countries down with it. The 1978 percentage is not available as this is written, but the U.S. percentage was certainly below 0.2%. Though the U.S. governmental contribution of aid is much the largest of any DAC country, as a percentage of GNP the U.S. aid was 13th on the list of 17 in 1977, exceeding only Japan

308

and three European countries whose aid effort has been termed "derisory" (see Table 18–2). As Table 18–2 also shows, three small European countries—Sweden, the Netherlands, and Norway—have become the leaders in giving economic aid. As a group, their average 1977 percentage of GNP was almost four times the average percentage of the three countries with the largest and strongest economies in the non-Communist world—the United States, West Germany, and Japan.

TABLE 18–2   Net official development assistance in 1977 from DAC countries to less developed countries and to multilateral agencies

United States aid looms large in absolute terms but small in relative terms.

| Country | Disbursement | |
	As Percentage of GNP	In $ Millions
Sweden	0.99%	$ 779
Netherlands	0.85	900
Norway	0.82	295
Denmark	0.60	258
France	0.60	2,267
Canada	0.51	991
Belgium	0.46	371
Australia	0.45	427
United Kingdom	0.37	914
New Zealand	0.35	53
West Germany	0.27	1,386
Austria	0.24	118
United States	0.22	4,156
Japan	0.21	1,424
Switzerland	0.19	119
Finland	0.17	49
Italy	0.10	186
Average and total	0.31%	$14,696

Source: Development Cooperation: 1978 Review (Paris: OECD, 1978), p. 191.

The centrally planned economies (primarily the USSR and China) have extended loans and grants. However, even including the Soviet Union's largest continuing aid to Cuba, the aid by these countries averaged only $1.1 billion per year from 1969 through 1976 (and fell to $0.7 billion in 1977).

Suddenly in the 1970s the oil countries emerged as large givers of economic aid. Aid disbursements by OPEC governments were above $5.5 billion in 1975, in 1976, and in 1977. During 1973–77 the aid of OPEC governments averaged more than 2% of their GNP. In recent years, Saudi

Arabia has been the world's second largest aid-giver, after only the United States. The OPEC countries have now formed important multilateral agencies. At first aid by OPEC countries was almost wholly to peoples with whom the Middle East oil countries had cultural ties, peoples of countries that neither suffered the most from the oil price increases nor were most needy. However, by 1978 in its spread and characteristics the aid granted by OPEC members was beginning to resemble that given by DAC members, and the two groups were cofinancing many projects. In 1979 there was some indication that OPEC aid might be declining.

Multilateral aid has increased steadily relative to bilateral aid, primarily because while some national legislatures, including the U.S. Congress, have wearied of aid-giving, the IBRD has been able to obtain large sums by selling bonds to the private financial markets and has ambitiously increased its lending programs. Yet multilateral aid is still much less than one half of total aid. Table 18–3 shows the volume of multilateral aid in 1977. Countries receiving aid have pressed to have their own regional development banks (funded, of course, by the highest income countries). Table 18–3 also shows the proliferation of these institutions.

TABLE 18–3   **Net disbursements by multilateral institutions to less developed countries, 1977 ($ millions)**

Most multilateral aid is by world institutions. Regional banks have been established in response to regional demand.

World Bank Group	3,102
Of which, IDA	1,132
United Nations	1,252
Regional institutions	
EEC	
European Development Fund }	501
European Investment Bank }	
OPEC banklike agencies	1,779
Of which, Gulf Organization for	
Development in Egypt	1,204
Regional development banks	
Inter-American Development Bank	687
Asian Development Bank	306
African Development Bank	66
Caribbean Development Bank	24
World Food Program and other	323
Total	6,971
Of which, concessional element	3,871
For comparison	
DAC bilateral	10,080
OPEC bilateral	3,760

Source: *Development Cooperation: 1978 Review* (Paris: OECD, 1978), p. 228.

The "Grant Element"

By definition, only concessional flows of resources are considered ODA. The concept of the "concessional element" in aid (also called the "grant element") needs explanation.

The concessional element is of course 100% if the aid is a grant. The concessional element in a loan is a rate of interest below commercial rates, often combined with a grace period during which no repayment of principal need be made and in most instances no interest is charged. The concessional element is greater if the repayment period of a loan made on these easy terms is long.

The value of the grant element of a loan may be calculated by calculating the present value of the required stream of repayments, discounted to the present at the prevailing commercial rate of interest. This present value is the amount of the comemrcial loan for which these repayments would be required. The excess of the actual loan over the amount of a commercial loan that the repayments would buy is the grant element. Of the $14.7 billion of aid funds extended by DAC member governments in 1977, the grant element was 89%. Almost all resource flows from the Communist countries and most of those from OPEC countries are also on concessional terms.

Why Do We Do It?

As the data of the preceding tables show, the absolute amount of economic aid is large. Why do we provide it?

Political motives have just been mentioned. They were certainly prominent in Harry Truman's early call for the initiation of an American aid program and in the affirmative response of the U.S. Congress. However, the purely humanitarian element in the motivation for aid should not be underestimated. Much aid has been provided out of the sense of guilt that high-income peoples felt because of their affluence, out of the belief that affluence created an obligation, or simply out of sympathy for the lower income peoples, whatever unconscious motivations underlay it. Perhaps the aid extended by the Scandinavian countries and the tiny amount extended by Switzerland arises most purely from humanitarian motives.

The humanitarian motive has sometimes been associated with the conception that the low-income peoples are less developed than we advanced ones, mentally and perhaps emotionally as well as technically, and that they need fatherly or perhaps schoolmasterly guidance. A veteran but maverick British colonial administrator in Burma thought that he saw in the post–World War II U.S. aid program the reappearance of the notion of the "white man's burden" to help inferior peoples.

In the United States the profit motive has been most conspicuous in agricultural commodity aid. The United States, with its huge agricultural productive capacity, has been the leader in providing food grains, cotton, and some other agricultural products to low-income countries with agricultural deficits. At times of U.S. agricultural surpluses, spokespersons reflecting the interests of U.S. farmers have seen agricultural commodity assistance as a remarkably beneficial program. American manufacturers have appeared in Washington singularly little to press for economic aid. Perhaps the prospective sales through economic aid of any one group of manufacturers have been too small to stimulate lobbying. Perhaps business lobbyists have been occupied with matters more important to their corporations. Members of Congress voting for foreign aid bills have often insisted that the aid must be "tied," that is, that funds loaned or granted must be used to purchase goods and services in the United States rather than elsewhere or to defray the local costs of development projects. Certain other countries have been more insistent on this. The United States has been more willing than some countries to abandon tying provisions if other countries would also do so. The vote of U.S. congressional supporters of foreign aid to tie it has often been motivated more by a desire to be able to report to voters that they were being alert to U.S. interests than by the urging of U.S. producers.

United States economic and military aid to most South American governments and to a ring of countries partly surrounding the Soviet Union; Soviet aid to the "people's republics" and to Cuba, Egypt, Iraq, and Syria; Chinese aid to North Korea, North Vietnam, and several African countries—all of these can be interpreted as a search for political advantage. So also can the British, French, Belgian, and Dutch emphasis on aid to former colonies, and the aid by Middle East oil countries to other Middle Eastern countries. The results have sometimes been disappointing to the aid-extenders. Gifts often do not buy friendship, especially when they are made in a patronizing manner, or when the recipients regard them as transfers to which they are entitled.

Whatever the mix of motives may be, if the results of aid are good, let us praise it.

SOME AID PROBLEMS

Tied Aid

A tied loan is worth less than its face value to the recipient, for the country making the loan may not be the most advantageous place in which to buy the materials and equipment for the project for which the loan was granted. A study of economic aid to Indonesia during 1967–69 estimated that on this account the tied aid granted was worth 19% less than untied aid would have been.[1] A similar percentage may apply elsewhere. Perhaps even more important, tying is likely to induce the recipient to frame projects

---

[1] Ichizo Miyamoto, "The Real Value of Tied Aid: The Case of Indonesia in 1967–1969," *Economic Development and Cultural Change,* 22 (April 1974), 436–52.

with as much import content as possible so that the loans will pay for as large a percentage as possible of the total project cost, and this is likely to induce the recipient to design projects that are as capital-intensive as possible. The projects will then create less employment and will be likely to have continuing import costs for their maintenance. On these counts too the recipient loses.

The DAC has been pressing its members to "untie" their aid, and it has had some success. In 1973 all DAC members agreed to untie their contributions to multilateral institutions. In 1974 eight major contributors agreed to permit their bilateral aid funds to be used for purchases in LDCs. In subsequent years more liberal financing of local costs was provided than had been provided previously. Thus a goodly part of the distorting effort of tying has been alleviated. But bilateral aid recipients are still not permitted to shop among Western Europe, the United States, and Japan to get the least expensive or the most suitable equipment and materials.

Agricultural Commodity Aid: Helpful or Harmful?

Since 1954, the United States has provided agricultural commodities on concessional terms as part of its economic development aid. Agricultural commodities can relieve starvation from famine or other causes; for this purpose the United States provides them as grants. They can also serve economic development, by relieving a country of the need to use its foreign exchange to increase its food supply, if development expenditures increase the demand for food by raising income. This effect was noted in Chapter 15.

More generally, if scarcity of resources or foreign exchange is a constraint on development, agricultural commodity aid can serve economic development as effectively as the provision of capital goods does, if resources can be shifted from agricultural into capital formation or into production for export to provide added foreign exchange. However, agricultural commodity aid from the United States under PL 480 cannot relieve a shortage of foreign exchange by substituting for commercial imports, at least from the United States, for PL 480 requires that the provision of agricultural aid be additional to previous U.S. sales to the country on commercial terms.

So far as it depresses the price of agricultural commodities within the recipient country, or prevents it increase, agricultural commodity aid has a retarding effect on the development of agriculture, which has long-run importance in economic growth. The degree of the effect is disputed. If food is distributed gratis or at subsidized prices to urban poor who could not otherwise afford it, this decreases little or not at all the demand for farm products. If agricultural commodity aid permits enlargement of the development program, that aid may increase the demand for farm products by raising urban and other incomes. There has been vigorous argument concerning preferred agricultural commodity aid policy, sometimes portrayed as between the hardhearted and doctrinaire and the humanitarian, sometimes as between the shortsighted and the longsighted. No general statement of desirable policy is possible; the choice depends on the conditions and the skill of administration in any given receipient country.

Counterpart Funds

In the past, agreements for the sale of agricultural commodities under PL 480 sometimes provided for payment in local currency. The local funds thus obtained were called "counterpart funds." Such agreements usually provided for use of the funds to pay U.S. embassy and related expenses, and beyond this to be lent to the recipient government for development uses agreed on by the United States and the recipient government. Economically, the provision was a sham, in two ways. Apart from their use for diplomatic expenses—which deprived the local government of foreign exchange—the counterpart funds did not actually repay the United States. Also, they did not constitute payment by the local government, for it could without any inflationary or other effect create the funds with which to make the payment, and it could borrow from its own banking system with precisely the same economic effects as if it borrowed from the U.S. government deposits that had been created. However, borrowing from counterpart funds, once they had been established, enabled the local government to tell its constituents that it was not engaging in deficit financing. And as noted, in the United States the provision permitted American legislators to tell their constituents that our food or other goods were not being given away.

Budget Distortion

The possibility that economic aid may cause or permit a country's revenues raised from domestic resources to be absorbed by nondevelopment purposes and so, in the long run, may impoverish the country's development program if aid ends, has been mentioned in Chapter 15. It is difficult to weigh the likelihood to the effect.

THE "LINK"

The International Monetary Fund was organized after World War II to manage, so far as might be possible, the world monetary system. When world liquidity seemed inadequate in the late 1960s, IMF members voted in 1969 to give the IMF authority to issue Special Drawing Rights (SDRs) to its members in proportion to their subscriptions in setting up the IMF. An 85% vote of the members must authorize each issuance. SDRs are like bank deposits. They can be used to make payments by the central bank of one country to that of another. In this sense they are a "world money." SDRs equivalent in amount to $9.5 billion were issued in 1970–72.

The lower income countries that are members of the IMF have formed a Committee of 77 (now representing not 77 but 125 countries, and active in the World Bank as well as the fund), which has pressed at successive IMF meetings for a link between the issuance of SDRs and economic aid. The IMF, they argue, should issue SDRs not to all member countries but to the lower income countries, directly or through development agencies. As the LDCs spent the funds, those funds would swell the international reserves of the industrial nations. The proposal has its logic.

Each member of the IMF casts votes in proportion to its subscription to the capital of the fund. The affluent nations thus cast a large majority. They have rejected the proposals for a "link," on the ground that international monetary management and economic aid should not be fused and confused. Now that the world is awash in a sea of Eurodollars, SDRs are no longer being issued. The IMF and its major members would like to see world liquidity decreased, not increased.

However, the IMF has taken some actions that are not unlike a "link." It has set up three funds, unofficially called "oil facilities," to make loans to nations whose balances of payments have run into deficit because of the increases in oil prices. These "facilities" meet only a very small fraction of the problem. They were funded by subscriptions of the high-income countries and the major oil exporters. In 1976 the IMF placed profits from gold sales in a trust fund to be used to aid LDCs with especially serious balance of payments problems.

DIRECT INVESTMENT

Private loans to LDCs were discussed in Chapter 17. The two other means of capital inflow are portfolio investment—the purchase of securities as an investment—and direct investment. There has been virtually no private portfolio investment in LDCs by MDC banks or other investors since World War II. Direct investment is discussed here.

Direct foreign investment in LDCs is by multinational corporations. The magnitude of the operations of MNCs was discussed in Chapter 11. Every such corporation believes that its operations are highly beneficial to the LDCs. Many persons in LDCs disagree. The governments of the larger Latin American countries, out of greater self-assurance and through a more "European" viewpoint, may welcome foreign enterprise, though sometimes the welcome is lukewarm, but the newer lower income nations are likely to look upon direct foreign investment as inimical to their welfare or at least exploitative. This section considers the economic aspects of this controversy.

The business firms note that they introduce added capital and an added productive enterprise into the country, and argue that in doing so they create added employment and income, introduce advanced techniques and management, train the country's workers, and, usually, increase the country's exports or decrease its import needs and thereby improve its balance of payments. The LDC asserts that the foreign firms drain income from the country, exploit the country's workers by paying them only the local level of wages, refuse to transmit their technical knowledge, often exhaust the country's resources, and if they do contribute any benefit, grasp exorbitant profits in return—and do all this in a patronizing and arrogant manner. In some instances, it is asserted, a foreign venture forecloses domestic investment in the same field, and by obtaining local loans uses scarce domestic resources that would otherwise be used effectively elsewhere. The validity of these claims may be sorted out to some degree.

Benefits?

Disregarding for the moment its effects on the balance of payments, direct foreign investment benefits the country economically if it yields a net increase in value added in the country. If, in addition to the profits and interest which it withdraws from the country, it yields a net increase in the incomes of the domestic workers plus the value added of the domestic suppliers, customer firms, and other domestic firms that its operations affect, then it makes an economic contribution. Note that it is the *increase* in wages and other value added that is in point. What should be considered is the *increase* in its workers' real wages over those that they were earning or that they could be earning in alternative employment. The foreign firm is expected to pay the country's highest wages, and probably does, to minimize labor trouble and to get the most capable workers. (It may still have the country's greatest labor troubles; its workers may be the most aggressive as well as the most capable, and they may have expansive notions of the wages that the firm should be able to pay.) If drawing those workers from their previous employment creates a chain of demand by which workers at progressively lower wage levels are drawn into jobs paying higher real wages, each moving up a notch in productivity, the entire sequence should be considered. If, on the other hand, the operation of the enterprise from which the workers were bid away is injured, its loss of value added is relevant. The argument ignores any effect on the distribution of income. That effect may be positive, a sequence of workers down to the lowest income levels moving up in income, or it may be negative—the operation, for example, may create unemployment in traditional, or at least less modern, enterprises. The income distribution effect and the aggregate value-added effect are incommensurable; there is no objective way in which one may be weighed against the other if their signs differ.

Training given by multinational corporations (MNCs) may be slight or considerable. A common complaint of LDCs is that the top managerial and technical positions are reserved for foreigners. The complaint is justified. Not only do multinational firms have difficulty in finding indigenous individuals whom they think capable of top jobs; often they are reluctant to place capable local individuals in positions in which these individuals will have access to company secrets, for example to production formulas or to accounting records that might bring into question the firms' profit reports to the local government.

The operations of foreign firms also affect the country's balance of payments. Some analysts balance the country's total current outflow of profits and interest against the current inflow of capital—both easily identifiable in the country's balance of payments accounts—and if the former is larger, these analysts conclude that foreign firms are siphoning away the country's wealth. The argument is spurious. Relevant considerations were stated earlier in this chapter in discussing the debt service problem. If the operations of a foreign firm increase the country's exports or decrease its imports by more than the amount of the outflow of dividends and interest, then they improve the balance of payments, even though the dividend and interest flows appear in the accounts as a large debit item and the effects on exports and imports are not identifiable.

Suppose, however, that the firm's operations create a net addition to value added plus a "consumer surplus," but require the import of material and neither decrease other imports nor increase exports, so that the balance of payments is adversely affected. It may be argued that because of the increase in the country's productivity its ability to export is indirectly increased. The argument is dubious; there is no assurance that improvement in the country's techniques of production and increase in its aggregate or per capita income will increase its ability to export. Increased income may result in an increased absolute amount of saving, even if not a higher share of income saved, but it need not create an increased ability to export. We may then again have an incommensurability; there is no objective way of weighing the adverse balance of payments effect against the favorable value-added effect—or the reverse, if that is the case.

It may be argued that if the country's choices thus create a deficit in the balance of payments, the currency should be devalued, that in the long run the adjustments in the economy resulting from the shifts in relative prices will maximize economic welfare. The argument is impeccable with respect to a well-functioning neoclassical system, but this may be of little comfort in the shorter run.

Factor Proportions; Transfer of Technology

Economists often accuse multinational corporations of transferring to LDCs capital-intensive methods that are uneconomic in a country that is capital-poor and labor-rich relative to the high-income economy in which the methods were appropriate, and uneconomic also relative to more labor-intensive methods of making the same or efficiently substitutable products, if these methods exist or can be devised. Certainly in this sense many methods introduced into LDCs by local as well as multinational corporations, and in many sectors rather than merely in manufacturing, are uneconomic. But research studies in India, Mexico, Puerto Rico, and the Central American Common Market have found that multinational corporations are less guilty in this respect than are local ones. The Indian study concluded that in comparable circumstances (i.e., with adjustment for the age of the factory and for differences in wage rates) American firms in India use more fixed capital but less capital overall, relative to labor, than do Indian firms. The other studies, using in general less complex analysis, also concluded that foreign firms use less capital-intensive methods than do local ones.[2] The implication is that local firms tend more strongly to simply imitate "modern" methods, multinational firms to be more adaptive when they face the new (to them) economic circumstances of LDCs. The reason asserted is that the managers of MNC plants are more likely to be engineers and so more competent or more confident in adapting the methods imported.

The transfer of technology from industrialized to less industrialized countries was discussed in Chapter 12. An important question concerning it is not merely the technology initially transferred, but whether it becomes frozen, so that continuing technical progress does not occur. Multinational firms are charged with being rigid in this respect. The accuracy of the charge seems unlikely, in view of the evidence that they use less capital-intensive methods than do local firms. Interestingly, the only direct empirical evidence relates to plantations rather than manufacturing.[3] Hla Myint, presumably out of his experience in Southeast Asia, charges that foreign firms introduce plantation methods that thereafter are never changed, and Clifford Geertz has described the evolution of a plantation system in Indonesia (the Dutch East Indies) in which methods so interlocked that technical change would have been possible only by massively scrapping cultivation schemes and starting over. Insofar as new techniques are transmitted to nationals, whether they become frozen depends on the degree of innovational energy of the receiving country.

---

[2] Larry Willmore, "Direct Foreign Investment in Central American Manufacturing," *World Development*, 4 (June 1976), 499–517; W. Paul Strassmann, *Technological Change and Economic Development: The Manufacturing Experience of Mexico and Puerto Rico* (Ithaca: Cornell University Press, 1968); and Danny M. Leipziger, "Production Characteristics in Foreign Enclave and Domestic Manufacturing: The Case of India," *World Development*, 4 (April 1976), 321–25.

[3] Hla Myint, "The Gains from International Trade and the Backward Countries," *Review of Economic Studies*, 22 (1954–55), 129–42; and Clifford M. Geertz, *Agricultural Involution: The Process of Ecological Change in Indonesia* (Berkeley: University of California Press, 1963).

Exploitation?

In any event, critics assert, multinational corporations that establish themselves in LDCs withdraw massive and unjustified profits. Even if they do good, they do it at exorbitant cost. Certainly it is difficult for the government of a low-income country to know whether a foreign corporation is reporting the true profit on its operations within the country and whether it is thereby paying the full tax for which it is liable. Multinational corporations on their part often regard local taxes as exorbitant, and they may have no compunction about evading them as they can. To minimize the profits of the subsidiary, the home office may charge the subsidiary high royalties for the use of patented processes. The transaction between this subsidiary and other divisions of the corporations are not at arm's length. There may be ample opportunity for such devices as transfer pricing, through which profits are transferred out of the country by setting high prices on goods sold to this subsidiary by other subsidiaries and by setting low prices on sales by this subsidiary to other subsidiaries in other countries. The transactions will of course be reported differently in those other countries. It is the standard practice of some reputable corporations to pay top staff members imported into a country only part of their salaries in the local currency, and to report only that part as the full salaries to the local government, in order to minimize local personal income taxes. The balance of salary is credited to the individuals' accounts at the head office or in banks of the home country. One may suppose that corporations which follow these practices may also resort to other methods, that have not become known, that will minimize the locally reported corporate profit.

The Effect on Growth

There may be other less easily identifiable effects of direct foreign investment on growth. Colin Stoneman has done an elaborate multiple regression analysis of the relationship to the average annual rate of growth in GDP in lower income countries of the following: gross domestic investment, net inflow on direct investment account, other net capital inflows, and the stock of foreign direct investment capital—all of these as proportions of GDP.[4] He used data from as early postwar dates as were available, for every LDC for which they were available, omitting only Bolivia and South Korea in the early 1950s, Zaire in the early 1960s, Nigeria and Cambodia in the late 1960s, and South Vietnam altogether. He grouped the countries into various groups, and he ran separate regressions for various

---

[4] "Foreign Capital and Economic Growth," *World Development*, 3 (January 1975), 11–26.

subperiods. He found high coefficients, statistically highly significant, for domestic saving and for "other capital inflows" (dominated by foreign aid); a low coefficient not statistically significant in most runs at the 5% level, for capital inflow on direct investment account; and a small but statistically significant negative coefficient for the stock of foreign direct investment capital. The statistical implication is that, other things being equal, a country with a stock of foreign capital in direct investments equal to 40% of GDP has a growth rate lower by 1% per year than it would be if the country had no foreign investment.

It is not easy to discern a causal relationship. Does technology diffuse more slowly from foreign-owned enterprises than from domestically owned ones? Do executives of foreign-owned enterprises "naturally" group with reactionary political elites in ways inimical to economic growth? Perhaps foreign firms, not facing the competition they face at home, do after all "freeze" their methods.

Stoneman accepts the reality of a causal influence. However, he argues that foreign investment is just one aspect of a country's situation in the world economic system, and he concludes that elimination by a country of the foreign investment in it would not be advisable unless a "positive substitute" for such investment can be found. It is difficult to follow this argument; presumably the statistical coefficient captured the net of all favorable as well as unfavorable effects.

CONTROLLING THE MNCs

A country may desire the activity proposed by a foreign corporation. The corporation wishes to enter the country. On what terms shall it enter? The terms least favorable to the company and most favorable to the country, from which both would nevertheless gain some benefit, may be far below the terms most favorable to the company and least favorable to the country on which both would also benefit. The process of determining the terms, within this range, is one of haggling between two large units.

The corporation of course has complete freedom of choice over whether to enter, and it may have the stronger hand in the haggling. However, once the corporation has sunk funds into facilities in the country, the relative power has shifted. Unless an agreement has been carefully spelled out, to prevent exploitation as it sees it the government may harass and control the company in various ways. It may increase the company's tax rates, and it may devise special taxes that rest on selected foreign firms alone. To avoid profit concealment, Brazil, Colombia, and Mexico no longer permit the deduction of royalties paid the home office, in the calculation of profits. The LDC may require that all foreign exchange earned be sold to the central bank, and at a specially designated foreign exchange rate, or that the purchase of foreign exchange for the transfer of dividends be at a special rate.

To force the hiring or promotion of local personnel, the government may refuse reentry visas to company executives who have left the country on home leave. None of these measures are rare. The company may have little recourse except to ask for diplomatic remonstrance by its government, to bribe the local officials concerned if they are susceptible, or in the extreme case to withdraw from the country, taking such a loss of sunk capital as it must.

In an increasing number of LDCs, before a foreign firm enters the country, the government and the firm now enter into an "entry contract," by which the company's right to obtain foreign exchange for the transfer of dividends and the repatriation of capital, its right to import materials, entry visas for its top staff, tariff or other protection against competing imports, tax liabilities, obligation to accept partial local ownership, obligation to train staff, and other important matters are spelled out. Only when the company and the country agree on a contract does the company enter the country. The practice gives some assurance to both the company and the government.

One of the matters that is usually settled before a multinational manufacturing corporation enters a country is the company's obligation to produce or purchase components within the country rather than import them. Thus a company entering upon the "screwdriver" manufacturing of a product within a country, that is, the "screwing together" of imported components, may have entered upon an obligation to produce or procure within the country within, say, 5 years, components having a value that is a certain percentage of the value of the final product; within 10 years, a larger share; within 15 years, a still larger one. As was noted in Chapter 11, the Andean countries of South America provided early in the 1970s that no foreign corporation producing within any of the Andean countries should be given the benefit of free trade among them unless it agreed to divest itself of ownership in favor of local purchasers within 15 years. No foreign-owned corporation has entered into such an agreement.

As noted earlier in this chapter, attached to the World Bank, but autonomous, is an International Center for Settlement of Investment Disputes. It has not been extremely active.

The cultures of many countries, and of low-income countries more often than of others, sanction benefits to government officials and employees from their positions beyond the receipt of salaries. Personal payments by foreign firms for privileges received are a natural extension of this situation. Bribes by foreign firms to influential officials have played a greater role in obtaining contracts to provide products or services than in arranging agreements to establish manufacturing operations. The United States has enacted a law forbidding American corporations to make such payments. Some other Western governments regard this as quixotic self-righteousness; why, they ask, should the United States attempt to regulate the morals of another country? In some instances the effect of the U.S. legislation is simply that a foreign firm gets the contract.

Expropriation

Expropriation may be of corporate property or of the property of individuals, for example, persons of Indian descent in Uganda or persons who are permitted to emigrate from the Soviet Union or Cuba. Only the expropriation of corporate property is considered here.

Expropriation by the government of an LDC may be for either domestic political reasons or for economic reasons. A foreign corporation is seen as exploitative. The people hail expropriation of its properties. The economic consequences are considered here. The country may benefit or suffer economically. Expropriations in Egypt, Chile, Bolivia, and oil-producing countries will illustrate the difficulties and the effects.

An immediate question is whether the government can arrange the continued operation of the enterprise without great loss of efficiency. When Egypt seized the Suez Canal properties, many Westerners predicted that there would soon be collisions between transiting ships, damage to canal machinery through technical mismanagement, and chaos, but Egyptian engineers and pilots proved competent to manage the operation and it went on efficiently, with appreciable increases in the country's foreign exchange earnings and in governmental revenues. When Chile seized copper mine properties owned by U.S. companies, many technical and administrative employees left the country (encouraged, it was asserted, by the copper-mining companies), workers relaxed, output fell sharply, and the country's foreign exchange earnings plummeted. Where expropriation is anticipated, the owners may minimize maintenance to maximize their withdrawal of funds. The owners of tin mines in Bolivia did this. In addition, the best veins of ore had been largely exhausted during the long life of the mines. The expropriated tin properties have been a large net burden to the Bolivian government.

The expropriation of oil properties has been carefully negotiated (in Libya, partly after seizure; elsewhere, in advance) to forestall physical deterioration and prevent the loss of needed management skills. When the protracted negotiations in Saudi Arabia are completed, the four American companies which now jointly hold 40% ownership of the properties will no doubt receive less capital compensation than they claim but will receive continuing management fees that may equal their present profits. Questions of Saudi Arabian participation in "downstream" activities are perhaps being negotiated. Parallel questions of marketing outlets may arise in other acts of expropriation.

The government will gain an immediate increase in its foreign exchange earnings in expropriation, if it is able to continue operation, or to restore operation after an interval, at a sufficiently efficient level. It will presumably lose some new foreign investment though if the expropriation took place in circumstances that need not be generalized, as was true of the expropriation of the Suez Canal and oil properties, other companies may not be frightened off. The Hickenlooper amendment to U.S. law authorizing foreign aid expenditures denies foreign aid to countries that have not reached agreements satisfactory to the former American owners, in any instances of expropriation. The World Bank, regional international banks, and commercial banks may be made reluctant lenders by disputes about compensation for property.

There will probably be further expropriations. These are most likely where revolt overthrows a government that has been regarded as in league with exploiters.

The Dream of International Regulation

United Nations agencies, the EEC, and the OECD have all drawn up codes of acceptable conduct for foreign investors. These have only moral force, and not very much of that. Officials of UNCTAD and of some LDCs have asserted the need to create a world organization with the duty of regulating the activities of multinational corporations and with power to enforce its decisions. The regulation would prevent transfer pricing, corruption, and, in one proposal or another, all of the practices asserted as abuses that have been mentioned in this chapter, and in general would protect weak countries against large corporations. The possible economic effects of such regulation need not be discussed here. The likelihood that such an organization will be established is extremely remote.

Not entirely unrelated are the discussions going on under United Nations auspices concerning the recovery and refining of mineral nodules that are known to lie in very deep waters in certain areas of the ocean floor. Some countries have proposed that their rights should extend far out from their shores. A proposal more generally representing the views of many LDCs is that a world organization should be formed which will hire companies to carry out the operations, and that through one channel or another its profits should be allocated to LDCs for economic development. American representatives have pointed to the very large amounts of capital that would have to be risked, and have argued that it is chimerical to believe that a world organization could hire corporations to do the job "on salary." Some American corporations have spent considerable sums in exploring methods by which the nodules could be recovered. In 1978 the American representatives in the protracted discussions stated that if satisfactory agreement is not soon arrived at the United States may authorize its corporations to proceed in certain areas of the Pacific and that it will protect their interests. A possible compromise is that certain areas will be opened to such private enterprise and that other areas will be assigned to an international organization for exploitation in whatever way the organization is able to arrange it.

There seems to be no likelihood that such an organization, if established, would become the forerunner of a World Economic Control Agency.

FOR FURTHER READING

Foreign Aid

The OECD annual publication *Development Cooperation* is the standard source of information and analysis of economic aid from all sources.

Edward S. Mason and R. E. Asher, *The World Bank since Bretton Woods* (Washington, D.C.: Brookings Institution, 1973), gives an exhaustive history of the World Bank up to about 1972. The World Bank annual reports and the annual address of the chairperson of the bank to the directors give analyses of development problems as well as factual information.

Jagdish Bhagwati and Richard S. Eckaus, eds., *Foreign Aid* (Baltimore: Penguin Books, 1970). A useful collection of articles published before that date.

In Jagdish Bhagwati, ed., *The New International Order*, see essays by John A. Edelman and Hollis B. Chenery on "Aid and Income Distribution," by John Williamson on "SDRs: The Link," and by Richard N. Cooper on "The Oceans as a Source of Revenue," the latter two with comments by Paul Streeten and Alexandre Kafka, respectively.

Peter T. Bauer, *Dissent on Development* (Cambridge, Mass: Harvard University Press, 1972), sees little that is beneficial in aid (pp. 95–135).

From a diametrically opposed viewpoint, Teresa Hayter, *Aid as Imperialism* (Baltimore: Penguin Books, 1971), mounts a Marxist criticism.

Private Foreign Investment

In two essays in Gerald K. Helleiner, *A World Divided*, C. V. Vaitsos and Edith Penrose take diverging views of the benefits and costs to recipient countries of direct foreign investment and of appropriate policies for recipient countries. In Edgar O. Edwards, *Employment in Developing Countries*, Vaitsos discusses the employment effects of foreign investment.

Richard E. Caves, "International Corporations: The Industrial Economics of Foreign Investment," *Economica*, 38 (February 1971), 1–27.

Albert O. Hirschman, "How to Divest in Latin America, and Why," in his *A Bias for Hope* (New Haven: Yale University Press, 1971). Reprint of *Princeton Essays in International Finance*, no. 76 (November 1969).

19

Trade and Development

This chapter deals with international trade in its relationship to economic growth.

In Chapters 4 and 7 it was shown that increasing exports may be a means by which technical progress, which of itself might cause disemployment of labor, may be converted into economic growth for the country as a whole.

THE EXPORTS OF THE LDCs

It was noted that in the 1960s and until the 1974–75 recession in the industrial countries, the rate of increase in the exports of LDCs as a group accelerated. During the 1950s the total exports of the nonoil LDCs were rising by only 0.8% per year. The last column of Table 19–1 shows the much increased growth rate of their exports and the especially rapid increase in their exports of manufactures that occurred after 1960. The figures are for physical volume. Because of inflation the value of exports increased faster.

As the table shows, the LDCs did not do very well in the export of agricultural products. A detailed analysis for the 1950s and 1960s showed an interesting fact concerning 21 important agricultural commodities and 5 important nonagricultural primary products. The faster the growth rate of the industrial nations' demand for a product was, the less was the LDCs' share of the increase in world exports.[1] This was not necessarily or wholly due to sluggishness in the LDCs' response to increasing world demand; the population of the LDCs, and hence their own demand for their primary

---

[1] B. I. Cohen and D. G. Sisler, "Exports of Developing Countries in the 1960s," *Review of Economics and Statistics,* 53 (November 1971), 354–61.

**TABLE 19-1   Growth of merchandise exports, 1960–1975
(average annual percentage growth rates, at 1975 prices)**
LDC exports of manufactures spurted after 1960.

	Total World Trade	Indus- trialized Coun- tries	Develop- ing Coun- tries
Food and beverages	4.1	5.2	2.8
Nonfood agricultural products	4.5	5.6	2.6
Nonfuel minerals and metals	3.9	3.1	4.8
Fuel and energy	6.3	4.2	6.2
Manufactures	8.9	8.8	12.3
Total merchandise	7.1	7.5	5.9

Reproduced from *World Development Report, 1978*, p. 9.
Sources: World Bank; United Nations *Yearbook of International Trade Statistics*, 1960, 1976; and *Handbook of International Trade and Development Statistics* (Geneva: UNCTAD, 1976).

products or at least for their agricultural products, increased rapidly during the 1960s.

The sharp increase in exports was in low-technology manufactures. The increase in the industrialized nations' imports of these was faster than the increase in their imports of all manufacturers, and the increase in their imports from the LDCs was faster than the increase in their imports from other high-income countries. Table 19–2 shows data for the 1950s and 1960s for six low-technology manufactures.

These average figures for all LDCs may be misleading. There was no general increase in LDC exports of manufactures at the rates shown in

**TABLE 19-2   Annual percentage change in imports
of low-technology manufactures, EEC, United States,
United Kingdom, Japan, and USSR, from 1950–1960
to 1967–1968**
LDC exports of low-technology manufactures rose especially rapidly in the 1960s.

	From the World	From LDCs
Clothing	13.3	18.7
Cotton fabrics	3.4	9.3
Footwear	11.7	15.6
Jute fabrics and jute	5.5	6.0
Pearls and precious stones	19.6	28.0
Veneer	7.3	19.0
Average for the six	12.0	15.0

Source: B. I. Cohen and D. G. Sisler, "Exports of Developing Countries in the 1960s," *Review of Economics and Statistics*, 53 (November 1971) computed from various issues of *International Financial Statistics*.

Tables 19-1 and 19-2. Rather, the increase occurred mainly in only a few more than a handful of countries, prominent among them South Korea, Taiwan, Hong Kong, India, Brazil, Spain, and Israel (the last two still considered "less developed" in the 1960s). Brazil is now even capable in the production of some higher technology products. The rates of growth of these countries, apart from India, were also among the highest in the world. India's manufacturing sector, though large in absolute terms among LDCs, is still small in relation to its total economy.

LDC total exports and LDC exports of low-technology manufactures rose rapidly for one main reason apart from the improvement in LDC capability: the unprecedentedly rapid rate of economic growth in the countries of Western Europe. As the incomes of those countries rose, their purchases rose. When their GNP slackened and turned negative in 1974-75, LDC exports and growth also slowed. Although the rate of growth in the high-income countries increased again in 1977 and 1978, it did not again reach its earlier booming rate. Neither did the growth rate of the LDCs as a group.

The increased willingness of the industrial nations to admit low-technology manufactures from the LDCs in the 1960s was not due solely to their willingness to aid those countries, though that motive should not be cynically disregarded. The European countries had run out of low-wage labor. While they were importing "guest workers" to perform their low-wage functions, including unskilled factory work, their own workers were moving to higher wage jobs in higher technology production. The importation of low-technology manufactures did not threaten their own workers to the degree that it would have previously. Only during and after the recession of 1974-75 did the industrial countries take marked protectionist measures.

The Importance of Demand

The course of world economic growth from 1960 to 1975 shows the complex dependence of growth at "the periphery" upon growth at "the center." (Slackening in aggregate demand by one high-income country also seriously affects the other high-income countries, but we are not concerned here with that impact.) In 1974 the aggregate income of the high-income countries as a group fell slightly, and in 1975 it fell by 1.4%. For countries with per capita incomes below $400 (in 1975), the results were great.

The average annual rate of growth in per capita income for the period 1970-75 fell below that for the immediately preceding period in 30 of the 36 countries above the $1,600 line. In fact, it fell in all of those countries except Iran, four Communist countries of Eastern Europe, and Trinidad and Tobago (where it remained constant). When this happened, it also fell in almost two thirds of the countries with 1975 per capita incomes below

$400. Table 19–3 dramatizes the facts by comparing growth rates for 1970–75 with growth rates for the period ending just before the 1974–75 recession.

TABLE 19-3   Change in the growth rate, 1960–1973 to 1970–1975 (number of countries)

Per capita income in almost all higher income countries and in many lower income countries grew more slowly during 1970–75 than during the 1960s.

Per Capita Income Class, 1975 (U.S. $)	Up	Down	No Change
Above 3,200	2	20	1
1,600–3,190	3	10	
800–1,590	10	8	
400– 790	15	8	
200– 390	7	13	
Below 200	8	15	

Note: Data rounded to nearest $10.
Source: *World Bank Atlases, 1975* and *1977.*

The recession did not cause per capita income in 1975 to fall below that of 1970 in any of the countries above the $1,600 per capita income line, but it did cause this result in 15 of the countries with per capita incomes below $400. This statement of causation must be qualified; the fourfold rise in the price of petroleum import was also a cause; but an important part of the causation was the decline in demand for the exports of the low-income countries.

Table 19–3 shows a remarkable related fact. From the 1960s to 1970–75, the rate of growth increased in most countries with incomes between $400 and $1,590 despite the recession in the high-income countries. By the time developing nations have reached that range of incomes they have apparently become more agile and less passively dependent on external demand.

The LDC export increase of the 1960s and early 1970s seems within limits to have been an adequate substitute for aid in providing resources for development. At any rate, all but a few of the LDCs thrived during this period. That they did indicates the importance of the foreign exchange gap. It reinforces the views of persons in LDCs who say that the high-income countries must give them either "trade or aid." The record suggests, indeed, that trade may be not only an adequate substitute for aid but a superior alternative to it. For there might not have been sufficient incentive to induce the capital formation of those years, even if enough economic aid had been available, if increases in aggregate income caused by increases in exports had not provided that incentive.

Trade Concessions

High-income countries impose lesser restrictions against the products of the LDCs than they impose against one another's products, and on the other hand they do not insist that in return the LDCs shall lower the very high tariffs or other barriers that most of them levy against manufactures. However, the comparison of tariff rates is not very meaningful, since the two groups of countries produce markedly differing though overlapping baskets of goods.

The restrictions of the industrial countries are least against primary products, which they need for their manufacturing. Of the 12 commodities designated by UNCTAD as "core commodities," discussed later in this chapter, the United States levies a tariff or other import restriction on only one, sugar. The industrial countries apply the "most favored nation" principle to all exports of the LDCs; that is, they admit those exports with the least restriction that they grant to any nation. When the European Economic Community was formed in 1958, the member countries agreed to admit without duty the products of the African countries that had been colonies of some of them.

The reciprocal tariff reductions agreed upon by the industrial nations in 1967 after a round of negotiations under the auspices of the General Agreement on Tariffs and Trade (GATT) related largely to trade among those nations. Following this agreement, UNCTAD negotiated an agreement with the industrial nations for a "Generalized System of Preferences" by which duties of the industrial nations on certain selected imports from the LDCs would be reduced below those offered to the most favored other nation. In 1971 and 1972 this system of preferences was adopted by all of the industrial nations of the non-Communist world except the United States and Canada. The United States was already more open to LDC manufactured goods than were the European countries or Japan. In 1975 the EEC agreed to accept certain products of 51 LDCs without duties.

However, though these various concessions combined apply to a considerable number of the commodities that the LDCs export, these are unimportant commodities, in value a small share of total LDC exports.

In April 1979, the industrialized nations announced the completion of a new agreement to liberalize trade, on which they had been negotiating for five years. (It is still subject to acceptance by national legislatures.) It is calculated that the agreement will reduce by an average of more than one third the already low customs duties of these nations. The LDCs complained bitterly that the agreement does little for them. It reduces the tariffs of industrial nations on LDC exports by only an average of some 15% to 20%. This complaint, however, overlooks the fact that as among the industrial countries the reductions are reciprocal; each nation expects its exports to increase while it grants easier imports. For the LDCs, the tariff reductions are net benefits. In this sense they gain more than do any of the industrial nations.

Perhaps the most important part of the "Tokyo Round" (the agreement was completed at Tokyo) is not the tariff reductions but the agreement to relax nontariff barriers by which various countries have reduced imports (special rules for valuing imported goods, which increase the price on which an ad valorem duty is calculated, supposed health and safety regulations, government procurement only from domestic suppliers, etc.). Some of these relaxations may considerably benefit LDCs, though not to the degree that the LDCs feel is due them.

Yet the industrial countries' acceptance of LDC exports is less than might appear from these formal arrangements. Since the recession of 1974–75, a cluster of protectionist measures have been adopted by the United States and the nations of the European Economic Community to prevent rapid displacement of workers in industries in which the newly industrializing LDCs offer cheap imports. The devices include, among others, "voluntary" restraints on LDC exports negotiated with the exporting country, import quotas, price floors on imports, countervailing duties, and subsidies to weak domestic industries. These devices have curtailed industrial country imports of clothing and other textile products, footwear, steel, TV sets, some food products and other agricultural products, and various other products. Some of the newly industrializing LDCs are versatile enough to turn to another product when one is restricted, but unless the protective measures are relaxed, future increase in the physical volume of LDC exports may be less rapid than it was during the dozen years preceding 1974. If so, the economic growth of the LDCs will suffer.

CARTELS

The LDCs are not content with an increase in their trade. They also want increases in the prices of their products.

The means of intervention in the market to raise prices are production, sale, and export quotas; export taxes; and price leadership. The term *cartel*, strictly defined, refers only to the first. Here all three are considered.

The Rationale: The Terms of Trade

An old reason, apart from the desire of most people to get as much income as they can, for the interest of LDCs in arrangements that will raise the price of their products is the belief of the LDCs that monopolies in the industrial countries have progressively raised their prices relative to the prices of the goods they buy, so that the terms of trade have turned progressively against the low-income countries during the past century and longer.

If the low-income countries' terms of trade had progressively deteriorated, it would not be necessary to refer to monopoly pricing to explain the trend. The differences in the income elasticity of demand for agricultural and nonagricultural products would be sufficient explanation, if the LDCs had been slow in moving out of agriculture. But in fact the supposed long-term deterioration of the LDCs' terms of trade is a myth.

The error began in the 1930s, when the deep fall in the prices of agricultural products during the Great Depression was mistaken for a secular change. The analytical mistake was reinforced by a study done shortly after World War II, which showed that during the preceding century or so the prices of primary products at London had declined relative to prices in general. In using this fact as evidence of deterioration of the terms of trade, it was overlooked that because steamships had replaced sailing vessels and because the construction of railroads had greatly reduced the cost of overland transportation, the cost of getting products to market had fallen by between two thirds and nine tenths, so that the prices of primary products at their points of origin had risen considerably relative to prices in general even while their prices in the London market had fallen.

The agricultural terms of trade fell during the 1880s and 1890s as new lands were opened to cultivation, rose to World War I, remained high in the 1920s but fell to the 1930s, rose until the end of World War II, and apart from oil have fallen considerably since then, but the data will not support the assertion of long-term deterioration.

There is also a moderately new reason for interest in price-raising arrangements. The lower income countries, now independent and their own masters, are now politically able to execute such arrangements. And there is a still newer reason. The success of OPEC has increased the belief of the lower income countries that they may be able to succeed.

Commodity agreements have been negotiated at one time or another since World War II for sugar, coffee, cocoa, wheat, olive oil, and tin. None of these agreements is in control of its market. Since 1973, associations have been formed or discussed for bauxite, mercury, bananas, iron ore, and oilseeds. Price actions concerning bauxite and bananas, discussed below, have been moderately successful. Although U.S. law forbids American firms to enter into agreements to fix prices or restrict production or sale and the EEC treaty forbids such agreements among companies of the member countries except with the permission of the EEC Commission, no provision of international law forbids or restricts them.

OPEC

The best known of existing cartels, though not the first, is that formed by the Organization of Petroleum Exporting Countries. OPEC itself was formed late in the 1960s by 12 major producers of oil for export, to strengthen their hand in negotiating with the international oil companies. (Later, a 13th country joined.) Until the 1940s, at a maximum the oil companies had paid royalties and profits taxes equal to, say, one fifth or one sixth of their gross earnings. The Creole Petroleum Company agreement with Venezuela—for approximately a 50–50 division—broke the pattern. During the postwar years the petroleum companies were progressively forced to yield larger shares, until before the end of the 1960s the governments were collecting two thirds or somewhat more of gross earnings in royalties, fees, and taxes. Then, in the early 1970s, the governments of the oil countries began moving to become part owners and later full owners of the oil companies' producing subsidiaries. The governments negotiated prices for the properties based mainly on the investment costs of the oil companies, not the market value of the properties, and paid for the properties out of oil revenues.

Then suddenly in 1973 the OPEC countries, acting in concert, approximately quadrupled the prices at which they would sell oil to the oil companies.[2] Only then were the OPEC countries acting as a cartel. In the following year they increased the price to quintuple the old price. In 1976 OPEC raised the price 10% further, in two steps, and in 1978 it announced another increase, of 14.5%, to take effect in four steps in 1979. After the disruption of Iranian oil production early in 1979 exacerbated the worldwide scarcity of oil, some OPEC countries raised their prices far above $14.55. In June 1979 OPEC officially recognized the new prices by establishing a base price of $18 per barrel for light crude and sanctioning prices up to $23.50 per barrel. "Spot prices"—the price for oil not sold under a contract—rose to as much as $40 per barrel. As had been true at the times of previous price increases, Saudi Arabia exerted a moderating force, and announced that the price for its light oil would be $18.

In the early 1970s the base price had been $1.60 per barrel.

The 1979 price increase owed much to world demand and supply as well as to the existence of OPEC. By this time, in spite of production on the "north slope" of Alaska and in the North Sea, the world supply of petroleum was increasing appreciably more slowly than demand. Because of depletion of some of their best oil deposits, a number of the oil-producing countries—Iran, Iraq, and Venezuela among them—could foresee a decline in their rate of production before the end of the 1980s. Even without any

---

[2] The oil countries were not without justification for some action, though cartels rarely need any. During a period of plentiful supply of oil a few years earlier, the oil companies had unilaterally reduced the "posted" price of petroleum. The posted price was the price on which their royalties were based.

To date the oil companies have not been hurt financially by the oil price increases. Their absolute margins in OPEC countries have on the average remained as high as before, their margins on North Sea and North Slope oil have been sufficient to add to their total profits, and the price they obtain for oil produced elsewhere has increased with the world price.

agreement among them, sensible national policy would have been to hold down the rate of production in order to prolong their receipt of revenues and to take advantage of the anticipated future greater scarcity. During the last years of the 1970s, therefore, oil prices would have risen sharply if OPEC had not existed. That they would have reached $23.50 per barrel is doubtful.

The Conditions for Success

OPEC illustrates conditions under which a cartel can flourish:

1. A small number of members producing a large share of the world supply and of world exports of the commodity. OPEC has a dangerously large number of members for a cartel, but this has not caused its disruption.

2. A durable commodity, one that is nonperishable if withheld from sale.

3. Increasing demand for the commodity. It is easier for members to agree if they do not have to reduce production in order to obtain an increased price.

4. Inelasticity of demand for the commodity with respect to price, because it or a substitute is indispensable and because at least in the short run and the intermediate run the substitution of other commodities or increase in production elsewhere is not possible.

5. OPEC is favored by a condition that does not pertain to any other commodity for which a cartel might be considered. The largest producer, Saudi Arabia, has not been able to use all of the revenues from its oil production, and has been willing to reduce its output well below capacity in order to let other members sell all the oil they wish to produce. (Saudi Arabia could also increase its capacity moderately within a few years of a decision to do so, and still more with a longer lead time.)

A cartel is more likely to be durable if its price action is moderate. That of OPEC has not been. The world reaction to the very large price increases illustrates the perils that a cartel faces. Even within five years there has been a marked reduction in petroleum consumption per unit of industrial output. That reduction will continue as adaptation to changed relative prices proceeds and as the price of petroleum in the United States is allowed to rise to world levels. The North Sea and (Alaskan) North Slope fields have been added to the world's supplying areas. Extremely large deposits have been discovered in Mexico. However, Mexico, warned by the internal inflation that has plagued other fast-spending oil countries, does not propose to exploit its deposits rapidly. Throughout the world exploration and preparation are going on in areas that it would not have been economic to consider at pre-1973 prices, and development in fields already known is going on more rapidly than it would have otherwise. Research proceeds into efficient and nonobjectionable ways of using the huge U.S. supplies of coal. Nuclear plants are being built.

However, after the accident at a nuclear power plant in Pennsylvania in 1979, public resistance to the proliferation of nuclear plants increased in both the United States and Europe. During at least the next 10 or 15 years the increase in the supply of energy from nonoil sources will seemingly not even equal the increase in world demand for energy. World demand for petroleum—and in spite of increases in petroleum production elsewhere, world demand for OPEC petroleum—will continue to increase. Moreover, even if a new government had not come into power in Iran, Iranian production would have decreased during the 1980s because of the exhaustion of fields, as will that of Venezuela. In these conditions, the prospects are that OPEC will flourish. These developments will occur unless drastic conservation measures are undertaken in the U.S.

Other Cartels

The experiences of the tin and coffee associations illustrate the problems that cartels may face. The oldest price-raising arrangement now in existence is in tin. The International Tin Council, formed in 1956, has as members the major producers shown in Table 19–4 plus several of the Communist satellite countries of Eastern Europe. The council has had little effect on the market, partly because its members could not agree on funds for more than a small stockpile. Late in the 1950s, sales of tin by the Soviet Union drove prices down through the floor that the council had agreed on. In the 1970s, large American purchases for a stockpile that was presumably for military security bid prices much above the agreed-on ceiling. Though

TABLE 19–4 Certain important minerals are possible candidates for cartelization

Mineral	Number of Major Producers	Percentage of World Supply	Names of Major Producers
Bauxite	6	70	Australia, Jamaica, Surinam, Guyana, France, Guinea
Tin	4	62	Malaysia, Bolivia, Indonesia, Thailand
Mercury	5	56	Spain, Italy, Mexico, Yugoslavia, Canada
Zinc	5	48	Canada, Japan, Australia, Peru, Mexico
Chromium	5	75	Soviet Union, South Africa, Turkey, Philippines, Rhodesia
Nickel	3	58	Canada, New Caledonia, Cuba

Source: *U.S. News & World Report,* May 6, 1974.

some of the stockpile has been sold, there is no conceivable military need for all that remains, but Congress refused to approve further sales, and prices remain high. Whether the cartel could maintain prices in normal market circumstances is uncertain. Opinions differ.

The international organization of coffee producers, which sets export quotas for its members, once almost foundered because of the rapidly growing production of new East African producers, together with an innovation that made their product acceptable. Their "robusta" coffee, though low in quality, was suitable for the new product, instant coffee. The cartel regained strength when the African producers were offered fairly generous quotas within it, and joined. The cartel has depended on the restraint of Brazil, the dominant producer; Brazil has been content to accept a steadily decreasing share of the coffee market in order to obtain the continued cooperation of other cartel members. Brazil's tactics have included accumulating very large stocks of coffee, burning some, and paying its producers to reduce the number of new trees planted to replace aging ones. When a severe drought in Brazil in 1976 destroyed a large part of the year's crop and killed many trees, raw coffee prices soared much above the agreed-on ceiling, but by early 1979 they had fallen by two thirds from their peak even though Brazil even resorted to buying back coffee that it had exported.

During the Korean War boom in coffee prices, the amount of coffee used per cup of the beverage fell and there was some shift to tea. These changes were not reversed when coffee prices fell. There may have been further similar changes since 1976, but these trends are countered by the growing population and affluence of coffee-drinking peoples, especially Americans, who are the major consumers. The cartel continues to function.

The International Bauxite Association was formed in 1973 by 11 producing countries under the leadership of Jamaica. There are many varieties of bauxite; it is not a standardized commodity. Jamaica has succeeded in imposing an 8½% export tax on its bauxite. The influence of other producers on bauxite prices is not clear.

Five Central American producers of bananas (if Panama is classed as Central American) increased banana prices by setting a common export tax of $1 per box. Colombia and Ecuador refused to join, but their production is not so great that it has as yet threatened the arrangement.

A cocoa cartel was formed in 1973. During its first five years, cocoa prices rose sharply, not because the cartel reduced the supply but because, while demand increased, marketing boards in the major cocoa-producing countries held the prices to producers constant and so offered them no incentive to increase production.

Price maintenance schemes have not been confined to the LDCs. There is an International Wheat Agreement. However, world wheat prices are held much above the level at which they would otherwise settle, not by the agreement but by the action of the United States and Canada. As noted in

Chapter 9, since the 1930s the United States has paid its farmers to reduce their acreages of major crops and has stored surpluses or lent farmers money to do so, in order to keep prices from falling through a legislated floor. American prices are thus maintained at a level much above world prices.

In addition to the general justifications given by LDCs for intervention in the market to obtain price increases, there is specific justification with respect to some of these commodities. Three firms handle 68% of the world's banana imports; the leading firm accounts for 25% of the world's tea purchases; and in the mid-1960s 12 firms handled 80% of the world's rubber trade.[3] In these circumstances one may assume that prices are not always competitively determined—indeed, that the firms may act as monopolists buying the commodities and as oligopolists in selling them. Barring some sort of international action to alter the situation, the application of countervailing power has its justification. However, it does not necessarily follow that it will be successful.

More Cartels?

Can producers of other commodities successfully unite in cartels?

Table 19-4 lists major producers of bauxite, tin, and four other metals, and their combined share of the total world supply. Still other minerals with concentrated production are manganese, phosphate rock, copper, tungsten, and cobalt. Rhodesia and the Soviet Union are the major producers of cobalt.

UNCTAD has designated ten commodities as "core" commodities, especially deserving of price stabilization and where possible price raising. They include the three tropical beverages; two of the minerals named above, copper and tin; and rubber, sugar, and three fibers. The ten commodities are listed in Table 19-5.

However, scrutiny of the two lists shows no obvious candidates for successful cartels. An attempt to form an association of the tea-growing countries failed because of inability to reach agreement on national quotas. Future success seems no more likely. Any marked increase in world sugar prices would probably trigger U.S. actions to increase domestic beet sugar production. The success of a sugar cartel is doubtful. The success of a rubber cartel is equally dubious. The Stevenson rubber price maintenance scheme of the 1920s collapsed because the price increase stimulated production in new areas. A price rise now would cause a further shift to the use of synthetic rubbers. The production of cotton, jute, and sisal and of competing synthetic fibers can readily be increased in countries outside any cartel.

Copper offers little prospect unless Canada and Australia should join a

---

[3] *Trade in Primary Commodities: Conflict or Cooperation?: A Tripartite Report* (Washington, D.C.: Brookings Institution, 1974).

TABLE 19–5   The ten "core" commodities
Primary commodity prices, even those of some minerals, fluctuate widely.

	Average Percentage Deviation from Seven-Year Moving Average (1975 prices)
Foods	
Cocoa	19.91
Coffee	8.41
Tea	3.06
Sugar	11.46
Fibers	
Cotton	3.93
Jute	12.54
Sisal	18.11
Rubber and metals	
Rubber	11.92
Copper	14.65
Tin	7.71

Source: Karsten Laursen, "The Integrated Programme for Commodities," *World Development*, 8 (April 1978), p. 424.

cartel, and perhaps not even then, because a quick, large, and continuing supply of copper scrap would be called forth by any considerable price increase.[4] Moreover, considerable substitution of aluminum for copper has occurred. More would occur if the price of copper rose significantly relative to that of aluminum and if it were thought likely that the price change would last for a long time. A successful copper cartel seems highly unlikely unless producers of bauxite join copper producers in a common cartel, and the difficulties of negotiation to that end are considerable.

The producers in the cases of mercury, zinc, chromium, and nickel seem unlikely bedfellows in view of either their political differences or their political relationships with the rest of the world. The high fixed cost of minerals production, which raises the unit cost if production is reduced, is also a deterrent. For these several reasons another cartel of metallic ore producers is not very likely. Yet the lure of higher prices is great, and it might cause the obstacles to be overcome. Of three recent assessments, one argues that other minerals cartels will appear and will succeed, a second that they will not.[5] A third was made by a group of 15 economists from Japan, Canada, the

---

[4] Marian Radetzki, "The Potential for Monopolistic Commodity Pricing by Developing Countries," in *A World Divided*, ed. G. K. Helleiner (London: Cambridge University Press, 1976).

[5] Fred C. Bergsten, "The New Era in World Commodity Markets," *Challenge*, September–October 1974 (pro); and Raymond F. Mikesell, "More Third World Cartels Ahead?," *Challenge*, November–December 1974, pp. 24–31 (con).

United States, and the European Economic Community, in a conference convened by the Brookings Institution to consider the possibility of additional cartels not merely in minerals but also in other commodities. The conclusion reached was that "the number of commodities on which collusion could be effective or feasible is small, the economic impact is likely to be limited and isolated rather than pervasive as with oil, and the prospects for sustained success over the medium term, to say nothing for the long term, are dim."[6]

Cartels and the LDCs as a Group

The successful formation of additional cartels of minerals producers would be injurious to the LDCs as a whole, as is the rise in the price of oil, for the large majority of LDCs are consumers, not producers, of minerals. It is estimated that from 1970–72 to 1975 the terms of trade loss resulting from the increased price of petroleum were as follows:

For all oil-importing countries with per capita GNP below $200, 14% of 1975 imports.
For all LDC oil importers with per capita GNP of $250 or above, 10% of 1975 imports.[7]

However, the cost to consuming countries of price increases in other minerals would be much less than that of the oil increase. In the case of other minerals, as of oil, the benefit of higher prices would be gained by a relatively few countries, and in the case of most metals mainly by medium-income countries rather than low-income countries. Even if the prices of all minerals were increased, most low- and medium-income countries would suffer; many fewer than one half would benefit.

Most mineral deposits are owned by small and already privileged groups in the producing countries. (Tin is an exception; there are many small tin mines.) In the cases of most metals, then, even in the producing countries the mass of the people would benefit from successful cartels only if the government took ownership of the mines or taxed the increased export proceeds and used them to provide public services, if the proceeds were used by the private recipients to increase investment and thereby the national product, or if the available foreign exchange made it possible for others to do so. Of course, in total these indirect benefits might be considerable.

---

[6] *Trade in Primary Commodities.*

[7] John Edelman and Hollis P. Chenery, in *The New International Economic Order*, ed. J. N. Bhagwati (Cambridge, Mass.: MIT Press, 1977), p. 47.

PRICE AND INCOME STABILIZATION

Lessening fluctuations in the income received by exporters of primary commodities has its virtues quite apart from change in the average level of prices.

Table 19–5 shows large fluctuations in the prices of eight of the ten core commodities. Instances of extreme fluctuations may readily be adduced. From mid-1973 to mid-1974, while the price of petroleum imported by Sri Lanka rose by 300%, the price of rice by 100%, and the prices of other imports by an average of 15%, the price of tea fell by 10% and that of rubber by 20%. Altogether, the real GNP of the country fell by between 20% and 25%.[8]

Single core commodities or other commodities provide a large share of the foreign exchange earnings of some countries. In 1975, 36 LDCs obtained more than one half of their export proceeds from their sales of a single primary product: 17, not too surprisingly, from petroleum and petroleum products; 3 from coffee; 1 from cocoa; 4 from sugar and honey; 2 from cotton; 2 from ores and concentrates of nonferrous metals grouped together; 2 from fertilizers; 2 from iron ore and iron ore concentrates; and 1 each from copper, pearls and precious stones, and live animals.[9] A similar list for 1953 had included 30 countries, the commodity in only four instances being petroleum.[10] Apart from petroleum, then, the number of countries thus dependent on a single export had decreased from 26 to 19, and the list of commodities had changed somewhat as diversification occurred in some countries and as surges into new products occurred in others. Yet the number of countries involved remained large.

Fluctuations in foreign exchange earnings cause economic cycles within the exporting country. If the exporters invest the increased proceeds within their country when export earnings rise, they may spend part of the foreign exchange abroad for the imports of capital goods but they must also sell part to the country's commercial banks to obtain domestic funds with which to pay the domestic cost of the investment. If they increase their consumption expenditures they must obtain domestic funds in the same way. The monetary effect is the same as if there were a burst of credit expansion by the country's commercial banks. By a multiplier effect, consumption as well as investment will increase. Moreover, by depositing in the central bank some or all of the foreign exchange they have received, the

---

[8] Reginald H. Green, in *A World Divided*, ed. Gerald K. Helleiner.

[9] Computed from United Nations *Yearbook of International Trade Statistics, 1977*, vol. 1 (New York: United Nations, 1978).

[10] P. Lamartine Yates, *Forty Years of Foreign Trade* (London: George Allen & Unwin, 1959).

commercial banks will also have the reserves to expand credit, thus pushing the boom higher. When foreign exchange earnings drop, the boom is cut off.

Remedies: Tax, Fiscal, Monetary

Tax, fiscal, and monetary policies of the country's government can do something to mitigate these violent swings. Assuming perfect foreknowledge of the course of a fluctuation, the action taken might be as follows. Taxes on exports, graduated with respect to the price of the exports, plus graduated income taxes, should be imposed. The domestic investment or consumption boom will thereby be curbed, even though not eliminated, and the government will also become the owner of some of the increased foreign exchange receipts. It should hold them until a fall in foreign exchange earnings occurs, then sell them to the central bank. The government can then counter the domestic deflation by increased spending (or by reducing personal taxes), and the central bank can make foreign exchange in excess of current earnings available to importers.

The difficulties with these policies, even assuming that the government can police exporters and capture the foreign exchange, are two. First, the fluctuations are not known in advance. Government agencies will be eager to spend the funds as they accumulate, and individuals will claim that the prosperity is not an excessive boom but only normal prosperity. These individuals may be correct in the sense that the boom may be doing no more than causing full employment.

Second, during the upswing the primary increase in investment or consumer spending will be by the exporters. The impact of the increased government spending after the downswing will be experienced elsewhere in the economy. Even if the fluctuations in aggregate national income were completely eliminated, there would be expansions and contractions within the economy. If the exporters spend for investment, these will be greater than if they consume their added income.

Remedies: Marketing Boards

A more drastic governmental intervention in private economic activity, designed to mitigate the fluctuations (and perhaps to raise governmental revenue), is for the government to take over the exporting function. Ideally, the government would then absorb all of the fluctuation. In that case, however, to the difficulties referred to above is added another: the need to be an efficient exporter.

A number of state trading boards were set up in LDCs after World War II. The rice marketing board of Burma, the cocoa marketing board of Ghana, a group of marketing boards in Nigeria, and similar boards in other West African countries are examples.

The extreme bad example is provided by Burma's State Agricultural Marketing Board. The board did stabilize the incomes of rice cultivators. It held them at a level which in real terms was below that of the prewar days of the foreign traders, while the board accumulated huge profits. The foreign exchange thus earned became income of the government, which not only spent but squandered it without regard to a possible future decline in receipts. The board cost the country enormous potential revenues by holding its rice for still higher prices while production in other countries recovered and prices fell, and by inefficient storage and handling which cost the country the benefit of grade differentials and permitted the rice to deteriorate in quality and in part to disappear.

The experience of the several Nigerian marketing boards presents a happier picture. The commodities handled were cocoa, groundnuts, palm oil, palm kernels, and cotton. Gerald Helleiner has analyzed the effects of these boards' operations during periods from about 1949 to about 1961.[11]

The Nigerian boards have had a high degree of success in holding prices stable throughout each marketing year, the only exception being cocoa in one year. The result has been a reduction of speculative marketing activity and improvement in the quality of the produce. The judgment of the marketing board managers with respect to year-to-year price changes has been good enough so that in all cases Nigerian prices have fluctuated less than world prices. But, perhaps surprisingly, because of changes in the quantities marketed and the failure of price changes to counteract them, incomes from cocoa and palm oil were about as unstable as if world prices had prevailed, incomes from groundnuts and cotton were more unstable, and only for sellers of palm kernels were incomes clearly stabilized. Helleiner concludes: "These results lend weight to the view that Nigerian marketing boards are better defended in their role as earners of tax revenues than in their role as stabilizing authorities." The comment applies to marketing boards in other countries as well.

International Price Stabilization Schemes

The agreement of the high-income nations to international stabilization schemes is important to the LDCs proposing such schemes both because the cooperation of the main consuming nations may lend added strength to the floor and ceiling provisions and, more important, because the LDCs hope that the industrial nations will contribute some of the capital needed to purchase buffer stocks and some of the costs of maintaining them.

In principle, by adding to or selling from a buffer stock as required, an international stabilization organization could fully prevent wide annual

---

[11] Gerald K. Helleiner, "Marketing Boards and Domestic Stabilization in Nigeria," *Review of Economics and Statistics*, 48 (February 1966), 69–78.

fluctuations in the prices of readily storable commodities, provided only that it had accumulated a sufficient stock before a world shortage appeared. The organization could prevent the price of, for example, tin or sugar from falling in any one year more than, say, 10% below the average price of the preceding year by buying all of the tin offered at a price reduced by that percentage. Conversely, by selling from its stock, the organization could prevent a price rise of more than 10%. Its operations need not interfere with secular trends. In case of a continuing secular fall in demand or increase in supply, it would simply let the price fall by a given percentage each year without limit. In the case of a severe continued secular downtrend, the arrangement would collapse from the weight of the accumulating stock, but the usual secular trend would cause a smaller average annual change than the permitted one, and thus would not occasion indefinitely continued accumulation. The width of the band within which price fluctuations are permitted must be enough to permit private traders to stock profitably from harvest to harvest or for one or two years. Otherwise the stabilization organization would find itself holding all of the world's working stocks at all times. Hence expert price management would be necessary and extreme price stabilization impossible.

The "Integrated Program for Commodities"

Under this heading UNCTAD has proposed an international program which would include, but not be limited to, price stabilization for the ten core commodities through international stocking. UNCTAD proposes raising a common fund to finance the accumulation of stocks, an improved compensatory financing arrangement for remaining income fluctuations in the export of primary commodities, and a grant element in the contribution of the high-income countries to the scheme.[12]

UNCTAD estimated that the capital fund needed to finance stocking the ten commodities would be $5 billion at 1975 prices. Another estimate concurs; a third estimate concludes that the required sum would be greater. Part would be obtained on the security of the stocks, once the scheme was in operation. The purpose of a common fund would be to lessen the total required, since the purchase of some commodities might be balanced by the simultaneous sale of others. Since funds beyond the initial guarantee would be borrowed only as needed, there seems to be little advantage in the arrangement.

Even with stocking of the ten commodities in full operation, there would be fluctuations in the revenues received, because of the permitted price variations and because of variations in quantities. Fluctuations in the reve-

---

[12] UNCTAD, *Commodities*, TD/184 (1976), together with supplements 1, 2, and 3 of the same.

nues from other commodities would also remain. The IMF has established a compensatory financing facility to counter short-run income fluctuations by loans to the exporting countries. In 1976, $1.2 billion was drawn from the funds of the facility. UNCTAD has proposed that the fund be enlarged (though by 1978 it had not been exhausted), and that not all of the loans be repaid, the high-income countries financing the balance.

Compensatory financing has advantages. It avoids the considerable annual cost of maintaining stocks, and it benefits all primary product exporters. It will not, of course, affect fluctuations in prices, but it will lessen fluctuations in incomes, which in many circumstances price stabilization will not do.

The operation of a buffer stock will not affect fluctuations in prices within the permitted price band. If a change in demand occurs that is sufficient without stabilization to pull prices above that band or push them below it, buffer stock operation will lessen the income fluctuation by lessening the price fluctuation. However, for annual crops the factor causing the price change is likely to be a change in supply, and this is sometimes true for minerals as well. In this case, if the price elasticity of demand is unity, then if no buffer stock interferes with the market, a change in the quantity supplied will be precisely balanced by an opposite change in price, and if demand elasticity is above unity, the quantity change will be at least partially balanced by a change in price, whereas buffer stock operation prevents this countering change in price (beyond the price band limits), and so de-stabilizes incomes. The unfettered market does better. If the elasticity of demand is less than unity, without price stabilization the change in price overcompensates for the change in the quantity supplied, and reductions in supply increase the income received, whereas increases in supply decrease it. But even in this case the percentage fluctuation in income occasioned by price stabilization is greater than the fluctuation in the opposite direction without it unless the elasticity of demand is 0.5 or less. (If this is not "intuitively" obvious, the reader may confirm it by algebraic manipulation or a few arithmetic examples. It is not obvious to all analysts, for some have said that buffer stock operation does better if the elasticity of demand is less than unity.)

Hence the case for price stabilization is not so strong as might at first be assumed. It is even weaker if one also considers the cost of maintaining the stocks. The case for income stabilization or at least compensatory financing is stronger.

In 1975 the countries of the EEC and 46 LDCs which had earlier been given preferential access to EEC markets entered into an agreement called the "Stabex" scheme. Under Stabex, the EEC will compensate any of the 46 countries if that country's receipts from sales of a specified list of commodities fall below a specified level. The commodities are not major ones, though they are important to individual countries. To date, there has been no comparable arrangement by a wider group of countries or concerning a more important group of commodities.

One may tend to assume that income stabilization or at least the receipt of a steady stream of foreign exchange would facilitate economic growth. However, this is not entirely obvious. Successive bursts of prosperity may stimulate investment and innovation more than a less exuberant steadier state does. Three econometric analyses have concluded that, as between stability and instability, stability fosters growth, but a more elaborate analysis concludes that growth proceeds more rapidly under instability.[13] If the comparison were between income instability and a sturdily maintained full employment, continuing full employment would be more likely to be found superior.

However this may be, no agreement between lower and higher income countries on an integrated commodities program has been reached, since the lower income countries negotiate for intervention in the market not merely to stabilize commodity prices but also to raise them above their secular trend level. The higher income countries reject the latter provision, on the grounds that it is unwarranted and that for some commodities it is impossible or extremely cumbersome. They also reject the notion of compensatory financing that is not fully repaid, and indeed it is difficult to rationalize special help for the selected countries that this would benefit as contrasted with the same amount of economic aid allocated on other grounds.

FOR FURTHER READING

General statements from the neoclassical viewpoint of the advantages of international specialization and the pursuance of the dictates of comparative advantage are made as lucidly and trenchantly in two works in the 1930s as in later statements: Gottfried Haberler, *The Theory of International Trade* (New York: Macmillan, 1937); and Jacob Viner, *Studies in the Theory of International Trade* (New York: Harper, 1937). In many later essays, both men have restated the argument and applied it to specific points in controversy. See, for example, J. Viner, *International Trade and Economic Development* (Glencoe, Ill.: Free Press, 1952); or G. Haberler, "Terms of Trade and Economic Development," in *Economic Development for Latin America*, ed. Howard S. Ellis and H. C. Wallich (New York: St. Martin's Press, 1961).

---

[13] Compare, for example, C. Glezakos, "Export Instability and Economic Growth: A Statistical Verification," *Economic Development and Cultural Change* (July 1973); D. Mathiesen and R. McKinnon, "Instability in Underdeveloped Countries: The Impact of International Economy," mimeographed (1972); and C. S. Voivodas, "The Effect of Foreign Exchange Stability on Growth," *Review of Economics and Statistics* (August 1974). On the other hand, a significant and positive correlation between instability and growth is reported in Odin Knudsen and Andrew Parnes, *Trade Instability and Economic Development: An Empirical Study* (Lexington, Mass.: D. C. Heath, 1976). All are cited in Karsten Laursen, "The Integrated Programme for Commodities," *World Development*, 8 (April 1978), 423–35. Laursen presents a useful analysis of the topic.

The basic sources of terms of trade data and their analysis are:

F. Hilgerdt, *Industrialization and Foreign Trade* (Geneva: League of Nations, 1945).

Charles P. Kindleberger, *The Terms of Trade: A European Case Study* (New York: MIT Press–Wiley, 1956).

Theodore Morgan, "The Long-Run Terms of Trade between Agriculture and Manufacturing," *Economic Development and Cultural Change*, 8 (October 1959), 1–23.

General Agreement on Tariffs and Trade, *International Trade* (annual report), Geneva.

The thesis of the inevitably falling terms of trade is presented in Raúl Prebisch, "The Economic Development of Latin America and Its Principal Problems," United Nations *Economic Bulletin for Latin America*, 7 *(February 1962), 1–22.*

LDC trade and commodity pricing problems are discussed in J. N. Bhagwati, ed., *The New International Order*, chaps. 6–9; G. K. Helleiner, ed., *A World Divided*, chaps 2–5; and G. M. Meier, ed., *Leading Issues in Development Economics*, chap. 11. The essays do not duplicate one another greatly. Among those excerpted by Meier are essays by Nurkse, Haberler, and Cairncross on the benefits of international trade and Sunkel's "Transnational Capitalism and National Disintegration," discussed in Chapter 6 of the present book. Helleiner's book presents Alfred Maizels and Marian Radetzki on commodity pricing, Paul Streeten on the new bargaining power of the LDCs, and Frances Stewart on LDC gains and losses in international trade. In Bhagwati's volume, Bhagwati discusses market disruption, means of compensation, and GATT reform; C. Fred Bergsten argues the potential disruption of DC access to supplies; Harald B. Malmgren surveys prospective trade policies of the DCs; and Harry G. Johnson critically analyzes LDC commodity demands. Other economists comment on the Bhagwati, Malmgren, and Johnson papers. See also:

Harry G. Johnson, *Money, Trade, and Economic Growth*, 2d ed. (London: Unwin University Books, 1964).

Gerald M. Meier, *Problems of Cooperation for Development* (New York: Oxford University Press, 1974), part 3, on trade preferences for imports from LDCs.

V

The Strategy and Tactics of Growth and Development

20

The Choice of Products
and the Choice of
Production Methods

Four questions remain. Given the natural resources, the state of techniques, the population, and the other circumstances of a given country's production, what products should the country select to produce in order to attain the best results in development? With what proportions of labor and capital should it produce each product? Should it aim at the domestic market or an international market—or in what proportions at each? And how should it guide the economy to achieve these desiderata? This chapter discusses the first two of these questions, and Chapters 21 and 22 the third and fourth.

"To attain the best results in development" is an ambiguous phrase. It is used here to mean to maximize material welfare. First, we summarize the general principles of the optimum choice of products and methods, as those principles are stated in general economic texts. These are mainly static principles; in the main they consider only the present, and not results over time; but in this section they are discussed (briefly) with emphasis on the choices they pose for a government in a developing country—a government that is concerned with the future. Then we turn to choice between agriculture and industry, and between capital-intensive and labor-intensive methods of production. In part this discussion is merely application of the general principles, but mainly it deals with dynamic considerations—with the effects that will follow as development proceeds.

INCOME DISTRIBUTION AND THE MAXIMIZATION OF WELFARE

We assume that the welfare that is to be maximized is the material welfare of all the members of the society, not the welfare of some select group or of the state somehow reified. We let each individual or each family express its choices in the marketplace. The aggregation of those choices, including the choices that the individuals choose to have the government make on their behalf, is then "the social choice." However, the influence that each individual will have upon the market depends on his or her income. If the distribution of income is changed—if, for example, the government redistributes the ownership of all agricultural land—then "the social choice" will have changed. A believer in an unqualified egalitarian ethic may argue that social welfare will be maximized if income is equally distributed—if every individual casts an equal "vote" in the marketplace. But this distribution of income will almost certainly lead to lesser aggregate production by some reasonable definition than will an unequal distribution of income. By some reasonable weighting of the welfare of every individual, inequality of control over productive resources and of income distribution may therefore yield an increase in the aggregate welfare of all individuals taken as a group. We leave this insoluble problem with the observation that welfare economics must make some assumption about the optimum distribution of income or the actual distribution of income to be accepted, and with this as a datum, it may then proceed.

LIMITATIONS OF THE MARKET AS ALLOCATOR

The problem of allocation among products is a problem of increasing the output of one good at the sacrifice of some output of another good. The shift should be made, and relative prices and profits opportunities will usually cause it to be made, though imperfectly, if the new basket of goods is valued more by the purchasers of the final products than was the old—if, that is, the value of aggregate output has been increased by the shift. The problem of choice among methods of production is the problem of using more of one productive resource (say, capital or labor) in order to reduce the amount of another (say, labor or capital) that is needed for the production of a given amount of output. Such a choice is usually made by any individual producer because it reduces his money cost of producing the output of a given total value. The resource released must then compete for employment elsewhere. The increased demand for one resource and the decreased demand for another will affect their relative prices (where the magnitude of the increase and the decrease is greater than infinitesimal), and so cause shifts in their use elsewhere. Welfare in the economy is increased if the aggregate result is an increase in the total output of the economy.

In a simple theoretical model, the shifts among products and among methods of production will cause the marginal value product of each input in production to become equal with that of every other input throughout the economic system, and this equalization will maximize output and thereby material welfare in the system.

The implication of the four questions that introduced this chapter is not that products and methods should be decided on and then decreed. Given the distribution of income, the market is a remarkably efficient allocator. Under certain conditions the "invisible hand" of the market, operating on thousands of individuals each of whom is seeking his or her own maximum economic advantage, will guide those individuals toward the production of products and the use of methods that maximize social benefit. The economist who believes that complete central direction of the economy will achieve maximum welfare must cope with the problem of how the central planners shall comprehend the complex interrelationships within the economy, guide every producer and worker to serve those interrelationships, and motivate each producer and worker. But the phrase "under certain conditions" in the second preceding sentence is not to be overlooked. We must ask what the limitations of the market as allocator are, and under what framework of constraints or inducements it will serve the members of the society better than if it is unconstrained. We ask, In what circumstances will the play of unconstrained market forces not bring about production of the optimum basket of goods and the optimum allocation of productive resources?

If some part of some productive resource (say, labor) is unemployed, and if rigidities prevent that resource from gaining employment by competing for it, then a problem of aggregate demand—the "Keynesian" problem—exists. We do not consider that problem here, but assume that the full employment of all productive resources exists. We are concerned with the allocation of those resources.

Monopoly

One deviation from the conditions that are presumed to lead to the optimum allocation of resources is the existence of monopoly. If monopoly exists, the price of the good produced will be held too high and too little will be produced, so that, at least in static theory monopoly not only distorts the distribution of income but reduces aggregate output. An exception exists where concentrating production in a single plant is necessary to attain the maximum economy of scale; in this case, regulated monopoly or governmental operation is beneficial. Schumpeter argued forcefully for another and more general benefit of monopoly: that it maximizes the rate of technical progress and thus of rise in income; for if a company can for a time have an exclusive gain from its technical advance, the incentive to technical progress will be greatly strengthened. The argument is cogent; permitting monopoly of the fruits of technical progress for a limited period, as for example by a patent system, no doubt raises a country's rate of growth. The argument does not apply to other types of monopoly, such as monopoly of a natural resource.

The problem of monopoly is faced in the early stages of industrialization in an acute form. The market for a given manufactured product is often no greater than can be served efficiently by one factory. The first factory is therefore free from competition; any prospective competitor knows that if he enters the field, both factories will lose money. If there are no close substitutes for an early industrial product, the producer may therefore be able to hold his price considerably higher than it would be otherwise. But the successful establishment of an early factory is a difficult and uncertain task, and the entrepreneur often would not attempt it if he anticipated competition, price regulation, or nationalization. In these circumstances, the rate of economic growth may be maximized by permitting private production without price regulation. The questions is an empirical one. No simple theoretical formula will answer it.

Imperfect Mobility

To maximize the marginal productivity or the marginal utility of outputs, competition among producers for inputs and among the suppliers of inputs must operate so as to bring the marginal product of each input to equality throughout the system and to equality with its price. So long as the opportunity cost of an input—the production in its present employment that will be lost by shifting it—is less in value than the production that may be gained by shifting it, the economy suffers if the shift is not made. This loss may occur if an input is not perfectly mobile.

If capital stays in the urban centers because risk is greater in agriculture, and workers stay on the farm because they feel that the higher money wages in town do not compensate for certain unpleasant features of urban life, then the marginal products are actually equal, for risk is a cost and psychic income is income. But if capital stays in town and loses the higher returns available in agriculture because its owners are not correctly informed about the opportunities for lending or investing in agriculture, and if workers stay on the farm and lose the higher wages available in the city because they are uninformed about urban opportunities or the conditions of urban life, then opportunities for increasing the country's production are being missed.

Both forms of imperfect mobility no doubt exist, but their presence may have often been exaggerated. To cite interest rates of 8% in urban lending and 30% in rural lending does not prove misallocation of capital until it is also known how much greater the cost of loan supervision is and how much more frequent defaults are in agriculture. And differences between rural and urban incomes do not demonstrate that factor immobility is at work. Migration from farms to cities, even when the immigrants face unemployment for part of the year, argues that the workers are mobile (see Chapter 4). Their competition for jobs simply fails to bring industrial wages down. The difficulty is institutional interference with factor prices rather than imperfect mobility.

Insofar as there is imperfect mobility, a recommendation for partial remedy is the improvement of transportation, communication, and information. A further remedy, economically sound but politically rarely possible, is the subsidization of industrial employment. For if the productivity of labor is 8 cents per hour in agriculture and 35 cents per hour in industry, but the labor will not be attracted to industry except at a wage of 45 cents per hour, then if the industrial employer is paid a subsidy of 10 cents per each worker-hour of newly recruited workers, the new workers will gain 37 cents, whoever bears the burden of the subsidy will lose 10 cents, and the two together, and the economy as a whole, will have gained 27 cents worth of output.

However, there is an economic disadvantage to increasing the flow of labor from agriculture to manufacturing: the need to use scarce resources to augment urban infrastructure. This will be a net cost, for the facilities needed in the villages, if they do not already exist, will be simpler.

The remedy which maximizes welfare may be to improve amenities in the villages: schools, health facilities, recreational facilities. Paradoxically, increasing the contentment of workers and preventing urban congestion may also maximize the rate of economic growth. In spite of the increase in the attractiveness of rural life, the concomitant increased information about the cities is likely to bring as large a flow of men and women to them as industrialization can absorb. The actual conditions and the optimum rates of course vary among countries.

Factor Price Rigidities: Shadow Prices

A more common hindrance to equalizing marginal productivity may be an opposite one.

It was stated above that what appears to be factor immobility may actually be a result of factor price rigidities. The market price of a factor in some use may deliberately be held at a level above its opportunity cost. Labor may have a much lower marginal product in one sector—for example, agriculture—than it would elsewhere, so that a shift of labor would increase aggregate output; yet by law or convention the minimum wage that can be offered elsewhere may be above the marginal product of added labor, and thus may prevent the shift, so that the surplus labor remains in agriculture and produces nothing. The development of industry in some LDCs is retarded by the requirement of unemployment compensation, sick pay, terminal leave, and the like, higher than can be afforded elsewhere in the economy. The labor costs imposed by law reduce the number of workers that industry will hire, and thereby force more workers to earn a poorer living elsewhere than would have to do so otherwise. If industrialists were allowed to pay only the wages (including fringe benefits) needed to attract workers from their low-productivity pursuits in agriculture or services, the value of aggregate output in the economy (at a constant price level) would be increased.

The conventional recommendation therefore is that the minimum wage or high fringe benefits should be eliminated, so that the marginal productivity of labor might reach equality everywhere apart from the differential needed to induce mobility.

This advice overlooks the problem of income distribution. The price elasticity of demand for labor in industry may be so low that industrial wages would be greatly reduced and agricultural and service incomes only slightly increased before the marginal productivity of labor was equalized across sectors. For production coefficients may be fixed in many industrial processes, so that a reduction in wage rates would induce no increase in the amount of labor employed. The inequality of income distribution, measured by either the Gini ratio or the income share of the lowest income 20% or 40% of the population, might be greatly worsened.

The ideal solution in an ideal economy would be to maximize aggregate output by eliminating barriers to marginal productivity equalization, then to decrease the inequality of income distribution by "secondary redistribution"—progressive taxation, direct governmental services to the poor, perhaps money subsidization of their incomes. If these measures are not possible because of public attitudes, administrative incapacity, or the political influence of the groups that would be taxed, then a second-best solution may be to tax industry to support expenditures enhancing the welfare of the nonindustrial low-income groups. If the government feels unable to assess and tax a company's profits, an excise tax is a third-best measure. But of course the political power of influential groups may bar this solution also.

Any of these policies may or may not serve the public welfare, somehow defined, better than would a policy of maximum encouragement to the equalization throughout the system of labor's marginal productivity. Since the results of that policy or of any of the three alternatives depend upon elasticities, rigidities, and social considerations that cannot be evaluated *a priori*, it is impossible without empirical investigation to state what may be the optimum feasible policy for any given country.

It is often asserted that the rigidity of social security requirements greatly discourages the expansion of industry, and especially discourages the use of labor-intensive methods. The major deterrent often seems to be the inability to lay off workers except at very high cost. To impose on employers the retention of unneeded workers is a crude device for fighting unemployment. Welfare would surely be increased if the government itself faced the problem of providing employment.

Institutional rigidities also often exist in the capital and foreign exchange markets.

Although capital may be scarce enough so that all the capital that is available can yield a marginal product of 18% per year, interest rates in certain uses may be limited by law to 10% per year. If enforced, the law will prevent those uses from getting capital even though the marginal product there is above 18%, and the capital will be used where its marginal product is less than 18%.

To encourage the import of modern equipment the foreign exchange rate may be set so low that eager bidders would like to buy more foreign exchange than is available, and foreign exchange must be rationed. Say the rate is set at 12 units of local currency to the U.S. dollar. Some uses in which imported equipment costing $1 may have marginal productivity of 20 units of local currency may not get the foreign exchange needed to buy it, whereas other uses in which the marginal productivity of equipment is only 12 units may get it. Similarly, the consumer goods admitted may not be those of the highest marginal utility.

Say the equilibrium exchange rate is 17 units of the local currency to the dollar. A common reason for setting the rate higher, so that foreign exchange must be rationed, is to encourage "modern" (capital-intensive) manufacturing. An importer to whom foreign exchange is allocated may then buy a $100,000 machine for 1,200,000 rather than 1,700,000 units of the local currency—a machine whose contribution to production is worth only 1,200,000 units. But it is then impossible to import all of the goods that would have contributed productivity or utility worth 1,700,000 units or more.

Other inputs, such as some natural resources, may also be overvalued or undervalued for institutional reasons.

In all of these cases, underneath the market price of the input an economic analyst may estimate its "shadow" price, the price for each factor which would be equal to its marginal productivity if every unit were employed optimally, so that no shift would increase its productivity. The shadow price is the opportunity cost. To maximize production, every input should be shifted from any use in which it is earning less than its shadow price to a use in which it will earn its shadow price, the only qualification being the one mentioned above about income distribution. Though complete freedom of international trade may not be an optimum condition, because there may be faster routes to future comparative advantage (see Chapter 21), to establish artificially exchange rates favorable to imports, and then of necessity to ration imports, is hardly the optimum policy.

Externalities

The concept of technological external economies has been present in economic literature for a long time. The productive activity carried on by one firm may confer a benefit on another producer or on a consumer for which the firm conferring it cannot collect payment, or may impose an uncompensated cost or burden (for example, pollution) on another producer or a consumer.

The marginal productivity to a private employer of a certain use of an input may not be identical with its marginal productivity to the society as a whole because of technological external economies and diseconomies. Private marginal productivity plus uncompensated benefits conferred and minus uncompensated burdens imposed on other parties is termed social marginal productivity. Production (that is, welfare) will be maximized if inputs are allocated so that social marginal productivity, not private marginal productivity, is maximized, for external economies and diseconomies must also be considered in evaluating whether a shift of a factor would increase welfare. The supposed existence of externalities often enters into argument about the advantages of industry compared to agriculture, capital-intensive methods compared to labor-intensive ones, and other allocation choices. The officials of some less developed countries attach less weight to the external diseconomies of manufacturing industry than do the industrial countries of the world. Japan has concentrated so single-mindedly on industrial growth that it permits pollution of its airways and waterways that would be intolerable in even the most negligent European or North American country. "Export your pollution-creating industries to us," Brazilian officials have said; "we will be glad to have their pollution along with them." It may be doubted whether these policies truly reflect the desires of publics that are fully informed about the future effects of present pollution.

There is a contrasting case in which the presence of technological external economies warrants governmental action to bring about technical advance more rapidly than the market would. This is the case which W. A. Lewis has termed "infant industralization," to distinguish it from the problems of infancy of a single industrial enterprise. If an industrial complex develops, the resulting "specialization, research, and learning" may reduce costs well below those that a single prospective industrialist could anticipate. Both single private investors and private investors as a group may be insufficiently bold to anticipate the effects of development of the entire complex. Hence, industrialization that will be economical may be retarded somewhat. (That it will be prevented for this reason is a limiting case that is less likely.) It may therefore be advantageous for the government to provide support and stimulus to induce an allocation of resources to industry sooner than the market would. The point should not be overemphasized. The government should not incur any costs of industrial development that private investors would not find it advantageous to incur themselves if they were sufficiently imaginative and could act in concert. In practice, an impatient government may waste resources in trying to accelerate the development of an industrial complex, for the government may overlook the conditions other than the mere absence of complementary firms that set a limit to the pace of industrialization. The attempt of the Italian government to foster rapid industrialization of the "heel" of Italy's boot provides a convenient example.

Economies of Scale: Public Goods

Policy measures to take advantage of economies of scale, not to counter their existence, are appropriate. The same is true of production of the type of goods called "public goods."

If a plant is enlarged, the cost per unit of the added units produced may be less than the pevious average cost in the plant. If so, then satisfaction in the economy as a whole is increased if the added goods are produced and are sold at their marginal cost, for productive resources will thereby be shifted from some use in which they are producing goods that yield lesser satisfaction per dollar of their price. But if the total output of the larger plant is sold at a price equal to marginal cost, the total costs will not be covered. Should the plant be erected if its operations as a whole are run at a loss which someone must bear?

A parallel case is that of indivisible costs or benefits. A lighthouse provides an excellent example. There may be no economies of scale in the ordinary sense; the physical volume of production is not increased; but if the light shines, an added ship may see it at no extra cost. The scale of consumption of the service, rather than of its provision, can be increased with zero added cost. Radio and television broadcasts are other examples. Samuelson uses the term *public goods* to describe goods whose provision to one recipient does not decrease the amount available to others. There are few other pure examples of public goods, but roads, bridges, national defense, education, police and fire protection (within a given geographic area), and certain other services usually provided by government approach the condition. If the price to the specific recipient should be zero, because the marginal cost is zero, by what criterion should the service be provided? No private producer would provide public goods or establish a plant in which there are economies of scale unless he expected to have a monopoly or an oligopolistic arrangement, so that competition would not drive the price down to the marginal cost.

The criterion in the case of either economies of scale or public goods is that the benefits to users in excess of the marginal cost ("rents" or "consumer surpluses") should in the aggregate equal the difference between receipts and the aggregate production cost. A government that provides a service of which this is not true is using resources for purposes that are less productive than other uses to which they might be put. Moreover, the cost should be collected from persons who benefit directly or indirectly (unless for reasons not related to this service it seems equitable to redistribute income from other taxpayers to these recipients, and providing this service happens to be a convenient way of redistributing it).

In almost all countries, public goods are provided by the government, since to maximize welfare they ought to be provided free. In the more developed Western countries, large private firms in some industries in which economies of scale prevail are allowed to gain the large profits that result from the inability of new firms (with small sales) to compete. The automobile industry is an example. Other industries, regarded as more essential or characterized by especially wasteful competition, are regulated in some countries and run by the government in others. This is true of the group of industries that are usually termed public utilities. In less developed countries, regulation is likely to be excessive, rather than deficient, if the public utility or the enterprise embodying economies of scale is foreign-owned. Perhaps a reasonable policy prescription would be parallel to that stated above for early monopolies. The public interest in the increase in productivity created by such enterprises is such that an enlightened government might well welcome them even if a pricing policy that would be optimum in a static economy cannot be enforced. As in other cases, the optimum policy decision in any given case depends on the specific circumstances.

SECULAR TRENDS: AGRICULTURE VERSUS INDUSTRY

Throughout this volume it has been assumed that the reader understands either "intuitively" or from the brief discussions in Chapters 2 and 7 that there will be and must be a continuing secular shift from agricultural to nonagricultural production. At this point the analysis is made more rigorous.

"Agriculture versus industry" is not quite the correct way of putting the problem. Every growth economist agrees that rising per capita income is associated with a greater or smaller degree of movement from the primary sector to the secondary and tertiary sectors.

Within the world as a whole, the lower income countries are the primary sector and the higher income countries the industrial sector. As noted in earlier chapters this broad statement must be accepted with care. Latin America, Asia other than Japan, and Africa together produce manufacturers worth perhaps six times the value of their imports of manufactures, and on the other hand the so-called industrial countries as a group produce more food than they import. But the net flow of primary products is in one direction and that of industrial products in the other, and the industrial products exports of the higher income countries to the lower income countries are much larger than their primary product exports, whereas the reverse is true in the other direction.

In sweeping terms, then, when one refers to the primary versus the secondary and tertiary sectors, one may think of the less developed countries versus the more developed countries. Yet the issue is agriculture versus industry within countries, or in the world as a whole, not one set of countries versus another.

Agriculture existed first. If manufacturing is to exist, it must draw workers from agriculture. Manufacturing is attractive to rural workers only if it promises incomes higher than those earned in rural pursuits. In a world in which the demand for manufactured goods is increasing relative to that for farm products, some volume of manufactures can be sold at prices that yield a sufficiently high value product per worker to permit and justify wages high enough to draw workers. A manufacturer who can satisfy that condition—who is able to operate a plant so that he can sell his products at a price at which consumers want to spend a segment of their income on them rather than on previously available products and who can cover his costs at that price—increases the national income. The higher the value product (distributed in profit, increased wages, or reduced sale prices), the greater is the increase in national income.

But importing the manufactured good may increase the national income still more. Suppose that the industrial good can be imported in exchange for the produce of 1,000 agricultural workers. Then if 1,100 workers must be diverted from agricultural to industrial production to produce it at home, its importation leaves 100 workers free to produce for export, and adds to national income more than does its domestic production. However, if only 950 workers must be diverted from agriculture to produce it, then its domestic production increases the national income the more. The latter situation, with due qualification concerning the difference between private and social marginal product and with due allowance for effects over time as well as immediate effects, is the basic and indeed the only justification for domestic manufacturing. Of course, if 1,100 workers were unemployed and they could be employed only by producing the industrial product, then its production would be advantageous even though relatively costly, but this is a third- or fourth-best solution whose adoption would indicate a country's ineptitude in its domestic economic policies.

The Importance of Elasticities

The trend over time in the relative demand for agricultural and industrial products, together with changes over time in productivity in their production, causes continuing change in comparative advantage. Consider the world as a whole as a single entity before taking the viewpoint of individual countries.

It was noted in Chapter 3 that the income elasticity of demand for industrial products in the entire range of LDCs taken as a group is, say, 1.2–1.4 and that that for food is 0.8 or less. The latter figure is probably a maximum estimate for the income elasticity of demand in these countries for all agricultural products. Since the income elasticity of demand for agricultural products declines as income rises, for the world as a whole the two elasticities may be about 0.7 and 1.4, respectively. Thus, as productivity and per capita income rise in the world as a whole, aggregate demand for the products of agriculture rises at a rate about one half (0.7/1.4) that for industrial products and services. (Note that this refers to the demand for agricultural products "at the farm gate." The expenditure for agricultural products at retail rises more than one half as fast as that for industrial products and services as a group, but this expenditure is for elaborate processing—for food, elaborate packaging, freezing, shipment over thousands of miles; for textiles, their manufacture; and so on—as well as for the agricultural products.)

The *price* elasticity of demand for agricultural products as a group is also below unity. A given percentage change in the price of agricultural products will cause a less than corresponding opposite change in the quantity wanted, or, to state the matter conversely, a given percentage change in the quantity supplied will cause a more than corresponding opposite change in the price. Thus a large harvest will yield farmers less aggregate revenue than a small one.

To avoid considering too many things at the same time, suppose that the farm and nonfarm populations and labor forces remain constant while economic growth proceeds. In this simple situation, consider the effect of increase in productivity on the distribution of income between the two sectors. Suppose that output per worker or per capita, and therefore aggregate output, increases at the same rate in agriculture and industry—say at 1% per year. The term *industry* is used here to include all nonagriculture.) Real world income therefore increases by 1%. But demand for nonagricultural products will be rising by 1.4% per year and that for agricultural products by only 0.7%. There will be an "excess" supply of farm products of 0.3% per year. Because the price elasticity of demand is below unity, the price of farm products will fall by more than 0.3% and farm income will rise by less than 0.4%. Conversely, the relative price of nonagricultural products, for which the demand has increased more than the supply, will rise. The terms of trade between agriculture and industry will steadily worsen for agriculture. The bulk of the increase in real world income will go to industry. The margin between per capita income in agriculture and industry will steadily increase.[1]

In this analysis, population was assumed constant. If the farm population is increasing faster than the nonfarm population, relative and absolute per capita income in agriculture will fare even worse.

This, in sharp analytical focus, is why in the world as a whole, industrial output will increase faster than agricultural output as per capita income rises, and why workers will be progressively driven from agriculture—or lured to industry.

---

[1] If the price elasticity of demand for farm products as a group is as low as 0.7 then there would be no increase in the absolute income of agriculture, and the entire benefit of technical progress would go to industry.

Paradoxically, this analysis indicates that farmers and farmland owners would benefit if in the world as a whole farm output rose very slowly. If world farm output were rising by less than the demand for it—by less than seven tenths as fast as the rise in income—then the low price elasticity of demand for farm products would work in favor of agriculturists. Agricultural prices would rise relative to industrial prices, and with them agricultural income would rise. If world farm output did not rise at all, cultivators or farmland owners would benefit mightily. The agriculturists of the world as a group would benefit by precisely the development that persons alarmed about the world's population growth fear: growing food scarcity. But from historic experience and any reasonable forecast of the future, it can be concluded that through intelligent human effort agricultural productivity is increasing steadily, and that through its increase world agricultural output is increasing fast enough so that on the worldwide average there must be steady and continuing migration from agriculture if per capita agricultural income is to increase as fast as nonfarm income (even if always remaining below it).

National Alternatives

Historically, the international migration of farm labor to "empty lands" or to industrial jobs in technically more advanced countries has been important. It will be important in the future in only a few situations: sparsely populated and affluent oil countries welcoming an increase in their labor forces; southern Europeans and North Africans working as "guests" performing the lowest paid work in West European countries; U.S. acceptance of migrants from the Caribbean to hold similar jobs; and the geographic accident of a long open border between Mexico and the United States, by virtue of which the United States too adopts a "guest worker" policy, though not by deliberate national decision. Apart from these instances, future intersectoral shifts of labor forces will be within individual countries, determined by the play of economic forces within each country. International migration will no longer provide an escape valve.

A rise in productivity in any sector of course increases average real income in the country as a whole, if other forces remain constant.[2] Sectoral differences in productivity and output affect the sectoral distribution of that income. If sales from agriculture to the nonagricultural sector lag in a country that cannot finance food imports or that can import food only at an increased unit food cost, the rise in food prices caused by the scarcity of food will benefit agriculture and will bear heavily on the nonfarm poor. If productivity and output in agriculture rise, in a country whose agricultural

---

[2] Barring the situation in which exports forming a large share of GDP are also such a large share of the world supply that increase in those exports materially worsens the terms of trade and in this way reduces GNP.

prices are above the world price and which therefore cannot export except at a reduced price, agricultural prices and aggregate agricultural income will fall. The nonfarm poor will benefit. The effects on the growth of industry will be mixed. There will be a cost effect and a demand effect. A rise in agricultural prices (an improvement from agriculture's viewpoint in the terms of trade between agriculture and industry) will enlarge the market for industrial products, but it will also increase the cost of industrial production, both directly if some of the agricultural materials are used and indirectly because industrial wages will presumably have to be increased. A worsening of agriculture's terms of trade will decrease industry's cost of production, but it will also decrease the market for industrial products. The two effects will be precisely identical in amount, except as the agricultural sector saves some of its added income or decreases saving if its income falls. Taking into account the change in savings, the price effect will be larger. Some growth economists overlook the price effect in their analysis. Others stress it. Even if the two quantities are identical, there may be a net effect on the growth of industry. No firm statement seems possible.

The adverse impact on agriculture of the differential income elasticities of demand is less in the lowest income countries, since the income elasticity of demand for food is closer to unity in those countries.

Even though in the world as a whole agriculture will derive the greatest direct benefit, the lower its production for the market, nevertheless the most advantageous position for any given group of cultivators would be to increase output rapidly while farm prices were high because other cultivators were not doing so. The more innovational cultivators, or those favored by better information about improved methods, will do so. The farmers who lag will suffer. Individual countries with especially favorable climatic conditions and soil will prosper by continuing to specialize in agriculture, particularly in the production of agricultural products for which the demand is high even at high incomes. For some types of agricultural production a high land-person ratio is also favorable. New Zealand's success in sheep raising provides an example. Denmark and the Netherlands have gained high incomes in the production and processing of dairy products and meat. No doubt some of the present lower income countries will provide other examples. Some countries may specialize advantageously in the production of certain fruits. But even these countries develop a good deal of manufacturing as their incomes rise (in some instances mainly in processing their agricultural specialties).

The Dynamics of Comparative Advantage

At the cost of some repetition, the application of the law of comparative advantage in dynamic conditions is summarized here. The principle is sometimes stated as though it condemned countries in which agriculture is now predominant to specialize in agriculture forever. That version of the law is fallacious.

The law of comparative advantage (or comparative costs) is based on the principle that the value of production is maximized by shifting each input to the production in which it has the highest marginal value productivity, until in equilibrium the marginal value productivity of all inputs in all uses is equal. On that basis, the law states that a country or region will maximize its income if it specializes in production of the goods in which it has the greatest comparative advantage. This will be production of the goods whose production uses relatively most of the inputs of which the country possesses relatively the greatest number. With free international trade, the forces of the market will equalize the price of each good throughout the world, and will lead every country to production which utilizes its full comparative advantage, thereby resulting in maximum welfare not only for the world as a whole but for each country. This conclusion holds on the same assumptions on which the market will maximize the value of production by equalizing marginal productivity: perfect competition, including perfect foresight and perfect mobility of factors within each country, so that each factor is paid the same income in all uses throughout the economy; no economies of scale; and no uncompensated externalities.

The formal proof of the law assumes not only unchanging techniques but the availability of the same techniques to all countries. In practice, economists who adduce the law of comparative advantage sometimes simply ignore international differences in the state of techniques.

On these assumptions, a country rich in agricultural land relative to its supply of labor or of capital (say Burma or Argentina) should specialize in producing commodities whose production is lowest cost when much land is used; a country with a large number of deft skilled workers (say Switzerland) should specialize in production requiring large numbers of skilled workers; and so on. And each country will be led by the relative prices of various products in the world market to do this—given the assumptions stated in the two preceding paragraphs.

The law, stated without reference to changes in the state of techniques, is backward-looking. It would have a country continue to do what it has always done. But technical and economic changes cause the comparative advantage of today to be the disadvantage of the day after tomorrow, if not of tomorrow.[3] Above all, techniques change, so that a country's relative cost of producing different products (say agricultural and manufactured products) from the same old natural resources changes drastically. As noted in Chapter 8, technical advance changes factor endowments. Changes in

---

[3] The definitive statement of the inadequacies of the static formulation of the law of comparative advantage is Romney Robinson, "Factor Endowments and Comparative Advantage," *Quarterly Journal of Economics,* 70 (May and August 1956), 169–92 and 346–63.

the world's relative demand for primary, secondary, and tertiary products as income rises also change comparative advantage.

Yet, though the law cannot be proved so rigorously when allowance is made for changes in the state of techniques, comparative advantage exists in a changing world as well as a static world, and comparative advantage in the very near future is the basis on which present allocation should be decided. Only if there is a sea change in resource availability and costs, such as the discovery of large new petroleum deposits and then later a quadrupling of petroleum prices, will comparative advantage change abruptly. Moreover, even with the aid of capital from petroleum exploitation a country does not move today to its comparative advantage 30 years from today. Rather, starting with the mix of products that has been advantageous in the past, a country's producers ask: "Considering the likely changes in our capabilities, in the resources available to us, and in the world economy, what comparative advantage five years from now shall we prepare for today? Ten years from now?" Except possibly for extremely long-lived infrastructure, it is futile to try to build the comparative advantage of, say, 25 years from now into structures now. Capital becomes obsolescent and is replaced by a new generation of equipment in shorter periods. And a cost incurred now to gain an advantage foreseen 25 years from now can mount prohibitively through compound interest during the 25-year interval.

On the basis of the considerations discussed so far in this chapter, as technical knowledge, technical and managerial experience, the availability of complementary production, and the availability of markets dictate, the gradual or rapid development of manufacturing and other nonagricultural industry becomes advantageous. The necessary sequence of its development, which makes it impossible to run before one can walk, was discussed in Chapter 6.

The Spurious Appeals of Industry

Because movement from agriculture to industry is advantageous over time as income rises, as techniques, experience, and markets make one and another industrial venture advantageous, some observers and some participants in the process of economic growth have leaped to the conclusion that manufacturing industry in general is advantageous at almost any time. They have then proceeded to rationalize that conclusion. Among the arguments and reasons advanced are the following:

1. "High-income countries have industry; therefore, establishing industry will give us high income." Or, another version of the same argument: "The value of output per worker is higher in industry than in agriculture. Therefore, emphasis on industry will raise per capita income." This notion of the inherent and absolute superior productivity of manufacturing industry die hard. It has no valid basis.

2. "Industry is modern." This is at times a way of stating some of the other reasons listed here, but often the desire to be modern and to overcome the humiliation of being looked down on by Western countries is so strong that a country's leaders are unable to understand that adopting and subsidizing methods that have a modern look, but for which the country does not yet have the basis, will reduce the country's level of living.

3. "Industrial life is associated with a modern outlook, an innovational spirit." This argument for forced industrialization overlooks two facts. First, the association cited is due in part to the fact that industrial life is a result of an innovational technical spirit. Trying to establish the external result will not establish the cause. Second, insofar as there is mutual causation and industrial life is a cause, it is industrial life, a complex phenomenon not to be evoked by building a factory, that is the cause.

Other arguments are more sophisticated.

4. "Industry has external economies that agriculture does not have." It spews out trained workers, has linkages which induce other industries to develop, and so on. For this reason, and because of the advantages of "growing points," it is argued that the concentration of investment at such points, even at the cost of relative starvation of primary production, will increase the rate of growth of GNP. Perhaps industry does yield greater external economies than agriculture. Certainly up to the point at which congestion outweighs the effect, the enterprises that gather together in growing points yield such economies to one another. But attempts to establish growing points artificially are likely to be futile.

5. "A high rate of investment will cause a high rate of growth. The development of industry leads to the development of a capital goods industry. If a large capital goods industry is estabished, there will be a high rate of investment, by definition. The economic fact is forced by the technical fact."

This argument is drawn from Soviet experience. The Soviet government decreed that there should be much capital goods production, and there was. But there will be no investors ready to buy the capital goods that are produced, unless a market for the products of the capital goods is seen. In the Soviet Union, the government provided that market in order to build capacity for producing still further capital goods and armaments. It prevented the income paid out in the process from creating a high demand for consumer goods, by taking a 40% markup on goods bought or produced by the state and sold to consumers. In any other country, a large volume of investment will follow a large volume of capital goods production only if, by some equivalent of the Soviet policies, the government buoys up the demand for capital goods.

The question of choice of products and the law of comparative advantage have been discussed here mainly in relation to the choice between agriculture and industry. But of course the principles that apply to that choice also apply to the choice of specific products and specific techniques within agriculture and within industry.

CAPITAL VERSUS LABOR

In the analysis of the techniques of production that will maximize output and welfare, the broadest question is, What relative amount of capital and labor should be used?

It has been said that economic growth has been urban and industrial, large-scale and capital-intensive in its methods, and of benefit to the upper class. The implication is that if there had been more concern for the mass of the people, economic growth would have been less urban, less industrial, smaller in scale, and less capital-intensive. The point may be accepted, but the problem is not quite that simple. In this section the question of the appropriate degree of capital-intensivity is examined.

As has been noted in earlier chapters, the capital-output ratio is about the same in low-income countries as in high-income countries. The labor-output ratio is much higher. This is just another way of saying that they are low-income countries. One way of summarizing the growth process is to state that as the ratio of capital embodying sufficiently improved techniques to labor is increased, output (hence income) per worker will increase, until when erstwhile low-income countries have as much capital per worker as present high-income countries now have, they will have as high per capita incomes as present high-income countries now have. This statement too is in the general direction of truth, though overly simple. The question considered here is whether the capital must be introduced in methods that use a "modern" degree of capital-intensivity and form a modern enclave, which is then gradually enlarged until it fills the economy, or whether it is better to spread the capital in thin doses more or less uniformly throughout the economy, capital-intensivity gradually rising everywhere.

Equalizing Marginal Productivity

Conventional economic theory supports the latter alternative. The conclusion follows from the theory of the diminishing marginal productivity of any factor as its amount is increased relative to those of other factors. If the first $1,000 of equipment per worker raises his output more than the second $1,000, and that more than the third, then aggregate output will be maximized by giving each of three workers $1,000 worth of equipment, not by buying a $3,000 machine for one worker alone.

Suppose that output in the economic system is homogeneous, so that its production can be pictured on a single production function. Then the argument can be stated simply in the terms of Figure 20–1. Assume that the capital inputs available in the economy are represented by OK_2, and the amount

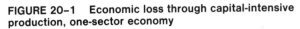

FIGURE 20–1   Economic loss through capital-intensive production, one-sector economy

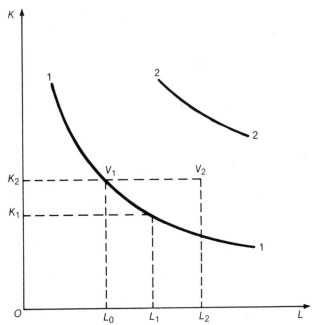

of labor by OL_2. If capital-intensive methods, which use relatively little labor, are used, production will be at V_1, and not all of the labor will find employment. If methods which use more labor per unit of capital are adopted, OK_1 of capital combined with OL_1 of labor will produce the same output, and since K_1K_2 of capital and L_1L_2 of labor remain, obviously total production can be increased. Aggregate production could be at V_2. If the perfect competition of economic theory prevails, the play of the market will bring output to the point V_2, for so long as some workers are unemployed, their competition for jobs will bring wages down relative to capital costs until all are employed, at which point the ratio between the two will be equal to the slope of the isoquant that passes through V_2.

If the economic system produces two commodities, say manufactured goods and agricultural products, then the situation is a little more complex. It is portrayed in Figure 20–2. The two production functions are drawn to the same scales. Suppose that the total amounts of capital and labor inputs in the economy are O_MK_1 and O_ML_1, respectively. Capital-intensive methods, employing O_MK_2 of capital inputs and only O_ML_2 of labor, are used in manufacturing, yielding output of M_1 on the MM isoquant. The remaining capital and labor inputs, K_1K_2 (= O_AK_3) and L_2L_1 (= O_AL_3), are available for use in agriculture, and are used there.

As the relatively steep negative slope of the isoquant MM at the point M_1

FIGURE 20–2 Economic loss through capital-intensive production, two-sector economy

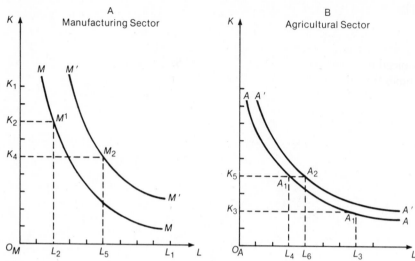

shows, production methods using a moderately smaller amount of capital (say K_2K_4 less) would not have to use much more labor to produce the same volume of output. On the other hand, if the capital saved were transferred to agriculture, the isoquant AA could be reached (at A'_1) with a much smaller amount of labor. If the net amount of labor thus saved (the difference between the labor freed in agriculture and that added in manufacturing, to maintain the same volume of output in each) were divided between agriculture and industry, output in both could be increased above the original output—to points M_2 and A_2, respectively.

In a geometric representation, no further shift will permit increased output in both sectors when production arrives at points at which the slopes of the two isoquants (drawn to the same scales) are equal. This is approximately true at M_2 and A_2. The statement that production in one industry is too capital-intensive and in another too labor-intensive, or that concentration of capital in one industry is starving another industry and reducing total output in the economy, means that in geometric terms production is at points such as M_1 and A_1, rather than M_2 and A_2.

As in the one-product economy of Figure 20–1, in a competitive system the play of the market will bring production of the two products of Figure 20–2 to the points M_2 and A_2, at which not merely will the slopes of the two isoquants be equal to each other, but the relative cost of capital and labor will be equal to that same slope. Competition will dictate that these points be chosen. A producer who produces with more capital-intensive (or for that matter more labor-intensive) methods will have higher costs, will find himself undersold, and, unless he mends his ways, will go bankrupt.

The "Factor Proportions Problem"

Why, then, are capital-intensive methods in use in some manufacturing enterprises in virtually every low-income country? One explanation is advanced in a well-known article by Richard S. Eckaus.[4] Economic theory assumes the possibility of an indefinitely large number of alternative methods of production, each using a little more or less capital, a little less or more labor, then another. But the history of economic growth in the West has been a history of the invention and introduction of more and more capital-intensive methods. Today, only capital-intensive methods are known in most Western manufacturing. As a result, production isoquants like those in Figures 20–1 and 20–2 may not exist. Rather, the situation may be as in Figure 20–3, sector M. The figure is adapted from Eckaus. M and A in the presentation here are thinly disguised representations of Manufacturing and Agriculture.

For convenience, the total amounts of capital and labor in the economy are indicated on the axes of sector M, at K_T and L_T. Sector M produces a product in considerable demand. The right-angled isoquants of sector M are not only highly capital-intensive; that they are right-angled indicates the use of unalterable proportions of capital and labor. No adaptations by which labor could be substituted for capital, or the reverse, are known; added labor (and also added capital) has zero marginal productivity.

Production in sector M is at M_1, on isoquant 6. $O_M K_1$ of capital is used,

FIGURE 20–3 Maximum output or maximum employment

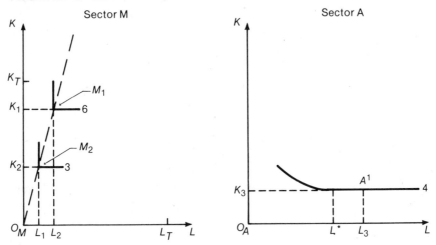

[4] "The Factor Proportions Problem in Underdeveloped Areas," *American Economic Review*, 45 (September 1955), 539–65.

leaving only K_1K_T (= O_AK_3) for sector A, but leaving a great deal of labor (L_2L_T, or O_AL_3). Sector A does know various alternative methods, and labor-intensive ones, but the amount of labor available is so great that its marginal productivity becomes zero.

In the situation of Figure 20–3, capital could not be shifted out of sector M by a change in production methods, since no less capital-intensive methods are known. The level of living could be raised by capital inflow, if absorptive capacity exists. Depending on who the consumers of the products of sector M are, the inequality of distribution might be lessened by levying a heavy tax on those products. Some capital formerly used in producing them might then be freed for use in sector A.

The Possibilities of Labor-Intensive Production

Eckaus's model offered an explanation of the large amount of labor with zero marginal productivity that was then thought to exist. However, it is not a necessary explanation of unemployment or underemployment. Technological disemployment, described in Chapter 4, offers an alternative explanation. And during the 20-some years since Eckaus's article was published, empirical investigations have produced increasing amounts of evidence that alternative methods of production of varying degrees of capital- and labor-intensivity are available in manufacturing. Double or triple shifts are possible to "stretch" capital. Japanese engineers have developed "minimachines," farm machines of many types which are so small that their use is economic even on farms of one–three hectares (about 2.5–7.5 acres), and machines run by hand power for processes which are performed by mechanical power in the West. In China a number of even simpler ingenious agricultural machines are in use. In Vietnam, insertion into a casing of the particular type of outboard motor that is useful in Vietnam's shallow inland channels has created an inexpensive type of tube-well pump. In Colombia, the writer has seen buildings as high as 13 stories constructed with cantilevered floors and curtain walls, with no steel rod or shape in the structure heavier than 1¼–1½-inch reinforcing rods.

All of these methods are capital-saving. Moreover, it is not necessary to ferret out such examples of ingenuity in order to find widely varying capital-labor ratios in production. Three English research workers studying this problem in Ghana and Ethiopia found that a large number of production methods, with differing capital-labor ratios, exist in each of a number of processes in vacuum-pan sugar production in Ghana and in shoe manufacturing in both countries.[5] A member of the same group of research workers found that a very great number of alternative processes were used in the

---

[5] James Pickett, D. J. C. Forsyth, and N. S. McBain, "The Choice of Technology," *World Development*, 2 (March 1974), 47–54.

production of cotton cloth in low-income countries.[6] A study of the manufacture of cigarettes, flashlight batteries, soft drinks, and tires in Indonesia found that labor-intensive, intermediate, and capital-intensive methods were used to make each of these products. The labor-intensive method or the intermediate method was usually the most economic, and the buyers noted no inferiority in quality when such methods were used.[7] A parallel study in Indonesia showed that five methods of rice milling of widely varying labor/capital intensity were available, and that although the most labor-intensive method, hand pounding, was no longer economically practical, the most labor-intensive of the other four methods was the most advantageous even at the market prices of capital and labor, and far more advantageous than any other at shadow prices (prices that reflected the relative scarcity of the two; shadow prices are discussed in Chapter 22).[8]

Why, then, are capital-intensive methods used in countries in which capital is costly and labor is cheap?

CAPITAL-INTENSIVE METHODS: WHY ARE THEY USED?

First, one should note that the cost per unit of output produced by capital-intensive methods may be less in some production and in some circumstances even though labor is very cheap. The more elaborate capital equipment may embody technical advances which outweigh its cost. In the central processes of some manufacturing, no method except a fairly capital-intensive one may be capable of producing the wanted product. This is true in some metallurgical manufacturing, where certain chemical transformations are involved, and in many other circumstances. And, as was noted in Chapter 11, even where labor-intensive methods are possible and labor is cheap capital-intensive methods may be cheaper in large-scale production.

As producers who have satisfied the home market with a rougher product turn to the export market, improvement in the substantive quality and adherence to precise specifications may become of increasing importance. In the trade-off between quality and price, improved quality in these respects may open up increasing segments of an international market. This is especially true with respect to producer goods. This has been noted in the cases of South Korea, Taiwan, and India,[9] and no doubt it is true more widely.

---

[6] J. Pickett and R. Robson, "Technology and Employment in the Production of Cotton Cloth," *World Development*, 5 (March 1977), 203–15.

[7] C. Peter Timmer, John W. Thomas, Louis T. Wells, and David Morawetz, *The Choice of Technology in Developing Countries* (Cambridge, Mass.: Harvard University Center for International Affairs [now the Harvard Institute for International Development], 1975). The study mentioned was by Wells.

[8] Ibid. Study by C. Peter Timmer.

[9] Alice H. Amsden, "The Division of Labour Is Limited by the Type of Market: The Case of the Taiwanese Machine Tool Industry," *World Development*, 5 (March 1977), 217–34.

Moreover, econometric studies in high- and low-income countries alike do record the responsiveness of labor-capital ratios to their relative cost.

In a 1974 article David Morawetz summarized the findings of 14 studies of the elasticity of substitution between capital and labor—the relationship between their relative cost and the amount of each used.[10] These varied from a study of a few broadly defined industries in one country to a study of five Latin American countries covering from 30 more narrowly defined industries in one country to 75 in another. Some of the studies compared different industries. Others compared the same industry at different time periods. Morawetz found elasticity of substitution of some degree revealed in all of the studies. The lower unit wage costs were in an industry relative to capital costs, the larger the amount of labor that was employed relative to the amount of capital. At least some of the employers involved must have used the degree of labor- versus capital-intensivity that yielded the lowest unit cost.

Yet this was not true in many of the individual cases studied in the research cited above. In many instances in Ghana, Ethiopia, and Indonesia, capital-intensive methods were in use even though more labor-intensive methods—in some cases the most labor-intensive of three groups of methods; in others, intermediate methods—were cheaper. This was also true of the tube wells in India discussed in Chapter 9. It has been found to be true in more casual observation in many other places.

Capital-intensive methods, it was said by some managers, produce goods of better quality. The question may be asked, Better in whose eyes? In instances noted by Wells in Indonesia, consumers, even discriminating consumers, noted no better quality. This is probably true much more generally. The better quality is present only in the aesthetics of the engineer.

This, assert Pickett, Forsyth, and McBain, generalizing from their field research, is the pervasive reason. There is an "engineering mentality."

> Engineers ... are professionally driven by what Schumpeter once called "the half-artistic joy in technically perfecting the productive apparatus." ... The engineer's interest is in technical efficiency—in extracting the maximum amount of sucrose from a given input of sugar cane; and from this standpoint machines are often more reliable than men.... A decision is taken, for example, to establish a plant of some given productive capacity in a developing country. Engineers trained according to developed country curricula are asked to design the plant. They produce blueprints for a limited number of alternatives, each of which is a variant on current "best-practice" technique. The alternatives are submitted to economic ... scrutiny, the most attractive chosen, and another capital-intensive, technologically inappropriate plant is established.

---

[10] David Morawetz, "Employment Implications of Industrialization in Developing Countries: A Survey," *Economic Journal*, 84 (September 1974), 491–542.

Closely related may be two tendencies of some, and perhaps many, indigenous entrepreneurs. One is a desire to be "modern." The other is a tendency to accept the most "advanced" design as the best, and to adopt it without scrutiny—for which in any event the indigenous entrepreneurs may not be technically competent. As has also been noted, some research has found that foreign investors use more capital-intensive methods than do indigenous ones in comparable processes, and other research has found that they use less capital-intensive methods. Where the latter has been found to be true, this is attributed to the fact that managers with engineering training, working in the field, understand better what substitutions are possible, and make labor-using substitutions to reduce costs.

One last question may be asked: Why does not competition drive the higher cost producers off the market? One answer, of course, must be that the market is not perfect. Another, not pertinent where two or more sets of methods exist side by side, but very generally pertinent in LDCs in which large amounts of low-productivity and low-income labor could readily be drawn into manufacturing, is that governments have created conditions in which either it is financially more advantageous for employers to use capital-intensive methods or there is no competitive pressure to force employers to greater efficiency. In the belief that the use of a large amount of capital equipment is "modern," governments grant tariff exemptions or especially low customs duties to machinery imports, and regulate interest rates so that those to industrial investors are artificially low, and on the other hand, ignoring the effect of relative labor and capital costs on employment, impose heavy social security costs on industrial producers and encourage and support the pressures that lead to industrial wage rates much above those needed to attract capable workers to industrial jobs. In these circumstances, the methods chosen are more capital-intensive than those that would be chosen in an undistorted market. Among the results are an undue use of foreign exchange for capital imports, reduced employment in manufacturing, and deterrence of the growth of manufacturing, whose prices are unduly high relative to other domestic prices and to prices on the world market, to which some manufacturers might at lower costs be able to sell. These measures are not necessary to protect domestic manufacturing. If it is desired to give protection, this can be done by methods that do not bias the selection of production techniques.

But by the protection provided, governments give sheltered markets to individual producers. In a market too small to provide opportunity for more than one producer, or a market in which a factory can be established only with a license and the first producer has been promised that he will be the only licensee, producers are able to adopt the methods that are most attractive, and relax.

This set of policies, adopted by governments eager to encourage the establishment of manufacturing enterprises, seems to be a very general cause of the use of nonoptimum methods of production.

FOR FURTHER READING

The articles by Robinson and Eckaus cited in notes 3 and 4 of this chapter present basic analyses.

Appropriate Technology

Morawetz's article cited in note 10.

The volume by Timmer, Thomas, Wells, and Morawetz cited in note 7.

World Development, 5, nos. 9/10 (May–June 1977). A set of articles, edited by James Pickett, on the work on "appropriate" technology of the University of Strathclyde David Livingstone Institute of Overseas Development Studies, of which he is the director.

A. H. Bhalla, ed., *Technology and Employment in Industry: A Case Study Approach* (Geneva: International Labor Office, 1975).

Amartya K. Sen, *Choice of Techniques: An Aspect of the Theory of Planned Economic Development*, 3d ed. (New York: A. M. Kelley, 1968).

In Edgar O. Edwards, *Employment in Developing Nations*, Frances Stewart, "Technology and Employment in LDCs," and Amir U. Khan, "Appropriate Technologies: Do We Transfer, Adapt, or Develop?"

E. F. Schumacher, *Small is Beautiful: Economics as if People Mattered* (New York: Harper & Row, 1973).

E. F. Schumacher, *Good Work* (New York: Harper & Row, 1979). A collection of Schumacher's essays and lectures, published after his death. Some provide examples of appropriate intermediate technology.

See also "For Further Reading," Chapter 12.

Sectoral Choice

Bruce F. Johnston and Peter Kilby, *Agriculture and Structural Transformation: Economic Strategies in Late-Developing Countries* (New York: Oxford University Press, 1975).

Herman M. Southworth and Bruce F. Johnston, eds., *Agricultural Development and Economic Growth* (Ithaca: Cornell University Press, 1967).

John W. Mellor, *The New Economics of Growth: A Strategy for India and the Developing World* (Ithaca: Cornell University Press for the Twentieth Century Fund, 1976).

21

Orientation:
Inward or Outward?

The question of the advisability of interference with market forces arises not only concerning the forces that determine the choice of products and production methods but also concerning the orientation that producers choose: What degree of orientation toward the domestic market, and what degree toward the international market? If there is to be interference, these questions arise: What degree of interference, and by what instruments? The instruments that are generally used to influence orientation may also influence the choice of products and methods, though not necessarily; one could be shaped without affecting the other. Those instruments have side effects that must be considered in deciding national policy. First the pure economics of the choice of orientation, then the administrative problems and the side effects, are considered here.

THE ECONOMICS OF MARKET ORIENTATION

Import Substitution

The first manufactures in a country are the ones mentioned in the scheme of stages of industrialization presented in Chapter 6: bricks, beer, cement, sugar, rice or wheat flour, and so on. In their production enterprisers move from handicraft industry to a scale and type of production that may be called manufacturing, with no protection against imports other than that provided by their closeness to the market and lower transportation costs. Presently it seems obvious to them and to their country that manufacturing of other types will emerge more rapidly if it is further protected, that fostering its speedier emergence is desirable, and that the appropriate protection is to restrict or bar, by means of tariffs or import quotas, the import of goods which someone is ready to try to manufacture.

In the judgment of the country's policymakers, the advantage of this "import substitution" (import replacement) policy is simply the fostering of manufacturing—not necessarily the most economic manufactures, and certainly at an increased cost to consumers in the short run and perhaps indefinitely, but at least manufacturing. The higher cost of production is partly offset by increased wage incomes to workers employed. In more sophisticated argument it is also asserted that the profits generated will increase saving and thus the country's resources for capital formation.

It is also argued that relying on the domestic market frees the country from the vagaries of the international market, relieves the country of the need to cope with multinational corporations, and in general lessens economic dependence on "the center." The argument concerning the vagaries of the international market is superficial, and that concerning economic dependence dubious, for a country that does not sell manufactures abroad must obtain foreign exchange for needed imports by selling primary products, and demand and price are much more volatile for these than for manufactured goods. Complete freedom from dependence requires autarky, and this, as noted in Chapter 6, can be achieved only at tremendous sacrifice in the level of living.

It is feared that if LDCs expand their exports of manufactured goods, even low-technology manufactured goods, they will find the markets of high-income countries closing to them. Those countries do resist the displacement of their workers in, for example, textile manufacturing, yet the rate of increase in their imports of manufactures, shown in Chapter 19, indicates that they accept them.

Lastly, it is argued that without a protected domestic market, manufacturing could not develop at all; that with free trade, imports of manufactures would smother the attempts of domestic producers to compete, and condemn the country to be forever an exporter of primary products. This is not an argument against an export orientation but an argument that a country's producers must manufacture for a protected home market before they can manufacture for the world. The question is discussed a little later in this chapter.

The Limit to Import Substitution

Good or bad, optimal or nonoptimal, except in large countries import substituion must in due time reach a limit. When a small country has fostered all of the manufacturing that is feasible within the country even with protection and other aids, without a change in policy it has nowhere to go. The contribution of manufacturing to its level of living, if there has been a contribution, must come to an end except as technical progress is possible even on the limited scale of production for which it has a market. Alfred Maizels analyzed the imports of industrial products by the industrial and the "semi-industrial countries" of the world, and the "rest of the world," in 1899 and 1959.[1] The classification "semi-industrial countries" includes all of the LDCs (as of about 1960) except those with no significant manufacturing sector. Those excluded, the "rest of the world," are most African countries, some smaller Latin American countries, and a few others. Maizel's data, with categories of goods somewhat consolidated, are shown in Table 21–1. In 1899, 55% of the manufactured imports of the "semi-industrial countries" had been textile and clothing. In 1959, these had fallen to 9%. What the "semi-industrial countries" were now importing in large volume were machinery and chemicals for use in their own production, and transportation equipment.

TABLE 21–1   Composition of manufactured imports, by country groups, 1899 and 1959

Most of the possibility of import substitution has been used up.

		Percentage Share			
	Year	Machinery, Transport Equipment, and Chemicals	Texiles and Clothing	Metals and Other Manufactures	Total Value ($ billions, 1955 prices)
Industrial countries	1899	17	38	45	5.1
	1959	47	11	42	22.6
Semi-industrial countries	1899	14	55	31	2.1
	1959	64	9	27	6.8
Rest of the world	1899	23	44	33	2.8
	1959	54	15	31	14.0

Source: Alfred Maizels, *Industrial Growth and World Trade* (Cambridge: Cambridge University Press, 1963).

A conclusion may be drawn: by 1959 the "semi-industrial countries" had done most of the import substitution that they could expect to do until they had arrived at the advanced stage of technical capability at which they could manufacture complex machines, electronic equipment, and chemicals. Import substitution was approaching a dead end. Even in the "rest of the world," it was also mostly complete. It could no longer be expected to contribute much to growth in LDCs above the lowest income level. Interestingly, manufactured imports of the industrial countries showed a simi-

---

[1] Alfred Maizels, *Industrial Growth and World Trade* (Cambridge: Cambridge University Press, 1963).

lar trend, though in less extreme degree. Their manufactured imports were almost wholly from each other in both years.

The results of a regression analysis done by Chenery are consistent with the facts presented by Maizels. Using postwar data, Chenery showed that as one moved from countries with per capita incomes of $100 to countries with per capita incomes of $600 (more than double those figures in 1980 prices), the ratio of domestic production of manufactured consumer goods rose little while that for investment and intermediate goods rose much more.[2] That is, between these two levels of postwar income there was not much import substitution in consumer goods. In light of the historical facts presented by Maizels, the explanation is simple: most feasible import substitution had already taken place, even in the lower income countries.

Export Promotion

The policy of import substitution was a mistake in any event, most economists state. A policy of export expansion would have brought faster and more beneficial economic growth in the past and will do so in the future. Instead of sheltering domestic manufacturing by restricting imports of manufactures, a country should devalue its currency. With each unit of foreign currency costing more units of the local currency, imports would be more expensive. With each unit of the local currency costing less foreign currency, domestic producers would be better able to offer exports to the international market. At an appropriate exchange rate, exports would equal imports without protectionism. The following benefits would follow:

1. Under import substitution, domestic manufacturers have monopolistic or quasi-monopolistic situations, and need not be efficient. With competition from foreign producers, they will be forced to be efficient, and the country's output and real income will rise.

2. Under import substitution, in all but the larger countries many manufacturers were unable to produce at the lowest-unit-cost scale of output. With the export market available, they will be able to do so.

3. As noted, import substitution eventually runs into a dead end. Within the scope of a country's resources, there is no limit to the expansion of its manufacturing production for the foreign market.

4. In the name of "modernity," protected production is likely to be capital-intensive. Government policies are likely to foster this tendency. If producers must compete in an international market, they will choose the products in whose production they can compete best, and they will use the lowest-cost factor proportions in producing them. That is, market forces will impel them to seek their greatest comparative advantage—which yields the greatest economic welfare for the country.

---

[2] Hollis B. Chenery, "Patterns of Industrial Growth," *American Economic Review*, 50 (September 1960), 624–54.

5. These choices will maximize employment.

6. The employment by producers of more labor relative to the amount of capital, where this is lower cost, will lessen the inequality of income distribution.

7. Success in exporting will increase foreign exchange earnings. Moreover, a country whose exports are increasing attracts foreign lenders and investors, since there will presumably be enough foreign exchange to service loans and to permit repatriation of dividends and capital. Hence the country will have ample capital with which to finance its economic growth.

Economics and Administration

Before we try to arrive at a verdict concerning these opposed policies, we should consider how the two work in practice.

Countries in which import substitution prevails seem always to be short of foreign exchange. Perhaps this is because when the producers of a country first bid for foreign exchange to finance the import of capital goods for development, this new demand unbalances the country's foreign exchange balance. Unless exports can be increased, other imports must fall. They can be reduced, and exports perhaps increased, by letting the foreign exchange value of the currency fall, but an alternative method, which does not burden importers with an increased cost and also, perhaps, better serves the country's vanity, is to maintain the foreign exchange value of the currency by imposing tariffs or quantitative restrictions on imports to reduce their volume. Quantitative restrictions are much preferred by would-be manufacturers, since they guarantee that there will not be competing imports, whereas a tariff merely makes the competing imports more expensive. Thus for a dual purpose a country drifts into a regime of quantitative import restrictions to support an exchange rate that is too high for foreign exchange equilibrium. Whether or not this is the main historical explanation, such a regime almost invariably results from an import substitution policy.

Competing claims will then arise for licenses to import, to obtain the materials and the intermediate goods that are necessary for manufacturing. Licenses may be allocated among industries by historic shares, by administrative decision concerning the relative importance of different manufacturing industries, by *ad hoc* bargaining, very probably by decisisons that depend on the greater access of one person than another to administrative officials, perhaps by the bribery of officials. There must be equity among firms, and small firms must not be discriminated against. If this policy is stressed, there may be allocation to firms that are all too small for efficient operation. An administratively defensible basis for allocation is according to the productive capacity of each firm; every firm is then likely to get materials and intermediate products in volumes that are too small for capacity operation. Yet with limited supply of the finished manufactured product, production will be profitable. Each firm will scheme to increase its capacity, as a basis for an increased allocation of materials; the economy of larger scale production will be adduced. Permits for capital goods imports for the establishment of too many firms may be granted, if not through corruption, because of a desire to increase competition or to widen entrepreneurship. Waste of capital to establish or increase capacity is almost assured. In a study of import substitution and export promotion regimes in ten countries, excess capacity in varying degree was found in Turkey, India, Ghana, Colombia, Chile, and Pakistan.[3] It will be necessary to forbid the sale of import licenses by one importer to another. The prohibition will be difficult to police. There will be periods when production must be halted in one plant or another because the import license system did not act smoothly enough to permit the import of needed supplies in time; and to avoid this situation there will be economically wasteful stocking of inventories. India is usually held up as the horrible example of these various results of maladministration,[4] but India has many companions, and while the situation varies in degree among countries, it is inherent in the system and not due merely to maladministration.

Thus an import substitution regime will not be the simply adminstered one that may be discussed in the abstract, but rather one that becomes a maze of economically irrational bureaucratic decisions and rules whose bias for imports against exports has no economic foundation and which discriminate among industries and firms without regard for the marginal productivity of each. When this realistic aspect of import substitution is considered, the economic case for ending it and turning to export promotion is strong, as is the economic-political-administrative case for at least ending the maze of rules and substituting price and cost inducements.

The shift from an import substitution to an export promotion regime then becomes a process that has been termed "liberalization," involving not only devaluation of the currency but also rationalization of the mass of rules and a shift from quantitative regulation to inducement through relative

---

[3] The National Bureau of Economic Research (NBER) commissioned a study of "Foreign Trade Regimes and Economic Development," directed by Jagdish N. Bhagwati and Anne O. Krueger. The ten countries studied were the six mentioned plus Israel, the Philippines, Brazil, and South Korea. In Brazil and South Korea, export expansion was going forward so vigorously at the time the studies were executed that the research probably did not examine whether there had been earlier excess capacity. A volume has been published on each country study except one of Pakistan that was not completed and that of Brazil. In addition, each of the two research directors wrote a summary volume: Jagdish N. Bhagwati, *Foreign Trade Regimes and Economic Development: Anatomy and Consequences of Exchange Control Regimes* (1978); and Anne O. Krueger, *Foreign Trade Regimes and Economic Development: Liberalization Attempts and Consequences* (1978). All of these volumes were published by the Ballinger Publishing Company, Cambridge, Massachusetts, for the National Bureau of Economic Research.

[4] Jagdish N. Bhagwati and T. N. Srinivasan, *Foreign Trade Regimes and Economic Development: India* (1976), presents a balanced survey of the experience of India.

prices and costs. Rationalization will consist of eliminating most, if not all, of the complex web of quantitative regulations. The variation among industries and firms in the protection provided will then end; those which use the nation's resources (human and other) most economically will then swim successfully; those that do not will sink. However, tariffs may be introduced or maintained to yield protection previously provided by quantitative import controls to enterprises that had an implied contract for protection when they were established and still need it; the tariff rate can be set to prevent monopolistic pricing that may have been possible within the absolute protection of a quantitative restriction on imports. In principle, a subsidy will provide that protection more equitably than a tariff, since the cost of the subsidy will be borne by the entire economy rather than by users of the product, but a tariff may be more feasible politically. A uniform tariff on all imports will hardly be in point, unless it is for revenue; the same effect on imports, without bias against exports, can be achieved by an added reduction in the exchange rate. However, a tariff for revenue may be among the more equitable collectible levies (see Chapter 16).

Liberalization, Exports, and Economic Growth

The authors of the NBER studies of ten foreign trade regimes tried to separate the effects of devaluation on exports from the effects of export subsidies and other incentives, changes in world prices of commodities, differences in the response of traditional and nontraditional exports, and so on. Professor Krueger notes in a summary volume: "Perhaps most striking is the fact that virtually all authors believed there were significant responses to changes in real EERs (effective exchange rates). . . . there is not one instance where doubt was expressed about the responsiveness of exports to real EERs. . . . The evidence that 'exchange rates matter,' at least when devaluation follows exchange controls, therefore seems fairly strong."[5] Krueger goes on, however, to emphasize the judgment that not merely devaluation and liberalization but the confidence of businesspersons that governmental policies and administrative decisions would consistently favor and support production for export were important contributors to the vigorous export activity.

This is an important addendum. South Korea is sometimes held up as evidence of the results of liberalization. South Korea devalued its currency once in 1961, at the same time offering subsidies to exports, and in 1964 devalued again (after rapid inflation had negated the effect of the former devaluation) and liberalized its entire system. Exports, valued in U.S. dollars, were $33 million in 1960, $119 million in 1964, $455 million in 1968, $1,624

---

[5] Krueger, *Foreign Trade Regimes: Liberalization Attempts*, pp. 198–99.

million in 1972, and $4,460 million in 1974. The average compound annual rate of growth in exports from 1960 to 1974 was more than 40% per year. But this effect was not achieved by foreign exchange liberalization alone. Military purchases by the United States and then U.S. economic aid poured liquidity and an unusually high and assured demand for exports into the country during the period. And the government provided such a basket of subsidies and other financial inducements to export that the village fool—provided that he had a talent for making new products—could hardly have failed to make large profits in producing for export. Larry Westphal and Kwang Suk Kim present the following estimates of the quantitative value of certain South Korean export incentives in 1968:

Form of Subsidy	Total Subsidy Payments as a Percentage of Total Commodity Exports
Tariff exemptions	14.4
Wastage allowance	2.4
Indirect tax exemptions	7.0
Overhead rate reductions	0.4
Direct tax exemptions	1.1
Interest subsidies	4.5
Total	29.8

The two authors note that exporters also seem to have been given a quasi-monopolistic privilege of charging higher prices for their products in the domestic market than for export.[6] In addition to these incentives, another analyst notes that exporters received a reduction of 50% on income taxes on profits earned from exports, export credit and loans for the purchase of raw materials and equipment at preferential rates, and through an export-import linkage system were permitted to import goods on the prohibited list (which were scarce and expensive) for their own use or for domestic resale.[7]

Among the ten countries studied, Brazil, Colombia, and Israel, along with South Korea, achieved the highest percentage rates of growth in non-traditional exports during the 1960s. These are also the four countries that offered the greatest subsidies and other financial incentives to exporters. In her summary volume Professor Krueger concedes that "the evidence ... strongly suggests that [a devaluation and liberalization policy]—by itself—would generally not have resulted in rapid and sustained export growth of the sort that was experienced over the longer run by Brazil, Israel, South

---

[6] Larry E. Westphal and K. S. Kim, "Industrial Policy and Development in Korea," draft version, mimeographed, 1973. These authors together with Charles R. Frank, Jr., wrote the later NBER study of South Korea.

[7] Bela Balassa, "Industrial Policies in Taiwan and Korea," *Weltwirtschaftliches Archiv*, band 106, heft 1 (1971), 13. I am indebted to Youngil Lim for calling my attention to this article and to the study by Westphal and Kim.

Korea, as well as by Colombian minor exports."[8] The countries that achieved the greatest success in expanding exports intervened as vigorously in the market as had the countries that had fostered import substitution.

However, the Philippines, Turkey, Egypt, and India, which adopted liberalized regimes without as great direct incentives, also did very well. The three economists who wrote the NBER book concerning South Korea estimated that the effect of exchange rate changes was greater than that of subsidies.[9] Such an estimate is judgmental, however, even though it is derived statistically and expressed in precise elasticities.

THE TRANSITION

Liberalization will inevitably hurt some of the business owners who, planning businesses for a protected market, have constructed business enterprises that use the wrong methods or produce the wrong product. As noted, some such investors who have depended on an explicit or implicit government assurance may be given continued protection through tariffs. This may be the cost of preserving a sense of social equity. There are two other possible adverse effects of liberalization that are purely transitional.

The transition may be difficult. Because a policy of liberalization is likely to be adopted only when an economic crisis forces action, the transition is likely to occur at a time when foreign exchange reserves have been depleted; it is impossible to service the nation's debt without rescheduling, and additional loans from abroad are available only on rather harsh terms; it has been necessary to curtail imports sharply, so that the country is "import-starved"; and inflation is occurring. A temporary surge in the demand for imports will follow liberalization. Even after this surge a permanent increase in the level of imports above the level during the import substitution period may be expected. Both of these developments will occur before exports increase. A foreign loan may therefore be necessary for successful liberalization. Obtaining one in the circumstances may be difficult.

Other things being equal, devaluation will cause an increase in the price of imported goods simply because more of the local currency is required to buy a given amount of foreign currency. However, the predevaluation price of goods protected against imports was high; otherwise the protection would not have been necessary. Even with devaluation the imported price may be lower. Hence the price level may not rise on account of the devaluation.

However, if the predevaluation inflation was caused by cost-push it will continue, and if it was caused primarily by excessive demand it will also continue unless imports are generously financed and markedly increase supply. The devaluation will reduce the price of domestically produced

---

[8] Krueger, *Foreign Trade Regimes: Liberalization Attempts*, p. 199.

[9] See note 6.

goods to foreign buyers, thus stimulating exports. But this benefit will disappear if there is continued inflation. If there is to be export promotion, there must be further devaluation to offset it. Speculation that there will be will cause funds to be transferred abroad, reducing the foreign exchange available for imports and forcing either the devaluation that was anticipated or a return to protectionism. To prevent this, some countries—notably Brazil—adopted a "crawling peg." This means that the currency was devalued frequently in small amounts—amounts so small that the difference between the buying and selling rates for foreign currency was as great as each "crawling" devaluation.

To counter inflation, the government may feel that it must adopt tight fiscal and monetary policies. The result may be depression. A marked increase in imports is itself deflationary. Deflation and depression may be caused in any event by the policies which the International Monetary Fund may insist upon as the price for providing a needed loan. The "IMF formula" for a condition of inflation and foreign exchange shortage is: devalue, reduce government expenditures, and curtail increase in the money supply. Depression may cause the government to abandon the tight fiscal and monetary policies; the inability to obtain enough foreign exchange may then cause a reversion to quantitative controls.

Thus a policy of liberalization is not always successful. Between 1956 and 1970, Brazil and Chile each devalued its currency three times; Colombia four times; South Korea, the Philippines, and Turkey twice; and Israel, having devalued in 1952, did so again in 1962. Most of these cases of repeated devaluation mark either the failure or the inadequacy of the earlier devaluation, though in a few cases exogenous circumstances forced the repetition. In her summary volume Krueger surveys the intermediate-term fate of 22 instances of attempted liberalization in the ten countries. In eight of these, there was almost immediate failure and reversion to restrictive regulation. In five others, liberalization was short-lived. Only in eight was liberalization a clear success for at least four years, and in six of the eight, for at least five years—Krueger's definition of intermediate term.[10]

MONETARY LIBERALIZATION THE KEY?

Edward S. Shaw, who was economic adviser to the government of South Korea during the two years following its adoption of a liberalization policy in 1964, regarded monetary liberalization as the key to success, in Korea and elsewhere. By monetary liberalization is meant, centrally, the release of ceilings on interest rates, so that they may rise as high as the demand for funds would pull them. In Korea they rose to 30% per year on one-year deposits, and to higher rates on shorter-term loans—rates much above the rate of inflation during the same period. A younger colleague of Shaw wrote a

---

[10] Krueger, *Foreign Trade Regimes: Liberalization Attempts*, p. 220.

book attempting to generalize the theory of the key role of financial liberalization to all countries.[11]

"Can one explain why economic wealth is high or rising in a fairly pervasive way in some countries, while other countries languish?," asked Ronald McKinnon in the introduction to his book. "Can one use a single frame of reference to explain why Japan has done better than India, Mexico better than Colombia, and Taiwan better than the Philippines." McKinnon's answer, stated throughout his book, is yes. He recognizes that liberalization in the broader sense is necessary, but argues that "once the monetary linchpin is put in place, appropriate strategies for liberalizing foreign trade and rationalizing domestic tax and expenditure policy follow naturally." Market-determined high interest rates, drawing funds into savings institutions, will end or curtail inflation by reducing demand without the deflationary effect of IMF policies, and will make unnecessary an inflow of funds from abroad to finance the transition. Indeed, "the absorption of substantial amounts of foreign capital during the liberalization process may ... be a serious mistake."

Shaw and McKinnon ignore the impressive web of government intervention in accounting for South Korea's export achievement and that of other countries. As is noted in this chapter, the NBER researchers found the facts and the problem of liberalization more complex. However, one can hardly doubt that interest rates much above the rate of inflation—which thus yield a positive real rate of interest—were important in inducing Korea's very high rate of saving, and that this was important in Korea's smooth transition. But as noted in Chapter 15, one should not attribute that saving rate to Korea's monetary policy alone. The very rapid rise in income was also a very important cause.

INFANT INDUSTRIALIZATION

Does this history prove that export promotion is superior to import substitution for industrialization and economic growth? A caveat must be noted. It is argued that where a country has very little industry—say, where it has not at least entered the third stage of industrialization sketched in Chapter 6—if the country is opened freely to the import of manufactures, their importation will smother nascent domestic manufacturing, so that the country will be condemned indefinitely to the production for export of nothing but primary products. The circumstance in point is not merely infant industry; it is, in W. Arthur Lewis's phrase, infant industrialization; what must be protected is not merely individual infant firms but the infancy of a manufacturing web. When the "Open Door" policy was forced upon

---

[11] Edward S. Shaw, *Financial Deepening in Economic Development* (London: Oxford University Press, 1973); and Ronald I. McKinnon, *Money and Capital in Economic Development* (Washington, D.C.: Brookings Institution, 1973).

China in the middle of the 19th century, the inflow of simple manufactures destroyed some Chinese cottage industries in some areas of the country, and Chinese manufacturing arose to take their place only two generations later, when China had regained its sovereignty sufficiently to regulate imports. One economist has argued vigorously that the manufacturers of no country can manufacture for export until they have first gained experience producing for the domestic market.[12] (This need not *necessarily* imply that that market shall be protected.)

In reply it is asserted that the manufacturers of South Korea have done precisely that, and that, as for infant industrialization, the advantage of low transportation costs and the need to perform some services to manufacturing locally will permit this basic early industrialization without artificial protection. In any event the question is moot for most of the present lower income countries, for most of them have already passed through that early stage.

FOR FURTHER READING

The basic sources for analysis of the question of "liberalization" are the volumes by Shaw and McKinnon (note 11), whose arguments are somewhat overdrawn, and the series of NBER studies under the direction of Bhagwati and Krueger, of which at least the volumes by Bhagwati and Krueger presenting synthesis and conclusions should be read (note 3). Since in making their argument, Shaw and McKinnon use South Korea as a prime illustration, the student exploring the topic should read the NBER case study of South Korea, by Charles R. Frank, Jr., Kwang Suk Kim, and Larry E. Westphal.

Bela Balassa, "Reforming the System of Incentives in Developing Countries," *World Development*, 3 (June 1975), 365–82, also presents an excellent summary analysis of measures to liberalize a system of quantitative import-restricting controls.

P. T. Bauer and B. S. Yamey, *The Economics of Underdeveloped Countries* (Chicago: University of Chicago Press, 1957), argue the case for leaving the whole matter of development to the market.

Relevant and good are:

Tun Wai, "Interest Rates in the Organized Money Markets of Underdeveloped Countries," and "Interest Rates outside the Organized Money Markets of Underdeveloped Countries," International Monetary Fund *Staff Papers*, August 1956 and November 1957, respectively.

Raymond W. Goldsmith, *Financial Structure and Development* (New Haven: Yale University Press, 1969).

Shaw's thesis and Tun Wai's articles are excerpted in Gerald M. Meier, *Leading Issues in Development Economics*, 3d ed., chap. 5, sec. D.

---

[12] Staffan B. Linder, *Trade and Trade Policy for Development* (New York: Praeger Publishing Co., 1967).

22

Planning

Development planning is the planning by government of measures that are intended to cause economic development to proceed better than it would have otherwise. In a parliamentary system of government the measures will be recommended to the parliament by the prime minister and acted on by the parliament. In a presidential system they will be adopted by the parliament or congress, with or without the recommendation of the president. Where the government is authoritarian, they will be promulgated by the dictator or the authoritarian group. These, then, are the final planners. However, plans are presented to them by someone. This chapter will take the viewpoint of a planning agency which reports to the chief executive. For convenience it will often be referred to simply as "the planner." Planning is a complex process. It will be considered step by step, each step leaving a problem unsettled. Ways of gathering the problems together and resolving them will then be discussed.

Development planning operates within a social and economic framework. The government and social usage have established a net of institutions which affect the relationships of individuals to one another and set a balance of one sort or another between individual rights and social responsibilities. The government deals with problems of externalities, monopoly, and "public goods" by prohibition, regulation, financial penalty or inducement, or perhaps the operation of enterprises by the government itself in fields in which monopoly is the most efficient form.[1] Government may operate other enterprises as well, in the belief that this serves the public interest

---

[1] "Public goods" are commonly provided by governments, if provided at all. Policy questions are more likely to arise with respect to monopolies and externalities.

in one way or another, or merely because authoritarian officials want the power. The planner will ordinarily accept this set of institutions and practices as his framework and work within it. If he has strong moral objections to the institutions set as the framework for planning and to the results that planning within those institutions will have, his choice must ordinarily be to resign his position.

Development planning is sometimes discussed merely as planning for the maximum rate of growth subject to the constraint that current consumption shall not be unduly depressed. The view is simplistic. The notion, for example, that the planner should be concerned with maximizing output and can leave to someone else concern for the distribution of the income created, is a notion possible only in a dream world. However, following conventional practice, the formal discussion of this chapter will deal almost wholly with the problem of maximizing material output. The reader is reminded at this point that in fact planning must also be molded to serve other economic objectives and noneconomic objectives, weighing each and compromising among them as well as may be, or simply subordinating one or more if compromise is not possible.

Principles that must underlie the planner's calculations aimed at maximizing the nation's output (as well as ameliorating the inequality of income distribution) have been discussed in the preceding two chapters. In principle those chapters might indeed have been incorporated into this one. The choice between an inward-looking orientation and an outward-looking orientation may be so deeply embedded in national preconceptions and vested interests that the planner must in the main accept it, but if his work is to have much meaning he must have some influence on the allocation of resources among sectors and among projects and on the choice of production methods. In his calculation of the allocation and choice that will maximize output, he will of course be guided by shadow prices and he will take externalities into account, rather than accept market prices and individual project profitability at face value. These considerations were discussed in Chapters 20 and 21 and are here "incorporated by reference."

MACROPLANNING

Macroplanning will start with the allocation of resources between consumption and capital formation. It must start, then, with a set of national income accounts. Suppose that on the output side these take the simple form for the year t, treated here as the present year:

$$Y(t) = C(t) + I(t), \tag{1}$$

where Y, C, and I refer to GNP, consumption, and capital formations, respectively. Capital formation includes both private and government.

The planner may then estimate GNP for the next time period if he has two additional facts—the estimated ICOR for the economy as a whole and the estimated lag between investment and the initiation of the flow of output from an investment project. Assume a lag of one-half year.[2] The planner may then write:

$$Y(t + 1) = Y(t) + 1/A[I(t)] \tag{2.1}$$

$$Y(t + 2) = Y(t + 1) + 1/A[I(t + 1)] \tag{2.2}$$

$$Y(t + 3) = Y(t + 2) + 1/A[I(t + 2)] \tag{2.3}$$

$$Y(t + n) = Y(t + n - 1) + 1/A[I(t + n - 1)] \tag{2.n}$$

or, more generally, for a period of years,

$$Y(t + n) = Y(t) + 1/A \left[\sum_{t=1}^{n-1} [I(t)] \right], \tag{3}$$

where A = the ICOR.

Even though explicitly only capital formation increases Y, this formulation does not regard capital as the only scarce input. Rather, A, the ICOR, estimated from the previous experience of the economy or from the experience of other economies, reflects an estimate of the impact of the amount of other inputs, increase in that amount, and technical progress. As was noted in Chapter 10, it is a crude conception, embodying a rough estimate—but the best estimate available.

One year is too short a period for planning, because of the vagaries of any single year and for other reasons that will be mentioned. But as one extends estimates beyond a few years, uncertainties compound. This is why planning is often for a five-year period.

In a closed economy, capital formation in equations (1) through (3) will be equal to domestic saving. In an open economy, resources for capital formation may be augmented by commercial capital inflow and foreign aid, and they may be diminished by a flow abroad of saving from the economy. In such an economy, from the saving-investment identity:

$$I_d = S + M - X$$
$$= S - I_f,$$

where I_d = domestic capital formation, M = imports, X = exports, and I_f = net investment abroad. Assuming for the moment that there is no capital inflow from foreign parties, M can exceed X only if residents of the country repatriate capital which they deposited or invested abroad in previous years, and an excess of X over M indicates that some proceeds from exports were deposited or invested abroad and hence are not avail-

---

[2] This is the average lag if the capital formation goes on throughout the year.

able for domestic capital formation. But of course in addition to a capital inflow there may be foreign aid grants. If so,

$$I_d = S - I_f + R,$$

where R = grants of foreign aid. I_f will be negative (so that the term $(-I_f)$ is positive), if commercial loans plus direct investment exceed net investment abroad by residents of the country.

The planner will count on this augmentation of the resources available for domestic capital formation if he can.

In a two-gap world, in which productive resources are not readily shiftable between the production of consumer goods and the production of capital goods or between production for domestic use and production for export, there would be a second constraint on I_d. Domestic investment would require a technically determined flow of imports because of inability to produce various types of investment goods within the economy. Let us assume that there is no substitutability whatever between investment goods produced at home and those imported. We must then write:

$$I_d = H_I + M_I,$$

where H_I = investment goods produced at home and M_I = investment goods imported. Quite separately from his estimate of the total resources available for investment, the planner must then estimate whether the necessary volume of capital goods imports in each year can be financed and whether the necessary volume of domestic saving will be forthcoming. To do so, he will have to estimate the volume of consumer goods imports (for both private and government use—two separate estimates).

The other part of the planning required in this first simple step (or, in this simple model) is the allocation of resources for investment among alternative uses. To maximize output, capital formation must be allocated to alternative uses so that the marginal productivity of each input is identical in all uses. The planner must anticipate the allocation of capital formation in order to estimate the volume of aggregate output in the following year, from which he will estimate the flow of saving in that year. (His anticipation of the allocation of capital formation will be reflected in his estimate of the ICOR.)

He will take neither the division of income between consumption and saving nor the availability of foreign exchange from the country's exports as data. He will propose measures to influence both. The consumption-saving division will be determined in part by the balance between the government's revenues and its consumption expenditures, both of which are subject to policy control. And governmental measures will influence the level of private saving.

The planner can of course recommend the allocation of governmental capital formation that will be most productive. Neither he nor the governmental authorities whom he serves can directly determine the allocation of private capital formation, unless all productive activity, though some of it is termed private, is controlled by government decree. Governmental measures, however, will influence the private allocation. That governmental expenditures and these governmental measures shall result in maximum possible output is one of the planner's concerns.

PROJECT PLANNING

Development activity is not carried out by sectors. It is carried out by individual projects. In principle, then, planning is project by project (including anticipated private projects). A sectoral plan is merely a summation of individual project plans, even though the project planning may lump anticipated individual private projects into categories, rather than considering them separately. The marginal productivity of every project must in principle be weighed against the marginal productivity of every other in every sector, so that throughout the economy the projects with the highest marginal productivity—and thereby, by definition, all projects with equal marginal productivity per unit of input—will be executed.

INTERINDUSTRY PLANNING

Implicitly, the discussion just above has assumed that all sectors and all firms produce final products and, furthermore, noncomplementary final products, so that the marginal productivity of each can be estimated separately from that of all others. One of the complexities of planning is that this is of course not true. Every sector also produces inputs for other sectors, and most individual firms produce inputs for other firms—some firms produce only inputs for other firms. To estimate marginal productivity the planner must estimate demand for the final products produced in the economy, but he cannot estimate marginal productivity unless he also estimates what inputs every sector and in principle every individual producer of the economy must obtain from every other.

There are few intermediate products for which the amount required as an input per unit of some other product is absolutely fixed, regardless of price. As a first approximation, however, in much of his planning the planner will assume that there are fixed coefficients. He will do so not merely to simplify his already complex job but also to avoid putting too much strain on the adaptability of producers. The required volume of an intermediate product used in only one other sector may be estimated by simple regression. But in general the output and input relations among sectors are much more complex than that. The needs of each sector can be estimated only by input-output analysis. (It is assumed that the reader understands this analysis.) If the planner has derived estimates of the coefficients of an input-output matrix, the interindustry flows needed in the production of any feasible final bill of goods can readily be calculated on a high-speed computer.

CRITICAL PATH ANALYSIS

Input-output analysis, however, is static. It deals only with relationships during a unit period of time. Efficient construction of any project must ensure that the various steps in construction are completed in sequence at appropriate times. If this is not done, a factory may stand idle because no power is available, or irrigation ditches may blow full of sand because they were dug two years before the deep wells to provide the water were completed, or because the nomads who were expected to become farmers do not choose to do so, or have not been taught how.

Programming must begin by considering the finished project and working backward to see what must be done when in order to bring it to coordinated completion. Take construction of a textile mill as an example. The questions must be asked: If a building, machinery, a power plant, access roads, a supply of intermediate- or long-staple cotton, management, and skilled workers will be required, what must be done with respect to each so that all will be ready at the year t? With respect to, say, the power plant, if it will take one year to install the turbines when the power plant is otherwise completed, then what things must be done by the time $t - 1$ (where the time unit is one year) in order that installation of the turbines can begin? When must the turbines be ordered if they are to be at the site by $t - 1$? When must dam construction begin to be ready at $t - 1$? Perhaps at $t - 3$, for a small dam. Then when must construction machinery be ordered so that it will be at the site at $t - 3$ as needed? Or when must construction tenders be asked for in order to enter into a contract at a time that will permit construction to begin by $t - 3$? Similarly for the access roads, the expansion of cotton production, the arrangement for management, the training of workers, the arrangements for marketing, and so on. Some of these segments may depend on others; access roads, for example, may have to be ready before dam construction can begin. If so, their construction time must be added to $t - 3$, and the elements in the road construction planned for completion within that prior period. In good project planning, the execution of all segments of a project will be programmed so that it is known what things must be done at $t - 5$ so that by $t - 4$ those things are done which will permit execution by $t - 3$ of the operations necessary to complete by $t - 2$ the things that must be done by then in order that the segments may be completed by $t - 1$ on whose execution by that date the completion of the whole by time t depends.

This multipronged, coordinated House-That-Jack-Built programming is termed critical path analysis or PERT. It is primarily physical or engineering planning rather than economic planning.

Programming, no matter how realistic its allowance for likely lags and delays, must be followed up, to see that each segment of the work proceeds at the pace that was programmed or, if it does not and the lag cannot be remedied, to readjust the program. A good reporting system to obtain prompt periodic reports of the rate of physical progress and the rate of expenditure is a necessary part of good project planning.

Most programming is not the concern of the planner. Insofar as the project is a private one, the entrepreneur must see to the programming. If it is a public one, the ministry or agency in charge has the responsibility. In year-to-year budgeting, the budget agency and the planning agency may hold the operating agency responsible for the failure of its planning during the preceding year, and in the next five-year plan the planner will take into account agency failures during the previous one, but beyond this the planning agency will do well not to become too involved in the programming of the projects of operating ministries or agencies.

ECONOMY-WIDE PROGRAMMING

But the planner must be involved in another way. That textile plant may not build its own power plant; it may depend on the governmental electrical network for power. Development will be retarded if port facilities, roads, the telecommunications network are not available by the times they are needed in expanding private production. Programming to prevent bottlenecks in these facilities is an essential part of governmental development planning. This programming must be not merely for individual projects but for the development plan of the entire economy. Each of the larger oil countries of the Middle East suffered serious harmful inflation during the early or mid-1970s because it did not begin to expand its port facilities or overland transportation facilities soon enough in anticipation of the construction projects, and the consumer demand resulting from expenditure for them, that it was so frenetically pushing ahead.

In principle, economy-wide programming must begin with a bill of goods for a future target year, say the fifth future year. That bill of goods must depend on the level of aggregate output that can be attained by that year $t + n$. This in turn will depend on the inputs that will be available, the sectors in which they will be employed, and the productivity that they will have attained in those sectors.

Increases in output in various industries—including housing, education, and so on, not merely manufacturing—will be needed to produce the $t + n$ bill of goods. The capacity of each industry will depend on the investment projects that have been completed by the year $t + n - 1$. Some of these will not be completed then unless they were in progress in the year $t + n - 2$ and unless other projects had been ready by that year. So on back to the present year, with the further important provision that the capital and consumption goods output that must be produced in the present year t in order to achieve the results in the year $t + 1$ that are needed to achieve the needed output in the year $t + 2$, and so on up to $t + n$, must be consistent with the productive capacity that exists in the year t. Perhaps the problem is not solvable. Perhaps, given the economy's capacity in the year t, there is no sequence by which the desired bill of goods for the year $t + n$ can be produced. To determine by successive approximations whether the problem is solvable and to determine the pattern of production from t to $t + n$ by which it can be solved would be impossibly complex except for the existence of high-speed computers.

Chenery wrote in 1971 that such matters could be handled, using linear relationships, for 200 sectors and a single time period, 10–30 sectors and 5–10 time periods, or 1 or 2 sectors and 100 time periods. Four years later, Chenery's statement was obsolete. The computational capacity of computers had doubled or tripled. In the four years after that, it more than tripled. The increase in the complexity of the models that can be handled will presumably continue to increase at this very rapid rate.

The appendix to this chapter outlines one programming model, that of Richard S. Eckaus and Kirit Parikh for India. It illustrates the problems of modeling mentioned above, and others. Even though now, a dozen years after the Eckaus-Parikh model was prepared, far more complex models are possible, three fundamental problems that constrained the model still remain.

First, the algebraic relationships assumed to exist in the economy must be linear. That is, one variable must not vary according to the second or higher power of another, which would make the relationship curvilinear if graphed. The direct incorporation into the model of income or price elasticities, economies of scale, and diminishing returns to investment is thereby ruled out. In some cases, linear approximations may substitute. If changes in input coefficients from year to year resulting from any of these factors, or from investment or technical advance, can be estimated, they can be allowed for by changing the coefficients in the model from year to year. (An input coefficient is the number of units of an input—which may be the output of another sector—required per unit of output.) Other rather awkward substitutes for nonlinear relationships may be devised. Exponential trends or relationships may be handled by means of logarithmic linearity.

Second, it is possible to design a pattern of investment and output, year by year, to construct the necessary set of equations to test whether the pattern is *consistent* with the availability of resources and the final bill of goods, and to solve the set of equations on a high-speed computer. If the pattern is not consistent, the planner can then prepare alternative patterns and submit them to the computer, one by one. However, the technique by which the computer could be given criteria and then asked to select the *optimum* pattern of investment and output—for example, to alter the pattern of investment so as to yield a different consumption mix as aggregate consumption or per capita consumption varied in amount, subject to constraints about total investment, government expenditures, exports, and imports year by year—involves computational requirements that are very large even for the latest electronic computers.

The other problem has little to do with computational capacity. Over any time period, because of technical advance, changes in input-output coefficients will occur that are not merely uniform increases in output per unit of each input. Because of these changes, the coefficients used in a matrix for the year $t + n$ will be considerably in error. Moreover, even in the most advanced economy, equipped with elaborate statistics, the computation of an input-output matrix requires several years because of the complexity of the data that must be gathered and analyzed. A set of coefficients available in the year t will be those of a year at least several years earlier, and will therefore be somewhat obsolete. The coefficients for a linear programming model will be even more obsolete. By the year $t + n$ they will be more obsolete because of technical changes that will have emerged in production in the meantime. The computation for the year $t + n$, in short, requires movement from obsolescing coefficients to speculative ones. There will therefore be considerable error.

Even if the planning matrix for a future year were in some sense precisely accurate, only an economy that was already superbly well developed technically and institutionally could respond to inducements, constraints, and administrative directions so as to fine-tune its performance in the ways indicated by an elaborate plan. Only an imaginary economy could comply with the programming involved in the use of an elaborate input-output matrix or linear programming model, even if all decision-making officials were ready to bow obediently to the computer.

It is apparent, then, that the conception of guiding development planning in a less developed economy by even an only modestly elaborate input-output matrix and programming based on it is a fantasy. By definition, the problem of economic development is the problem of the absence of the necessary administrative, managerial, entrepreneurial, and technical ability, and in any event the necessary information for so elaborate a technoeconomic operation. Even in the Soviet Union the planning process is at present much cruder than the process described above.

Yet the *concept* of an input-output matrix is of use in planning in all but the least developed countries. A picture in the minds of officials involved with development planning that output in any sector requires flows from other sectors may remind the officials of questions they ought to ask. Will we have enough power in that region if these projects are carried out? Will there be enough water for both the factory and the power plant? Where will the cement be obtained? Will there be repair and service facilities for the machinery we intend to make available to farmers? Will our port facilities and transportation from the ports be adequate? Etc.

It is rare that the precision of requirements indicated in an input-output matrix of, say, 40 sectors has much relevance to the development problems of a low-income country. The judgment of a judicious planner concerning where the bottlenecks will be—skilled workers, steel capacity, port congestion, ability to budget—may be as good a guide to needed action as the indications given by the input-output matrix, or by the best linear programming model that the available data make possible. Yet the model may be a powerful aid. The model is not a substitute for the planner's judgment, but a way of quantifying that judgment, of testing his "intuitions." Its purpose is to indicate to officials the indirect economic technical requirements and results of their programs.

A mental schema that will always place in the minds of planners the nagging question "What have I overlooked?" is an invaluable adjunct to planning. This, one may judge, is the main value of the concept of input-output matrices and economy-wide programming in all or almost all of the LDCs of the world. Implicitly, the planner is filling in the matrix, and even if the filling in must be by the crudest of subjective judgment, it is important that the need to do it be realized.

COEFFICIENTS AND PRICES

At this point the Chapter 7 discussion of balanced versus unbalanced growth may recur in the mind of the reader. There are virtually no completely fixed coefficients in production. Producers seeking to minimize costs economize on inputs whose prices have risen. And the high prices stimulate increased production of the inputs and draw in increased quantities of the inputs from abroad. These are the social purposes of prices. Growth occurs through unbalance.

But the price elasticity of demand and supply of some inputs and some final products is less than that of others. Only in extreme circumstances is unloading cement by helicopter from ships lying out in the harbor a good substitute for unloading it at a dock. The supply response to the high price of flour is relatively fast, if the price has risen sufficiently to justify unloading by helicopters obtained from around the world, but a telephone system is not built in a day, even if communication is in very short supply. The price system is not at its best in calling forth increased supplies of goods whose production requires a long lead time. Most of the services provided by infrastructure are of this sort. This is why the conception of the economy as an input-output system or a programming model is an important part of the mental equipment of the planner.

MULTIPLE SOCIAL OBJECTIVES AND TRADE-OFFS

The discussion to this point has been simplified in a way that must now be remedied. A country's objective is not merely economic growth or economic growth subject to a consumption constraint. Various groups in the country and various governmental authorities will have other social objectives. These will relate to the distribution of income, the maintenance of full employment, the maintenance of price stability, the degree of economic interdependence with other nations, defense, the allocation of economic and other benefits among geographic regions of the country, appearing modern, national prestige. There are others. Some means will be taken as ends and will become social objectives. Import substitution is an example. These objectives will not only compete for resources; some of them may conflict more directly with others. The "objective function" of the planner—the function which states his objectives—must reflect the relative weight of each objective.

Constructing such a function is no easy matter. The individual whom the planner serves, or the individuals whom that superior serves, may not clearly appreciate that more of some of these objectives must mean less of others. The planner must struggle with the inconsistencies. The objective function of planning is sometimes thought of as that of maximizing growth in output subject not only to a consumption constraint but to all these other constraints. This, however, is an economist's conceit. These are not merely constraints. Planning must be treated as having multiple objectives. The planner can be most effective only if he can present to the decision-makers the trade-offs involved. He must prepare several alternative development programs, saying, for example: "These measures will foster the development of several manufacturing enterprises for the domestic market. With this protection private enterprisers will probably invest in them. The cost of living will be increased slightly. This alternative program will stimulate many petty manufacturing enterprises. About the same infrastructure expenditure will be required for both, though the infrastructure programs will differ in these ways. . . . The results of the first development programs will be evident more quickly. The second will, if successful, create more employment and raise the incomes of a fairly low income segment of the population." Or, "If you want this airline and this big steel mill, for which the country has only low-grade iron ore, the economy will probably achieve only a 4½% per year rate of growth during the coming five years. If instead the funds are spent in this alternative way, the growth rate will probably be 5%, for these reasons . . ."

Michael Roemer, arguing for this procedure, refers to it as planning by "revealed preference"—inducing the decision-makers to make choices, with the implications of the choices exposed.[3] The procedure may seem to multiply the planner's work, but it probably hastens the later stages of planning sufficiently to compensate for the additional initial work, and it certainly makes the planning more effective.

---

[3] "Planning by 'Revealed Preference': An Improvement on the Traditional Method," *World Development*, 4 (September 1976), 775–82.

Planning by revealed preference avoids the preparation, by a planning agency insulated from the nation's political processes, of a planning document which gathers dust on a shelf.

PERSPECTIVE PLANNING

A "perspective plan" containing a vision of the goals for, say, 15 years in the future is a necessary frame for the five-year plan. The vision must be a fairly specific statement of goals, goals not only of output and its composition, but of the degree to which the various social objectives will have been attained. The perspective plan must be affirmed by the political authorities and thought feasible by the planner. Such a plan will guide the five-year plan and, specifically, indicate the directions of change that should be embodied in the five-year plan. It will help to make the goals for the end of the five-year plan dynamic rather than static.

CONCLUDING COMMENTS

The planning that has been discussed here is fairly advanced planning. In many of the least developed countries, comprehensive planning is impossible or can be only symbolic, for the elementary facts of gross national product and its composition, population size and rate of growth, and the like, are only imperfectly known, and the view of planning held by the officials of these countries is similarly undeveloped. In such countries planning may consist mainly of the consideration of individual projects and only vaguely of comparison among projects, for projects may occur to the decision-making officials and to the planners one at a time. The questions asked are whether a proposed project seems worth its cost in an absolute sense— whether its contribution to GNP or the nation's welfare is positive—and whether it can be financed. The calculus is like that which may be employed by a banker in deciding whether to make a loan. The planning of the International Bank for Reconstruction and Development was almost wholly at this level—with the addition of some regard for the allocation of its funds among countries—during the first decade and more of its existence.

Project planning at a level of sophistication one step higher will include selection among projects by comparison of their expected yields or returns in some broad sense, with less or more careful recognition that the government's project expenditures must fit into a budget total. Expenditures for roads, schools, dams, and agricultural extension services may be weighed against one another. This planning, then, shades into interindustry planning, programming, and planning by revealed preference.

The greater the degree to which individuals regard a program as their own, the less threatening and the more interesting they will find it, and the more likely they will be to execute it. This fact may be of especial importance in "traditional" societies, in which it is perhaps of even more importance to each minister that his prerogatives not be infringed on than it is in "modern" societies. For this reason, a plan worked out in cooperation with the operating agencies that looks highly imperfect to a development economist may achieve much more than a "better" plan worked out solely by more capable individuals in the planning agency. The problem is compounded if the plan was worked out by foreign advisers rather than by indigenous officials.

But a plan must be worked out with the operating agencies, not merely collected from them. A plan cannot be the sum of what individual ministries wish to do, not merely because the sum of ministry proposals may exceed what is possible but because of the intersectoral relationships that have figured prominently in the discussion of this chapter. One duty of the planner or of the decision-making officials above him is therefore to create an understanding in each ministry of those interrelationships and thereby of the need for each ministry to adjust its plans to take account of the needs of development projects and programs in other ministries. That is, the traditional prerogative of each minister to have the little qualified right to do what he pleases within his area of authority with the resources available to him must be infringed on. To succeed in this infringement, to convert rival ministries into cooperating ones, is a requirement for the most effective planning.

Yet planning is not detailed budgeting. "Insofar as governments continue to value their development goals and appreciate the usefulness of systematic attention to longer and larger issues that lurk beneath the surface of day-to-day business, they will preserve some detachment for their planners and insist, nevertheless, that the products of that detachment get factored into the political process."[4]

There is no economic reason, but only a political one, why the nation-state should be the planning unit. In a large country whose parts are not closely integrated economically, the planning areas may appropriately be separate regions of the country, trade among regions being treated somewhat as foreign trade is treated in a national plan. This would have been appropriate in China and the Soviet Union in the past, and considerable delegation of planning to regional authorities is still appropriate in those countries and in India. On the other hand, a very small country which has only specialized resources, as is likely to be true of very small countries, can plan effectively only in collaboration with its neighbors. As the world productive system becomes more integrated, multinational planning becomes more imperative for all nations, large or small, but that is a limited sort of planning and a question that is separate from the concerns of this chapter.

---

[4] John P. Lewis, "Development Planning: Some Lessons from Experience," paper presented to the Rehovot Conference on Economic Growth in Developing Countries, September 2–11, 1973.

APPENDIX

Multisector planning models occupied the attention of economists more in the 1960s than in the 1970s. One by Richard S. Eckaus and Kirit Parikh is outlined briefly here.[5]

Within the limitations stated in the text and the limitations of available data, the feasibility or consistency of a proposed production program—for example, a five-year plan—can be checked by linear programming.

It is also possible by linear programming to calculate the most efficient allocation of resources to meet given objectives, in a similarly aggregated and simplified model for the economy. The simplifications made necessary by the requirement of linearity are such that the procedure will usually evaluate only rather gross allocational alternatives, but even this evaluation may indicate significant implications of development programs that are not revealed by other analysis. The method, and both its limitations and its value, may be illustrated by outlining the Eckaus-Parikh linear programming analysis of India's third Five Year Plan, for the period 1961–62 to 1966–67.[6]

The model has 11 sectors: agriculture and plantations; mining and metals; equipment; chemicals and fertilizers; cement, glass, and wood; food and clothing manufacturers; electrical generation; transportation; construction; housing; and other and margin. The only scarce inputs other than the intersectoral inputs and productive capacity (capital equipment) at the beginning of the plan period are capital and foreign exchange; labor is treated as available in excess supply.

Each sector's input coefficients of capital, imports, and outputs of other sectors were estimated from Indian data. The model takes as one constraint the increase in productive capacity in each sector during the five-year period stated or implicit in the Five Year Plan. The model assumes that to yield productive capacity in any year t, one third of the investment indicated by the capital coefficient (the incremental fixed-capital-output ratio) must be made in year $t - 3$, one third in $t - 2$, and one third in $t - 1$.

Other constraints are increase in inventories (estimated as a ratio to in-

[5] Examples are: S. Chakravarty and Louis Lefeber, "An Optimizing Planning Model," *Economic Weekly* (Bombay), 17 (February 1965), 237–52; Alan Manne and Thomas E. Weisskopf, "A Dynamic Multi-Sector Model for India: 1967–1975," in *Applications of Input-Output Analysis*, ed. A. P. Carter and A. Brody (Amsterdam: North Holland Publishing Co., 1969); M. Bruno, M. Fraenkel, and C. Daugherty, "Dynamic Input-Output, Trade, and Development," mimeographed (Jerusalem: Bank of Israel and Hebrew University, 1968); and Richard S. Eckaus and Kirit Parikh, *Planning for Growth* (Cambridge, Mass.: MIT Press, 1967). A summary is presented, with comments by E. S. Mason and A. S. Manne, in *National Economic Planning*, ed. M. F. Millikan (New York: Columbia University Press, 1967).

[6] I am grateful to Professor Eckaus for comments on the first draft of my summary of the nature of the Eckaus-Parikh model. He bears no other responsibility for the final draft.

crease in output in each sector), exports from various sectors (estimated at a constant 4% rate of annual increase from the initial level), government consumption of the products of each sector (estimated at a 2.5% rate of annual increase from the initial level), and the replacement of capital fully depreciated in the given year (estimated exogenously), if the calculations show that the replacement of the capacity for later use is justified. The initial conditions are capacity in each sector, that coming into being during the first years of the plan period from earlier investment, and the initial levels of imports, exports, and government consumption. The terminal conditions are enough capital formation going on at the end of the plan to sustain in the postplan period the programmed rate of growth of output during the plan period. Imports not competitive with Indian production are estimated at ratios to output in the importing sectors; the remaining foreign exchange available from exports plus foreign aid (assumed to be $500 million per year) is allocated among other imports in ratios proportional to the previous quantities of these imports, with the qualification that not more than a given share may go to any sector. These are competitive imports; they augment the supply of inputs to the various productive sectors.

Consumption is treated as a single composite good composed of output from the various consumer goods sectors in fixed proportions. (In view of the fairly slow increase in per capita incomes, no annual variation in the weights of the components to reflect differing income elasticities was thought necessary.) The result is that in the initial model the total estimated consumption in each year is limited by the consumer goods output capacity of any sector that is a bottleneck, even though excess capacity exists in other consumer goods sectors.

The model is programmed to maximize the weighted value of consumption during the five-year period subject to these constraints. A rate of discount of 10% per year is used, to weight the consumption of the various years. One difficulty typical of models of this general nature arose: the model tended to concentrate all production of consumer goods in the last years of the period if any rate of discount up to a certain rate was used, then to concentrate it all in the first years at higher rates of discount. At a 10% discount rate, the latter occurred. This "flip-flop" behavior was prevented by a "monotonicity constraint": the model was instructed to increase consumption from each year to the next by not less than a specified percentage. Such a constraint is of course reasonable on social welfare grounds; it was not introduced merely to prevent a flip-flop.

The solution of such a model yields the optimum allocation price of each primary input (in this case, capital and foreign exchange); the price of imports derived from the world price and the shadow foreign exchange rate; and from the cost of the inputs, the shadow price (what might be termed the shadow cost) of each sector's output. Subject to the capital needs in sectors in which the model is instructed to produce specified amounts of output (for government, exports, etc.), and to the need to maximize over the period a steadily increasing level of output, the model allocates capital to bottleneck sectors until bottlenecks are broken, and thereafter to all sectors in such a way as to maximize the weighted value of total consumption. Where excess capacity is shown in any year, investment is allocated to a sector only if the calculations show that investment to increase capacity for later use is justified relative to investment in other sectors.

The solution showed that no possible allocation of productive resources, even with consumption at zero, would yield the 5% per year increase in aggregate productive capacity implicit in the Five Year Plan. The main reasons no doubt were the magnitude of the capacity increase targeted, the existence of capacity bottlenecks in some sectors, and the assumption of lags before investment would remove them. Because of the assumption of fixed-input coefficients, plus the assumption that capital already in place in one industry could not be shifted to another, neither imports nor excess capacity in other sectors could be applied to remove the bottlenecks, and even massive investment in the first year would not necessarily remove them until the fourth. In the first year a bottleneck in the construction industry prevented full utilization of capacity in any other sector, and until the last year bottlenecks in the construction, equipment, and mining and metals sectors prevented full utilization of capacity in any sector except these three.

A reduction of the planned growth in aggregate productive capacity of 4%, or from 5% to about 4.15% per year, made the plan technically feasible, but with average aggregate annual consumption only a little more than one half that in 1959–60. When the assumption of fixed-input coefficients was abandoned, and the idle capacity in the major consumer goods sectors was allocated among the various sectors, the model showed that with the reduced growth target consumption could be maintained at an average annual rate of a little above the 1959–60 level—too little above to hold per capita consumption constant with a population increase of 2% per year. If 100% of the planned growth rate were to be achieved in the model, consumption would have to be appreciably lower, even if it were assumed that idle productive capacity in one industry could be immediately shifted to increase production of the products of another sector. Thus the model suggests that the plan's targets were inconsistent with a politically feasible level of consumption. Specifically, the model brings the capital-output ratios implicit in the plan into question. The model indicates that to attain output capacity equal to 96% of the Third Plan targets, net investment of more than 160 billion rupees would have been required, whereas the plan estimated a need of only 100 billion rupees to achieve the full targets.

The authors programmed various other alternative "runs." In some of these they increased exports, to finance increased imports. This turned out to make the attainment of a higher growth rate (or higher consumption) possible, even though it simultaneously reduced the amount of domestic resources available for investment and thus left the saving rate unchanged. That is, in this Indian model, as in most of the alternative cases of the simpler Chenery-Strout model, the import gap is greater than the saving gap.

The model is, of course, rather inflexible. The inability of the model to allow for adaptations in consumption and production occasioned by the relative scarcity of some inputs and some goods is very unrealistic. So also is not permitting the use of idle capacity in some consumer goods industries because of the low level of capacity in others—but not as unrealistic as it might seem, for a chief bottleneck industry in the model was food production, and Indian consumers did in fact divert income from other uses to food purchases when food scarcity caused food prices to rise. Moreover, the inflexibilities were allowed for by the authors in a rough way in the supplementary runs after the first runs had shown excess capacity. The aggregative input coefficients have wide margins of error. But this is because of inadequacy of data, not because of the programming technique; if more precise capital-output ratios are not available for use in a programming model, they are not available for any other use. The authors did not allow for changes in input coefficients made possible by investment and by technical advances. Neither did they take into account many policy alternatives.[7] However, in any other planning procedure these changes in coefficients and the possible effects of these policy alternatives can be allowed for only in a rough-and-ready way, and similar allowances can be made in the results shown by the programming model. In spite of its inflexibility, linear programming can improve the basis for planning by showing in precise quantitative form the implications of whatever is known about input coefficients.

FOR FURTHER READING

The two books edited by Chenery and by Blitzer and others, listed immediately below, present by far the best introduction to planning models. The Chenery volume has certain formal aspects that the Blitzer volume does not have, but the latter has an appraisal of the state of planning that is of much wider scope.

Hollis B. Chenry, ed., *Studies in Development Planning* (Cambridge, Mass.: Harvard University Press, 1971).

Charles R. Blitzer, Peter B. Clark, and Lance Taylor, eds., *Economy-Wide Models and Development Planning* (London: Oxford University Press, 1975). Eleven essays surveying the state of economic planning. Excellent bibliographies. Lance Taylor gives an excellent 76-page appraisal of the state and limitations of the technique.

Two articles in *Scientific American* by W. W. Leontief expound the input-out-

---

[7] E. S. Mason lists many of these limitations of the model in his "Comments" in *National Economic Planning*, ed. M. F. Millikan.

put method: "Input-Output Economics," October 1951, and "The Structure of Development," September 1963.

Albert Waterston, *Development Planning: Lessons of Experience* (Baltimore: Johns Hopkins Press, 1965), draws upon World Bank experience to discuss planning—not planning models—in a wide range of countries.

Peter Bauer, *Dissent on Development* (Cambridge, Mass.: Harvard University Press), attacks national planning along with various other deliberate national and international development measures.

Two sources listed in the suggested readings following Chapter 20 should also be listed here:

Ian M. D. Little and J. A. Mirrlees, *Project Appraisal and Planning for Developing Countries* (New York: Basic Books, 1974), gives judicious, commonsense, and technically soundly based analysis.

The reader should examine not only recent issues but also earlier issues of the annual publication *Benefit-Cost and Policy Analysis* (Chicago: Aldine).

In chap. 7 of his *Money, Trade, and Economic Growth*, 2d ed. (London: Unwin University Books, 1964), Harry G. Johnson presents a brief, sharp analysis of the market and planning in relationship to each other in economic development.

Gerald M. Meier, *Leading Issues in Development Economics*, 3d ed., gives well-selected excerpts from Johnson on this topic, plus excerpts from a number of essays on policy models and planning experience not mentioned above.

Index of Names of Persons

403

Subject Index

J-L

M

This book has been set CRT in 10 and 9 point Caledonia, leaded 2 points. Part numbers are 48 point Bodoni and part titles are 24 point Baskerville italic. Chapter numbers are 48 point Baskerville and chapter titles are 18 point Baskerville bold. The size of the type page is 27 by 45½ picas.